WEALTH AND POVERTY IN AMERICA

Wealth and Poverty in America

A Reader

Edited by
Dalton Conley

Blackwell
Publishing

Editorial material and organization © 2003 by Dalton Conley

350 Main Street, Malden, MA 02148-5018, USA
108 Cowley Road, Oxford OX4 1JF, UK
550 Swanston Street, Carlton South, Melbourne, Victoria 3053, Australia
Kurfürstendamm 57, 10707 Berlin, Germany

First published 2003 by Blackwell Publishers Ltd, a Blackwell Publishing company

Library of Congress Cataloging-in-Publication Data has been applied for.

ISBN 0-631-23179-X (hardback); ISBN 0-631-23180-3 (paperback)

A catalogue record for this title is available from the British Library.

Set in 9.5 on 11.5 pt Photina
by SNP Best-set Typesetter Ltd., Hong Kong

For further information on
Blackwell Publishing, visit our website:
http://www.blackwellpublishing.com

Contents

127634

Acknowledgments

The editor and publishers gratefully acknowledge the following for permission to reproduce copyright material:

Bruce Ackerman and Anne Alstott, for material from *The Stakeholder Society* by Bruce Ackerman and Anne Alstott (1999), pp. 1–17. Copyright © 1999 by Yale University, by permission of Yale University Press;

Elijah Anderson, for "The Code of the Streets," *The Atlantic Monthly*, 273:5 (1994), pp. 80–94. Copyright © 1994 by Elijah Anderson, by permission of the author;

David Brooks, for material from *Bobos in Paradise: The New Upper Class and How They Got There* by David Brooks, pp. 25–34, 35–43, 48–53. Copyright © 2000 by David Brooks, by permission of Simon & Schuster, Inc.;

Dalton Conley, for material from *Being Black, Living in the Red: Race, Class, and Property in America* by Dalton Conley, pp. 1–17. Copyright © 1999 Dalton C. Conley, by permission of the University of California Press;

Mitchell Duneier, for material from 'Sidewalk Sleeping' from *Sidewalk* by Mitchell Duneier. Copyright © 1999 Mitchell Duneier, by permission of Farrar Straus & Giroux, LLC;

Robert H. Frank and Philip J. Cook, for material from *The Winner-Take-All Society: How More and More Americans Compete for Ever Fewer and Bigger Prizes, Encouraging Economic Waste, Income Inequality, and an Impoverished Cultural Life* by Robert H. Frank and Philip J. Cook, pp. 1–22. Copyright © 1995 by Robert H. Frank and Philip J. Cook, by permission of The Free Press, a Division of Simon & Schuster, Inc.;

Christopher Jencks et al., for material from *Inequality: A Reassessment of the Effect of Schooling in America* by Christopher Jencks, pp. 3–11. Copyright © 1972 by Basic Books, Inc., by permission of Basic Books, a member of Perseus Books, LLC;

Michael B. Katz, for material from *In the Shadow of the Poor House: A Social History of Welfare in America* by Michael B. Katz, pp. 3–35. Copyright © 1986 by Basic Books, Inc., by permission of Basic Books, a member of Perseus Books, LLC;

Jay MacLeod, for material from *Ain't No Makin' It: Leveled Aspirations in a Low Income Neighborhood* by Jay MacLeod (1987), pp. 3–7, 250–9. Copyright © 1987 by Westview Press, Inc., by permission of Westview Press, a member of Perseus Books, LLC;

Karl Marx, for material from *Capital*, vol. 1 by Karl Marx, first published 1954, (1986), pp. 476–85, by permission of Lawrence & Wishart;

Susan E. Mayer, for material from *What Money Can't Buy: Family Income and Children's Life Chances* by Susan E. Mayer (1997), pp. 45–54. Copyright © 1997 by the President and Fellows of Harvard College, by permission of Harvard University Press;

C. Wright Mills, for material from *The Power Elite* by C. Wright Mills, new edition (2000), pp. 94–117. Copyright © 1956, 2000 by Oxford University Press, Inc., by permission of Oxford University, Inc.;

Mary Pattillo-McCoy, for material from *Black Picket Fences: Privilege and Peril Among the Black Middle Class* (1999), pp. 13–30, by permission of The University of Chicago Press;

George Simmel, for "The Miser and the Spendthrift" in *George Simmel: On Individuality and Social Forms*, ed. David Levine (1971), pp. 179–86, by permission of The University of Chicago Press;

Adam Smith, for notes from *An Inquiry into the Nature and Causes of the Wealth of Nations* by Adam Smith (1976), pp. 7–16, by permission of The University of Chicago Press;

Carol Stack, for material from *All Our Kin: Strategies for Survival in a Black Community* by Carol Stack (1983), pp. 32–44. Copyright © 1983 by Carol Stack, by permission of Basic Books, a member of Perseus Books, LLC;

Alexis de Tocqueville, for material from *Democracy in America* by Alexis de Tocqueville, ed. J. P. Mayer and Max Lerner, trans. George Lawrence (1965), pp. 530–4, 535–8. Copyright © 1965 by Harper & Row Publishers, Inc., by permission of HarperCollins Publishers, Inc.;

Loïc Wacquant, for "Whores, Slaves and Stallions: Languages of Exploitation and Accommodation Among Prizefighters," *Body and Society*, 7:4 (2001), by permission of Sage Publications Ltd;

Michael Walzer, for material from *Spheres of Justice: A Defense of Pluralism and Equality* by Michael Walzer (1983), pp. 295–303. Copyright © 1983 by Basic Books, Inc., by permission of Basic Books, a member of Perseus Books, LLC, and Blackwell Publishers;

Max Weber, for material from *The Protestant Ethic and the Spirit of Capitalism* by Max Weber, Routledge (Allen & Unwin) (1930), pp. 170–83, by permission of Taylor & Francis Books Ltd;

Bruce Western, Becky Petit and Josh Guetzkow, for "Black Economic Progress in the Era of Mass Imprisonment" from *Invisible Punishment: The Consequences of Mass Imprisonment*, ed. Meda Chesney-Lind and Marc Mauer (2002), by permission of The New Press;

William Julius Wilson, for material from *The Truly Disadvantaged* by William Julius Wilson (1985), pp. 149–64, by permission of The University of Chicago Press;

The publishers apologize for any errors or omissions in the above list and would be grateful to be notified of any corrections that should be incorporated in the next edition or reprint of this book.

Introduction: Wealth and Poverty in the Affluent Society

What does it mean to be poor in America at the dawn of the twenty-first century? For that matter, what does it mean to be rich? And how are the two related to each other? At first glance these appear to be relatively simple questions. But upon careful reflection, they present enormous theoretical and empirical challenges to any student or social scientist.

Let's start with poverty: What does it mean to be poor in a rich country such as the United States? The difficulties of conceptualizing poverty amid plenty are perhaps best illustrated by a speech given by a member of the Forbes 400 richest Americans, Thomas Monaghan, founder of the Domino's Pizza chain, who himself rose to great wealth from meager origins. "To me one of the most exciting things in the world is being poor," he began. To explain what he meant, Monaghan cited a study that concluded that a family of four could survive on $68 per year back around 1970 (which would make it $256 today). "Now you're probably wondering how you can live on $68 a year. The first thing you do is go to the Farm Bureau and buy a hundred-pound bag of powdered milk . . . While you're at the Farm Bureau you buy yourself a bushel of oats or wheat or corn, and you mash that stuff up . . . And you grow some vegetables and you get a few vitamin pills to supplement your diet. And I think that's exciting." He went on to talk about how cheaply he lived in a house trailer, calling it "the greatest living I ever did." He concluded his speech with a rhetorical appeal: "Oh gosh," Monaghan said, "I'd love to talk to all these people who say they can't get by."[1]

We could debate the actual numbers – that is, exactly how cheaply someone could live in the contemporary United States – and we could question the hypocrisy of a man worth hundreds of millions of dollars castigating the poor for their implied whining, but that would miss the deeper point that Monaghan raises. Namely, what does it mean to be poor in a country when starvation and death from the elements is rare?

And what about wealth, for that matter? What does it mean to be wealthy when the assets once associated only with the robber baron elite – such as stocks, bonds, and homes – are now quite widespread across most groups in society (with some notable exceptions). For example, despite ups and downs in share prices, participation in the stock market is at a record high in the United States – and keeps rising. In 1983, 24 percent of Americans held stock directly or indirectly through their employer's retirement plan. By 1999, that figure had doubled to 48 percent. This rise comes after a remarkable increase in the rate of home ownership in the United States; now a full two-thirds of Americans own the house or apartment in which they live. The result of all this is that the culture of wealth and ownership – once confined to the elite – is now part of mainstream America.

Of course, this generalization obscures the paradoxical fact that while more and more people own *something*, inequalities in wealth and income have reached levels not seen since the early twentieth century. In other words, the very rich of today are a lot wealthier compared to the rest of us than were the rich of decades past. Folk statistics vividly illustrate the extent of this inequality: If the world were reduced to 100 people, six people would own half the world's wealth (and those six would be Americans). Bill Gates owns as much wealth as the bottom 40 percent of Americans combined.

As a group that exerts a disproportionate amount of influence on economics, politics, and culture, the rich deserve more attention from students and scholars than they generally receive. Hardly ever do social scientists ask: "Why are the rich wealthy?" in the same way we often ask why the poor are poor. Part of the reason for this is that given their power, it is much easier for the rich to protect themselves from social inquiry and scientific study. In fact, it is in their interest to remain mysterious and under-studied. If the rest of us were to know how concentrated wealth actually is in the United States we might call for policies that would tax riches more heavily, for instance. Or if we learned the ways through which the rich preserve their assets and generate profits we might get into the game, too, and drive down what economists call "rent" – profits that result from a prime position in the market. Another part of the explanation for the lopsided amount of scholarship on poverty and wealth is that our public discourse associates poverty with moral failing – and thus makes it the subject of scientific study and social critique. Wealth, on the other hand, is what we all supposedly aspire to. There is no shortage of how-to books explaining the way to become rich. There is less literature, however, in the way of critical social inquiry about the rich.

This point leads us to the third question motivating this reader: How are poverty and wealth related to each other in America? Perhaps because the rich are under-observed, the social sciences sorely lack theoretical linkages between wealth and poverty. In other words, we tend to conceptualize the problems surrounding poverty as distinct from the causes and consequences of great wealth. Rarely do social scientists ask how the rich and poor are similar. Hardly ever do we make causal connections between poverty and wealth; that is, not often do we grasp how the poverty of some is directly related to – and even causal of – the wealth of others (and vice versa). The ideologies of equal opportunity and individual responsibility that dominate American culture tend to obscure such linkages. Uncovering these connections is one of the leitmotifs of the readings presented in this volume.

Part I, entitled "On the Origins and Causes of Wealth and Poverty," presents classic and contemporary selections that form theories of where wealth comes from – for example, the division of labor, the exploitation of labor, and the Protestant ethic – and why wealth tends to be concentrated in the hands of the few – for instance, through winner-take-all markets. This set of readings deals with wealth creation (or appropriation) at a more systemic, rather than individual, level. For example, Adam Smith explains how through the division of labor a single pin maker who initially produced between one and twenty pins per day when he was fabricating the pin from start to finish is able to produce upwards of 48,000 pins a day with nine other workers when the task is broken down to its constituent parts, and each worker devotes himself to specializing in a specific task to the larger end. The result of this increased efficiency, according to Smith, is greater wealth for all. For Marx, however, the division of labor – which should lead to shorter work days through this greater productivity – instead leads to the extraction of this "surplus labor" by the capitalist (owner) in the form of profits. The result for workers is not greater wealth but rather increasing poverty and progressively larger ranks. Writing largely in response to Marx, Weber brings the "ideal" or spiritual realm into these economic accounts. In *The Protestant Ethic and the Spirit of Capitalism*, he argues that institution of double-entry bookkeeping combines with the ecclesiastical orientation of Protestantism to spur economic development. Whereas in Catholicism, poverty was seen as a virtue ("the meek shall inherit the Earth") in Protestantism, work and the material rewards of work belong to the virtuous ("Lose no time. Be always employ'd in something useful" [Benjamin Franklin]). Weber sees cultural differences such as these as not merely the reflection of underlying economic systems but as themselves part of the causal story in explaining development among various societies.

Most of this scholarship in the political economy tradition prior to 1900 had been focused on the transition from precapitalism to capitalism (or premodernism to modernism). While there is still a strong research tradition concerned with this question (as well as critiquing it), much of the debate during the twentieth century shifted to structural explanations of why levels of inequality have varied across time and place. The Davis and Moore article presented in Part I is perhaps the most influential ever written in this tradition. The functionalist account of inequality that these authors present offers an enticing – if tautological and ultimately flawed – explanation of why inequality not only persists, but is necessary. Davis and Moore are operating heavily under the influence (perhaps unconsciously) of nineteenth-century thinkers who saw society as an organism and used biological metaphors to account for social facts. In this vein, Davis and Moore viewed inequality as a necessary condition to induce the most talented individuals to fill the most "functionally" important and demanding jobs in society. In this paradigm, society has needs like you and I. The last reading in this section presents a contemporary account of how increased communication and centralization of markets results in "winner-take-all markets." Frank and Cook make a convincing case that when markets expand so that everyone consumes in a large national (or international) pool, the rewards for the very best become inflated and very fine distinctions in "quality" become magnified. Why settle for listening to the fourteenth highest rate violinist in the world when – thanks to compact discs, mass production, cable television and so on – you can now listen to the top rated violinist? The fourteenth is out of luck but the top dog is living larger than ever before.

Part II of the reader deals with the question of why certain individuals – based on position in the economy, or accident of birth – can expect to have greater or lesser life chances of being rich (or poor). In other words, they are about how inequality gets reproduced. Christopher Jencks et al.'s *Inequality* sets the agenda by asking how much inequality we are willing to tolerate. They argue that the commonly given reasons for disparate fortunes do not go very far in explaining the overall level of inequality in society. It is not just genes or cognitive skill; nor is it schooling; nor is it family environment primarily. Rather who makes it is largely attributable to unmeasureable attributes; they take a stab and call them "competence" and "luck."

The echoes of this argument can be heard two decades later in the work of Susan Mayer (a student of Jencks) who argues that rich and poor kids differ in fundamental ways and that the actual effect of income on children's outcomes is much smaller than most social scientists (or liberals) would be willing to admit. In other words, it's the parents that matter, not how much money they have. Her analysis is based on the assumption that many attributes that result in parents earning good wages are also the attributes that make for good outcomes among children. Giving poor parents more money, then, will not do much to affect the long-term outcomes of their children. This analysis is based on a number of technical assumptions that go beyond the scope of this text. Briefly stated, however, her research largely results from looking at how income *changes* over time in a family affect (or don't affect) kids. They appear to have little impact. But it might be the case that economic resources matter in subtler ways such that the overall trajectory or class position of a family is what matters for structuring kids' opportunities and confidence (or lack thereof) in the world. This is essentially what I argue in the next selection, which is taken from *Being Black, Living in the Red: Race, Wealth and Social Policy in America*. Here, I suggest that net worth or asset level – more than income – is a better measure of the overall class position of families in America. When we view wealth and poverty through the lens of net worth, a new socioeconomic landscape emerges. In particular, the unequal starting points of blacks and whites comes into focus. Whites own about eight times the assets of blacks, a gap that is larger than any other socioeconomic indicator in the United States. This excerpt fleshes out the implications of this equity–inequity for the life chances of blacks and whites in contemporary America. The next selection, taken from Mary Pattillo-McCoy's *Black Picket Fences: Privilege and Peril among the Black Middle Class* shows in real, personified terms how this racial wealth inequality plays itself out. Namely, being black and middle class as traditionally defined by income is quite a different reality than being white and middle class. The black middle class community that she studied lacks the geographic and social buffers between themselves and poorer folk that the white middle classes are able to erect. This difference is largely a result of racial residential segregation and both reflects and is reflected in the lower African American net worth figures (since housing is the primary asset for most American families). The result is greater environmental hazards and worse schools for African American middle-class kids, which in turn, makes it more difficult for them to reproduce (or exceed) their parents' socioeconomic attainment. The section concludes with another ethnographic piece from Jay MacLeod's, *Ain't No Making It: Aspirations and Attainment in a Low-Income Community*, which documents some of the invisible structural and cultural forces that socialize low-income teenagers into reproducing their parents' class status. The fact that neither the Hallway Hangers (pessimistic, poor white teenagers) or the Brothers (optimistic, poor black teenagers) have much in the way of opportunities works to show how aspirations are not enough to make it out of poverty when social structures are so strongly pushing a kid in that direction. This selection demonstrates another powerful way in which parental class status – be it income, wealth, occupation or education – acts to structure the life chances of adolescents in a way that reaches beyond material conditions.

Part III, "Lifestyles of the Rich and Famous," offers a series of readings intended to accentuate some of the more important classic and contemporary writings on the upper class. It starts with three short pieces excerpted from de Tocqueville's classic text, *Democracy in America*. Each of these selections describe his observations about the particular manifestation of wealth in America. De Tocqueville argues that in a country like the US – which lacks a stable, hereditary aristocracy – people enjoy the physical rewards of riches much more since they do not take them for granted. He also argues that in a democratic country like the America he documents, physical pleasures take on a more subtle nature and give "less rein to any great disorderly passion." Democracy, in other words, restrains the indulgence of great wealth. However, in the subsequent piece he argues that these same democratic conditions make for a certain restlessness. Small differences in wealth are magnified in more equal times. Also, recency of wealth takes away from the sense of security it might otherwise bring. Today, however, the United States has the most unequal distribution of income and wealth among the Western democracies. Hence, de Tocqueville's observations deserve revisiting. From *Democracy in America*, we then shift to an essay by the German social philosopher Georg Simmel, which makes a good lens through which to consider de Tocqueville's observations. In "The Miser and the Spendthrift," Simmel follows his tradition of outlining "social types" or forms. The remarkable aspect of his analysis of these two ideal types is not the obvious ways in which they differ, but rather the similarities that Simmel draws between them. Neither a miser nor a spendthrift is satisfied by the possession of material goods or the satisfaction of earthly desires. For both, money itself is the end, rather than the means to the end; money fulfills an almost spiritual role in their social orders.

We then move ahead to C. Wright Mills's book *The Power Elite* in which he describes an American society in the 1950s that is largely controlled by three sets of elites – the economic elite, the political elite, and the military elite. He describes the linkages between these groups and the mechanisms by which they control American society. The particular section we focus on describes the monied elite, "The Very Rich." This makes for an interesting contrast to the next piece taken from David Brooks's *Bobos in Paradise: The New Upper Class and How They Got There*. This is a bit of almost-comic, yet sociologically insightful journalism that describes how the elite has changed since the time of Mills. Brooks describes an upper class that is largely meritocratic (or at least more meritocratic than that of the old Protestant establishment described by Mills or Baltzell).[2] He describes how the social mores of this new elite arise out of a merger between the old, bourgeois elite and the bohemian movements of the 1960s counter-culture. Hence the name "bobos" – bourgeois bohemians. The last piece in Part III describes – in a very concrete way – a situation in which the concentration of wealth in the hands of a small minority affects the life choices of the rest of us. Michael Walzer describes the situation of Pullman, Illinois when a single rich man owned an entire town that housed his workers. Walzer walks us through the implications for local democracy and the quality of life in general.

Part IV, "Lifestyles of the Poor and Anonymous," deals with the daily, lived experience of being poor in America. The readings start with one from Carol Stack's *All Our Kin*. In "Swapping," Stack shows us how many poor people weave their own safety net, of sorts. Through informal exchange the poor residents of "The Flats" are able to fashion a system of mutual obligation and social insurance. This network of trading and sharing turns out to be a key to survival. However, it also may serve to hold back individuals or families that might have otherwise made it out of The Flats through upward mobility. This is because resources tend to be seen as belonging to the community as a whole. So if a lucky individual comes into some money through work or inheritance, for example, then there is a whole network of obligations and community needs that draw on these new resources, which might have otherwise been used toward the purchase of mobility enhancing assets such as a car for commuting to a more rewarding job or a home in a better situated neighborhood or even additional formal education.

Carol Stack is followed up by Elijah Anderson's essay, *The Code of the Street*, which describes the social mores in certain poor, violence-ridden communities. The "code" that Anderson describes could not be more different than the social norms described by Stack in "Swapping." Put simply, the "code of the street," which according to Anderson, is prevalent in the inner-city ghetto, functions as a way for poor African American youth to maintain social order in neighborhoods that have been abandoned by formal institutions such as the police. However, unlike other social codes that informally regulate public space in mainstream American culture, a violation of the code of the street can put an individual at potentially life-threatening risk. According to Anderson, these norms of the street grow out of an opposition to mainstream culture, which itself is a response to the alienation of poor, black inner-city residents from the economic and social institutions of a predominantly white society and which is linked to the drug trade on the streets. Mitchell Duneier's informants in *Sidewalk*, meanwhile, are also predominantly black men, but they are generally older than the youth that Anderson describes – in fact, many have come out the other side of the drug wars that Anderson describes. Duneier's *Sidewalk* respondents are also plying an informal – but legal – trade on the streets: selling books and other printed matter. But they are doing it in a wealthy neighborhood. Hence the social norms – the "code" – for these poor African American men is quite different from that of Anderson's youth. In fact, it is all about honing to the perceived mainstream norms of "decency" upon which their economic activity depends. For the vendors whose entire lives are public ones – i.e. many sleep and live on the streets – this is particularly challenging.

"Lifestyles of the Poor and Anonymous" concludes with Loïc Wacquant's article on boxers in the inner city, "Whores, Slaves, and Stallions: Languages of Exploitation and Accommodation among Prizefighters." The boxers about which Wacquant writes literally "embody" the exploitative relationships that characterize ghetto poverty. That is, in their own words, the boxers' flesh and blood are peddled by "pimps," "slave masters," and "livestock traders." While the boxers talk in very knowing terms about the exploitation they experience, Wacquant shows us that for a variety of reasons they are forced to accommodate this exploitation – rationalizing along the way that such exploitation is rife everywhere. At the same time, however, by combining a spirit of entrepreneurship, a notion of individual exceptionalism and assertions of bodily masculinity, the boxers are able to create integrity within themselves through participation in the blood sport. Like Duneier's sidewalk entrepreneurs, Wacquant's boxers make moral meaning (and marginal earnings) where "mainstream" opportunities to do so are absent – peddling themselves rather than magazines. As is the case for Anderson's respondents, violence plays an important role; however, in Wacquant's gym, the two forces of "self-made" work and violence come together in an organized fashion that yields a durable, corporeal integrity along with a moral purpose.

The challenge for the reader is to link Parts III and IV about the "lived" consequences of wealth and poverty, respectively, to the preceding parts on the systemic and individual determinants of socioeconomic status. How do the conditions of the creation of wealth and deprivation directly affect the lifestyles of those who benefit and suffer from those systems? Conversely, how do the lifestyles of the rich and poor affect their very own life chances embedded within those systems of inequality (if at all)? The answers of MacLeod and Patillo-McCoy may differ substantially from those of Jencks and Mayer. These questions provide the backdrop for the final part entitled, "What is to be Done? Wealth, Poverty, and Public Policy." Part V is meant to open up the horizons of what is possible in terms of the distribution of material rewards in America. Before presenting new policy ideas and possibilities, however, it is first necessary to view American social policy through the historical lens presented by Michael Katz's *In the Shadow of the Poorhouse*. Katz shows how American social policy has long been driven by a conception of poverty as pauperism, that is, as a condition largely resulting from the behavioral deficiencies of the poor themselves. The result of seeing the poor as responsible for their own plight is a social policy that predominantly ranges from rehabilitative to punitive – that is, focusing on the individual, proximate causes rather than the social, systemic roots shown in the first section.

Equipped with the readings of the first four parts of the volume, along with an understanding of the past history of American welfare, we can advance onward to consider contemporary politics and policy possibilities ranging from William Julius Wilson's savvy way of expanding the welfare state through "targeted universalism"; to Bruce Ackerman's and Anne Alstott's idea for transforming it by creating a trust fund for every American as they enter adulthood; to the dark reality of a recent, rapid expansion of the prison system, which Bruce Western, Becky Pettit, and Josh Guetzkow view as a (pseudo-)welfare state structure that regulates the labor market while both obscuring and contributing to ongoing racial inequality.

Readers should not read Part V as an afterthought to the rest of the volume. Public policy is not just reactive to material conditions and distributions but creates them as well. Take for example, the case of the trade-off between work and welfare. Since American welfare policy is generally means-tested – that is, recipients need to have recorded incomes below a certain cutoff point in order to qualify – those who work full time for low wages do not benefit from welfare or from Medicaid health insurance for that matter (though they do benefit from the earned income tax credit, which augments their wages). If welfare and health benefits were universal rather than means-tested, these strange incentive structures would not result. The tendency to means-test – to divide the so-called deserving poor from the so-called undeserving poor from everyone else – enjoys a long tradition in American social policy as Katz shows us in his essay. However, the result is that many welfare recipients are actually working off the books in order to survive on the meager benefits provided by the government. At the same time, many officially employed "working poor" are caught between a rock and a hard place. They are doing what society expects of them – confounding stereotypes of shiftlessness and incompetency among the poor – yet they do not seem to be able to escape poverty. They are held up as heroes by politicians, but are largely forgotten about when it comes to social support. As it turns out, however, the boundary between these two groups is more porous than we may wish to believe; often they live in the same household; other times a given individual may cross the line from "deserving" (yet unsupported) working poor to "undeserving" (yet benefit-qualifying) poor. Such earnings patterns and moral contradictions are made, in part, by social policy.

Also, social policy plays an even more fundamental role than affecting resource flows and incentives; it creates entire classes and categories of people. In fact, there is a whole other way of thinking about poverty that we have not yet discussed. The classical German sociologist Georg Simmel offers perhaps the most robust definition of "the poor" across time and place: they are the group in society whose private suffering becomes a matter of public concern. In his own words, "what makes one poor is not a lack of means. The poor person, sociologically speaking, is the individual who receives assistance because of this lack of means."[3] This is a definition that focuses not on what the poor lack, but on what they receive. Public policy, in other words, may be the creator of, not the reactor to, the poor.

Two final points: First, as represented by its very title, this volume frames the question of social stratification in terms of the ends of the distribution, seemingly neglecting the great middle classes. This constitutes a purposeful analytic choice to draw out contrasts and to emphasize the degree of inequities in modern American society that are consistently underestimated by the population itself. Further, in surveys, very few American respondents identify themselves as anything other than "middle class." This has led many scholars to claim that subjective class status has little meaning in the US context or to even go so far as to suggest that America is a classless society. The selections in this volume should lead readers to sharply question that claim and contemplate the various reasons for the persistence of that particularly American myth of a classless society. All this said, the reader should note that what is true for rich and poor is also true for everyone else who falls somewhere in the middle – once we recognize that the rich and the poor are *us* and not some far off class of people.

Secondly, the reader should keep in mind that the focus of this volume is on the distribution of material resources – its causes and consequences and future possibilities in America. That is not meant to take lightly the distribution of other sorts of resources like symbolic or political power, honor, prestige, cultural capital, social ties, or authority – to name a few other dimensions of stratification. However, the reader will note in the texts presented that these other aspects of inequality are inextricably linked to the material distribution of resources and rewards (see, e.g., Walzer's selection). Material wealth (or lack thereof) merely provides the springboard for the reader to understand, comparatively, other forms of social stratification, for it is almost impossible in a modern, monetized, marketized society to talk about any dimension of stratification without starting from or arriving at money as the primary axis upon which hierarchies form and reform. Or, as a character in a popular film says, "Follow the money."[4]

NOTES

1   For the text of the speech, see p. 22 of *Harpers* (August 1990).
2   See E. Digby Baltzell, *The Protestant Establishment: Aristocracy and Caste in America* (New York: Random House, 1964).
3   P. 178 of Georg Simmel, "The Poor," in Donald N. Levine, ed., *Georg Simmel: On Individuality and Social Forms* (Chicago: University of Chicago Press, 1971).
4   This is a reference to Alan Pakula's *All the President's Men*.

Editor's note: In most instances throughout the readings that follow, we have made efforts to eliminate references that authors make to other parts of their own texts. In a few instances, it was not possible to entirely eliminate those cross-references and in these cases we have alerted the reader to the original publication. This is particularly true for references made in the notes to chapter 3. Intrepid readers are referred to the original text, *The Protestant Ethic and the Spirit of Capitalism* (translated by Talcott Parsons, with an introduction by Anthony Giddens; London: Allen and Unwin, 1930).

Part I

On the Origins and Causes of Wealth and Poverty: Systemic Explanations

1

Of the Division of Labour

Adam Smith (1723–1790)

In 1751 Adam Smith was appointed professor of logic at Glasgow University but in 1752 became the chair of moral philosophy, teaching a range of subjects from ethics to law to political economy. In 1759, at the age of 36, he published the *Theory of Moral Sentiments*. In 1776, he moved to London, the same year that *The Wealth of Nations* was published. Two years later he was appointed to the post of commissioner of customs in Edinburgh, Scotland where he fell ill and died on July 17, 1790. At the end of his life, it was discovered that Smith had devoted a large portion of his income to anonymous acts of charity.

The greatest improvement[1] in the productive powers of labour, and the greater part of the skill, dexterity, and judgment with which it is any where directed, or applied, seem to have been the effects of the division of labour.

The effects of the division of labour, in the general business of society, will be more easily understood, by considering in what manner it operates in some particular manufactures. It is commonly supposed to be carried furthest in some very trifling ones; not perhaps that it really is carried further in them than in others of more importance: but in those trifling manufactures which are destined to supply the small wants of but a small number of people, the whole number of workmen must necessarily be small; and those employed in every different branch of the work can often be collected into the same workhouse, and placed at once under

the view of the spectator. In those great manufactures, on the contrary, which are destined to supply the great wants of the great body of the people, every different branch of the work employs so great a number of workmen, that it is impossible to collect them all into the same workhouse. We can seldom see more, at one time, than those employed in one single branch. Though in such manufactures,[2] therefore, the work may really be divided into a much greater number of parts, than in those of a more trifling nature, the division is not near so obvious, and has accordingly been much less observed.

To take an example, therefore,[3] from a very trifling manufacture; but one in which the division of labour has been very often taken notice of, the trade of the pin-maker; a workman not educated to this business (which the division of labour has rendered a distinct trade),[4] nor acquainted with the use of the machinery employed in it (to the invention of which the same division of labour has probably given occasion), could scarce, perhaps, with his utmost industry, make one pin in a day, and certainly could not make twenty. But in the way in which this business is now carried on, not only the whole work is a peculiar trade, but it is divided into a number of branches, of which the greater part are likewise peculiar trades. One man draws out the wire, another straights it, a third cuts it, a fourth points it, a fifth grinds it at the top for receiving the head; to make the head requires two or three distinct operations; to put it on, is a peculiar business, to whiten the pins is another; it is even a trade by itself to put them into the paper; and the important business of making a pin is, in this manner, divided into about eighteen distinct operations, which, in some manufactories, are all performed by distinct hands, though in others the same man will sometimes perform two or three of them.[5] I have seen a small manufactory of this kind where ten men only were employed, and where some of them consequently performed two or three distinct operations. But though they were very poor, and therefore but indifferently accommodated with the necessary machinery, they could, when they exerted themselves, make among them about twelve pounds of pins in a day. There are in a pound upwards of four thousand pins of a middling size. Those ten persons, therefore, could make among them upwards of forty-eight thousand pins in a day. Each person, therefore, making a tenth part of forty-eight thousand pins, might be considered as making four thousand eight hundred pins in a day. But if they had all wrought separately and independently, and without any of them having been educated to this peculiar business, they certainly could not each of them have made twenty, perhaps not one pin in a day; that is, certainly, not the two hundred and fortieth, perhaps not the four thousand eight hundredth part of what they are at present

capable of performing, in consequence of a proper division and combination of their different operations.

In every other art and manufacture, the effects of the division of labour are similar to what they are in this very trifling one; though, in many of them, the labour can neither be so much subdivided, nor reduced to so great a simplicity of operation. The division of labour, however, so far as it can be introduced, occasions, in every art, a proportionable increase of the productive powers of labour. The separation of different trades and employments from one another, seems to have taken place, in consequence of this advantage. This separation too is generally carried furthest in those countries which enjoy the highest degree of industry and improvement; what is the work of one man in a rude state of society, being generally that of several in an improved one. In every improved society, the farmer is generally nothing but a farmer; the manufacturer, nothing but a manufacturer. The labour too which is necessary to produce any one complete manufacture, is almost always divided among a great number of hands. How many different trades are employed in each branch of the linen and woollen manufactures, from the growers of the flax and the wool, to the bleachers and smoothers of the linen, or to the dyers and dressers of the cloth! The nature of agriculture, indeed, does not admit of so many subdivisions of labour, nor of so complete a separation of one business from another, as manufactures. It is impossible to separate so entirely, the business of the grazier from that of the corn-farmer, as the trade of the carpenter is commonly separated from that of the smith. The spinner is almost always a distinct person from the weaver; but the ploughman, the harrower, the sower of the seed, and the reaper of the corn, are often the same. The occasions for those different sorts of labour returning with the different seasons of the year, it is impossible that one man should be constantly employed in any one of them. This impossibility of making so complete and entire a separation of all the different branches of labour employed in agriculture, is perhaps the reason why the improvement of the productive powers of labour in this art, does not always keep pace with their improvement in manufactures. The most opulent nations, indeed, generally excel all their neighbours in agriculture as well as in manufactures; but they are commonly more distinguished by their superiority in the latter than in the former. Their lands are in general better cultivated, and having more labour and expence bestowed upon them, produce more in proportion to the extent and natural fertility of the ground. But this[6] superiority of produce is seldom much more than in proportion to the superiority of labour and expence. In agriculture, the labour of the rich country is not always much more productive than that of the poor; or, at least, it is never so much more productive, as it commonly is in manufactures. The corn of the rich country, therefore, will not always, in the same degree of goodness, come cheaper to market than that of the poor. The corn of Poland, in the same degree of goodness, is as cheap as that of France, notwithstanding the superior opulence and improvement of the latter country. The corn of France is, in the corn provinces, fully as good, and in most years nearly about the same price with the corn of England, though, in opulence and improvement, France is perhaps inferior to England. The corn-lands of England, however, are better cultivated than those of France, and the corn-lands[7] of France are said to be much better cultivated than those of Poland. But though the poor country, notwithstanding the inferiority of its cultivation, can, in some measure, rival the rich in the cheapness and goodness of its corn, it can pretend to no such competition in its manufactures; at least if those manufactures suit the soil, climate, and situation of the rich country. The silks of France are better and cheaper than those of England, because the silk manufacture, at least under the present high duties upon the importa-

tion of raw silk, does not so well suit the climate of England as that of France.[8] But the hard-ware and the coarse woollens of England are beyond all comparison superior to those of France, and much cheaper too in the same degree of goodness.[9] In Poland there are said to be scarce any manufactures of any kind, a few of those coarser household manufactures excepted, without which no country can well subsist.

This great increase of the quantity of work which, in consequence of the division of labour, the same number of people are capable of performing,[10] is owing to three different circumstances; first to the increase of dexterity in every particular workman; secondly, to the saving of the time which is commonly lost in passing from one species of work to another; and lastly, to the invention of a great number of machines which facilitate and abridge labour, and enable one man to do the work of many.[11]

First, the improvement of the dexterity of the workman necessarily increases the quantity of the work he can perform; and the division of labour, by reducing every man's business to some one simple operation, and by making this operation the sole employment of his life, necessarily increases very much the dexterity of the workman. A common smith, who, though accustomed to handle the hammer, has never been used to make nails, if upon some particular occasion he is obliged to attempt it, will scarce, I am assured, be able to make above two or three hundred nails in a day, and those too very bad ones.[12] A smith who has been accustomed to make nails, but whose sole or principal business has not been that of a nailer, can seldom with his utmost diligence make more than eight hundred or a thousand nails in a day. I have seen several boys under twenty years of age who had never exercised any other trade but that of making nails, and who, when they exerted themselves, could make, each of them, upwards of two thousand three hundred nails in a day.[13] The making of a nail, however, is by no means one of the simplest operations.

The same person blows the bellows, stirs or mends the fire as there is occasion, heats the iron, and forges every part of the nail: In forging the head too he is obliged to change his tools. The different operations into which the making of a pin, or of a metal button,[14] is subdivided, are all of them much more simple, and the dexterity of the person, of whose life it has been the sole business to perform them, is usually much greater. The rapidity with which some of the operations of those manufactures are performed, exceeds what the human hand could, by those who had never seen them, be supposed capable of acquiring.

Secondly, the advantage which is gained by saving the time commonly lost in passing from one sort of work to another, is much greater than we should at first view be apt to imagine it. It is impossible to pass very quickly from one kind of work to another; that is carried on in a different place, and with quite different tools. A country weaver,[15] who cultivates a small farm, must lose a good deal of time in passing from his loom to the field, and from the field to his loom. When the two trades can be carried on in the same workhouse, the loss of time is no doubt much less. It is even in this case, however, very considerable. A man commonly saunters a little in turning his hand from one sort of employment to another. When he first begins the new work he is seldom very keen and hearty: his mind, as they say, does not go to it, and for some time he rather trifles than applies to good purpose. The habit of sauntering and of indolent careless application, which is naturally, or rather necessarily acquired by every country workman who is obliged to change his work and his tools every half hour, and to apply his hand in twenty different ways almost every day of his life; renders him almost always slothful and lazy, and incapable of any vigorous application even on the most pressing occasions. Independent, therefore, of his deficiency in point of dexterity, this cause alone must always reduce considerably the quantity of work which he is capable of performing.

Thirdly, and lastly, every body must be sensible how much labour is facilitated and abridged by the application of proper machinery. It is unnecessary to give any example.[16] I shall only observe, therefore,[17] that the invention of all those machines by which labour is so much facilitated and abridged, seems to have been originally owing to the division of labour. Men are much more likely to discover easier and readier methods of attaining any object, when the whole attention of their minds is directed towards that single object, than when it is dissipated among a great variety of things. But in consequence of the division of labour, the whole of every man's attention comes naturally to be directed towards some one very simple object. It is naturally to be expected, therefore, that some one or other of those who are employed in each particular branch of labour should soon find out easier and readier methods of performing their own particular work, wherever the nature of it admits of such improvement. A great part of the machines made use of[18] in those manufactures in which labour is most subdivided, were originally the inventions of common workmen, who, being each of them employed in some very simple operation, naturally turned their thoughts towards finding out easier and readier methods of performing it. Whoever has been much accustomed to visit such manufactures, must frequently have been shown very pretty machines, which were the inventions of such[19] workmen, in order to facilitate and quicken their own particular part of the work. In the first fire-engines,[20] a boy was constantly employed to open and shut alternately the communication between the boiler and the cylinder, according as the piston either ascended or descended. One of those boys, who loved to play with his companions, observed that, by tying a string from the handle of the valve which opened this communication to another part of the machine, the valve would open and shut without his assistance, and leave him at liberty to divert himself with his play-fellows. One of the greatest improvements that has been made upon this machine, since it was first invented, was in this manner the discovery of a boy who wanted to save his own labour.[21]

All the improvements in machinery, however, have by no means been the inventions of those who had occasion to use the machines. Many improvements have been made by the ingenuity of the makers of the machines, when to make them became the business of a peculiar trade; and some by that of those who are called philosophers or men of speculation, whose trade it is not to do any thing, but to observe every thing; and who, upon that account, are often capable of combining together the powers of the most distant and dissimilar objects.[22] In the progress of society, philosophy or specu-lation becomes, like every other employ-ment, the principal or sole trade and occupation of a particular class of citizens. Like every other employment too, it is subdi-vided into a great number of different branches, each of which affords occupation to a peculiar tribe or class of philosophers; and this subdivision of employment in phi-losophy, as well as in every other business, improves dexterity, and saves time. Each individual becomes more expert in his own peculiar branch, more work is done upon the whole, and the quantity of science is considerably increased by it.[23]

It is the great multiplication of the pro-ductions of all the different arts, in con-sequence of the division of labour, which occasions, in a well-governed society, that universal opulence which extends itself to the lowest ranks of the people. Every workman has a great quantity of his own work to dispose of beyond what he himself has occasion for; and every other workman being exactly in the same situation, he is enabled to exchange a great quantity of his own goods for a great quantity, or, what comes to the same thing, for the price of a great quantity of theirs. He supplies them abundantly with what they have occasion for, and they accommodate him as amply with what he has occasion for, and a general plenty diffuses itself through all the different ranks of the society.

Observe the accommodation of the most common artificer or day-labourer in a civi-lized and thriving country, and you will perceive that the number of people of whose industry a part, though but a small part, has been employed in procuring him this ac-commodation, exceeds all computation. The woollen coat, for example, which covers the day-labourer, as coarse and rough as it may appear, is the produce of the joint labour of a great multitude of workmen. The shep-herd, the sorter of the wool, the wool-comber or carder, the dyer, the scribbler, the spinner, the weaver, the fuller, the dresser, with many others, must all join their differ-ent arts in order to complete even this homely production. How many merchants and carriers, besides, must have been employed in transporting the materials from some of those workmen to others who often live in a very distant part of the country! How much commerce and navigation in particular, how many ship-builders, sailors, sail-makers, rope-makers, must have been employed in order to bring together the dif-ferent drugs made use of by the dyer, which often come from the remotest corners of the world! What a variety of labour too is necessary in order to produce the tools of the meanest of those workmen! To say nothing of such complicated machines as the ship of the sailor, the mill of the fuller, or even the loom of the weaver, let us consider only what a variety of labour is requisite in order to form that very simple machine, the shears with which the shepherd clips the wool. The miner, the builder of the furnace for smelting the ore, the feller of the timber, the burner of the charcoal to be made use of in the smelting-house, the brick-maker, the brick-layer, the workmen who attend the furnace, the mill-wright, the forger, the smith, must all of them join their different arts in order to produce them. Were we to examine, in the same manner, all the different parts of his dress and household furniture, the coarse linen shirt which he wears next his skin, the shoes which cover his feet, the bed which he lies on, and all the different parts which compose it, the kitchen-grate at which he prepares his victuals, the coals which he makes use of for that purpose, dug from the bowels of the earth, and brought to him perhaps by a long sea and a long land carriage, all the other utensils of his kitchen, all the furniture of his table, the knives and forks, the earthen or pewter plates upon which he serves up and divides his victuals, the different hands employed in preparing his bread and his beer, the glass window which lets in the heat and the light, and keeps out the wind and the rain, with all the knowledge and art requisite for preparing that beautiful and happy invention, without which these northern parts of the world could scarce have afforded a very comfortable habitation, together with the tools of all the different workmen employed in producing those different conveniencies; if we examine, I say, all these things, and consider what a variety of labour is employed about each of them, we shall be sensible that without the assistance and co-operation of many thousands, the very meanest person in a civilized country could not be provided, even according to what we very falsely imagine, the easy and simple manner in which he is commonly accommodated. Compared, indeed, with the more extravagant luxury of the great, his accommodation must no doubt appear extremely simple and easy; and yet it may be true, perhaps, that the accommodation of an European prince does not always so much exceed that of an industrious and frugal peasant, as the accommodation of the latter exceeds that of many an African king, the absolute master of the lives and liberties of ten thousand naked savages.[24]

NOTES

This phrase ["Of the Division of Labour"], if used at all before this time, was not a familiar one. Its presence here is probably due to a passage in Mandeville, *Fable of the Bees*, pt. ii. (1729), dial. vi., p. 335: 'CLEO. . . . When once men come to be governed by written laws, all the rest comes on apace . . . No number of men, when once they enjoy quiet, and no man needs to fear his neighbour, will be long without learning to divide and subdivide their labour. HOR. I don't understand you. CLEO. Man, as I have hinted before, naturally loves to imitate what he sees others do, which is the reason that savage people all do the same thing: this hinders them from meliorating their condition, though they are always wishing for it: but if one will wholly apply himself to the making of bows and arrows, whilst another provides food, a third builds huts, a fourth makes garments, and a fifth utensils, they not only become useful to one another, but the callings and employments themselves will, in the same number of years, receive much greater improvements, than if all had been promiscuously followed by every one of the five. HOR. I believe you are perfectly right there; and the truth of what you say is in nothing so conspicuous as it is in watch-making, which is come to a higher degree of perfection than it would have been arrived at yet, if the whole had always remained the employment of one person; and I am persuaded that even the plenty we have of clocks and watches, as well as the exactness and beauty they may be made of, are chiefly owing to the division that has been made of that art into many branches.' The index contains, 'Labour, The usefulness of dividing and subdividing it'. Joseph Harris, *Essay upon Money and Coins*, 1757, pt. i., § 12, treats of the 'usefulness of distinct trades,' or 'the advantages accruing to mankind from their betaking themselves severally to different occupations,' but does not use the phrase 'division of labour'.

1 Ed. 1 reads 'improvements'.
2 Ed. 1 reads 'Though in them'.
3 Another and perhaps more important reason for taking an example like that which follows is the possibility of exhibiting the advantage, of division of labour in statistical form.
4 This parenthesis would alone be sufficient to show that those are wrong who believe

Smith did not include the separation of employments in 'division of labour'.

5   In Adam Smith's *Lectures*, p. 164, the business is, as here, divided into eighteen operations. This number is doubtless taken from the *Encyclopédie*, tom. v. (published in 1755), *s.v.* Épingle. The article is ascribed to M. Delaire, 'qui décrivait la fabrication de l'épingle dans les ateliers même des ouvriers,' p. 807. In some factories the division was carried further. E. Chambers, *Cyclopædia*, vol. ii., 2nd ed., 1738, and 4th ed., 1741, *s.v.* Pin, makes the number of separate operations twenty-five.

6   Ed. 1 reads 'the'.

7   Ed. 1 reads 'the lands' here and line preceding.

8   Ed. 1 reads 'because the silk manufacture does not suit the climate of England'.

9   In *Lectures*, p. 164, the comparison is between English and French 'toys,' i.e., small metal articles.

10   Ed. 1 places 'in consequence of the division of labour' here instead of in the line above.

11   'Pour la célérité du travail et la perfection de l'ouvrage, elles dépendent entièrement de la multitude des ouvriers rassemblés. Lorsqu'une manufacture est nombreuse, chaque opération occupe un homme différent. Tel ouvrier ne fait et ne fera de sa vie qu'une seule et unique chose; tel autre une autre chose: d'où il arrive que chacune s'exécute bien et promptement, et que l'ouvrage le mieux fait est encore celui qu'on a à meilleur marché. D'ailleurs le goût et la façon se perfectionnent nécessairement entre un grand nombre d'ouvriers, parce qu'il est difficile qu'il ne s'en rencontre quelques-uns capables de réfléchir, de combiner, et de trouver enfin le seul moyen qui puisse les mettre audessus de leurs semblables; le moyen ou d'épargner la matière, ou d'allonger le temps, ou de surfaire l'industrie, soit par une machine nouvelle, soit par une manœuvre plus commode.' – *Encyclopédie*, tom i. (1751), p. 717, *s.v.* Art. All three advantages mentioned in the text above are included here [in the original publication].

12   In *Lectures*, p. 166, 'a country smith not accustomed to make nails will work very hard for three or four hundred a day and those too very bad'.

13   In *Lectures*, p. 166, 'a boy used to it will easily make two thousand and those incomparably better'.

14   In *Lectures*, p. 255, it is implied that the labour of making a button was divided among eighty persons.

15   The same example occurs in *Lectures*, p. 166.

16   Examples are given in *Lectures*, p. 167: 'Two men and three horses will do more in a day with the plough than twenty men without it. The miller and his servant will do more with the water mill than a dozen with the hand mill, though it too be a machine.'

17   Ed. 1 reads 'I shall, therefore, only observe'.

18   Ed. 1 reads 'machines employed'.

19   Ed. 1 reads 'of common'.

20   I.e., steam-engines.

21   This pretty story is largely, at any rate, mythical. It appears to have grown out of a misreading (not necessarily by Smith) of the following passage: 'They used before to work with a buoy in the cylinder enclosed in a pipe, which buoy rose when the steam was strong, and opened the injection, and made a stroke; thereby they were capable of only giving six, eight or ten strokes in a minute, till a boy, Humphry Potter, who attended the engine, added (what he called scoggan) a catch that the beam Q always opened; and then it would go fifteen or sixteen strokes in a minute. But this being perplexed with catches and strings, Mr. Henry Beighton, in an engine he had built at Newcastle-on-Tyne in 1718, took them all away, the beam itself simply supplying all much better.' – J. T. Desaguliers, *Course of Experimental Philosophy*, vol. ii., 1744, p. 533. From pp. 469, 471, it appears that hand labour was originally used before the 'buoy' was devised.

22   In *Lectures*, p. 167, the invention of the plough is conjecturally attributed to a farmer and that of the hand-mill to a slave, while the invention of the water-wheel and the steam engine is credited to philosophers. Mandeville is very much less favourable to the claims of the philosophers: 'They are very seldom the same sort of people, those that invent arts and improvements in them and those that inquire into the reason of things: this latter is most commonly practised by such as are idle and indolent, that are fond of retirement, hate business and

take delight in speculation; whereas none succeed oftener in the first than active, stirring and laborious men, such as will put their hand to the plough, try experiments and give all their attention to what they are about.' – *Fable of the Bees*, pt. ii. (1729), dial. iii., p. 151. He goes on to give as examples the improvements in soap-boiling, grain-dyeing, etc.

23 The advantage of producing particular commodities wholly or chiefly in the countries most naturally fitted for their production is recognised below [p. 480 of original publication], but the fact that division of labour is necessary for its attainment is not noticed. The fact that division of labour allows different workers to be put exclusively to the kind of work for which they are best fitted by qualities not acquired by education and practice, such as age, sex, size and strength, is in part ignored and in part denied below [pp. 19, 20 of original publication]. The disadvantage of division of labour or specialisation is dealt with below [vol. ii., pp. 302–4 of original publication].

24 This paragraph was probably taken bodily from the MS. of the author's lectures. It appears to be founded on Mun, *England's Treasure by Forraign Trade*, chap. iii., at end; Locke, *Civil Government*, § 43; Mandeville, *Fable of the Bees*, pt. i., Remark P, 2nd ed. 1723, p. 182, and perhaps Harris, *Essay upon Money and Coins*, pt. i., § 12. See *Lectures*, pp. 161–2 and notes.

2

Absolute and Relative Surplus Value

Karl Marx (1818–1883)

Karl Heinrich Marx was born into a comfortable middle-class home in Trier, Germany on May 5, 1818. Finding a university position inaccessible, Marx became a journalist and, in 1842, became editor of the influential newspaper *Rheinische Zeitung*. However, the Prussian government soon closed the paper in response to many of his articles, at which time Marx emigrated to France. In Paris, Marx set down his views in a series of writings known as the *Economic and Philosophical Manuscripts* (1844), which remained unpublished until the 1930s. Marx was soon exiled from Paris, and with his co-author, Frederick Engels, moved to Brussels in 1844 where he stayed for three years. At a conference of the League in London at the end of 1847, Marx and Engels were commissioned to write a short treatise. *The Communist Manifesto* had just been published when a spate of revolutions broke out across Europe in 1848. By 1857 he had produced an 800-page tome on capital, landed property, wage labor, the state, foreign trade and the world market. The *Grundrisse* (or Outlines) was not published until 1941. In the 1860s, he devoted himself to *Capital*; the third volume remained unfinished at the time of his death in 1883.

In considering the labour-process, we began [see Chapter VII of original publication] by treating it in the abstract, apart from its historical forms, as a process between man and Nature. We there stated [p. 176 of original publication]: "If we examine the whole process from the point of view of its result, the product, it is plain that both the instruments and the subject of labour, are means of production, and that the labour itself is productive labour." And in Note 2, same page [of original publication], we further added: "This method of determining, from the standpoint of the labour-process alone, what is productive labour, is by no means directly applicable to the case of the capitalist process of production." We now proceed to the further development of this subject.

So far as the labour-process is purely individual, one and the same labourer unites in himself all the functions, that later on become separated. When an individual appropriates natural objects for his livelihood, no one controls him but himself. Afterwards he is controlled by others. A single man cannot operate upon Nature without calling his own muscles into play under the control of his own brain. As in the natural body head and hand wait upon each other, so the labour-process unites the labour of the hand with that of the head. Later on they part company and even become deadly foes. The product ceases to be the direct product of the individual, and becomes a social product, produced in common by a collective labourer, i.e., by a combination of workmen, each of whom takes only a part, greater or less, in the manipulation of the subject of their labour. As the co-operative character of the labour-process becomes more and more marked, so, as a necessary consequence, does our notion of productive labour, and of its agent the productive labourer, become extended. In order to labour productively, it is no longer necessary for you to do manual work yourself; enough, if you are an organ of the collective labourer, and perform one of its subordinate functions. The first definition given above of productive labour, a definition deduced from the very nature of the production of material objects, still remains correct for the collective labourer, considered as a whole. But it no longer holds good for each member taken individually.

On the other hand, however, our notion of productive labour becomes narrowed. Capitalist production is not merely the production of commodities, it is essentially the production of surplus-value. The labourer produces, not for himself, but for capital. It no longer suffices, therefore, that he should simply produce. He must produce surplus-value. That labourer alone is productive, who produces surplus-value for the capitalist, and thus works for the self-expansion of capital. If we may take an example from outside the sphere of production of material objects, a schoolmaster is a productive labourer, when, in addition to belabouring the heads of his scholars, he works like a horse to enrich the school proprietor. That the latter has laid out his capital in a teaching factory, instead of in a sausage factory, does not alter the relation. Hence the notion of a productive labourer implies not merely

a relation between work and useful effect, between labourer and product of labour, but also a specific, social relation of production, a relation that has sprung up historically and stamps the labourer as the direct means of creating surplus-value. To be a productive labourer is, therefore, not a piece of luck, but a misfortune. In Book IV [of original publication], which treats of the history of the theory, it will be more clearly seen, that the production of surplus-value has at all times been made, by classical political economists, the distinguishing characteristic of the productive labourer. Hence their definition of a productive labourer changes with their comprehension of the nature of surplus-value. Thus the Physiocrats insist that only agricultural labour is productive, since that alone, they say, yields a surplus-value. And they say so because, with them, surplus-value has no existence except in the form of rent.

The prolongation of the working-day beyond the point at which the labourer would have produced just an equivalent for the value of his labour-power, and the appropriation of that surplus-labour by capital, this is production of absolute surplus-value. It forms the general groundwork of the capitalist system, and the starting-point for the production of relative surplus-value. The latter pre-supposes that the working-day is already divided into two parts, necessary labour, and surplus-labour. In order to prolong the surplus-labour, the necessary labour is shortened by methods whereby the equivalent for the wages is produced in less time. The production of absolute surplus-value turns exclusively upon the length of the working-day; the production of relative surplus-value, revolutionises out and out the technical processes of labour, and the composition of society. It therefore pre-supposes a specific mode, the capitalist mode of production, a mode which, along with its methods, means, and conditions, arises and develops itself spontaneously on the foundation afforded by the formal subjection of labour to capital. In the course of this development, the formal sub-jection is replaced by the real subjection of labour to capital.

It will suffice merely to refer to certain intermediate forms, in which surplus-labour is not extorted by direct compulsion from the producer, nor the producer himself yet formally subjected to capital. In such forms capital has not yet acquired the direct control of the labour-process. By the side of independent producers who carry on their handicrafts and agriculture in the tradi-tional old-fashioned way, there stands the usurer or the merchant, with his usurer's capital or merchant's capital, feeding on them like a parasite. The predominance, in a society, of this form of exploitation excludes the capitalist mode of production; to which mode, however, this form may serve as a transition, as it did towards the close of the middle ages. Finally, as is shown by modern "domestic industry," some intermediate forms are here and there reproduced in the background of Modern Industry, though their physiognomy is totally changed.

If, on the one hand, the mere formal sub-jection of labour to capital suffices for the production of absolute surplus-value, if, e.g., it is sufficient that handicraftsmen who pre-viously worked on their own account, or as apprentices of a master, should become wage-labourers under the direct control of a capitalist; so, on the other hand, we have seen, how the methods of producing rela-tive surplus-value, are, at the same time, methods of producing absolute surplus-value. Nay, more, the excessive prolongation of the working-day turned out to be the peculiar product of Modern Industry. Gen-erally speaking, the specifically capitalist mode of production ceases to be a mere means of producing relative surplus-value, so soon as that mode has conquered an entire branch of production; and still more so, so soon as it has conquered all the impor-tant branches. It then becomes the general, socially predominant form of production. As a special method of producing relative surplus-value, it remains effective only, first,

in so far as it seizes upon industries that pre-viously were only formally subject to capital, that is, so far as it is propagandist; secondly, in so far as the industries that have been taken over by it, continue to be revolu-tionised by changes in the methods of production.

From one standpoint, any distinction between absolute and relative surplus-value appears illusory. Relative surplus-value is absolute, since it compels the absolute pro-longation of the working-day beyond the labour-time necessary to the existence of the labourer himself. Absolute surplus-value is relative, since it makes necessary such a development of the productiveness of labour, as will allow of the necessary labour-time being confined to a portion of the working-day. But if we keep in mind the behaviour of surplus-value, this appearance of identity vanishes. Once the capitalist mode of production established and become general, the difference between absolute and relative surplus-value makes itself felt, whenever there is a question of raising the rate of surplus-value. Assuming that labour-power is paid for at its value, we are confronted by this alternative: given the pro-ductiveness of labour and its normal inten-sity, the rate of surplus-value can be raised only by the actual prolongation of the working-day; on the other hand, given the length of the working-day, that rise can be effected only by a change in the relative magnitudes of the components of the working-day, viz., necessary labour and surplus-labour; a change which, if the wages are not to fall below the value of labour-power, pre-supposes a change either in the productiveness or in the intensity of the labour.

If the labourer wants all his time to produce the necessary means of subsistence for himself and his race, he has no time left in which to work gratis for others. Without a certain degree of productiveness in his labour, he has no such superfluous time at his disposal; without such superfluous time, no surplus-labour and therefore no capitalists, no slave-owners, no feudal lords, in one word, no class of large proprietors.[1]

Thus we may say that surplus-value rests on a natural basis; but this is permissible only in the very general sense, that there is no natural obstacle absolutely preventing one man from disburdening himself of the labour requisite for his own existence, and burdening another with it, any more, for instance, than unconquerable natural obstacles prevent one man from eating the flesh of another.[2] No mystical ideas must in any way be connected, as sometimes happens, with this historically developed productiveness of labour. It is only after men have raised themselves above the rank of animals, when therefore their labour has been to some extent socialised, that a state of things arises in which the surplus-labour of the one becomes a condition of existence for the other. At the dawn of civilisation the productiveness acquired by labour is small, but so too are the wants which develop with and by the means of satisfying them. Further, at that early period, the portion of society that lives on the labour of others is infinitely small compared with the mass of direct producers. Along with the progress in the productiveness of labour, that small portion of society increases both absolutely and relatively.[3] Besides, capital with its accompanying relations springs up from an economic soil that is the product of a long process of development. The productiveness of labour that serves as its foundation and starting-point, is a gift, not of Nature, but of a history embracing thousands of centuries.

Apart from the degree of development, greater or less, in the form of social production, the productiveness of labour is fettered by physical conditions. These are all referable to the constitution of man himself (race, &c.), and to surrounding Nature. The external physical conditions fall into two great economic classes, (1) Natural wealth in means of subsistence, i.e., a fruitful soil, waters teeming with fish, &c., and (2), natural wealth in the instruments of labour, such as waterfalls, navigable rivers, wood,

metal, coal, &c. At the dawn of civilisation, it is the first class that turns the scale; at a higher stage of development, it is the second. Compare, for example, England with India, or in ancient times, Athens and Corinth with the shores of the Black Sea.

The fewer the number of natural wants imperatively calling for satisfaction, and the greater the natural fertility of the soil and the favourableness of the climate, so much less is the labour-time necessary for the maintenance and reproduction of the producer. So much greater therefore can be the excess of his labour for others over his labour for himself. Diodorus long ago remarked this in relation to the ancient Egyptians. "It is altogether incredible how little trouble and expense the bringing up of their children causes them. They cook for them the first simple food at hand; they also give them the lower part of the papyrus stem to eat, so far as it can be roasted in the fire, and the roots and stalks of marsh plants, some raw, some boiled and roasted. Most of the children go without shoes and unclothed, for the air is so mild. Hence a child, until he is grown up, costs his parents not more, on the whole, than twenty drachmas. It is this, chiefly, which explains why the population of Egypt is so numerous, and, therefore, why so many great works can be undertaken."[4] Nevertheless the grand structures of ancient Egypt are less due to the extent of its population than to the large proportion of it that was freely disposable. Just as the individual labourer can do more surplus-labour in proportion as his necessary labour-time is less, so with regard to the working population. The smaller the part of it which is required for the production of the necessary means of subsistence, so much the greater is the part that can be set to do other work.

Capitalist production once assumed, then, all other circumstances remaining the same, and given the length of the working-day, the quantity of surplus-labour will vary with the physical conditions of labour, especially with the fertility of the soil. But it by no means follows from this that the most fruitful soil is the most fitted for the growth of the capitalist mode of production. This mode is based on the dominion of man over Nature. Where Nature is too lavish, she "keeps him in hand, like a child in leading-strings." She does not impose upon him any necessity to develop himself.[5] It is not the tropics with their luxuriant vegetation, but the temperate zone, that is the mother-country of capital. It is not the mere fertility of the soil, but the differentiation of the soil, the variety of its natural products, the changes of the seasons, which form the physical basis for the social division of labour, and which, by changes in the natural surroundings, spur man on to the multiplication of his wants, his capabilities, his means and modes of labour. It is the necessity of bringing a natural force under the control of society, of economising, of appropriating or subduing it on a large scale by the work of man's hand, that first plays the decisive part in the history of industry. Examples are, the irrigation works in Egypt,[6] Lombardy, Holland, or in India and Persia where irrigation by means of artificial canals, not only supplies the soil with the water indispensable to it, but also carries down to it, in the shape of sediment from the hills, mineral fertilisers. The secret of the flourishing state of industry in Spain and Sicily under the dominion of the Arabs lay in their irrigation works.[7]

Favourable natural conditions alone, give us only the possibility, never the reality, of surplus-labour, nor, consequently, of surplus-value and a surplus-product. The result of difference in the natural conditions of labour is this, that the same quantity of labour satisfies, in different countries, a different mass of requirements,[8] consequently, that under circumstances in other respects analogous, the necessary labour-time is different. These conditions affect surplus-labour only as natural limits, i.e., by fixing the points at which labour for others can begin. In proportion as industry advances, these natural limits recede. In the midst of our West European society, where the labourer purchases the right to work for his own livelihood only by paying for it in surplus-labour, the idea easily takes root that it is an inherent quality of human labour to furnish a surplus-product.[9] But consider, for example, an inhabitant of the eastern islands of the Asiatic Archipelago, where sago grows wild in the forests. "When the inhabitants have convinced themselves, by boring a hole in the tree, that the pith is ripe, the trunk is cut down and divided into several pieces, the pith is extracted, mixed with water and filtered: it is then quite fit for use as sago. One tree commonly yields 300 lbs., and occasionally 500 to 600 lbs. There, then, people go into the forests, and cut bread for themselves, just as with us they cut fire-wood."[10] Suppose now such an eastern bread-cutter requires 12 working-hours a week for the satisfaction of all his wants. Nature's direct gift to him is plenty of leisure time. Before he can apply this leisure time productively for himself, a whole series of historical events is required; before he spends it in surplus-labour for strangers, compulsion is necessary. If capitalist production were introduced, the honest fellow would perhaps have to work six days a week, in order to appropriate to himself the product of one working-day. The bounty of Nature does not explain why he would then have to work 6 days a week, or why he must furnish 5 days of surplus-labour. It explains only why his necessary labour-time would be limited to one day a week. But in no case would his surplus-product arise from some occult quality inherent in human labour.

Thus, not only does the historically developed social productiveness of labour, but also its natural productiveness, appear to be productiveness of the capital with which that labour is incorporated.

Ricardo never concerns himself about the origin of surplus-value. He treats it as a thing inherent in the capitalist mode of production, which mode, in his eyes, is the natural form of social production. Whenever he discusses the productiveness of labour, he seeks in it, not the cause of surplus-value, but the cause that determines the magnitude of that value. On the other hand, his school has openly proclaimed the productiveness of labour to be the originating cause of profit (read: surplus-value). This at all events is a progress as against the mercantilists who, on their side, derived the excess of the price over the cost of production of the product, from the act of exchange, from the product being sold above its value. Nevertheless, Ricardo's school simply shirked the problem, they did not solve it. In fact these bourgeois economists instinctively saw, and rightly so, that it is very dangerous to stir too deeply the burning question of the origin of surplus-value. But what are we to think of John Stuart Mill, who, half a century after Ricardo, solemnly claims superiority over the mercantilists, by clumsily repeating the wretched evasions of Ricardo's earliest vulgarisers?

Mill says: "The cause of profit is that labour produces more than is required for its support." So far, nothing but the old story; but Mill wishing to add something of his own, proceeds: "To vary the form of the theorem; the reason why capital yields a profit, is because food, clothing, materials and tools, last longer than the time which was required to produce them." He here confounds the duration of labour-time with the duration of its products. According to this view, a baker whose product lasts only a day, could never extract from his workpeople the same profit, as a machine maker whose products endure for 20 years and more. Of course it is very true, that if a bird's nest did not last longer than the time it takes in building, birds would have to do without nests.

This fundamental truth once established. Mill establishes his own superiority over the mercantilists. "We thus see," he proceeds, "that profit arises, not from the incident of exchange, but from the productive power of labour; and the general profit of the country is always what the productive power of

labour makes it, whether any exchange takes place or not. If there were no division of employments, there would be no buying or selling, but there would still be profit." For Mill then, exchange, buying and selling, those general conditions of capitalist production, are but an incident, and there would always be profits even without the purchase and sale of labour-power!

"If," he continues, "the labourers of the country collectively produce twenty per cent. more than their wages, profits will be twenty per cent., whatever prices may or may not be." This is, on the one hand, a rare bit of tautology; for if labourers produce a surplus-value of 20% for the capitalist, his profit will be to the total wages of the labourers as $20:100$. On the other hand, it is absolutely false to say that "profits will be 20%." They will always be less, because they are calculated upon the *sum total* of the capital advanced. If, for example, the capitalist have advanced £500, of which £400 is laid out in means of production and £100 in wages, and if the rate of surplus-value be 20%, the rate of profit will be $20:500$, i.e., 4% and not 20%.

Then follows a splendid example of Mill's method of handling the different historical forms of social production. "I assume, throughout, the state of things which, where the labourers and capitalists are separate classes, prevails, with few exceptions, universally; namely, that the capitalist advances the whole expenses, including the entire remuneration of the labourer." Strange optical illusion to see everywhere a state of things which as yet exists only exceptionally on our earth. But let us finish – Mill is willing to concede, "that he should do so is not a matter of inherent necessity."[11] On the contrary: "the labourer might wait, until the production is complete, for all that part of his wages which exceeds mere necessaries: and even for the whole, if he has funds in hand sufficient for his temporary support. But in the latter case, the labourer is to that extent really a capitalist in the concern, by supplying a portion of the funds necessary for carrying it on." Mill might have gone further and have added, that the labourer who advances to himself not only the necessaries of life but also the means of production, is in reality nothing but his own wage-labourer. He might also have said that the American peasant proprietor is but a serf who does enforced labour for himself instead of for his lord.

After thus proving clearly, that even if capitalist production had no existence, still it would always exist, Mill is consistent enough to show, on the contrary, that it has no existence, even when it does exist. "And even in the former case" (when the workman is a wage-labourer to whom the capitalist advances all the necessaries of life, he the labourer), "may be looked upon in the same light" (i.e., as a capitalist), "since, contributing his labour at less than the market-price, (!) he may be regarded as lending the difference (?) to his employer and receiving it back with interest, &c."[12] In reality, the labourer advances his labour gratuitously to the capitalist during, say one week, in order to receive the market-price at the end of the week, &c., and it is this which, according to Mill, transforms him into a capitalist. On the level plain, simple mounds look like hills; and the imbecile flatness of the present bourgeoisie is to be measured by the altitude of its great intellects.

NOTES

1 "The very existence of the master-capitalists, as a distinct class, is dependent on the productiveness of industry." (Ramsay, 1. c., p. 206.) "If each man's labour were but enough to produce his own food, there could be no property." (Ravenstone, 1. c., pp. 14, 15.)

2 According to a recent calculation, there are yet at least 4,000,000 cannibals in those parts of the earth which have already been explored.

3 "Among the wild Indians in America, almost everything is the labourer's, 99 parts of a

hundred are to be put upon the account of labour. In England, perhaps, the labourer has not $^2/_3$." ("The Advantages of the East India Trade, &c.," p. 73.)

4 Diodorus, 1. c., 1. 1., c. 80.

5 "The first (natural wealth) as it is most noble and advantageous, so doth it make the people careless, proud, and given to all excesses; whereas the second enforceth vigilancy, literature, arts and policy." ("England's Treasure by Foreign Trade. Or the Balance of our Foreign Trade is the Rule of our Treasure. Written by Thomas Mun of London, merchant, and now published for the common good by his son John Mun." London, 1669, pp. 181, 182.) "Nor can I conceive a greater curse upon a body of people, than to be thrown upon a spot of land, where the productions for subsistence and food were, in great measure, spontaneous, and the climate required or admitted little care for raiment and covering . . . there may be an extreme on the other side. A soil incapable of produce by labour is quite as bad as a soil that produces plentifully without any labour." ("An Enquiry into the Causes of the Present High Price of Provisions." Lond. 1767, p. 10.)

6 The necessity for predicting the rise and fall of the Nile created Egyptian astronomy, and with it the dominion of the priests, as directors of agriculture. "Le solstice est le moment de l'année où commence la crue du Nil, et celui que les Egyptiens ont dû observer avec le plus d'attention. . . . C'était cette année tropique qu'il leur importait de marquer pour se diriger dans leurs opérations agricoles, Ils durent donc chercher dans le ciel un signe apparent de son retour." (Cuvier: "Discours sur les révolutions du globe," ed. Hoefer, Paris, 1863, p. 141.)

7 One of the material bases of the power of the State over the small disconnected producing organisms in India, was the regulation of the water supply. The Mahometan rulers of India understood this better than their English successors. It is enough to recall to mind the famine of 1866, which cost the lives of more than a million Hindus in the district of Orissa, in the Bengal presidency.

8 "There are no two countries which furnish an equal number of the necessaries of life in equal plenty, and with the same quantity of

labour. Men's wants increase or diminish with the severity or temperateness of the climate they live in; consequently, the proportion of trade which the inhabitants of different countries are obliged to carry on through necessity cannot be the same, nor is it practicable to ascertain the degree of variation farther than by the degrees of Heat and Cold; from whence one may make this general conclusion, that the quantity of labour required for a certain number of people is greatest in cold climates, and least in hot ones; for in the former men not only want more clothes, but the earth more cultivating than in the latter." ("An Essay on the Governing Causes of the Natural Rate of Interest." Lond. 1750, p. 59.) The author of this epoch-making anonymous work is J. Massie. Hume took his theory of interest from it.

9 "Chaque travail doit (this appears also to be part of the droits et devoirs du citoyen) laisser un excédant." Proudhon.

10 F. Schouw: "Die Erde, die Pflanzen und der Mensch," 2. Ed. Leipz. 1854, p. 148.

11 On the basis of a suggestion Marx made to N. F. Danielson (Nikolai – on) in his letter of November 28, 1878, the part of this paragraph which begins with the words "Strange optical illusion" and ends with the words "inherent necessity" should read as follows: "Mr. Mill is willing to concede that it is not absolutely necessary for it to be so, even under an economic system where the labourers and capitalists are separate classes." – *Note by the Institute of Marxism–Leninism in the Russian edition.*

12 J. St. Mill. "Principles of Pol. Econ.," Lond. 1868, pp. 252–3.

3

The Protestant Ethic and the Spirit of Capitalism

Max Weber (1864–1920)

Max Weber was born near Erfurt, Saxony (in central Germany). The father of "interpretive" sociology, he has emphasized the importance of the "meaning" of social action to the actors themselves as a subject of study. In this vein, he has argued for the causal power of "ideal interests" (i.e. culture), thereby moving away from a technologically or economically deterministic view of history. Weber was trained as a lawyer; however, he began studying the conditions of agricultural workers in East Prussia in 1892 and in 1894 became a professor of economics. His teaching career was interrupted by World War I, and after returning to the academy briefly in the post-war period, he caught pneumonia in 1920 and died at age 56. His most major works include, *The Protestant Ethic and the Spirit of Capitalism* (1902), *Economy and Society* (1922), and *The Methodology of the Social Sciences* (1949).

Although we cannot here enter upon a discussion of the influence of Puritanism in all these directions, we should call attention to the fact that the toleration of pleasure in cultural goods, which contributed to purely æsthetic or athletic enjoyment, certainly always ran up against one characteristic limitation: they must not cost anything. Man is only a trustee of the goods which have come to him through God's grace. He must, like the servant in the parable, give an account of every penny entrusted to him,[1] and it is at least hazardous to spend any of it for a purpose which does not serve the glory of God but only one's own enjoyment.[2] What person, who keeps his eyes open, has not met representatives of this view-point even in the present?[3] The idea of a man's duty to his possessions, to which he subordinates himself as an obedient steward, or even as an acquisitive machine, bears with chilling weight on his life. The greater the possessions the heavier, if the ascetic attitude toward life stands the test, the feeling of responsibility for them, for holding them undiminished for the glory of God and increasing them by restless effort. The origin of this type of life also extends in certain roots, like so many aspects of the spirit of capitalism, back into the Middle Ages.[4] But it was in the ethic of ascetic Protestantism that it first found a consistent ethical foundation. Its significance for the development of capitalism is obvious.[5]

This worldly Protestant asceticism, as we may recapitulate up to this point, acted powerfully against the spontaneous enjoyment of possessions; it restricted consumption, especially of luxuries. On the other hand, it had the psychological effect of freeing the acquisition of goods from the inhibitions of traditionalistic ethics. It broke the bonds of the impulse of acquisition in that it not only legalized it, but (in the sense discussed) looked upon it as directly willed by God. The campaign against the temptations of the flesh, and the dependence on external things, was, as besides the Puritans the great Quaker apologist Barclay expressly says, not a struggle against the rational acquisition, but against the irrational use of wealth.

But this irrational use was exemplified in the outward forms of luxury which their code condemned as idolatry of the flesh,[6] however natural they had appeared to the feudal mind. On the other hand, they approved the rational and utilitarian uses of wealth which were willed by God for the needs of the individual and the community. They did not wish to impose mortification[7] on the man of wealth, but the use of his means for necessary and practical things. The idea of comfort characteristically limits the extent of ethically permissible expenditures. It is naturally no accident that the development of a manner of living consistent with that idea may be observed earliest and most clearly among the most consistent representatives of this whole attitude toward life. Over against the glitter and ostentation of feudal magnificence which, resting on an unsound economic basis, prefers a sordid elegance to a sober simplicity, they set the clean and solid comfort of the middle-class home as an ideal.[8]

On the side of the production of private wealth, asceticism condemned both dishonesty and impulsive avarice. What was condemned as covetousness, Mammonism, etc., was the pursuit of riches for their own sake. For wealth in itself was a temptation. But here asceticism was the power "which ever seeks the good but ever creates evil"[9]; what was evil in its sense was possession and its temptations. For, in conformity with the Old Testament and in analogy to the ethical valuation of good works, asceticism looked upon the pursuit of wealth as an end in itself as highly reprehensible; but the attainment of it as a fruit of labour in a calling was a sign of God's blessing. And even more important: the religious valuation of restless, continuous, systematic work in a worldly calling, as the highest means to asceticism, and at the same time the surest and most evident proof of rebirth and genuine faith, must have been the most powerful conceivable lever for the expansion of that attitude toward life which we have here called the spirit of capitalism.[10]

When the limitation of consumption is combined with this release of acquisitive activity, the inevitable practical result is obvious: accumulation of capital through ascetic compulsion to save.[11] The restraints which were imposed upon the consumption of wealth naturally served to increase it by making possible the productive investment of capital. How strong this influence was is not, unfortunately, susceptible of exact statistical demonstration. In New England the connection is so evident that it did not escape the eye of so discerning a historian as Doyle.[12] But also in Holland, which was really only dominated by strict Calvinism for seven years, the greater simplicity of life in the more seriously religious circles, in combination with great wealth, led to an excessive propensity to accumulation.[13]

That, furthermore, the tendency which has existed everywhere and at all times, being quite strong in Germany to-day, for middle-class fortunes to be absorbed into the nobility, was necessarily checked by the Puritan antipathy to the feudal way of life, is evident. English Mercantilist writers of the seventeenth century attributed the superiority of Dutch capital to English to the circumstance that newly acquired wealth there did not regularly seek investment in land. Also, since it is not simply a question of the purchase of land, it did not there seek to transfer itself to feudal habits of life, and thereby to remove itself from the possibility of capitalistic investment.[14] The high esteem for agriculture as a peculiarly important branch of activity, also especially consistent with piety, which the Puritans shared, applied (for instance in Baxter) not to the landlord, but to the yeoman and farmer, in the eighteenth century not to the squire, but the rational cultivator.[15] Through the whole of English society in the time since the seventeenth century goes the conflict between the squirearchy, the representatives of "merrie old England", and the Puritan circles of widely varying social influence.[16] Both elements, that of an unspoiled naïve joy of life, and of a strictly regulated, reserved self-control, and conventional ethical conduct are even to-day combined to form the English national character.[17] Similarly, the early history of the North American Colonies is dominated by the sharp contrast of the adventurers, who wanted to set up plantations with the labour of indentured servants, and live as feudal lords, and the specifically middle-class outlook of the Puritans.[18]

As far as the influence of the Puritan outlook extended, under all circumstances – and this is, of course, much more important than the mere encouragement of capital accumulation – it favoured the development of a rational bourgeois economic life; it was the most important, and above all the only consistent influence in the development of that life. It stood at the cradle of the modern economic man.

To be sure, these Puritanical ideals tended to give way under excessive pressure from the temptations of wealth, as the Puritans themselves knew very well. With great regularity we find the most genuine adherents of Puritanism among the classes which were rising from a lowly status,[19] the small bourgeois and farmers, while the *beati possidentes*, even among Quakers, are often found tending to repudiate the old ideals.[20] It was the same fate which again and again befell the predecessor of this worldly asceticism, the monastic asceticism of the Middle

Ages. In the latter case, when rational economic activity had worked out its full effects by strict regulation of conduct and limitation of consumption, the wealth accumulated either succumbed directly to the nobility, as in the time before the Reformation, or monastic discipline threatened to break down, and one of the numerous reformations became necessary.

In fact the whole history of monasticism is in a certain sense the history of a continual struggle with the problem of the secularizing influence of wealth. The same is true on a grand scale of the worldly asceticism of Puritanism. The great revival of Methodism, which preceded the expansion of English industry toward the end of the eighteenth century, may well be compared with such a monastic reform. We may hence quote here a passage[21] from John Wesley himself which might well serve as a motto for everything which has been said above. For it shows that the leaders of these ascetic movements understood the seemingly paradoxical relationships which we have here analysed perfectly well, and in the same sense that we have given them.[22] He wrote:

I fear, wherever riches have increased, the essence of religion has decreased in the same proportion. Therefore I do not see how it is possible, in the nature of things, for any revival of true religion to continue long. For religion must necessarily produce both industry and frugality, and these cannot but produce riches. But as riches increase, so will pride, anger, and love of the world in all its branches. How then is it possible that Methodism, that is, a religion of the heart, though it flourishes now as a green bay tree, should continue in this state? For the Methodists in every place grow diligent and frugal; consequently they increase in goods. Hence they proportionately increase in pride, in anger, in the desire of the flesh, the desire of the eyes, and the pride of life. So, although the form of religion remains, the spirit is swiftly vanishing away. Is there no way to prevent this – this continual decay of pure religion? We ought not to prevent people from being diligent and frugal; *we must exhort all Christians to gain all they can, and to save all they can; that is, in effect, to grow rich.*[23]

There follows the advice that those who gain all they can and save all they can should also give all they can, so that they will grow in grace and lay up a treasure in heaven. It is clear that Wesley here expresses, even in detail, just what we have been trying to point out.[24]

As Wesley here says, the full economic effect of those great religious movements, whose significance for economic development lay above all in their ascetic educative influence, generally came only after the peak of the purely religious enthusiasm was past. Then the intensity of the search for the Kingdom of God commenced gradually to pass over into sober economic virtue; the religious roots died out slowly, giving way to utilitarian worldliness. Then, as Dowden puts it, as in *Robinson Crusoe*, the isolated economic man who carries on missionary activities on the side[25] takes the place of the lonely spiritual search for the Kingdom of Heaven of Bunyan's pilgrim, hurrying through the market-place of Vanity.

When later the principle "to make the most of both worlds" became dominant in the end, as Dowden has remarked, a good conscience simply became one of the means of enjoying a comfortable bourgeois life, as is well expressed in the German proverb about the soft pillow. What the great religious epoch of the seventeenth century bequeathed to its utilitarian successor was, however, above all an amazingly good, we may even say a pharisaically good, conscience in the acquisition of money, so long as it took place legally. Every trace of the *deplacere vix potest* has disappeared.[26]

A specifically bourgeois economic ethic had grown up. With the consciousness of standing in the fullness of God's grace and being visibly blessed by Him, the bourgeois business man, as long as he remained within the bounds of formal correctness, as long as his moral conduct was spotless and the use to which he put his wealth was not objectionable, could follow his pecuniary interests as he would and feel that he was fulfilling a duty in doing so. The power of religious asceticism provided him in addition with sober, conscientious, and unusually industrious workmen, who clung to their work as to a life purpose willed by God.[27]

Finally, it gave him the comforting assurance that the unequal distribution of the goods of this world was a special dispensation of Divine Providence, which in these differences, as in particular grace, pursued secret ends unknown to men.[28] Calvin himself had made the much-quoted statement that only when the people, i.e. the mass of labourers and craftsmen, were poor did they remain obedient to God.[29] In the Netherlands (Pieter de la Court and others), that had been secularized to the effect that the mass of men only labour when necessity forces them to do so. This formulation of a leading idea of capitalistic economy later entered into the current theories of the productivity of low wages. Here also, with the dying out of the religious root, the utilitarian interpretation crept in unnoticed, in the line of development which we have again and again observed.

Mediæval ethics not only tolerated begging but actually glorified it in the mendicant orders. Even secular beggars, since they gave the person of means opportunity for good works through giving alms, were sometimes considered an estate and treated as such. Even the Anglican social ethic of the Stuarts was very close to this attitude. It remained for Puritan Asceticism to take part in the severe English Poor Relief Legislation which fundamentally changed the situation. And it could do that, because the Protestant sects and the strict Puritan communities actually did not know any begging in their own midst.[30]

On the other hand, seen from the side of the workers, the Zinzendorf branch of Pietism, for instance, glorified the loyal worker who did not seek acquisition, but lived according to the apostolic model, and was thus endowed with the *charisma*[31] of the disciples.[32] Similar ideas had originally been prevalent among the Baptists in an even more radical form.

Now naturally the whole ascetic literature of almost all denominations is saturated with the idea that faithful labour, even at low wages, on the part of those whom life offers no other opportunities, is highly pleasing to God. In this respect Protestant Asceticism added in itself nothing new. But it not only deepened this idea most powerfully, it also created the force which was alone decisive for its effectiveness: the psychological sanction of it through the conception of this labour as a calling, as the best, often in the last analysis the only means of attaining certainty of grace.[33] And on the other hand it legalized the exploitation of this specific willingness to work, in that it also interpreted the employer's business activity as a calling.[34] It is obvious how powerfully the exclusive search for the Kingdom of God only through the fulfilment of duty in the calling, and the strict asceticism which Church discipline naturally imposed, especially on the propertyless classes, was bound to affect the productivity of labour in the capitalistic sense of the word. The treatment of labour as a calling became as characteristic of the modern worker as the corresponding attitude toward acquisition of the business man. It was a perception of this situation, new at his time, which caused so able an observer as Sir William Petty to attribute the economic power of Holland in the seventeenth century to the fact that the very numerous dissenters in that country (Calvinists and Baptists) "are for the most part thinking, sober men, and such as believe that Labour and Industry is their duty towards God".[35]

Calvinism opposed organic social organization in the fiscal-monopolistic form which it assumed in Anglicanism under the Stuarts, especially in the conceptions of Laud, this alliance of Church and State with the monopolists on the basis of a Christian-social ethical foundation. Its leaders were universally among the most passionate opponents of this type of politically privileged commercial, putting-out, and colonial capitalism. Over against it they placed the individualistic motives of rational legal acquisition by virtue of one's own ability and initiative. And, while the politically privileged monopoly industries in England all disappeared in short order, this attitude played a large and decisive part in the development of the industries which grew up in spite of and against the authority of the State.[36] The Puritans (Prynne, Parker) repudiated all connection with the large-scale capitalistic courtiers and projectors as an ethically suspicious class. On the other hand, they took pride in their own superior middle-class business morality, which formed the true reason for the persecutions to which they were subjected on the part of those circles. Defoe proposed to win the battle against dissent by boycotting bank credit and withdrawing deposits. The difference of the two types of capitalistic attitude went to a very large extent hand in hand with religious differences. The opponents of the Nonconformists, even in the eighteenth century, again and again ridiculed them for personifying the spirit of shopkeepers, and for having ruined the ideals of old England. Here also lay the difference of the Puritan economic ethic from the Jewish; and contemporaries (Prynne) knew well that the former and not the latter was the bourgeois capitalistic ethic.[37]

One of the fundamental elements of the spirit of modern capitalism, and not only of that but of all modern culture: rational conduct on the basis of the idea of the calling, was born – that is what this discussion has sought to demonstrate – from the spirit of Christian asceticism. One has only to re-read the passage from Franklin, quoted at the beginning of this essay, in order to see that the essential elements of the attitude which was there called the spirit of capitalism are the same as what we have just shown to be the content of the Puritan worldly asceticism,[38] only without the religious basis, which by Franklin's time had died away. The idea that modern labour has an ascetic character is of course not new. Limitation to specialized work, with a renunciation of the Faustian universality of man which it involves, is a condition of any valuable work in the modern world; hence deeds and renunciation inevitably condition each other to-day. This fundamentally ascetic trait of middle-class life, if it attempts to be a way of life at all, and not simply the absence of any, was what Goethe wanted to teach, at the height of his wisdom, in the *Wanderjahren*, and in the end which he gave to the life of his *Faust*.[39] For him the realization meant a renunciation, a departure from an age of full and beautiful humanity, which can no more be repeated in the course of our cultural development than can the flower of the Athenian culture of antiquity.

The Puritan wanted to work in a calling; we are forced to do so. For when asceticism was carried out of monastic cells into everyday life, and began to dominate worldly morality, it did its part in building the tremendous cosmos of the modern economic order. This order is now bound to the technical and economic conditions of machine production which to-day determine the lives of all the individuals who are born into this mechanism, not only those directly concerned with economic acquisition, with irresistible force. Perhaps it will so determine them until the last ton of fossilized coal is burnt. In Baxter's view the care for external goods should only lie on the shoulders of the "saint like a light cloak, which can be thrown aside at any moment".[40] But fate decreed that the cloak should become an iron cage.

Since asceticism undertook to remodel the world and to work out its ideals in

the world, material goods have gained an increasing and finally an inexorable power over the lives of men as at no previous period in history. To-day the spirit of religious asceticism – whether finally, who knows? – has escaped from the cage. But victorious capitalism, since it rests on mechanical foundations, needs its support no longer. The rosy blush of its laughing heir, the Enlightenment, seems also to be irretrievably fading, and the idea of duty in one's calling prowls about in our lives like the ghost of dead religious beliefs. Where the fulfilment of the calling cannot directly be related to the highest spiritual and cultural values, or when, on the other hand, it need not be felt simply as economic compulsion, the individual generally abandons the attempt to justify it at all. In the field of its highest development, in the United States, the pursuit of wealth, stripped of its religious and ethical meaning, tends to become associated with purely mundane passions, which often actually give it the character of sport.[41]

No one knows who will live in this cage in the future, or whether at the end of this tremendous development entirely new prophets will arise, or there will be a great rebirth of old ideas and ideals, or, if neither, mechanized petrification, embellished with a sort of convulsive self-importance. For of the last stage of this cultural development, it might well be truly said: "Specialists without spirit, sensualists without heart; this nullity imagines that it has attained a level of civilization never before achieved."

But this brings us to the world of judgments of value and of faith, with which this purely historical discussion need not be burdened. The next task would be rather to show the significance of ascetic rationalism, which has only been touched in the foregoing sketch, for the content of practical social ethics, thus for the types of organization and the functions of social groups from the conventicle to the State. Then its relations to humanistic rationalism,[42] its ideals of life and cultural influence; further to the development of philosophical and scientific empiricism, to technical development and to spiritual ideals would have to be analysed. Then its historical development from the mediæval beginnings of worldly asceticism to its dissolution into pure utilitarianism would have to be traced out through all the areas of ascetic religion. Only then could the quantitative cultural significance of ascetic Protestantism in its relation to the other plastic elements of modern culture be estimated.

Here we have only attempted to trace the fact and the direction of its influence to their motives in one, though a very important point. But it would also further be necessary to investigate how Protestant Asceticism was in turn influenced in its development and its character by the totality of social conditions, especially economic.[43] The modern man is in general, even with the best will, unable to give religious ideas a significance for culture and national character which they deserve. But it is, of course, not my aim to substitute for a one-sided materialistic an equally one-sided spiritualistic causal interpretation of culture and of history. Each is equally possible,[44] but each, if it does not serve as the preparation, but as the conclusion of an investigation, accomplishes equally little in the interest of historical truth.[45]

NOTES

1 Charnock, *Self-Examination* (*Works of the Puritan Divines*, p. 172): "Reflection and knowledge of self is a prerogative of a rational nature." Also the footnote: "Cogito, ergo sum, is the first principle of the new philosophy."

2 This is not yet the place to discuss the relationship of the theology of Duns Scotus to certain ideas of ascetic Protestantism. It never gained official recognition, but was at best tolerated and at times proscribed. The later specific repugnance of the Pietists to Aristotelean philosophy was shared by Luther, in a somewhat different sense, and also by Calvin in conscious antagonism to Catholicism (cf. *Instit. Christ*, II, chap. xii, p. 4; IV, chap. xvii, p. 24). The "primacy of the will", as Kahl has put it, is common to all these movements.

3 Thus, for instance, the article on "Asceticism" in the Catholic *Church Lexicon* defines its meaning entirely in harmony with its highest historical manifestations. Similarly Seeberg in the *Realenzyklopädie für protestantische Theologie und Kirche*. For the purpose of this study we must be allowed to use the concept as we have done. That it can be defined in other ways, more broadly as well as more narrowly, and is generally so defined, I am well aware.

4 In Hudibras (*1st Song*, 18, 19) the Puritans are compared with the bare-foot Franciscans. A report of the Genoese Ambassador, Fieschi, calls Cromwell's army an assembly of monks.

5 In view of the close relationship between otherworldly monastic asceticism and active worldly asceticism, which I here expressly maintain, I am surprised to find Brentano (*Die Anfänge des modernen, Kapitalismus* (Munich, 1916), p. 134 and elsewhere) citing the ascetic labour of the monks and its recommendation against me. His whole "Exkurs" against me culminates in that. But that continuity is, as anyone can see, a fundamental postulate of my whole thesis: the Reformation took rational Christian asceticism and its methodical habits out of the monasteries and placed them in the service of active life in the world. Compare the following discussion, which has not been altered.

6 So in the many reports of the trials of Puritan heretics cited in Neal's *History of the Puritans* and Crosby's *English Baptists*.

7 Sanford, *Studies and Reflections of the Great Rebellion* (and both before and after him many others), has found the origin of the ideal of reserve in Puritanism. Compare on that ideal also the remarks of James Bryce on the American college in Vol. II of his *American Commonwealth*. The ascetic principle of self-control also made Puritanism one of the fathers of modern military discipline. (On Maurice of Orange as a founder of modern army organization, see Roloff,

Preuss. Jahrb., 1903, III, p. 255.) Cromwell's Ironsides, with cocked pistols in their hands, and approaching the enemy at a brisk trot without shooting, were not the superiors of the Cavaliers by virtue of their fierce passion, but, on the contrary, through their cool self-control, which enabled their leaders always to keep them well in hand. The knightly storm-attack of the Cavaliers, on the other hand, always resulted in dissolving their troops into atoms. See Firth, *Cromwell's Army*.

8 See especially Windelband, *Ueber Willensfreiheit*, pp. 77 ff.

9 Only not so unmixed. Contemplation, sometimes combined with emotionalism, is often combined with these rational elements. But again contemplation itself is methodically regulated.

10 According to Richard Baxter everything is sinful which is contrary to the reason given by God as a norm of action. Not only passions which have a sinful content, but all feelings which are senseless and intemperate as such. They destroy the countenance and, as things of the flesh, prevent us from rationally directing all action and feeling to God, and thus insult Him. Compare what is said of the sinfulness of anger (*Christian Directory*, second edition, 1698, p. 285. Tauler is cited on p. 287). On the sinfulness of anxiety, *Ebenda*, I, p. 287. That it is idolatry if our appetite is made the "rule or measure of eating" is maintained very emphatically (ibid., I, pp. 310, 316, and elsewhere). In such discussions reference is made everywhere to the Proverbs and also to Plutarch's *De tranquilitate Animi*, and not seldom to ascetic writings of the Middle Ages: St. Bernard, Bonaventura, and others. The contrast to "who does not love wine, women, and song . . ." could hardly be more sharply drawn than by the extension of the idea of idolatry to all sensuous pleasures, so far as they are not justified by hygienic considerations, in which case they (like sport within these limits, but also other recreations) are permissible. Please note that the sources referred to here and elsewhere are neither dogmatic nor edifying works, but grew out of practical ministry, and thus give a good picture of the direction which its influence took.

11 I should regret it if any evaluation of one or the other form of religion should be read into this discussion. We are not concerned with that here. It is only a question of the influence of certain things which, from a purely religious point of view, are perhaps incidental, but important for practical conduct.

12 On this, see especially the article "Moralisten, englische", by E. Troeltsch, in the *Realenzyklopädie für protestantische Theologie und Kirche*, third edition.

13 How much influence quite definite religious ideas and situations, which seem to be historical accidents, have had is shown unusually clearly by the fact that in the circles of Pietism of a Reformed origin the lack of monasteries was occasionally directly regretted, and that the communistic experiments of Labadie and others were simply a substitute for monastic life.

14 As early even as several confessions of the time of the Reformation. Even Ritschl (*Pietismus*, I, p. 258 f.) does not deny, although he looks upon the later development as a deterioration of the ideas of the Reformation, that, for instance, in *Conf. Gall.* 25, 26, *Conf. Belg.* 29, *Conf. Helv.* post, 17, the true Reformed Church was defined by definitely empirical attributes, and that to this true Church believers were not accounted without the attribute of moral activity.

15 "Bless God that we are not of the many" (Thomas Adams, *Works of the Puritan Divines*, p. 138).

16 The idea of the birthright, so important in history, thus received an important confirmation in England. "The firstborn which are written in heaven. . . . As the firstborn is not to be defeated in his inheritance, and the enrolled names are never to be obliterated, so certainly they shall inherit eternal life" (Thomas Adams, *Works of the Puritan Divines*, p. xiv).

17 The Lutheran emphasis on penitent grief is foreign to the spirit of ascetic Calvinism, not in theory, but definitely in practice. For it is of no ethical value to the Calvinist; it does not help the damned, while for those certain of their election, their own sin, so far as they admit it to themselves, is a symptom of backwardness in development. Instead of repent-

ing of it they hate it and attempt to overcome it by activity for the glory of God. Compare the explanation of Howe (Cromwell's chaplain 1656–8) in *Of Men's Enmity against God and of Reconciliation between God and Man* (*Works of English Puritan Divines*, p. 237): "The carnal mind is enmity against God. It is the mind, therefore, not as speculative merely, but as practical and active that must be renewed", and, p. 246: "Reconciliation . . . must begin in (1) a deep conviction . . . of your former enmity. . . . I have been alienated from God. . . . (2) (p. 251) a clear and lively apprehension of the monstrous iniquity and wickedness thereof." The hatred here is that of sin, not of the sinner. But as early as the famous letter of the Duchess Renata d'Este (Leonore's mother) to Calvin, in which she speaks of the hatred which she would feel toward her father and husband if she became convinced they belonged to the damned, is shown the transfer to the person. At the same time it is an example of what was said above [pp. 104–6] of how the individual became loosed from the ties resting on his natural feelings, for which the doctrine of predestination was responsible.

18 "None but those who give evidence of being regenerate or holy persons ought to be received or counted fit members of visible Churches. Where this is wanting, the very essence of a Church is lost", as the principle is put by Owen, the Independent-Calvinistic Vice-Chancellor of Oxford under Cromwell (*Inv. into the Origin of Ev. Ch.*). Further, see the following essay (not translated here. – Translator).

19 See following essay.

20 *Cat. Genev.*, p. 149. Bailey, *Praxis pietatis*, p. 125: "In life we should act as though no one but Moses had authority over us."

21 "The law appears to the Calvinist as an ideal norm of action. It oppresses the Lutheran because it is for him unattainable." In the Lutheran catechism it stands at the beginning in order to arouse the necessary humility, in the Reformed catechism it generally stands after the Gospel. The Calvinists accused the Lutherans of having a "virtual reluctance to becoming holy" (Möhler), while the Lutherans accused the Calvinists of an "unfree servitude to the law", and of arrogance.

22 *Studies and Reflections of the Great Rebellion*, pp. 79 f.

23 Among them the Song of Songs is especially noteworthy. It was for the most part simply ignored by the Puritans. Its Oriental eroticism has influenced the development of certain types of religion, such as that of St. Bernard.

24 On the necessity of this self-observation, see the sermon of Charnock, already referred to, on 2 Cor. xiii. 5, *Works of the Puritan Divines*, pp. 161 ff.

25 Most of the theological moralists recommended it. Thus Baxter, *Christian Directory*, II, pp. 77 ff., who, however, does not gloss over its dangers.

26 Moral book-keeping has, of course, been widespread elsewhere. But the emphasis which was placed upon it as the sole means of knowledge of the eternal decree of salvation or damnation was lacking, and with it the most important psychological sanction for care and exactitude in this calculation.

27 This was the significant difference from other attitudes which were superficially similar.

28 Baxter (*Saints' Everlasting Rest*, chap. xii) explains God's invisibility with the remark that just as one can carry on profitable trade with an invisible foreigner through correspondence, so is it possible by means of holy commerce with an invisible God to get possession of the one priceless pearl. These commercial similes rather than the forensic ones customary with the older moralists and the Lutherans are thoroughly characteristic of Puritanism, which in effect makes man buy his own salvation. Compare further the following passage from a sermon: "We reckon the value of a thing by that which a wise man will give for it, who is not ignorant of it nor under necessity. Christ, the Wisdom of God, gave Himself, His own precious blood, to redeem souls, and He knew what they were and had no need of them" (Matthew Henry, *The Worth of the Soul, Works of the Puritan Divines*, p. 313).

29 In contrast to that, Luther himself said: "Weeping goes before action and suffering excells all accomplishment" (*Weinen geht vor Wirken und Leiden übertrifft alles tun*).

30 This is also shown most clearly in the development of the ethical theory of

Lutheranism. On this see Hoennicke, *Studien zur altprotestantischen Ethik* (Berlin, 1902), and the instructive review of it by E. Troeltsch, *Gött. Gel. Anz.*, 1902, No. 8. The approach of the Lutheran doctrine, especially to the older orthodox Calvinistic, was in form often very close. But the difference of religious background was always apparent. In order to establish a connection between morality and faith, Melanchthon had placed the idea of repentance in the foreground. Repentance through the law must precede faith, but good works must follow it, otherwise it cannot be the truly justifying faith – almost a Puritan formula. Melanchthon admitted a certain degree of perfection to be attainable on earth. He had, in fact, originally taught that justification was given in order to make men capable of good works, and in increasing perfection lay at least the relative degree of blessedness which faith could give in this world. Also later Lutheran theologians held that good works are the necessary fruits of faith, that faith results in a new external life, just as the Reformed preachers did. The question in what good works consist Melanchthon, and especially the later Lutherans, answered more and more by reference to the law. There remained of Luther's original doctrines only the lesser degree of seriousness with which the Bible, especially the particular norms of the Old Testament, was taken. The decalogue remained, as a codification of the most important ideas of the natural moral law, the essential norm of human action. But there was no firm link connecting its legal validity with the more and more strongly emphasized importance of faith for justification, because this faith had a fundamentally different psychological character from the Calvinistic.

The true Lutheran standpoint of the early period had to be abandoned by a Church which looked upon itself as an institution for salvation. But another had not been found. Especially was it impossible, for fear of losing their dogmatic foundation (*sola fide!*), to accept the ascetic rationalization of conduct as the moral task of the individual. For there was no motive to give the idea of proof such a significance as it attained in Calvinism through the doctrine of predestination. Moreover, the magical interpretation of the sacraments, combined with the lack of this doctrine, especially the association of the *regeneratio*, or at least its beginning with baptism, necessarily, assuming as it did the universality of grace, hindered the development of methodical morality. For it weakened the contrast between the state of nature and the state of grace, especially when combined with the strong Lutheran emphasis on original sin. No less important was the entirely forensic interpretation of the act of justification which assumed that God's decrees might be changed through the influence of particular acts of repentance of the converted sinner. And that was just the element to which Melanchthon gave increasing emphasis. The whole development of his doctrine, which gave increasing weight to repentance, was intimately connected with his profession of the freedom of the will. That was what primarily determined the *unme*thodical character of Lutheran conduct.

Particular acts of grace for particular sins, not the development of an aristocracy of saints creating the certainty of their own salvation, was the necessary form salvation took for the average Lutheran, as the retention of the confession proves. Thus it could develop neither a morality free from the law nor a rational asceticism in terms of the law. Rather the law remained in an unorganic proximity to faith as an ideal, and, moreover, since the strict dependence on the Bible was avoided as suggesting salvation by works, it remained uncertain, vague, and, above all, unsystematic in its content. Their conduct remained, as Troeltsch has said of their ethical theory, a "sum of mere beginnings which never quite materialized"; which, "taught in particular, uncertain, and unrelated maxims", did not succeed in "working out an articulate system of conduct", but formed essentially, following the development through which Luther himself (see above) had gone, a resignation to things as they were in matters both small and great. The resignation of the Germans to foreign cultures, their rapid change of nationality, of which there is so much complaint, is clearly to be attributed, along with certain political circumstances in the history of the nation, in part to the results of this influence, which still affects all aspects of our life. The subjective assimilation of culture remained weak because it took place primarily by means of a passive absorption of what was authoritatively presented.

31 On these points, see the gossipy book of Tholuck, *Vorgeschichte des Rationalismus*.

32 On the quite different results of the Mohammedan doctrine of predestination (or rather predetermination) and the reasons for it, see the theological dissertation (Heidelberg) of F. Ullrich, *Die Vorherbestimmungslehre im Islam u. Ch.*, 1912. On that of the Jansenists, see P. Honigsheim, *Die Staats- und Soziallehren der Französischen Jansenisten im 17ten Jahrhundert* (Heidelberg Historical Dissertation, 1914).

33 See the following essay [in original publication].

34 Ritschl, *Geschichte des Pietismus*, I, p. 152, attempts to distinguish them for the time before Labadie (only on the basis of examples from the Netherlands) (1) in that the Pietists formed conventicles; (2) they held the doctrine of the "worthlessness of existence in the flesh" in a "manner contrary to the Protestant interests in salvation"; (3) "the assurance of grace in the tender relationship with the Lord Jesus" was sought in an un-Calvinistic manner. The last criterion applies for this early period only to one of the cases with which he deals. The idea of worthlessness of the flesh was in itself a true child of the Calvinistic spirit, and only where it led to practical renunciation of the world was it antagonistic to normal Protestantism. The conventicles, finally, had been established to a certain extent (especially for catechistic purposes) by the Synod of Dordrecht itself. Of the criteria of Pietism analysed in Ritschl's previous discussion, those worth considering are (1) the greater precision with which the letter of the Bible was followed in all external affairs of life, as Gisbert Voet for a time urged; (2) the treatment of justification and reconciliation with God, not as ends in themselves, but simply as means toward a holy ascetic life as can be seen perhaps in Lodensteyn, but as is also suggested by Melanchthon [see above, note 30]; (3) the high value placed on repentance

as a sign of true regeneration, as was first taught by W. Teellinck; (4) abstention from communion when unregenerate persons partake of it (of which we shall speak in another connection). Connected with that was the formation of conventicles with a revival of prophecy, i.e. interpretation of the Scriptures by laymen, even women. That went beyond the limits set by the canons of Dordrecht.

Those are all things forming departures, sometimes considerable, from both the doctrine and practice of the Reformers. But compared with the movements which Ritschl does not include in his treatment, especially the English Puritans, they form, except for No. 3, only a continuation of tendencies which lay in the whole line of development of this religion. The objectivity of Ritschl's treatment suffers from the fact that the great scholar allows his personal attitude towards the Church or, perhaps better, religious policy, to enter in, and, in his antipathy to all peculiarly ascetic forms of religion, interprets any development in that direction as a step back into Catholicism. But, like Catholicism, the older Protestantism included all sorts and conditions of men. But that did not prevent the Catholic Church from repudiating rigorous worldly asceticism in the form of Jansenism; just as Pietism repudiated the peculiar Catholic Quietism of the seventeenth century. From our special view-point Pietism differs not in degree, but in kind from Calvinism only when the increasing fear of the world leads to flight from ordinary economic life and the formation of monastic-communistic conventicles (Labadie). Or, which has been attributed to certain extreme Pietists by their contemporaries, they were led deliberately to neglect worldly duties in favour of contemplation. This naturally happened with particular frequency when contemplation began to assume the character which Ritschl calls Bernardism, because it suggests St. Bernard's interpretation of the Song of Songs: a mystical, emotional form of religion seeking the *unio mystica* with an esoteric sexual tinge. Even from the viewpoint of religious psychology alone this is undoubtedly something quite different from Calvinism, including its ascetic form exemplified by men like Voet. Ritschl, however, everywhere attempts to connect this quietism with the Pietist asceticism and thus to bring the latter under the same indictment; in doing so he puts his finger on every quotation from Catholic mysticism or asceticism which he can find in Pietist literature. But English and Dutch moralists and theologians who are quite beyond suspicion cite Bernard, Bonaventura, and Thomas à Kempis. The relationship of all the Reformation Churches to the Catholic past was very complex and, according to the point of view which is emphasized, one or another appears most closely related to Catholicism or certain sides of it.

35   The illuminating article on "Pietism" by Mirbt in the third edition of the *Realenzyklopädie für protestantische Theologie und Kirche*, treats the origin of Pietism, leaving its Protestant antecedents entirely on one side, as a purely personal religious experience of Spener, which is somewhat improbable. As an introduction to Pietism, Gustav Freytag's description in *Bilder der deutschen Vergangenheit* is still worth reading. For the beginnings of English Pietism in the contemporary literature, compare W. Whitaker, *Prima Institutio disciplinaque pietatis* (1570).

36   It is well known that this attitude made it possible for Pietism to be one of the main forces behind the idea of toleration. At this point we may insert a few remarks on that subject. In the West its historical origin, if we omit the humanistic indifference of the Enlightenment, which in itself has never had great practical influence, is to be found in the following principal sources: (1) Purely political expediency (type: William of Orange). (2) Mercantilism (especially clear for the City of Amsterdam, but also typical of numerous cities, landlords, and rulers who received the members of sects as valuable for economic progress). (3) The radical wing of Calvinism. Predestination made it fundamentally impossible for the State really to promote religion by intolerance. It could not thereby save a single soul. Only the idea of the glory of God gave the Church occasion to claim its help in the suppression of heresy. Now the greater the emphasis on the membership of the preacher, and all those that partook of the communion, in the elect, the more intol-

erable became the interference of the State in the appointment of the clergy. For clerical positions were often granted as benefices to men from the universities only because of their theological training, though they might be personally unregenerate. In general, any interference in the affairs of the religious community by those in political power, whose conduct might often be unsatisfactory, was resented. Reformed Pietism strengthened this tendency by weakening the emphasis on doctrinal orthodoxy and by gradually undermining the principle of *extra ecclesiam nulla salus*.

Calvin had regarded the subjection of the damned to the divine supervision of the Church as alone consistent with the glory of God; in New England the attempt was made to constitute the Church as an aristocracy of proved saints. Even the radical Independents, however, repudiated every interference of temporal or any sort of hierarchical powers with the proof of salvation which was only possible within the individual community. The idea that the glory of God requires the subjection of the damned to the discipline of the Church was gradually superseded by the other idea, which was present from the beginning and became gradually more prominent, that it was an insult to His glory to partake of the Communion with one rejected by God. That necessarily led to voluntarism, for it led to the believers' Church the religious community which included only the twice-born. Calvinistic Baptism, to which, for instance, the leader of the Parliament of Saints Praisegod Barebones belonged, drew the consequences of this line of thought with great emphasis. Cromwell's army upheld the liberty of conscience and the parliament of saints even advocated the separation of Church and State, because its members were good Pietists, thus on positive religious grounds. (4) The Baptist sects, which we shall discuss later, have from the beginning of their history most strongly and consistently maintained the principle that only those personally regenerated could be admitted to the Church. Hence they repudiated every conception of the Church as an institution (*Anstalt*) and every interference of the temporal power. Here also it was for positive religious reasons that unconditional toleration was advocated.

The first man who stood out for absolute toleration and the separation of Church and State, almost a generation before the Baptists and two before Roger Williams, was probably John Browne. The first declaration of a Church group in this sense appears to be the resolution of the English Baptists in Amsterdam of 1612 or 1613: "The magistrate is not to middle with religion or matters of conscience . . . because Christ is the King and Law-giver of the Church and conscience." The first official document of a Church which claimed the positive protection of liberty of conscience by the State as a right was probably Article 44 of the Confession of the Particular Baptists of 1644.

Let it be emphatically stated again that the idea sometimes brought forward, that toleration as such was favourable to capitalism, is naturally quite wrong. Religious toleration is neither peculiar to modern times nor to the West. It has ruled in China, in India, in the great empires of the Near East in Hellenistic times, in the Roman Empire and the Mohammedan Empires for long periods to a degree only limited by reasons of political expediency (which form its limits to-day also!) which was attained nowhere in the world in the sixteenth and seventeenth centuries. Moreover, it was least strong in those areas which were dominated by Puritanism, as, for instance, Holland and Zeeland in their period of political and economic expansion or in Puritan old or New England. Both before and after the Reformation, religious intolerance was peculiarly characteristic of the Occident as of the Sassanian Empire. Similarly, it has prevailed in China, Japan, and India at certain particular times, though mostly for political reasons. Thus toleration as such certainly has nothing whatever to do with capitalism. The real question is, Who benefited by it? Of the consequences of the believers' Church we shall speak further in the following article.

37 This idea is illustrated in its practical application by Cromwell's tryers, the examiners of candidates for the position of preacher. They attempted to ascertain not only the knowledge of theology, but also the subjective state of grace of the candidate.

38 The characteristic Pietistic distrust of Aristotle and classical philosophy in general is suggested in Calvin himself (compare *Instit. Christ*, II, chap. ii, p. 4; III, chap. xxiii, p. 5; IV, chap. xvii, p. 24). Luther in his early days distrusted it no less, but that was later changed by the humanistic influence (especially of Melanchthon) and the urgent need of ammunition for apologetic purposes. That everything necessary for salvation was contained in the Scriptures plainly enough for even the untutored was, of course, taught by the Westminster Confession (chap. i, No. 7.), in conformity with the whole Protestant tradition.

39 The official Churches protested against this, as, for example, in the shorter catechism of the Scotch Presbyterian Church of 1648, sec. vii. Participation of those not members of the same family in family devotions was forbidden as interference with the prerogatives of the office. Pietism, like every ascetic community-forming movement, tended to loosen the ties of the individual with domestic patriarchalism, with its interest in the prestige of office.

40 We are here for good reasons intentionally neglecting discussion of the psychological, in the technical sense of the word, aspect of these religious phenomena, and even its terminology has been as far as possible avoided. The firmly established results of psychology, including psychiatry, do not as present go far enough to make them of use for the purposes of the historical investigation of our problems without prejudicing historical judgments. The use of its terminology would only form a temptation to hide phenomena which were immediately understandable, or even sometimes trivial, behind a veil of foreign words, and thus give a false impression of scientific exactitude, such as is unfortunately typical of Lamprecht. For a more serious attempt to make use of psychological concepts in the interpretation of certain historical mass phenomena, see W. Hellpach, *Grundlinien zu einer Psychologie der Hysterie*, chap. xii, as well as his *Nervosität und Kultur*. I cannot here attempt to explain that in my opinion even this many-sided writer has been harmfully influenced by certain of Lamprecht's theories. How completely worthless, as compared with the

older literature, Lamprecht's schematic treatment of Pietism is (in Vol. VII of the *Deutsche Geschichte*) everyone knows who has the slightest acquaintance with the literature.

41 Thus with the adherents of Schortinghuis's *Innige Christendom*. In the history of religion it goes back to the verse about the servant of God in Isaiah and the 22nd Psalm.

42 This appeared occasionally in Dutch Pietism and then under the influence of Spinoza.

43 Labadie, Teersteegen, etc.

44 Perhaps this appears most clearly when he (Spener!) disputes the authority of the Government to control the conventicles except in cases of disorder and abuses, because it concerns a fundamental right of Christians guaranteed by apostolic authority (*Theologische Bedenken*, II, pp. 81 f.). That is, in principle, exactly the Puritan standpoint regarding the relations of the individual to authority and the extent to which individual rights, which follow *ex jure divino* and are therefore inalienable, are valid. Neither this heresy, nor the one mentioned farther on in the text, has escaped Ritschl (*Pietismus*, II, pp. 115, 157). However unhistorical the positivistic (not to say philistine) criticism to which he has subjected the idea of natural rights to which we are nevertheless indebted for not much less than everything which even the most extreme reactionary prizes as his sphere of individual freedom, we naturally agree entirely with him that in both cases an organic relationship to Spener's Lutheran standpoint is lacking.

The conventicles (*collegia pietitatis*) themselves, to which Spener's famous *pia desideria* gave the theoretical basis, and which he founded in practice, corresponded closely in essentials to the English prophesyings which were first practised in John of Lasco's London Bible Classes (1547), and after that were a regular feature of all forms of Puritanism which revolted against the authority of the Church. Finally, he bases his well-known repudiation of the Church discipline of Geneva on the fact that its natural executors, the third estate (*status œconomicus*: the Christian laity), were not even a part of the organization of the Lutheran Church. On the other hand, in the discussion of excommunication the lay members' recognition of the Consistorium appointed by the prince as representatives of the third estate is weakly Lutheran.

45 The name Pietism in itself, which first occurs in Lutheran territory, indicates that in the opinion of contemporaries it was characteristic of it that a methodical business was made out of *pietas*.

4

Some Principles of Stratification

Kingsley Davis (1908–1997) and Wilbert Moore

Kingsley Davis was a world-renowned expert on population trends. He held a BA from the University of Texas and a Ph.D. from Harvard University. He first taught at Clark University and then later at Pennsylvania State University, Princeton University and ultimately, the Bureau of Applied Social Research at Columbia University. He is also the first sociologist to be elected to the National Academy of Sciences. He is best known for coining the terms "population explosion" and "zero population growth." His specific studies of American society led him to work on a general science of world society. He is author of, among other works, *A Crowding Hemisphere: Population Change in the Americas* (1958) and *World Urbanization: 1950–70* (Vol. I and II, 1969–72).

Influenced by the social theorists Talcott Parsons and Pitirim Sorokin, Wilbert Moore is best known for his work on "structural-functionalism," a theoretical paradigm that views society as a whole as having needs, functions, and tensions within it. These inherent properties of an anthropomorphized society generate social stability and change from within. In fact, Moore, who was a professor in the sociology/anthropology department of Princeton University, has called society a system of "tension management." Within this paradigm, inequality itself has a functional role. Among Moore's works are *Social Change* (1963) and *Order and Change* (1967).

In a previous paper some concepts for handling the phenomena of social inequality were presented.[1] In the present paper a further step in stratification theory is undertaken – an attempt to show the relationship between stratification and the rest of the social order.[2] Starting from the proposition that no society is "classless," or unstratified, an effort is made to explain, in functional terms, the universal necessity which calls forth stratification in any social system.

Next, an attempt is made to explain the roughly uniform distribution of prestige as between the major types of positions in every society. Since, however, there occur between one society and another great differences in the degree and kind of stratification, some attention is also given to the varieties of social inequality and the variable factors that give rise to them.

Clearly, the present task requires two different lines of analysis – one to understand the universal, the other to understand the variable features of stratification. Naturally each line of inquiry aids the other and is indispensable, and in the treatment that follows the two will be interwoven, although, because of space limitations, the emphasis will be on the universals.

Throughout, it will be necessary to keep in mind one thing – namely, that the discussion relates to the system of positions, not to the individuals occupying those positions. It is one thing to ask why different positions carry different degrees of prestige, and quite another to ask how certain individuals get into those positions. Although, as the argument will try to show, both questions are related, it is essential to keep them separate in our thinking. Most of the literature on stratification has tried to answer the second question (particularly with regard to the ease or difficulty of mobility between strata) without tackling the first. The first question, however, is logically prior and, in the case of any particular individual or group, factually prior.

The Functional Necessity of Stratification

Curiously, however, the main functional necessity explaining the universal presence of stratification is precisely the requirement faced by any society of placing and motivating individuals in the social structure. As a functioning mechanism a society must somehow distribute its members in social positions and induce them to perform the duties of these positions. It must thus concern itself with motivation at two different levels: to instill in the proper individuals the desire to fill certain positions, and, once in these positions, the desire to perform the duties attached to them. Even though the social order may be relatively static in form, there is a continuous process of metabolism as new individuals are born into it, shift with age, and die off. Their absorption into the positional system must somehow be arranged and motivated. This is true whether the system is competitive or non-

competitive. A competitive system gives greater importance to the motivation to achieve positions, whereas a non-competitive system gives perhaps greater importance to the motivation to perform the duties of the positions; but in any system both types of motivation are required.

If the duties associated with the various positions were all equally pleasant to the human organism, all equally important to societal survival, and all equally in need of the same ability or talent, it would make no difference who got into which positions, and the problem of social placement would be greatly reduced. But actually it does make a great deal of difference who gets into which positions, not only because some positions are inherently more agreeable than others, but also because some require special talents or training and some are functionally more important than others. Also, it is essential that the duties of the positions be performed with the diligence that their importance requires. Inevitably, then, a society must have, first, some kind of rewards that it can use as inducements, and, second, some way of distributing these rewards differentially according to positions. The rewards and their distribution become a part of the social order, and thus give rise to stratification.

One may ask what kind of rewards a society has at its disposal in distributing its personnel and securing essential services. It has, first of all, the things that contribute to sustenance and comfort. It has, second, the things that contribute to humor and diversion. And it has, finally, the things that contribute to self respect and ego expansion. The last, because of the peculiarly social character of the self, is largely a function of the opinion of others, but it nonetheless ranks in importance with the first two. In any social system all three kinds of rewards must be dispensed differentially according to positions.

In a sense the rewards are "built into" the position. They consist in the "rights" associated with the position, plus what may be called its accompaniments or perquisites.

Often the rights, and sometimes the accompaniments, are functionally related to the duties of the position. (Rights as viewed by the incumbent are usually duties as viewed by other members of the community.) However, there may be a host of subsidiary rights and perquisites that are not essential to the function of the position and have only an indirect and symbolic connection with its duties, but which still may be of considerable importance in inducing people to seek the positions and fulfil the essential duties.

If the rights and perquisites of different positions in a society must be unequal, then the society must be stratified, because that is precisely what stratification means. Social inequality is thus an unconsciously evolved device by which societies insure that the most important positions are conscientiously filled by the most qualified persons. Hence every society, no matter how simple or complex, must differentiate persons in terms of both prestige and esteem, and must therefore possess a certain amount of institutionalized inequality.

It does not follow that the amount or type of inequality need be the same in all societies. This is largely a function of factors that will be discussed presently.

The Two Determinants of Positional Rank

Granting the general function that inequality subserves, one can specify the two factors that determine the relative rank of different positions. In general those positions convey the best reward, and hence have the highest rank, which (a) have the greatest importance for the society and (b) require the greatest training or talent. The first factor concerns function and is a matter of relative significance; the second concerns means and is a matter of scarcity.

Differential functional importance

Actually a society does not need to reward positions in proportion to their functional importance. It merely needs to give sufficient reward to them to insure that they will be filled competently. In other words, it must see that less essential positions do not compete successfully with more essential ones. If a position is easily filled, it need not be heavily rewarded, even though important. On the other hand, if it is important but hard to fill, the reward must be high enough to get it filled anyway. Functional importance is therefore a necessary but not a sufficient cause of high rank being assigned to a position.[3]

Differential scarcity of personnel

Practically all positions, no matter how acquired, require some form of skill or capacity for performance. This is implicit in the very notion of position, which implies that the incumbent must, by virtue of his incumbency, accomplish certain things.

There are, ultimately, only two ways in which a person's qualifications come about: through inherent capacity or through training. Obviously, in concrete activities both are always necessary, but from a practical standpoint the scarcity may lie primarily in one or the other, as well as in both. Some positions require innate talents of such high degree that the persons who fill them are bound to be rare. In many cases, however, talent is fairly abundant in the population but the training process is so long, costly, and elaborate that relatively few can qualify. Modern medicine, for example, is within the mental capacity of most individuals, but a medical education is so burdensome and expensive that virtually none would undertake it if the position of the M.D. did not carry a reward commensurate with the sacrifice.

If the talents required for a position are abundant and the training easy, the method of acquiring the position may have little to do with its duties. There may be, in fact, a virtually accidental relationship. But if the skills required are scarce by reason of the rarity of talent or the costliness of training, the position, if functionally important, must have an attractive power that will draw the necessary skills in competition with other positions. This means, in effect, that the position must be high in the social scale – must command great prestige, high salary, ample leisure, and the like.

How variations are to be understood

In so far as there is a difference between one system of stratification and another, it is attributable to whatever factors affect the two determinants of differential reward – namely, functional importance and scarcity of personnel. Positions important in one society may not be important in another, because the conditions faced by the societies, or their degree of internal development, may be different. The same conditions, in turn, may affect the question of scarcity; for in some societies the stage of development, or the external situation, may wholly obviate the necessity of certain kinds of skill or talent. Any particular system of stratification, then, can be understood as a product of the special conditions affecting the two aforementioned grounds of differential reward.

Major Societal Functions and Stratification

Religion

The reason why religion is necessary is apparently to be found in the fact that human society achieves its unity primarily through the possession by its members of certain ultimate values and ends in common. Although these values and ends are subjective, they influence behavior, and their integration enables the society to operate as a system. Derived neither from inherited nor from external nature, they have evolved as a part of culture by communication and moral pressure. They must, however, appear to the members of the society to have some reality, and it is the role of religious belief and ritual to supply and reinforce this appearance of reality. Through belief and ritual the common ends and values are connected with an imaginary world symbolized by concrete sacred objects, which world in turn is related in a meaningful way to the facts and trials of the individual's life. Through the worship of the sacred objects and the beings they symbolize, and the acceptance of supernatural prescriptions that are at the same time codes of behavior, a powerful control over human conduct is exercised, guiding it along lines sustaining the institutional structure and conforming to the ultimate ends and values.

If this conception of the role of religion is true, one can understand why in every known society the religious activities tend to be under the charge of particular persons, who tend thereby to enjoy greater rewards than the ordinary societal member. Certain of the rewards and special privileges may attach to only the highest religious functionaries, but others usually apply, if such exists, to the entire sacerdotal class.

Moreover, there is a peculiar relation between the duties of the religious official and the special privileges he enjoys. If the supernatural world governs the destinies of men more ultimately than does the real world, its earthly representative, the person through whom one may communicate with the supernatural, must be a powerful individual. He is a keeper of sacred tradition, a skilled performer of the ritual, and an interpreter of lore and myth. He is in such close contact with the gods that he is viewed as possessing some of their characteristics. He is, in short, a bit sacred, and hence free from some of the more vulgar necessities and controls.

It is no accident, therefore, that religious functionaries have been associated with the very highest positions of power, as in theocratic regimes. Indeed, looking at it from this point of view, one may wonder why it is that they do not get *entire* control over their societies. The factors that prevent this are worthy of note.

In the first place, the amount of technical competence necessary for the performance of religious duties is small. Scientific or artistic capacity is not required. Anyone can set himself up as enjoying an intimate relation with deities, and nobody can successfully dispute him. Therefore, the factor of scarcity of personnel does not operate in the technical sense.

One may assert, on the other hand, that religious ritual is often elaborate and religious lore abstruse, and that priestly ministrations require tact, if not intelligence. This is true, but the technical requirements of the profession are for the most part adventitious, not related to the end in the same way that science is related to air travel. The priest can never be free from competition, since the criteria of whether or not one has genuine contact with the supernatural are never strictly clear. It is this competition that debases the priestly position below what might be expected at first glance. That is why priestly prestige is highest in those societies where membership in the profession is rigidly controlled by the priestly guild itself. That is why, in part at least, elaborate devices are utilized to stress the identification of the person with his office – spectacular costume, abnormal conduct, special diet, segregated residence, celibacy, conspicuous leisure, and the like. In fact, the priest is always in danger of becoming somewhat discredited – as happens in a secularized society – because in a world of stubborn fact, ritual and sacred knowledge alone will not grow crops or build houses. Furthermore, unless he is protected by a professional guild, the priest's identification with the supernatural tends to preclude his acquisition of abundant wordly goods.

As between one society and another it seems that the highest general position awarded the priest occurs in the medieval type of social order. Here there is enough economic production to afford a surplus, which can be used to support a numerous and highly organized priesthood; and yet the populace is unlettered and therefore credulous to a high degree. Perhaps the most extreme example is to be found in the Buddhism of Tibet, but others are encountered in the Catholicism of feudal Europe, the Inca regime of Peru, the Brahminism of India, and the Mayan priesthood of Yucatan. On the other hand, if the society is so crude as to have no surplus and little differentiation, so that every priest must be also a cultivator or hunter, the separation of the priestly status from the others has hardly gone far enough for priestly prestige to mean much. When the priest actually has high prestige under these circumstances, it is because he also performs other important functions (usually political and medical).

In an extremely advanced society built on scientific technology, the priesthood tends to lose status, because sacred tradition and supernaturalism drop into the background. The ultimate values and common ends of the society tend to be expressed in less anthropomorphic ways, by officials who occupy fundamentally political, economic, or educational rather than religious positions. Nevertheless, it is easily possible for intellectuals to exaggerate the degree to which the priesthood in a presumably secular milieu has lost prestige. When the matter is closely examined the urban proletariat, as well as the rural citizenry, proves to be surprisingly god-fearing and priest-ridden. No society has become so completely secularized as to liquidate entirely the belief in transcendental ends and supernatural entities. Even in a secularized society some system must exist for the integration of ultimate values, for their ritualistic expression, and for the emotional adjustments required by disappointment, death, and disaster.

Government

Like religion, government plays a unique and indispensable part in society. But in contrast to religion, which provides integration in terms of sentiments, beliefs, and rituals, it organizes the society in terms of law and authority. Furthermore, it orients the society to the actual rather than the unseen world.

The main functions of government are, internally, the ultimate enforcement of norms, the final arbitration of conflicting interests, and the overall planning and direction of society; and externally, the handling of war and diplomacy. To carry out these functions it acts as the agent of the entire people, enjoys a monopoly of force, and controls all individuals within its territory.

Political action, by definition, implies authority. An official can command because he has authority, and the citizen must obey because he is subject to that authority. For this reason stratification is inherent in the nature of political relationships.

So clear is the power embodied in political position that political inequality is sometimes thought to comprise all inequality. But it can be shown that there are other bases of stratification, that the following controls operate in practice to keep political power from becoming complete: (a) The fact that the actual holders of political office, and especially those determining top policy must necessarily be few in number compared to the total population. (b) The fact that the rulers represent the interest of the group rather than of themselves, and are therefore restricted in their behavior by rules and mores designed to enforce this limitation of interest. (c) The fact that the holder of political office has his authority by virtue of his office and nothing else, and therefore any special knowledge, talent, or capacity he may claim is purely incidental, so that he often has to depend upon others for technical assistance.

In view of these limiting factors, it is not strange that the rulers often have less power and prestige than a literal enumeration of their formal rights would lead one to expect.

Wealth, property, and labor

Every position that secures for its incumbent a livelihood is, by definition, economically rewarded. For this reason there is an economic aspect to those positions (e.g. political and religious) the main function of which is not economic. It therefore becomes convenient for the society to use unequal economic returns as a principal means of controlling the entrance of persons into positions and stimulating the performance of their duties. The amount of the economic return therefore becomes one of the main indices of social status.

It should be stressed, however, that a position does not bring power and prestige *because* it draws a high income. Rather, it draws a high income because it is functionally important and the available personnel is for one reason or another scarce. It is therefore superficial and erroneous to regard high income as the cause of a man's power and prestige, just as it is erroneous to think that a man's fever is the cause of his disease.[4]

The economic source of power and prestige is not income primarily, but the ownership of capital goods (including patents, good will, and professional reputation). Such ownership should be distinguished from the possession of consumers' goods, which is an index rather than a cause of social standing. In other words, the ownership of producers' goods is properly speaking, a source of income like other positions, the income itself remaining an index. Even in situations where social values are widely commercialized and earnings are the readiest method of judging social position, income does not confer prestige on a position so much as it induces people to compete for the position. It is true that a man who has a high income as a result of one position may find this money helpful in climbing into another position as well, but this again reflects the effect of his initial, economically advantageous status, which exercises its influence through the medium of money.

In a system of private property in productive enterprise, an income above what an individual spends can give rise to possession of capital wealth. Presumably such possession is a reward for the proper management of one's finances originally and of the productive enterprise later. But as social differentiation becomes highly advanced and yet the institution of inheritance persists, the phenomenon of pure ownership, and reward for pure ownership, emerges. In such a case it is difficult to prove that the position is functionally important or that the scarcity involved is anything other than extrinsic and accidental. It is for this reason, doubtless, that the institution of private property in productive goods becomes more subject to criticism as social development proceeds toward industrialization. It is only this pure, that is, strictly legal and functionless ownership, however, that is open to attack; for some form of active ownership, whether private or public, is indispensable.

One kind of ownership of production goods consists in rights over the labor of others. The most extremely concentrated and exclusive of such rights are found in slavery, but the essential principle remains in serfdom, peonage, encomienda, and indenture. Naturally this kind of ownership has the greatest significance for stratification, because it necessarily entails an unequal relationship.

But property in capital goods inevitably introduces a compulsive element even into the nominally free contractual relationship. Indeed, in some respects the authority of the contractual employer is greater than that of the feudal landlord, inasmuch as the latter is more limited by traditional reciprocities. Even the classical economics recognized that competitors would fare unequally, but it did not pursue this fact to its necessary conclusion that, however it might be acquired, unequal control of goods and services must give unequal advantage to the parties to a contract.

Technical knowledge

The function of finding means to single goals, without any concern with the choice between goals, is the exclusively technical sphere. The explanation of why positions requiring great technical skill receive fairly high rewards is easy to see, for it is the simplest case of the rewards being so distributed as to draw talent and motivate training. Why they seldom if ever receive the highest rewards is also clear: the importance of technical knowledge from a societal point of view is never so great as the integration of goals, which takes place on the religious, political, and economic levels. Since the technological level is concerned solely with means, a purely technical position must ultimately be subordinate to other positions that are religious, political, or economic in character.

Nevertheless, the distinction between expert and layman in any social order is fundamental, and cannot be entirely reduced to other terms. Methods of recruitment, as well as of reward, sometimes lead to the erroneous interpretation that technical positions are economically determined. Actually, however, the acquisition of knowledge and skill cannot be accomplished by purchase, although the opportunity to learn may be. The control of the avenues of training may inhere as a sort of property right in certain families or classes, giving them power and prestige in consequence. Such a situation adds an artificial scarcity to the natural scarcity of skills and talents. On the other hand, it is possible for an opposite situation to arise. The rewards of technical position may be so great that a condition of excess supply is created, leading to at least temporary devaluation of the rewards. Thus "unemployment in the learned professions" may result in a debasement of the prestige of those positions. Such adjustments and readjustments are constantly occurring in changing societies; and it is always well to bear in mind that the efficiency of a stratified structure may be affected by the modes of recruitment for positions. The social order itself, however, sets limits to the inflation or deflation of the prestige of experts: an oversupply tends to debase the rewards and discourage recruitment or produce revolution, whereas an under-supply tends to increase the rewards or weaken the society in competition with other societies.

Particular systems of stratification show a wide range with respect to the exact position of technically competent persons. This range is perhaps most evident in the degree of specialization. Extreme division of labor tends to create many specialists without high prestige since the training is short and the required native capacity relatively small. On the other hand it also tends to accentuate the high position of the true experts – scientists, engineers, and administrators – by increasing their authority relative to other functionally important positions. But the idea of a technocratic social order or a government or priesthood of engineers or social scientists neglects the limitations of knowledge and skills as a basic for performing social functions. To the extent that the social structure is truly specialized the prestige of the technical person must also be circumscribed.

Variation in Stratified Systems

The generalized principles of stratification here suggested form a necessary preliminary to a consideration of types of stratified systems, because it is in terms of these principles that the types must be described. This can be seen by trying to delineate types according to certain modes of variation. For instance, some of the most important modes (together with the polar types in terms of them) seem to be as follows:

(a) The degree of specialization

The degree of specialization affects the fineness and multiplicity of the gradations in power and prestige. It also influences the extent to which particular functions may be emphasized in the invidious system, since a given function cannot receive much emphasis in the hierarchy until it has achieved structural separation from the other func-

tions. Finally, the amount of specialization influences the bases of selection. Polar types: *Specialized, Unspecialized.*

(b) The nature of the functional emphasis

In general when emphasis is put on sacred matters, a rigidity is introduced that tends to limit specialization and hence the development of technology. In addition, a brake is placed on social mobility, and on the development of bureaucracy. When the preoccupation with the sacred is withdrawn, leaving greater scope for purely secular preoccupations, a great development, and rise in status, of economic and technological positions seemingly takes place. Curiously, a concomitant rise in political position is not likely, because it has usually been allied with the religious and stands to gain little by the decline of the latter. It is also possible for a society to emphasize family functions – as in relatively undifferentiated societies where high mortality requires high fertility and kinship forms the main basis of social organization. Main types: *Familistic, Authoritarian (Theocratic* or sacred, and *Totalitarian* or secular), *Capitalistic.*

(c) The magnitude of invidious differences

What may be called the amount of social distance between positions, taking into account the entire scale, is something that should lend itself to quantitative measurement. Considerable differences apparently exist between different societies in this regard, and also between parts of the same society. Polar types: *Equalitarian, Inequalitarian.*

(d) The degree of opportunity

The familiar question of the amount of mobility is different from the question of the comparative equality or inequality of rewards posed above, because the two criteria may vary independently up to a point.

For instance, the tremendous divergences in monetary income in the United States are far greater than those found in primitive societies, yet the equality of opportunity to move from one rung to the other in the social scale may also be greater in the United States than in a hereditary tribal kingdom. Polar types: *Mobile* (open), *Immobile* (closed).

(e) The degree of stratum solidarity

Again, the degree of "class solidarity" (or the presence of specific organizations to promote class interests) may vary to some extent independently of the other criteria, and hence is an important principle in classifying systems of stratification. Polar types: *Class organized, Class unorganized.*

External Conditions

What state any particular system of stratification is in with reference to each of these modes of variation depends on two things: (1) its state with reference to the other ranges of variation, and (2) the conditions outside the system of stratification which nevertheless influence that system. Among the latter are the following:

(a) The stage of cultural development

As the cultural heritage grows, increased specialization becomes necessary, which in turn contributes to the enhancement of mobility, a decline of stratum solidarity, and a change of functional emphasis.

(b) Situation with respect to other societies

The presence or absence of open conflict with other societies, of free trade relations or cultural diffusion, all influence the class structure to some extent. A chronic state of warfare tends to place emphasis upon the military functions, especially when the opponents are more or less equal. Free trade, on the other hand, strengthens the hand of the trader at the expense of the warrior and priest. Free movement of ideas generally has an equalitarian effect. Migration and conquest create special circumstances.

(c) Size of the society

A small society limits the degree to which functional specialization can go, the degree of segregation of different strata, and the magnitude of inequality.

Composite Types

Much of the literature on stratification has attempted to classify concrete systems into a certain number of types. This task is deceptively simple, however, and should come at the end of an analysis of elements and principles, rather than at the beginning. If the preceding discussion has any validity, it indicates that there are a number of modes of variation between different systems, and that any one system is a composite of the society's status with reference to all these modes of variation. The danger of trying to classify whole societies under such rubrics as *caste, feudal,* or *open class* is that one or two criteria are selected and others ignored, the result being an unsatisfactory solution to the problem posed. The present discussion has been offered as a possible approach to the more systematic classification of composite types.

NOTES

1 Kingsley Davis, "A Conceptual Analysis of Stratification," *American Sociological Review.* 7: 309–21, June, 1942.
2 The writers regret (and beg indulgence) that the present essay, a condensation of a longer study, covers so much in such short space that adequate evidence and qualification cannot be given and that as a result what is actually very tentative is presented in an unfortunately dogmatic manner.

3 Unfortunately, functional importance is difficult to establish. To use the position's prestige
to establish it, as is often unconsciously done,
constitutes circular reasoning from our point
of view. There are, however, two independent
clues: (a) the degree to which a position is
functionally unique, there being no other
positions that can perform the same function
satisfactorily; (b) the degree to which other
positions are dependent on the one in question. Both clues are best exemplified in organized systems of positions built around one
major function. Thus, in most complex societies the religious, political, economic, and
educational functions are handled by distinct
structures not easily interchangeable. In
addition, each structure possesses many different positions, some clearly dependent on, if
not subordinate to, others. In sum, when an
institutional nucleus becomes differentiated
around one main function, and at the same
time organizes a large portion of the population into its relationships, the *key* positions in
it are of the highest functional importance.
The absence of such specialization does not
prove functional unimportance, for the whole
society may be relatively unspecialized; but it
is safe to assume that the more important
functions receive the first and clearest structural differentiation.

4 The symbolic rather than intrinsic role of
income in social stratification has been succinctly summarized by Talcott Parsons, "An
Analytical Approach to the Theory of Social
Stratification," *American Journal of Sociology.*
45: 841–62, May, 1940.

5

Winner-Take-All Markets

Robert H. Frank and Philip J. Cook

Robert Frank is Professor of Economics at the Johnson School and also Goldwin Smith Professor of Economics, Ethics, and Public Policy in the College of Arts and Sciences, Cornell University. He was a Peace Corps Volunteer in rural Nepal from 1966 to 1968, chief economist for the Civil Aeronautics Board from 1978 to 1980, and a Fellow at the Center for Advanced Study in the Behavioral Sciences in 1992–3. Professor Frank's books include *Choosing the Right Pond*; *Passions Within Reason*; and *Luxury Fever*. *The Winner-Take-All Society*, co-authored with Philip Cook, was named a Notable Book of the Year by the *New York Times*, and was included in *Business Week*'s list of the ten best books for 1995.

Philip Cook joined the Economics faculty of Duke University in 1973 after completing his Ph.D. at the University of California, Berkeley. He holds a joint appointment in Public Policy Studies (now the Terry Sanford Institute), of which he served as Director from 1985 to 1989 and from 1996 to 1999, and in the Department of Economics. His ongoing research projects include such topics as the costs and benefits of alcohol control measures, the effects of abortion legalization and subsidy, and how markets for handguns influence crime. His most recent book (co-authored with Jens Ludwig) is *Gun Violence: The Real Costs* (Oxford University Press, 2000).

Rabo Karabekian, the protagonist of Kurt Vonnegut's novel *Bluebeard*, is an abstract expressionist painter of modest renown ("a footnote in Art History," as he describes himself). He recognizes that he was "obviously born to draw," just as others are born to tell stories, sing, dance, or be leaders, athletes, and scientists. Speculating on the historical origins of such talents, Rabo muses:

I think that could go back to the time when people had to live in small groups of relatives – maybe fifty or a hundred people at the most. And evolution or God or whatever arranged things genetically, to keep the little families going, to cheer them up, so that they could all have somebody to tell stories around the campfire at night, and somebody else to paint pictures on the walls of the caves, and somebody else who wasn't afraid of anything and so on.[1]

But Rabo also recognizes that most of these talented people face diminished opportunities in modern societies:

> of course a scheme like that doesn't make sense anymore, because simply moderate giftedness has been made worthless by the printing press and radio and television and satellites and all that. A moderately gifted person who would have been a community treasure a thousand years ago has to give up, has to go into some other line of work, since modern communications has put him or her into daily competition with nothing but the world's champions. . . . The entire planet can get along nicely now with maybe a dozen champion performers in each area of human giftedness.[2]

Now that most of the music we listen to is recorded, the world's best soprano can literally be everywhere at once. And since it costs no more to stamp out compact discs from Kathleen Battle's master recording of Mozart arias than from her understudy's, most of us listen to Battle. Millions of us are each willing to pay a few cents extra to hear her rather than another singer who is only marginally less able; and this enables Battle to write her own ticket.

Rabo Karabekian and Kathleen Battle sell their services in what we call "winner-take-all markets." So do Boris Becker, P. D. James, Carl Sagan, Kazuo Ishiguro, Hakeem Olajuwon, Gabriel García Márquez, Gerard Depardieu, Oksana Baiul, Alan Dershowitz, Alberto Tomba, John Madden, Mel Gibson, Mick Jagger, George Soros, Kip Keino, Jacques Derrida, Sonia Braga, Diane Sawyer, Gary Kasparov, Giorgio Armani, Stephen Hawking, Michael Jordan, Andrew Lloyd Webber, Elle Macpherson, John Cleese, Katerina Witt, Peter Høeg, George Will, Kimiko Date, Arnold Schwarzenegger, and

John Grisham. The markets in which these people and others like them work are very different from the ones economists normally study. We call them winner-take-all markets because the value of what gets produced in them often depends on the efforts of only a small number of top performers, who are paid accordingly.

For example, although thousands of people are involved in making a major motion picture, the difference between commercial success and failure usually hinges on the performances of only a handful – the director, the screenwriter, the leading actors and actresses, and perhaps a few others.

Similarly, although thousands of players compete each year in professional tennis, most of the industry's television and endorsement revenues can be attributed to the drawing power of just the top ten players. For example, the Australian Wally Masur, among the top fifty players in the world for many years, in 1993 was a semifinalist at the U.S. Open. At no time during his career, however, did manufacturers offer tennis shoes or racquets bearing his signature.

Since most of the markets we will be talking about have more than one winner, it would be more accurate to call them "those-near-the-top-get-a-disproportionate-share markets." But this is a mouthful, and hence our simpler, if somewhat less descriptive, label.

The winner-take-all reward structure has long been common in entertainment, sports, and the arts. But, as sociologist William Goode clearly recognized, the phenomenon that gives rise to it is by no means confined to celebrity labor markets. "The failure of the somewhat less popular" is how he referred to this phenomenon: "Grocery stores have only so much shelf space and thus only so much for each type of soap, cornflakes, or maple syrup . . . obviously the most popular of any class of products or programs will shoulder the less popular off, although in quality these may be close to the most successful in popularity."[3]

The cars that succeed in the marketplace are often only marginally more stylish or better built than those that fail. And even experts sometimes argue about whether the stereo loudspeaker that sweeps the market is really better than the ones buyers rejected.

When only barely perceptible quality margins spell the difference between success and failure, the buying public may have little at stake in the battles that decide which products win. But to the manufacturers the stakes are often enormous – the difference between liquidation and the continuation of multibillion-dollar annual revenues.

These high stakes have created a new class of "unknown celebrities": those pivotal players who spell the difference between corporate success and failure. Because their performance is crucial, and because modern information technology has helped build consensus about who they are, rival organizations must compete furiously to hire and retain them. In the automobile industry, for example, this might mean bidding for an especially talented designer or a highly innovative engineer, or even, in one notorious case, a ruthlessly effective purchasing agent. Little known to the buying public, these individuals often enjoy superstar status in their respective industries.

The markets in which they toil have become an increasingly important feature of modern economic life. They have permeated law, journalism, consulting, medicine, investment banking, corporate management, publishing, design, fashion, and even the hallowed halls of academe. And, although many of the examples we cite are drawn from an American context, the forces that give rise to winner-take-all markets are also at work in other industrial economies – indeed, even in countries in the earliest stages of economic development.

The revolution in electronic communications and data processing, for example, has transformed labor markets not just in the United States, the United Kingdom, France, Germany, and Japan, but also in China, India, Brazil, and Indonesia. The same kinds of trade agreements that have brought workers in Toronto into direct competition with workers in Chicago have also brought workers in Kyoto into direct competition with workers in Munich and Johannesburg. And each year a growing share of people in all these places will read books by the same authors, see films by the same directors, and buy clothing by the same designers.

Winner-take-all markets have already wrought profound changes in economic and social life. And because many of the forces that create these markets are intensifying, even more dramatic changes loom ahead. Some of these changes are for the better. Consumers clearly gain, for example, when modern technology allows the most talented people to serve ever wider audiences. Once the compositor's work is done, a renowned author's manuscript costs no more to reproduce than a hack's. Once the world's hospitals are linked by high-speed data transmission networks, the world's most gifted neurosurgeons can assist in the diagnosis and treatment of patients thousands of miles away – patients whose care would otherwise be left to less talented and less experienced physicians.

But winner-take-all markets also entail many negative consequences, and these will be our primary focus. Winner-take-all markets have increased the disparity between rich and poor. They have lured some of our most talented citizens into socially unproductive, sometimes even destructive, tasks. In an economy that already invests too little for the future, they have fostered wasteful patterns of investment and consumption. They have led indirectly to greater concentration of our most talented college students in a small set of elite institutions. They have made it more difficult for "late bloomers" to find a productive niche in life. And winner-take-all markets have molded our culture and discourse in ways many of us find deeply troubling.

Growing Income Inequality

Despite a flurry of denials from Bush administration officials when burgeoning income inequality first made headlines in the late 1980s, there is now little doubt that the top U.S. earners have pulled sharply away from all others. For example, the incomes of the top 1 percent more than doubled in real terms between 1979 and 1989, a period during which the median income was roughly stable and in which the bottom 20 percent of earners saw their incomes actually fall by 10 percent.[4]

Growing inequality is by no means confined to the United States. In the United Kingdom, for example, the richest 20 percent earned seven times as much as the poorest 20 percent in 1991, compared with only four times as much as in 1977.[5] The British gap between males with the highest wage rates and those with the lowest is larger now than at any time since the 1880s, when U.K. statistics on wages were first gathered systematically.[6]

As in other times and places, the growing gap between rich and poor has increasingly strained our bonds of community. The top earners are richer now than ever before, yet few among them can feel proud of the social environment we have bequeathed to our children.

Despite a recent spate of books on income inequality, there remains little consensus about why it has grown so sharply. Some commentators mention changes in public policy, citing the Reagan–Thatcher program of tax cuts for the wealthy and program cuts for the poor. Others emphasize the decline of labor unions, the downsizing of corporations, and the growing impact of foreign trade. Still others – notably former Harvard president Derek Bok in his widely discussed book *The Cost of Talent* – mention imperfect competition and cultural factors. Bok sees powerful elites who are insulated from competition and able to set their own terms in a world increasingly unrestrained by inhibitions about greed.

We will argue that the runaway salaries of top performers have not resulted from the policy changes of the Reagan–Bush and Thatcher–Major administrations, or from the decline of labor unions. Expanding trade, along with cultural forces, may have played a role, but only a supporting one. And if any one thing is certain, it is that growing income inequality has not resulted from any weakening of competitive forces.

On the contrary, global and domestic competition have never been more intense than now. Our claim is that the explosion of top salaries has stemmed largely from the growing prevalence of winner-take-all markets, which, we will argue, is tied closely to the growth of competitive forces. We will describe changes that have made the most productive individuals more valuable, and at the same time have led to more open bidding for their services.

In professional sports, for example, the most productive athletes have become more valuable because of the large influx of television revenue. What is more, owners of sports teams are now forced to compete with one another for the most talented athletes because of "free agency" – athletes' freedom to choose which teams to play for, which resulted from the string of legal decisions that struck down earlier restrictions on mobility. The result has been that much of the new revenue has found its way into the salaries of top players. The San Francisco Giants offered Barry Bonds a $43,750,000 contract in 1992 not because team owner Peter Magowan was stupid but because Bonds's presence helped fill the stands and land a more lucrative TV contract.[7] Bonds was a free agent when he signed with the Giants, and making him a smaller offer would have risked losing his drawing power to a rival bidder.

Growth in productivity of the top performers and the more open bidding for their services have occurred for different reasons in different markets. In broad terms, however, the story in other winner-take-all markets largely resembles the one we have seen in professional sports. Disney CEO Michael Eisner was paid more than $200 million in 1993 not because he duped shareholders but because he delivered an unprecedented increase in the company's value at a time when the mobility of chief executives has made them increasingly like the free agents of professional sports. And Danielle Steel gets $12 million apiece for her novels not because conglomerate publishing houses have deep pockets and limited business acumen, but because she sells millions of copies. If Dell/Delacorte had failed to bid accordingly for her manuscripts. Steel could simply have signed with a rival publisher.

The widening gap between the winners and losers is apparently not new. Writing more than a century ago, the British economist Alfred Marshall observed that "the relative fall in the incomes to be earned by moderate ability, however carefully trained, is accentuated by the rise in those that are obtained by many men of extraordinary ability. There never was a time at which moderately good oil paintings sold more cheaply than now, and there never was a time at which first-rate paintings sold so dearly."[8]

What *is* new is that the phenomenon has spread so widely and that so many of the top prizes have become so spectacular. The lure of these prizes, we will argue, has produced several important distortions in modern industrial economies. Perhaps the most important of these involves the influence of market signals on career choices.

The Misallocation of Talent

For any nation to prosper in the face of growing international competition, it must somehow allocate its most talented citizens to its most important jobs. It must steer its best executives to the enterprises that add greatest value, its most creative scientists to the most pressing technical problems, its ablest public servants to the most important cabinet positions. If the economic collapse of the communist countries can be traced to any single factor, it is their dismal performance in these critical assignment tasks. The critics of communism were right all along: The allocation of talent by central bureaucracy is a recipe for economic disaster.

Market economies have done much better by simply letting people decide for themselves which careers to pursue. Although social critics often question the recent wave of multimillion-dollar salaries on ethical grounds, there can be no doubt that these salaries have attracted our best and brightest people. Competition for the top prizes is intense, and those fortunate enough to land them are almost invariably the survivors of a series of increasingly demanding elimination tournaments.

The aspiring major-league baseball player, for example, starts with T-ball, moves on to Little League and then, if he shows enough talent and determination, to Babe Ruth League. Only the best from Babe Ruth League can hope to start for the most competitive high school teams, and only a fraction of those players go on to the minor leagues, where formidable hurdles remain before landing a shot at the majors. Even then, most players who make it onto a major-league roster ultimately fail to land a starting berth, and only a small fraction of starters go on to become stars. As we will see, competition for top positions in other sectors of the economy is no less intense. Almost without exception, the survivors of these competitions are people of enormous talent, energy, and drive.

One of our central claims is that although the competition for top slots in winner-take-all markets does indeed attract our most talented and productive workers, it also generates two forms of waste: first, by attracting too many contestants, and second, by giving rise to unproductive patterns of consumption and investment as contestants vie with one another for top positions.

Consider first the matter of overcrowding. Winner-take-all markets attract too many contestants in part because of a common human frailty with respect to gambling – namely, our tendency to overestimate our chances of winning. Becoming a contestant in a winner-take-all market entails a decision to pit one's own skills against a largely unknown field of adversaries. An intelligent decision obviously requires a well-informed estimate of the odds of winning. Yet people's assessments of these odds are notoriously inaccurate. Survey evidence consistently shows, for example, that some 80 percent of us think we are better-than-average drivers, and that even more of us think of ourselves as more productive than the average worker.[9] We will describe evidence that many people are similarly overconfident about their odds of prevailing in winner-take-all contests. When people overestimate their chances of winning, the number who forsake productive occupations in traditional markets to compete in winner-take-all markets will be larger than could be justified on traditional cost–benefit grounds.

It is not surprising that there are bad outcomes when people make important decisions on the basis of inaccurate information. What is perhaps less expected is that too many contestants tend to compete in winner-take-all markets even when people have completely accurate assessments of their odds of winning.

The explanation lies in an incentive problem similar to the one that gives rise to excessive environmental pollution. In deciding whether to buy an air-conditioner, for example, people weigh the benefits of their added comfort against the cost of buying and operating it. From the individual buyer's point of view, the relevant operating expense is the cost of the electricity the machine uses. But the machine's operation also imposes an additional cost on others. The more we run the air-conditioner, the more electricity we must generate, and the more we pollute the air in the process. In

the absence of regulation, individuals are free to ignore this additional cost, and most of them do so. As a result, when people are driven exclusively by market incentives, we tend to get too little clean air.

By the same token, potential contestants in winner-take-all markets generally ignore an important cost imposed on others by their entry – namely that each additional contestant reduces the odds that someone already in the contest will win. This zero-sum feature leads too many people to compete in winner-take-all markets, and too few to seek productive careers in traditional markets. Thus we will argue that our national income would be higher if some students abandoned their ambitions to become multimillionaire plaintiffs' attorneys in favor of the more modest but more predictable paychecks of electrical engineers.

The winner-take-all payoff structure encourages another form of waste in that it invites – indeed, virtually compels – competitors to take costly steps to enhance their prospects of winning. Book publishing is a lottery of the purest sort, with a handful of best-selling authors receiving more than $10 million per book while armies of equally talented writers earn next to nothing. Under these circumstances, authors naturally jump at any chance to increase their visibility and sales. Witness, for example, this excerpt from Judith Krantz's description of her promotional tour for her best-selling novel *Scruples*:

Touring for a book – it's the literary equivalent of war. I remember my hardcover tour. I'd hit a city – say, Cleveland – at night, unpack, steam out the clothes that were wrinkled, and, the next morning, get up at six. Because there's always an "A.M. Show," a "Good Morning Show," a "Hello Show" in every city in the country. . . . When you leave that hotel early in the morning, you have to be packed up and all checked out – the publisher has a limo to get you to the studio, and your suitcase is going to be in that limo all day while you make your sixteen different stops. Your arrival at the studio is at seven-thirty or eight, and the author invariably goes on last, but you have to be there an hour ahead of time in order to keep them from going crazy. Then, after I went on, I'd do a whole day of media in Cleveland, finishing up at six o'clock, just in time to catch a plane to Detroit, and the departure gate is *always* at the very end of the airport. You do all that day after day and enough weeks in a row, and you get so that you feel you can hardly function.[10]

That promotional tours like Krantz's are crucial in deciding which fifteen books make it onto the *New York Times* fiction best-seller list cannot be denied. Yet, no matter how much time and effort Krantz and other authors devote to these tours, a simple truth remains: Only fifteen books can make the list each week. Because one author moves up only if another moves down, the rewards of investing in book tours loom much larger for authors as individuals than they do for authors as a whole.

If promotional efforts involve a measure of social waste, they may also help people make marginally better decisions about which books to buy, which films to see, and so on. Many other competitive maneuvers, however, have no such redeeming feature. Consumption of anabolic steroids by professional athletes, for instance, not only does not add to social value, it almost surely diminishes it. National Football League (NFL) fans have little reason to prefer watching games in which each team's linemen average 300 pounds rather than 250. Yet the advantage to any team of having larger players than its opponent can be decisive. And so, in the absence of effective drug testing, widespread ingestion of steroids, with all the attendant health risks, is inevitable.

The incentives for authors to go on book tours and for athletes to consume anabolic steroids are much like the incentives for rival nations to engage in military arms races. Each side suffers an unacceptable loss of position if it buys no arms while its rival does. Yet weaponry is costly, and when both sides buy arms, both do worse than if neither had. We will argue that winner-take-all markets spawn a host of what might be called "positional arms races," which augment the losses stemming from overcrowding.

The Contest for Elite Educational Credentials

Lawyers on Wall Street who specialize in corporate takeovers receive just a small percentage of the total amount of money involved in these transactions. But the amounts involved are often staggeringly large. The RJR–Nabisco buyout, for instance, was consummated at a price of $25 billion. So even when forty lawyers split just one-quarter of 1 percent, we are still talking about a great deal of money for what often amounts to only a few weeks' or months' work.

When such sums are conspicuously reported in the media, bright and ambitious young people naturally ask themselves, "How can I get a job as a Wall Street lawyer?" With so many applicants vying for each entry-level opening, Wall Street firms must be extremely choosy. Even to land an interview at some firms, it is necessary to hold a degree from one of only a handful of prestigious law schools. And how does one gain admission to one of these law schools? The surest route is to have been a leading student at one of a handful of elite undergraduate institutions.

Indeed, the day has already arrived when failure to have an elite undergraduate degree closes certain doors completely, no matter what other stellar credentials a student might possess. Harvard's graduate program in economics, for example, recently rejected an applicant from a small Florida college, despite her straight-A transcript and glowing recommendations from professors who described her as by far the best student they had ever taught. Her problem was that the committee also had a file drawer full of applications from straight-A students with strong letters from schools like Stanford, Princeton, and MIT. On the evidence, the Florida applicant *might* have been as good or better than the others. But committees are forced to play the odds, which tell us clearly that the best students from the best schools are better, on average, than the best students from lesser schools.

The nation's elite educational institutions have become, in effect, the gatekeepers for society's most sought-after jobs. Those who fail to pass through their doors often never have a chance. We will present evidence that realization of this truth has spread widely among our best and brightest high school seniors. Years ago many top students attended state universities close to home, where they often received good educations at reasonable expense to their families. Today these same students are far more likely to apply to, be accepted by, and matriculate at one of a handful of the nation's most prestigious universities, most of which are located in the Northeast. When the rejection letters from these schools are sent out each year in April, recipients increasingly have grounds for feeling downcast. Though many of them are barely seventeen, some of life's most important doors have already closed in their faces.

Of course, there are some obvious advantages to concentrating the best students in a few top schools, just as there are advantages to tracking the best students into separate classrooms in the elementary schools. But tracking also entails costs, and the central question in each case is, How much tracking is best? The debate rages on in the public schools, where the alternatives are usually a limited amount of tracking within each school or no tracking at all. But those are not the choices we face in higher education.

There we must choose between tracking at the local or regional level (for example, by putting the best students into honors programs in the state universities) and tracking at the national level (by sending the best students to a small number of elite institutions). The second option is the one we are heading for, yet it is by no means clear that it dominates the first.

In recent years a number of books have lambasted the supposedly cushy working conditions of university professors. *ProfScam* author Charles Sykes offers this blustery indictment:

> They are overpaid, grotesquely underworked, and the architects of academia's vast empires of waste. . . . They insist that their obligations to research justify their flight from the college classroom despite the fact that fewer than one in ten ever makes any significant contribution to their field. Too many – maybe even a vast majority – spend their time belaboring tiny slivers of knowledge, utterly without redeeming social value except as items on their résumés. . . . In tens of thousands of books and hundreds of thousands of journal articles, they have perverted the system of academic publishing into a scheme that serves only to advance academic careers and bloat libraries with masses of unread, unreadable, and worthless pabulum.[11]

Although much of this criticism is overblown (after all, students from around the world increasingly clamor for admission to American universities), it also contains a kernel of truth in several areas. We will argue that the objects of most severe criticism – namely growing salaries and shrinking teaching loads – are best understood as natural consequences of positional arms races in higher education.

Realizing the importance of prestige in attracting top students, schools across the country have attempted to mimic the strategy of elite universities by bidding for the distinguished and visible faculty whose research accomplishments are perhaps the most important emblems of academic distinction. In the process, a superstar phenomenon – albeit a relatively mild one – has emerged in academia: Top researchers' salaries have escalated more rapidly than those of their lesser-ranked rivals, even as the teaching loads of top faculty have shrunk. The quest for academic prestige has also motivated universities to bid aggressively for top administrators, fund-raisers, and others who have demonstrated the capacity to attract and manage resources.

In a world with unlimited resources, these developments might not be cause for concern. But we live in a world in which educational costs have rapidly been outpacing the costs of other goods and services. Undergraduate tuition at the Ivy League schools (*excluding* room, board, and other expenses) – which stood at less than $3,000 per year in 1970 – has now reached $20,000, and similar escalation has occurred in tuitions elsewhere. Political pressure has been mounting to control these costs, but unless we understand the forces that give rise to them, we risk costly errors. Excellence in higher education is a critical source of economic advantage, and if costs are to be cut, it must be done in a way that does not compromise this advantage. The winner-take-all perspective suggests a number of practical policy changes that might serve this goal.

Contests for Relative Position in Everyday Life

The winner-take-all markets we have mentioned so far are high-visibility arenas in which people, many with celebrity status, compete for enormous financial rewards. These contests affect the lives of ordinary citizens to the extent that they mold our system of higher education, alter the distribution of income, increase the prices of what we buy, and so on.

But there are also many other arenas in which ordinary citizens are themselves confronted directly with rewards that depend on relative, rather than absolute, performance. The ability to purchase many goods and services, for example, is constrained less by the absolute amount of one's earnings than by how much one earns relative to others. In Los Angeles most people would like to have a home with a commanding view, and yet only a small fraction – say 10 percent – of the home sites there can satisfy that demand. If each family is willing to pay the same fraction of its income for the privilege, the allocation of home sites with views will be settled by relative income alone. If everyone's income were to double, or to fall by half, the winning bidders would be the same – those with incomes in the highest ten percent.

Because many important rewards in life depend on relative, not absolute, income, people have a strong interest in seeing that their incomes keep pace with community standards. This incentive structure leads to a variety of winner-take-all contests in everyday life.

To land a job, for example, an applicant is well advised to "look good." But what, exactly, does that mean? On reflection, any realistic definition turns out to depend almost completely on context. To look good means simply to look better than most other applicants. One way to do so is to spend more than others on clothing. Since the same incentives clearly apply to all applicants, however, an escalating stand-off inevitably ensues. At leading law and business schools, many students don't dare appear for an interview wearing a suit that costs less than six hundred dollars. Yet when all students spend that amount, their attractiveness rankings are no different than if all had spent only three hundred dollars. In either case, only one person in ten can exceed the ninetieth percentile on the attractiveness scale.

As wasteful as escalating expenditures on clothing might seem, the stakes become even higher once cosmetic surgery emerges as a weapon in the competition to look good. Such surgery is expensive, is painful, and entails a small risk of serious side effects. Its use is increasing rapidly and, in some areas of the country, it has already become widespread. In Southern California, for example, morticians now complain that the noncombustible silicone sacks used in chin, breast, and buttocks augmentation have begun to clog their crematoria.

Although surgical enhancement of appearance often clearly serves an individual's goals, its social utility is highly questionable. Indeed, once it becomes the norm, its principal effect is merely to shift the standards that define normal appearance. Many people who would once have been described, nonjudgmentally, as being slightly overweight or having slightly thinning hair now feel increasing pressure to undergo liposuction or hair-transplant surgery.

Agreements to Limit Wasteful Competition

It would be surprising if no one had ever noticed that people and firms often find themselves embroiled in wasteful positional arms races, and more surprising still if no steps had ever been taken to curb them. People often are aware, at least implicitly, of these wasteful processes, and have implemented a host of strategies for keeping them under control. Because they function like treaties that limit military weapons, we call these strategies "positional arms control agreements."

The governmental regulations we will identify as positional arms control agreements (whether originally adopted for that purpose or not) come in many forms and apply in many arenas. These include restrictions on the top prizes that individuals may receive – such as income taxes, consumption taxes, and luxury taxes; campaign finance laws; safety regulations, both in the

workplace and in product markets; regulations that limit working hours; regulations, or "blue laws," that limit retail business hours; and even laws that prohibit polygamy.

Many such limiting agreements do not involve the force of law. Retail merchant associations, for example, sometimes agree collectively to limit business hours (although enforcement difficulties often lead to a breakdown of these agreements). Private and parochial schools often limit clothing expenditure by imposing uniform requirements or dress codes. Sports leagues impose roster limits, pay caps, drug bans, and revenue-sharing arrangements. And where the antitrust laws permit, industry associations often work out elaborate agreements for sharing the fruits of basic research.

Even informal social norms are sometimes employed to limit wasteful competition. We will offer this interpretation, for example, of social norms that limited the casualties from dueling in eighteenth-century Europe; of contemporary norms in many communities, especially small ones, that frown on conspicuous consumption; and of social norms that discourage cosmetic surgery and other practices regarded as vain.

Some Winner-Take-All Markets Are Worse Than Others

Our claims that winner-take-all markets attract too many resources and generate wasteful spending patterns rest on the standard economic premise that the social value of a product or service is well measured by what the market is willing to pay for it. The top prizes in many winner-take-all markets, however, significantly overstate the social value added by top performers. In these instances the tendency to attract too many resources may be greatly amplified.

The legal profession is a case in point. Without denying that lawyers perform a number of tasks that are indispensable for a well-ordered society, we note that many lawyers appear to receive salaries that far exceed their social value. This is especially the case for lawyers involved in litigation, which usually does less to create new wealth than to redistribute existing wealth.[12] As economist Kenneth Boulding once described the problem:

> [F]or any individual person there is a payoff in having the best lawyer. Under these circumstances, it is not surprising that the law attracts some of the ablest minds of our society and that the payoffs for high ability are probably as great in the law as in any other profession if not greater. If, however, we could achieve a kind of intellectual disarmament and agree that nobody would be allowed in the legal profession with an IQ above a hundred, the result would be almost exactly similar; people would still try to buy the best lawyers they could, but a valuable intellectual resource would be economized.[13]

We may suspect that when Boulding made this fanciful proposal, almost thirty years ago, he had little inkling of how attractive it might someday seem to a society ravaged by the modern tort system.

Winner-Take-All Markets and Norms of Fairness

Winner-take-all markets have implications not only for efficiency but also for norms of fairness. The economist's theory of wages, which holds that workers are paid in proportion to the value of their productive contributions, was never intended to justify market income distributions on ethical grounds. Nonetheless, many see a certain rough justice when pay is distributed on that basis, for the system rewards not only talent but also the willingness to expend effort. In winner-take-all markets, however, pay dis-

tributions will be more spread out – often dramatically so – than the underlying distributions of effort and ability. It is one thing to say that people who work 10 percent harder or have 10 percent more talent should receive 10 percent more pay. But it is quite another to say that such small differences should cause pay to differ by 10,000 percent or more. Olympic gold medalists go on to receive millions in endorsements while the runners-up are quickly forgotten – even when the performance gap is almost too small to measure: "The miler who triumphs in the Olympic Games, who places himself momentarily at the top of the pyramid of all milers, leads a thousand next-best competitors by mere seconds. The gap between best and second-best, or even best and tenth-best, is so slight that a gust of wind or a different running shoe might have accounted for the margin of victory."[14] The realization of how winner-take-all markets contribute to income inequality may affect the extent to which society tries to alter market distributions in the name of fairness.

Media and Culture in the Winner-Take-All Society

Social critics have long complained that market imperatives have degraded our culture. What these critics have consistently failed to offer, however, is a reasoned account of *why* this should be so. If the market system is the best mechanism for producing the cars and houses we want, why isn't it also best for books, movies, and television programming?

Still, it is difficult to deny that the critics have a point. The films and books that media conglomerates urge on us will all too rarely speak well of us to future generations. Consider again Judith Krantz, who in the spring of 1994 published her eighth best-seller, a romance entitled *Lovers*. Just what is Krantz urging us to read on these frantic book tours of hers? *The New Yorker*'s critic Anthony Lane quoted the following sentence in support of his claim that *Lovers* was one of eight abominable books among the top ten sellers on a recent *New York Times* list: "Did his cousin Billy Winthrop also take a pair of bodyguards with her wherever she went, Ben Winthrop asked himself in mild surprise as he leaned out of his car to give his name to the guard at the gatehouse that stood squarely at the driveway entrance to Billy's estate in Holmby Hills."[15] If passages like these ever find their way onto the reading list of a freshman writing seminar, it will be to illustrate what Lane describes as the difficulty of trying "to cram twice as much information into a single sentence as it was designed to bear."[16]

Of course, defenders of popular culture can cite counterexamples like the novels of John Le Carré, which are consistently best-sellers and yet also consistently draw praise from even the toughest critics. And there, typically, the culture debate bogs down, an apparently unresolvable quarrel over tastes.

The winner-take-all perspective suggests a possible way of moving beyond this stalemate. We start with the observation that, as social beings, people have a keen interest in reading the same books others read, and in seeing the same movies. Consider a book buyer's choice between two books that, on the available evidence, are of equal quality: Both are on subjects of interest, both have been favorably reviewed, and so on. If one of these books happens to have made the best-seller list and the other hasn't, this tends to tip the balance. After all, we like to discuss books with friends, and a book's presence on the best-seller list means that friends will be more likely to have read it.

As we will see, this success-breeds-success feature is common in many winner-take-all markets, but never more so than in markets for popular culture. Positive-feedback effects in the marketing of books and movies mean that a big launch has become an essential ingredient in the process of becoming a hit. A book that fails to achieve large early sales quickly lands on the remainder tables, and a film that fails to open big is unlikely to survive for long in the theaters.

We will argue that it is the financial imperatives of achieving *quick* market success that have shaped popular culture in the ways that critics find so distasteful. Publishers have learned that the surest way to achieve large early sales is to promote books by authors who have already written several best-sellers. Studios have learned that the surest route to a big opening weekend is to produce a sequel to a recent hit movie. The financial incentives strongly favor sensational, lurid, and formulaic offerings; these incentives could not have been consciously designed to be more hostile to innovative, quirky, or offbeat works, whose charms generally take longer to communicate. The winner-take-all reward structure is especially troubling in light of evidence that, beginning in infancy and continuing throughout life, the things we see and read profoundly alter the kinds of people we become.

The Challenges Posed by Winner-Take-All Markets

Whereas free marketeers maintain that market incentives lead to socially efficient results, our claim is that winner-take-all markets attract too many contestants, result in inefficient patterns of consumption and investment, and often degrade our culture. If these costs are to be avoided, firms and individuals must somehow be restrained from taking advantage of readily available profit opportunities.

This does not mean, however, that detailed, prescriptive government regulation is the cure for all social ills. As conservatives have ably demonstrated, such regulations entail pitfalls all their own, often doing more harm than the problems they were designed to overcome.

The problems we attribute to winner-take-all markets stem largely from participants' failure to take account of the costs they impose on others. In this sense these problems are much like those associated with pollution, and our experience with pollution control offers useful guidance about how best to curb the waste that arises in winner-take-all markets.

The best remedies seldom involve bureaucratic attempts to regulate behavior directly. Rather, alternative policies that require individuals to take into account the full costs of their actions have generally proved simpler, more effective, and less intrusive. Thus, a group of northeastern states eliminated a major source of environmental litter virtually overnight simply by enacting deposit laws for soft-drink containers.

Our search will be for remedies in this mold. Our goal is to discover ways to bring individual and social incentives more closely into line, at the same time preserving freedom of choice to the greatest possible degree. If there are too many attorneys and too few engineers, we are more likely to solve this problem by altering the reward structure than by trying to regulate career choices directly.

But regulation with a light touch is still regulation, and many free marketeers will object to some of the remedies we propose. To these skeptics, we concede that people have every right to seek their fortunes in winner-take-all markets. Yet in an economy permeated by these markets, there can be no general presumption that private market incentives translate self-interested behavior into socially efficient outcomes. Precisely the same logic that justifies community intervention to curb environmental pollution also supports the community's right to restructure the winner-take-all reward system for the common good.

Does Greater Equality Necessarily Reduce Growth?

In virtually every society, we hear of the "agonizing trade-off" between equity and efficiency. Conservative American economists of the supply-side school, in particular,

are fond of saying that although they would not mind seeing a more progressive tax system on equity grounds, such a move would produce devastating effects on growth.

The winner-take-all perspective poses a sharp challenge to this argument. The overcrowding problem in winner-take-all markets arises because participation in these markets is misleadingly attractive to individuals. To the extent that many, if not most, of society's highest incomes are the direct result of winner-take-all processes, the effect of higher taxes on these incomes would be to reduce the overcrowding problem.

Moreover, the people most likely to drop out would be those whose odds of making it into the winner's circle were smallest to begin with. Thus the value of what gets produced in winner-take-all markets would not be much reduced if higher taxes were levied on winners' incomes; more important, whatever reductions did occur would tend to be more than offset by increased output in traditional markets. To the extent that most of society's top earners are participants in winner-take-all markets, it follows that a more progressive tax structure would not reduce but actually increase economic efficiency!

As today's young economists look back to the early years of the Great Depression, most are astonished to realize that, less than a lifetime ago, their predecessors thought that the cure for a stagnant economy was to reduce the supply of money. We now know better, of course. For several decades, the Federal Reserve has boosted the money supply at the slightest indication of an economic downturn, and this has helped keep the economy on a remarkably even keel by historical standards.

We may all hope that, one lifetime from now, economists will look back in similar astonishment at the notions that guided late-twentieth-century economic and social policy. The problem of our time is not depression but the multiple evils of rising inequality, budget deficits, and slow growth. Yet the quintessential conservative policy prescription of this era – tax cuts for middle- and upper-income people – is no more likely to cure these problems than monetary contraction was likely to cure the Great Depression. Advocates of tax cuts sometimes concede their negative impact on inequality and budget deficits, but they see these as costs worth bearing in order to stimulate economic growth.

Our claim is that this trickle-down theory simply does not apply in economies pervaded by winner-take-all markets. This is a good thing, too, for it means that the very same policies that promote both fiscal integrity and equality are also likely to spur economic growth. The time-honored trade-off between equity and efficiency is far less agonizing than it appears.

NOTES

1   Vonnegut, 1987, pp. 74, 75.
2   Ibid., p. 75.
3   Goode, 1978, p. 72.
4   For a detailed discussion, see Krugman, Fall 1992.
5   *The Economist*, November 5, 1994, p. 19.
6   Ibid.
7   *Fortune*, April 19, 1993, p. 162.
8   Marshall, 1947 (1890), p. 685.
9   Evidence for these and other similar tendencies is discussed in Gilovich, 1991, chap. 5.

10 Quoted by Whiteside, 1981, pp. 158, 159.
11 Sykes, 1988, pp. 5, 6.
12 See Ashenfelter and Bloom, 1990.
13 Boulding, 1966, p. 110.
14 Gleick, 1992, p. 128.
15 Lane, 1994, p. 90.
16 Ibid., p. 90.

REFERENCES

Ashenfelter, Orly, and David Bloom. "Lawyers as Agents of the Devil in a Prisoner's Dilemma Game," Working Paper #270, Industrial Relations Section, Princeton University, 1990.

Boulding, Kenneth. *The Impact of the Social Sciences*, Rutgers, N.J.: Rutgers University Press, 1966.

Gilovich, Thomas. *How We Know What Isn't So*. New York: Free Press, 1991.

Gleick, James. *Genius*. New York: Pantheon, 1992.

Goode, William J. *The Celebration of Heroes*, Berkeley: University of California Press, 1978.

Krugman, Paul R. "The Right, the Rich, and the Facts." *The American Prospect* 11 (Fall 1992): 19–31.

Lane, Anthony. "The Top Ten." *The New Yorker*, June 27 & July 4, 1994, pp. 79–92.

Marshall, Alfred. *Principles of Economics, Eighth Edition*. New York: Macmillan, 1947.

Sykes, Charles J. *ProfScam: Professors and the Demise of Higher Education*. Washington, D.C.: Regnery Gateway, 1988.

Vonnegut, Kurt. *Bluebeard*. New York: Delacorte Press, 1987.

Whiteside, Thomas. *The Blockbuster Complex*. Middletown, Conn.: Wesleyan University Press, 1981.

Part II

Who's Rich, Who's Poor:
How Resources Affect Life Chances

6

Inequality

Christopher Jencks (with the assistance of Marshall Smith, Henry Acland, Mary Jo Bane, David Cohen, Herbert Gintis, Barbara Heyns, and Stephan Michelson)

Christopher "Sandy" Jencks is the Malcolm Wiener Professor of Social Policy at Harvard University. He has also taught at Northwestern University, the University of Chicago, and the University of California at Santa Barbara. In an earlier life he was a fellow of the Institute for Policy Studies in Washington (1963–7) and Editor of *The New Republic* (1961–3). He is currently a member of the Editorial Board of *The American Prospect*. His recent research has dealt with changes in the material standard of living over the past generation, homelessness, the effects on children of growing up in poor neighborhoods, welfare reform, and poverty measurement. He is currently writing a book, with Susan Mayer, tentatively titled, *Did We Really Lose the War on Poverty?* His earlier books include *The Academic Revolution* (with David Riesman); *Inequality; Who Gets Ahead?; The Urban Underclass* (with Paul Peterson); *Rethinking Social Policy; The Homeless;* and *The Black White Test Score Gap* (with Meredith Phillips).

Most Americans say they believe in equality. But when pressed to explain what they mean by this, their definitions are usually full of contradictions. Many will say, like the Founding Fathers, that "all men are created equal." Many will also say that all men are equal "before God," and that they are, or at least ought to be, equal in the eyes of the law. But most Americans also believe that some people are more competent than others, and that this will always be so, no matter how much we reform society. Many also believe that competence should be rewarded by success, while incompetence should be punished by failure. They have no commitment to ensuring that everyone's job is equally desirable, that everyone exercises the same amount of political power, or that everyone receives the same income.

But while most Americans accept inequality in virtually every sphere of day-to-day life, they still believe in what they often call "equal opportunity." By this they mean that the rules determining who succeeds and who fails should be fair. People are, of course, likely to disagree about precisely what is "fair" and what is "unfair." Still, the general principle of fair competition is almost universally endorsed.

During the 1960s, many reformers devoted enormous effort to equalizing opportunity. More specifically, they tried to eliminate inequalities based on skin color, and to a lesser extent on economic background. They also wanted to eliminate absolute deprivation: "poverty," "ignorance," "powerlessness," and so forth. But only a handful of radicals talked about eliminating inequality per se. Almost none of the national legislation passed during the 1960s tried to reduce disparities in adult status, power, or income in any direct way. There was no significant effort, for example, to make taxation more progressive, and very little effort to reduce wage disparities between highly paid and poorly paid workers. Instead, attention focused on helping workers in poorly paid jobs to move into better paid jobs. Nor was there much effort to reduce the social or psychological distance between high- and low-status occupations. Instead, the idea was to help people in low-status occupations leave these occupations for more prestigious ones. Even in the political arena, "maximum feasible participation" implied mainly that more "leaders" should be black and poor, not that power should be equally distributed between leaders and followers.

Because the reforms of the 1960s did not tackle the problem of adult inequality directly, they accomplished only a few of their goals. Equalizing opportunity is almost impossible without greatly reducing the absolute level of inequality, and the same is true of eliminating deprivation.

Consider the case of equal opportunity. One can equalize the opportunities available to blacks and whites without equalizing anything else, and considerable progress was made in this direction during the late 1960s. But equalizing the opportunities available to different children of the same race is far more difficult. If a society is competitive and rewards adults unequally, some parents are bound to succeed while others fail. Successful parents will then try to pass along their advantages to their children. Unsuccessful parents will inevitably pass along some of their disadvantages. Unless a society completely eliminates ties between parents and children, inequality among parents guarantees some degree of inequal-

ity in the opportunities available to children. The only real question is how serious these inequalities must be.

Or consider the problem of deprivation. When the war on poverty began in late 1963, it was conceived as an effort to raise the living standards of the poor. The rhetoric of the time described the persistence of poverty in the midst of affluence as a "paradox," largely attributable to "neglect." Official publications all assumed that poverty was an absolute rather than a relative condition. Having assumed this, they all showed steady progress toward the elimination of poverty, since fewer and fewer people had incomes below the official "poverty line."

Yet despite all the official announcements of progress, the feeling that lots of Americans were poor persisted. The reason was that most Americans define poverty in relative rather than absolute terms. Public opinion surveys show, for example, that when people are asked how much money an American family needs to "get by," they typically name a figure about half what the average American family actually receives. This has been true for the last three decades, despite the fact that real incomes (i.e. incomes adjusted for inflation) have doubled in the interval.

Political definitions of poverty have reflected these popular attitudes. During the Depression, the average American family was living on about $30 a week. A third of all families were living on less than half this amount, i.e. less than $15 a week. This made it natural for Franklin Roosevelt to speak of "one third of a nation" as ill-housed, ill-clothed, and ill-fed. One third of the nation was below what most people then regarded as the poverty line.

By 1964, when Lyndon Johnson declared war on poverty, incomes had risen more than fivefold. Even allowing for inflation, living standards had doubled. Only about 10 percent of all families had real incomes as low as the bottom third had had during the Depression. But popular conceptions of what it took to "get by" had also risen since the Depression. Mean family income was about $160 a week, and popular opinion now held that it took $80 a week for a family of four to make ends meet. About a quarter of all families were still poor by this definition. As a matter of political convenience, the Administration set the official poverty line at $60 a week for a family of four rather than $80, ensuring that even conservatives would admit that those below the line were poor. But by 1970 inflation had raised mean family income to about $200 a week, and the National Welfare Rights Organization was rallying liberal support for a guaranteed income of $100 a week for a family of four.

These political changes in the definition of poverty were not just a matter of "rising expectations" or of people's needing to "keep up with the Joneses." The goods and services that made it possible to live on $15 a week during the Depression were no longer available to a family with the same "real" income (i.e. $40 a week) in 1964. Eating habits had changed, and many cheap foods had disappeared from the stores. Most people had enough money to buy an automobile, so public transportation had atrophied, and families without automobiles were much worse off than during the Depression. The labor market had also changed, and a person without a telephone could not get or keep many jobs. A home without a telephone was more cut off socially than when few people had telephones and more people "dropped by." Housing arrangements had changed, too. During the Depression, many people could not afford indoor plumbing and "got by" with a privy. By the 1960s, privies were illegal in most places. Those who could not afford an indoor toilet ended up in buildings which had broken toilets. For this they paid more than their parents had paid for privies.

Examples of this kind suggest that the "cost of living" is not the cost of buying some fixed set of goods and services. It is the cost of participating in a social system. The cost of participation depends in large part on how much other people habitually spend to participate. Those who fall far below the norm, whatever it may be, are excluded. It follows that raising the incomes of the poor will not eliminate poverty if the incomes of other Americans rise even faster. If people with incomes less than half the national average cannot afford what "everyone" regards as "necessities," the only way to eliminate poverty is to make sure everyone has an income at least half the average.

This line of reasoning applies to wealth as well as poverty. The rich are not rich because they eat filet mignon or own yachts. Millions of people can now afford these luxuries, but they are still not "rich" in the colloquial sense. The rich are rich because they can afford to buy other people's time. They can hire other people to make their beds, tend their gardens, and drive their cars. These are not privileges that become more widely available as people become more affluent. If all workers' wages rise at the same rate, the highly paid professional will have to spend a constant percentage of his income to get a maid, a gardener, or a taxi. The number of people who are "rich," in the sense of controlling more than their share of other people's time and effort, will therefore remain the same, even though consumption of yachts and filet mignon is rising.

If the distribution of income becomes more equal, as it did in the 1930s and 1940s, the number of people who are "rich" in this sense of the term will decline, even though absolute incomes are rising. If, for example, the wages of domestic servants rise faster than the incomes of their prospective employers, fewer families will feel they can afford full-time servants. This will lower the living standards of the elite to some extent, regardless of what happens to consumption of yachts and filet mignon.

This same logic applies not only to income but to the cognitive skills taught in school. Young people's performance on standardized tests rose dramatically between World War I and World War II, for example. But the level of competence required for many adult roles rose too. When America was a polyglot nation of immigrants, all sorts of jobs were open to those who could not read English. Such people could, for example, join the army, drive a truck, or get a job in the construction industry. Today, when almost everyone can read English, the range of choices open to nonreaders has narrowed. The military no longer takes an appreciable number of illiterates, a driver's license requires a written examination, and apprenticeships in the construction trades are restricted to those who can pass tests. Those who cannot read English are at a disadvantage, simply because they are atypical. America is not organized with their problems in mind. The same thing applies to politics. If the average citizen's vocabulary expands, the vocabulary used by politicians and newspapers will expand too. Those with very limited vocabularies relative to their neighbors will still have trouble following events, even though their vocabulary is larger than, say, their parents' vocabulary was.

Arguments of this kind suggest that it makes more sense to think of poverty and ignorance as relative than as absolute conditions. They also suggest that eliminating poverty and ignorance, at least as these are usually defined in America, depends on eliminating, or at least greatly reducing, inequality. This is no simple matter. Since a competitive system means that some people "succeed" while others "fail," it also means that people will end up unequal. If we want to reduce inequality, we therefore have two options. The first possibility is to make the system less competitive by reducing the benefits that derive from success and the costs paid for failure. The second possibility is to make sure that everyone enters the competition with equal advantages and disadvantages.

The basic strategy of the war on poverty during the 1960s was to try to give everyone entering the job market or any other competitive arena comparable skills. This meant placing great emphasis on education.

Many people imagined that if schools could equalize people's cognitive skills this would equalize their bargaining power as adults. In such a system nobody would end up very poor – or, presumably, very rich.

This strategy rested on a series of assumptions which went roughly as follows:

1 Eliminating poverty is largely a matter of helping children born into poverty to rise out of it. Once families escape from poverty, they do not fall back into it. Middle-class children rarely end up poor.
2 The primary reason poor children do not escape from poverty is that they do not acquire basic cognitive skills. They cannot read, write, calculate, or articulate. Lacking these skills, they cannot get or keep a well-paid job.
3 The best mechanism for breaking this vicious circle is educational reform. Since children born into poor homes do not acquire the skills they need from their parents, they must be taught these skills in school. This can be done by making sure that they attend the same schools as middle-class children, by giving them extra compensatory programs in school, by giving their parents a voice in running their schools, or by some combination of all three approaches.

So far as we can discover, each of these assumptions is erroneous.

1 Poverty is not primarily hereditary. While children born into poverty have a higher-than-average chance of ending up poor, there is still an enormous amount of economic mobility from one generation to the next. Indeed, there is nearly as much economic inequality among brothers raised in the same homes as in the general population. This means that inequality is recreated anew in each generation, even among people who start life in essentially identical circumstances.
2 The primary reason some people end up richer than others is not that they have

more adequate cognitive skills. While children who read well, get the right answers to arithmetic problems, and articulate their thoughts clearly are somewhat more likely than others to get ahead, there are many other equally important factors involved. Thus there is almost as much economic inequality among those who score high on standardized tests as in the general population. Equalizing everyone's reading scores would not appreciably reduce the number of economic "failures."

3   There is no evidence that school reform can substantially reduce the extent of cognitive inequality, as measured by tests of verbal fluency, reading comprehension, or mathematical skill. Neither school resources nor segregation has an appreciable effect on either test scores or educational attainment.

Our work suggests, then, that many popular explanations of economic inequality are largely wrong. We cannot blame economic inequality primarily on genetic differences in men's capacity for abstract reasoning, since there is nearly as much economic inequality among men with equal test scores as among men in general. We cannot blame economic inequality primarily on the fact that parents pass along their disadvantages to their children, since there is nearly as much inequality among men whose parents had the same economic status as among men in general. We cannot blame economic inequality on differences between schools, since differences between schools seem to have very little effect on any measurable attribute of those who attend them.

Economic success seems to depend on varieties of luck and on-the-job competence that are only moderately related to family background, schooling, or scores on standardized tests. The definition of competence varies greatly from one job to another, but it seems in most cases to depend more on personality than on technical skills. This makes it hard to imagine a strategy for equalizing competence. A strategy for equalizing luck is even harder to conceive.

The fact that we cannot equalize luck or competence does *not* mean that economic inequality is inevitable. Still less does it imply that we cannot eliminate what has traditionally been defined as poverty. It only implies that we must tackle these problems in a different way. Instead of trying to reduce people's capacity to gain a competitive advantage on one another, we would have to change the rules of the game so as to reduce the rewards of competitive success and the costs of failure. Instead of trying to make everyone equally lucky or equally good at his job, we would have to devise "insurance" systems which neutralize the effects of luck, and income-sharing systems which break the link between vocational success and living standards.

This could be done in a variety of ways. Employers could be constrained to reduce wage disparities between their best- and worst-paid workers. The state could make taxes more progressive, and could provide income supplements to those who cannot earn an adequate living from wages alone. The state could also provide free public services for those who cannot afford to buy adequate services in the private sector. Pursued with vigor, such a strategy would make "poverty" (i.e. having a living standard less than half the national average) virtually impossible. It would also make economic "success," in the sense of having, say, a living standard more than twice the national average, far less common than it now is. The net effect would be to make those with the most competence and luck subsidize those with the least competence and luck to a far greater extent than they do today.

This strategy was rejected during the 1960s for the simple reason that it commanded relatively little popular support. The required legislation could not have passed Congress. Nor could it pass today. But that does not mean it was the wrong strategy. It simply means that until we change the political and moral premises on which most Americans now operate, poverty and inequality of opportunity will persist at pretty much their present level.

At this point the reader may wonder whether trying to change these premises is worthwhile. Why, after all, should we be so concerned about economic equality? Is it not enough to ensure equal opportunity? And does not the evidence we have described suggest that opportunities are already quite equal in America? If economic opportunities are relatively equal, and if the lucky and the competent then do better for themselves than the unlucky and incompetent, why should we feel guilty about this? Such questions cannot be answered in any definitive way, but a brief explanation of our position may help avoid misunderstanding.

We begin with the premise that every individual's happiness is of equal value. From this it is a short step to Bentham's dictum that society should be organized so as to provide the greatest good for the greatest number. In addition, we assume that the law of diminishing returns applies to most of the good things in life. In economic terms this means that people with low incomes value extra income more than people with high incomes. It follows that if we want to maximize the satisfaction of the population, the best way to divide any given amount of money is to make everyone's income the same. Income disparities (except those based on variations in "need") will always reduce overall satisfaction, because individuals with low incomes will lose more than individuals with high incomes gain.

The principal argument against equalizing incomes is that some people contribute more to the general welfare than others, and that they are therefore entitled to greater rewards. The most common version of this argument is that unless those who contribute more than their share are rewarded (and those who contribute less than their share punished) productivity will fall and everyone will be worse off. A more sophisti-cated version is that people will only share their incomes on an equal basis if all decisions that affect these incomes are made collectively. If people are left free to make decisions on an individual basis, their neighbors cannot be expected to pay the entire cost of their mistakes.

We accept the validity of both these arguments. We believe that men need incentives to contribute to the common good, and we prefer monetary incentives to social or moral incentives, which tend to be inflexible and very coercive. We believe, in other words, that virtue should be rewarded, and we assume that there will be considerable variation in virtue from one individual to another. This does not, however, mean that incomes must remain as unequal as they are now. Even if we assume, for example, that the most productive fifth of all workers accounts for half the Gross National Product, it does not follow that they need receive half the income. A third or a quarter might well suffice to keep both them and others productive.

Most people accept this logic to some extent. They believe that the rich should pay more taxes than the poor, although they often disagree about how much more. Conversely, they believe that the poor should not starve, even if they contribute nothing to the general welfare. They believe, in other words, that people should not be rewarded solely for their contribution to the general welfare, but that other considerations, such as need, should also be taken into account. Our egalitarianism is simply another way of saying that we think need should play a larger role than it now does in determining what people get back from society. We do not think it can or should be the sole consideration.

When we turn from the distribution of income to the distribution of other things, our commitment to equality is even more equivocal. We assume, for example, that occupational prestige resembles income in that those who have low-prestige occupations usually value additional prestige more than those who have high-prestige occupations. Insofar as prestige is an end in itself, then, the optimal distribution is again egalitarian. But occupational prestige derives from a variety of factors, most of which are more difficult to redistribute than income. We cannot imagine a social system in which all occupations have equal prestige, except in a society where all workers are equally competent. Since we do not see any likelihood of equalizing competence, we regard the equalization of occupational prestige as a desirable but probably elusive goal.

When we turn from occupational prestige to educational attainment and cognitive skills, the arguments for and against equality are reversed. If schooling and knowledge are thought of strictly as ends in themselves, it is impossible to make a case for distributing them equally. We can see no reason to suppose, for example, that people with relatively little schooling value additional schooling more than people who have already had a lot of schooling. Experience suggests that the reverse is the case. Insofar as schooling is an end in itself, then, Benthamite principles imply that those who want a lot should get a lot, and those who want very little should get very little. The same is true of knowledge and cognitive skills. People who know a lot generally value additional knowledge and skills more than those who know very little. This means that insofar as knowledge or skill is valued for its own sake, an unequal distribution is likely to give more satisfaction to more people than an equal distribution.

The case for equalizing the distribution of schooling and cognitive skill derives not from the idea that we should maximize consumer satisfaction, but from the assumption that equalizing schooling and cognitive skill is necessary to equalize status and income. This puts egalitarians in the awkward position of trying to impose equality on people, even though the natural demand for both cognitive skill and schooling is very unequal. Since we have found rather modest relationships between cognitive skill and schooling on the one hand and status and income on the other, we are much less concerned than most egalitarians with making sure that people end up alike in these areas.

Our commitment to equality is, then, neither all-embracing nor absolute. We do not believe that everyone can or should be made equal to everyone else in every respect. We assume that some differences in cognitive skill and vocational competence are inevitable, and that efforts to eliminate such differences can never be 100 percent successful. But we also believe that the distribution of income can be made far more equal than it is, even if the distribution of cognitive skill and vocational competence remains as unequal as it is now. We also think society should get on with the task of equalizing income rather than waiting for the day when everyone's earning power is equal.

7

What Money Can't Buy: Family Income and Children's Life Chances

Susan Mayer

Susan E. Mayer is an associate professor at the lrving B. Harris Graduate School of Public Policy Studies and at the College at the University of Chicago, and is the past director and current deputy director of the Northwestern University/University of Chicago Joint Center for Poverty Research. She also serves as a faculty affiliate with the University's Center for Human Potential and Public Policy. She is the author of the book, *What Money Can't Buy: Family Income and Children's Life Chances* (Harvard University Press) and co-editor with Paul Peterson of the book, *Earning and Learning: How Schools Matter* (Brookings Institution Press). Mayer's current research is on economic mobility across generations and the role of non-cognitive skills on social and economic success.

Why Parental Income Might Be Important

Americans disagree about the relative importance of parental income and other parental characteristics in shaping children's outcomes. Folk theories do not always correspond with social science theory, but in this case the ideas of the educators I interviewed summarize the main theoretical positions of social scientists on the importance of income. Two theories of the relationship between parental income and children's well-being dominate social science. I refer to them as the "investment" theory and the "good-parent" theory. These theories lead to different predictions about how additional parental income influences children.

The investment theory

Some people argue that money is important because it buys the things that children need, such as food and medical care. Most Americans agree that children whose basic material needs are not met have a hard time acquiring the skills that help them succeed. One teacher told me, "We have kids who have no food. We had two kids we knew were not getting any food at home. They were only getting the breakfast and lunch at school. We called [the state] Social Services and they said, 'Well that's ok. They are getting two meals a day.' Can you believe that they said that? We gave those kids peanut butter and bread every week." An assistant principal in a mostly middle-class school in the South gave this example: "We had a little girl who had a toothache – her tooth was just rotting, and it really hurt. We couldn't find anyone to see her because Medicaid doesn't pay for dental. How could she learn in school?" Her colleague was more blunt, "You can't do without money, can you?"

The investment theory dominates economics and is usually associated with Gary Becker and his colleagues (Becker 1981; Becker and Tomes 1986). In this theory the relationship between parents' and children's economic success is the result of biological and other endowments that parents pass on to their children, combined with what parents invest in their children. Endowments include both genetic endowments, such as a child's sex and race, as well as "cultural" endowments, such as the value parents place on their children's education. Parents invest both time and money in their children's "human capital," especially by investing in their education, but also by purchasing health care, good neighbors, and other "inputs" that improve children's future well-being.

How much parents invest in their children is determined by their own values and norms, their ability to finance investments (which is influenced by their income and their access to capital), and the availability of alternative sources of investment, such as government programs. Since the return on investments depends on children's biological endowments, these also influence how much parents are willing to invest.

The investment theory holds that children raised in affluent families succeed more often than those raised in poor families, both because rich parents pass on superior endowments and because they can invest more in their children. In theory, income transfers (or other policies that equalize access to capital) could equalize parents' investments in their children. If investments were equal, the remaining differences in the life chances of children would be due to endowments and "luck." Since endowments are all the things parents pass on to their

children, including biological, social, and psychological attributes, the remaining differences might be quite large unless, as some social scientists believe, income transfers could also equalize parents' social and psychological attributes.

As Becker and others have noted, government transfers to parents might be an inefficient way to increase investments in poor children. Parents are likely to spend at least some transfer income on themselves or on other goods and services that do not increase their children's human capital. One study finds that, on average, households spend only about 38 percent of their income on children. The remaining 62 percent is spent on the adults (Lazear and Michael 1988). This is partly because of short-term egalitarianism. In many realms children, at least before adolescence, need less than adults. They eat less and their clothes and entertainment cost less. Thus if a family tries to ensure that all members' needs are met equally, it will spend more on adults than on children. In addition, parents are not completely altruistic in their expenditure decisions. This same study finds that rich parents allocate a smaller proportion of their expenditures to children than poor parents. The fact that poor parents spend a higher fraction of their money on their children implies that transferring income from rich to poor parents would increase the aggregate amount spent on children. But it is not clear that this would result in improved child outcomes. If the additional money spent on children went for fast food or fancy gym shoes, the long-term benefits to children might be small.

Even if the government provides specific goods and services, such as education, to improve children's human capital, parents are likely to redirect some of what they would have spent on providing these things to other forms of consumption that do not improve their children's human capital. For example, if the government provides free health care for children, parents will switch some of what they would have spent on health care to other forms of consumption. Thus though transferring income or noncash benefits to parents will likely increase investments in low-income children, it will also increase the amount low-income parents spend on themselves. The political attractiveness of transfers depends on one's willingness to finance poor parent's expenditures on themselves in order to increase expenditures on children. This in turn depends on how much additional expenditures on children improve their outcomes.

The Good-Parent Theory

In contrast to the investment theory, the good-parent theory holds that low income reduces parents' ability to be good parents, not because poor families have less money to invest in their children, but because low income decreases the quality of nonmonetary investments, such as parents' interactions with their children. This in turn hurts children's chances for success. One teacher I talked to used her own experience to make this point. She explained that at one time she had been a single mother with two children. "Money is an issue, I mean it makes a big difference. I can remember being in school and what I was really thinking about was whether a check was going to bounce. I can remember, my kids were sick and I knew their father was supposed to pay for their medical things, but I knew he wouldn't pay unless I paid it first, then hassled him to get it back. I worried, was it worth doing that? Do they really need to see the doctor? Are they sick enough? It was hard. Being poor is not easy."

There are at least two versions of the good-parent theory: the parental-stress version and the role-model version. The parental-stress version, which dominates psychology, holds that poverty is stressful and that stress diminishes parents' ability to provide "supportive, consistent, and involved parenting" (McLoyd 1990). Poor parenting, in turn, hurts the social and emotional development of children, which limits their educational and social opportunities. This theory implies that transferring income to poor families should alleviate stress, improve parenting, and thus improve children's outcomes.

The transactional theory of child development is a closely related elaboration of the stress theory (Parker et al. 1988; Sameroff and Chandler 1975; Scarr and McCartney 1983). It holds that children's characteristics, such as their cognitive ability, temperament, and health, shape their responses to the environment, and that these responses in turn transform the environment. A student teacher made this point. In describing why some children fail and others succeed, she said, "Well I know that it's not always just the parents. I come from a home, I mean my parents are always on me about my work, and they expect the same from my brothers and sisters. But my sister is determined she's just not going to do what she's supposed to. Every night my daddy, he'd say, 'Let me see your homework,' and she'd say, 'Oh we didn't have any today.' He'd call the teachers. I mean he knew she had to have some homework. It came to a point where there was nothing he could do. They went to counseling. They tried everything. But they couldn't take her hand and make her do it. So I know it isn't just the parents."

The example psychologists often use to describe the transactional theory is a child born prematurely to a poor single mother. The premature birth and the prospect of rearing a child alone with little money depress the mother. Because the child is immature, she is often passive. The child's passivity makes the mother feel inadequate, which deepens her depression. Because she is depressed, the mother is unresponsive to the child. The child gets little stimulation from the environment, and eventually stops seeking it. This further deepens the mother's feelings of inadequacy. By the time the child is two or three years old, she is behind in language and cognitive development (Parker et al. 1988). But no one factor in this scenario is the sole "cause" of the developmental delay – the child's low birth weight, her mother's depression, and the family's poverty all play a role.

This reasoning has led to the notion that children's success depends on the number of "risk factors" they face. Risk factors include such things as a poor home environment, poor health, and poverty. Some researchers treat poverty as a "marker" for risk factors, that is, as a correlate but not necessarily a cause of risks such as stress, poor health, weak social support, and maternal depression (Parker et al. 1988). Others treat poverty as a cause of such risks (Houston et al. 1994). The distinction is important. If poverty causes depression, transferring income to parents can alleviate their depression. But if parents who are depressed are poor because depression makes it hard to earn a living, transferring money to them will not reduce their depression. In this case we would have to treat parental depression directly.

Psychologists differ as to the relative importance of various risk factors. Some seem to believe that all risk factors are equally important. In the example of the premature child, they view the mother's poverty and the child's birth weight as equally important, because changing either would change the child's development by the same amount. Had we transferred money to the mother, she would have been less anxious about her child's birth and, therefore, less depressed and more responsive to the child. Yet a medical intervention that increased the child's birth weight would have gotten the same result, because the child would then have been more responsive, leading the mother to be less depressed and more responsive in return. Others suggest that because all risk factors are equally important, interventions must address all of them simultaneously. Advocates of this approach suggest interventions that address the material, emotional, and psychological needs of poor families.

Some researchers try to estimate the relative importance of various risk factors, usually by estimating their additive effect. If risk factors are additive, each one has the same effect regardless of other characteristics of parents and their children. The transaction theory suggests, however, that poverty interacts with other factors. When risk factors interact, the effect of a risk factor depends on other characteristics of parents and children. For example, an additive model assumes that parental depression has the same effect on children regardless of parents' income. An interaction model assumes that parental depression is more (or less) harmful for children when their parents are poor. No data set has enough cases to estimate all the potential interactions implied by such hypotheses.

The role-model version of the good-parent theory also emphasizes parents' interactions with their children, but it does not necessarily imply that poor parents are stressed. Instead, it usually holds that because of their position at the bottom of the social hierarchy, low-income parents develop values, norms, and behaviors that are "dysfunctional" for success in the dominant culture. This could be because the parents are unusually stressed, because their deviant values help reduce stress, or for reasons that have little to do with stress.

A common variation of this hypothesis is that behaviors which appear to be dysfunctional from the point of view of the middle class are in fact a rational response to poverty. An assistant principal in a school in which nearly all the students are economically disadvantaged described it this way: "A lot of time the parents want to have expectations for their kids. But they think it doesn't do any good to have expectations if you don't think it's ever going to be in the reach of the child. So they don't follow through. Lack of hope. That is one of the most profound things. Simply the lack of hope. You take most of the parents that we work with and they would like to hope that their child will go to college, but they don't really see a way that they are going to make that happen."

A teacher in an affluent suburb of Chicago who tutored students on the impoverished west side of the city saw the same thing. "The expectation there was that your kid – no matter how bright your kid was – he was going to fail. I mean that was the expectation. To be streetwise was a much better value. Most of them thought that they were going to live in that part of the city where they had been brought up for the rest of their lives. And that was just the way it was. It was almost like it was preordained was the feeling I got from the parents and the kids. They had the idea that . . . no matter what they did they were going to fail." If parents believe that their children cannot succeed in school, not valuing education will reduce feelings of failure. Since children tend to model their own values and behavior on those of their parents, parents' "dysfunctional" values and behaviors are transmitted to their children. As a result, poor parents are "bad" role models for their children. If generations of irregular employment and discrimination result in street skills seeming more valuable than academic skills, parents will be more likely to encourage their children to acquire street skills than to study or stay in school.

This version of the good-parent theory implies that neither increasing parents' incomes nor providing parents with the means to invest in their children's human capital is likely to improve children's life chances in the short run. Instead, parents' values, attitudes, and behavior must be changed, a process that is likely to require a permanent change in the opportunity structure. This version of the role-model hypothesis is usually called the "culture of poverty" hypothesis and has been politically controversial. Conservatives argue that if parental values and norms account for both parents' poverty and the failures of their children, transferring income to poor parents without changing their attitudes and behaviors will

not only fail to help poor children but could actually hurt the children by reinforcing the parental values that result in poverty. They argue that the values and attitudes of the poor will change only in response to the right incentives. Liberals agree that the incentives should be changed, but by this they usually mean that the government must work to change the structural circumstances that reinforce "dysfunctional" values and behavior, including racism, economic segregation, and segmented labor markets. Once the structural changes create a "level playing field," parents will change (Ogbu 1981; Wilson 1987).[1]

The role-model hypothesis applies mainly to families experiencing long-term poverty. For families experiencing short-term poverty, stress is likely to be high but changes in basic values are likely to be rare. Indeed, the role-model hypothesis often assumes that low-income parents change their values over the long run precisely because this is an effective way of reducing the stress caused by economic stringency and deprivation.

All these theories try to describe how income influences children's outcomes. But it is possible that the problems associated with poor children are a result not of low income but of parental characteristics that cause their income to be low and also influence their children's outcomes. In this view, parents' attitudes, values, and behavior influence children's chances for success. One teacher at a school in Georgia was typical of those with this view. She told me emphatically, "The amount of money that somebody makes does not determine [how well his or her child does in school]. It's what they do with their money and the time they spend with their children." She attributed her own success growing up in a family without much money to parents who had high expectations for her. "They were responsible. They made sure I was clothed and fed, and then they expected me, when I went to school, to do well. They checked up on me to make sure I was doing well. They

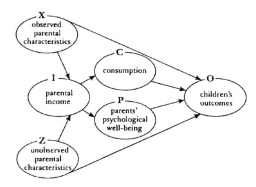

Figure 7.1 Heuristic income model

were involved in school. They always went to PTA. They kept up with my report cards. They expected me to behave. They wanted more for me than they had."

Some folk theories still hold that poverty improves character. A young student teacher thought her family's poverty led her to a college education. She explained that because of her family's poverty, "I didn't fit in (with other children) style-wise. I've never fit in style-wise, I mean – clothes-wise. So I decided to fit in with the smart crowd. That's why I made good grades and all. I thought if I can't fit in with a crowd that is popular and has money, I'll fit in with this other crowd." Nevertheless, almost no empirical evidence supports the idea that poverty benefits children.

Figure 7.1 is a schematic overview of these theories about how parental income affects children's outcomes. It shows that observed parental characteristics (X) affect both parental income (I) and children's outcomes (O). Many parental characteristics that we cannot measure, what I call unobserved parental characteristics (Z), also affect both parental income and children's outcomes. The investment theory holds that income affects children's outcomes by affecting a family's consumption and investments in its children (C). The parental-stress theory holds that income affects parents' psychological well-being (P), which in turn affects children's outcomes.

Children from low-income families score lower on tests of cognitive skill than children from affluent families, are more likely to have babies as teenagers or become young single mothers, and are more likely to drop out of high school and receive fewer years of education. Young men raised in low-income families work fewer hours and earn lower wages than those raised in affluent families. Social scientists have developed several hypotheses about why poor children fare worse than affluent children, most of which imply that parental income per se affects children's outcomes.

All the social science theories about the influence of parental income on children's outcomes recognize that poor parents differ from rich parents in many ways besides their income. In order to determine the true relationship between parental income and children's outcomes, we would need to compare children whose families have different incomes but are alike on all the characteristics that affect both parental income and children's well-being.

NOTE

1 The "culture of poverty" hypothesis (Lewis 1966) is the version of the role-model hypothesis that has received the most attention from both academics and policy makers. More recently John Ogbu (1981) has emphasized that cultural traits are adaptations to poverty that reproduce poverty as well.

REFERENCES

Becker, Gary. 1981. *A Treatise on the Family.* Cambridge, Mass.: Harvard University Press.

Becker, Gary, and Nigel Tomes. 1986. "Human Capital and the Rise and Fall of Families." *Journal of Labor Economics* 4(2), part 2:S1–S139.

Houston, Aletha, Vonnie McLoyd, and Cynthia Coll. 1994. "Children and Poverty: Issues in Contemporary Research." *Child Development* 65:275–82.

Lazear, Edward, and Robert T. Michael. 1988. *Allocation of Income within the Household.* Chicago: The University of Chicago Press.

Lewis, Oscar. 1966. "The Culture of Poverty." *Scientific American* 215(4):19–25.

McLoyd, Vonnie. 1990. "The Impact of Economic Hardship on Black Families and Children: Psychological Distress, Parenting, and Socioemotional Development." *Child Development* 61: 311–46.

Ogbu, John. 1981. "Origins of Human Competence: A Cultural-Ecological Perspective." *Child Development* 52:413–29.

Parker, Steven, Steven Greer, and Barry Zuckerman. 1988. "Double Jeopardy: The Impact of Poverty on Early Child Development." *Pediatric Clinics of North America* 35(6):1227–40.

Sameroff, Arnold, and M. Chandler. 1975. "Reproductive Risk and the Continuum of Caretaking Casualty." *Review of Child Development*, ed. F. D. Horowitz, M. Hetherington, S. Scarr-Salapateck, and G. Seigel. Chicago: University of Chicago Press.

Scarr, Sandra, and Kathleen McCartney. 1983. "How People Make Their Own Environments: A Theory of Genotype – > Environment Effects." *Child Development* 54:424–35.

Wilson, William Julius. 1987. *The Truly Disadvantaged: The Inner City, the Underclass, and Public Policy.* Chicago: The University of Chicago Press.

8

Being Black, Living in the Red: Race, Wealth, and Social Policy in America

Dalton Conley

Dalton Conley is Associate Professor of Sociology and Director of the Center for Advanced Social Science Research at New York University. Previously he taught at Yale University in the Departments of Sociology and African American Studies. His research explores race and class dynamics in the contemporary United States. He is author of *Being Black, Living in the Red: Race, Wealth and Social Policy in America* (California, 1999; winner of the American Sociological Association 1997 Dissertation Award), *Honky* (California, 2000; Vintage, 2001), a sociological memoir, and with Neil Bennett and Kate Strully, the forthcoming book, *The Starting Gate: Health and Life Chances Across Generations*. He is currently working on a book entitled *The Pecking Order* that examines class differences among siblings from the same family of origin and is supported by the Robert Wood Johnson Foundation (Investigator Award in Health Policy Research) and the NSF (CAREER Award). In addition to academic journals, Conley has written for *The New York Times Magazine*, *Time* Magazine, *The Nation*, *Urban Latino Magazine*, *Salon*, *Feed Magazine*, *Le Monde Diplomatique* and various other trade publications.

Property is theft.   *Pierre Joseph Proudhon, 1809–65*

If I could cite one statistic that inspired this study, it would be the following: in 1994, the median white family held assets worth more than seven times those of the median non-white family. Even when we compare white and minority families at the same income level, whites enjoy a huge advantage in wealth. For instance, at the lower end of the income spectrum (less than $15,000 per year), the median African American family has no assets, while the equivalent white family holds $10,000 worth of equity. At upper income levels (greater than $75,000 per year), white families have a median net worth of $308,000, almost three times the figure for upper-income African American families ($114,600).[1]

Herein lie the two motivating questions of this study. First, why does this wealth gap exist and persist over and above income differences? Second, does this wealth gap explain racial differences in areas such as education, work, earnings, welfare, and family structure? In short, this book examines where race *per se* really matters in the post–civil rights era and where race simply acts as a stand-in for that dirty word of American society: class. The answers to these questions have important implications for the debate over affirmative action and for social policy in general.

An alternative way to conceptualize what this study is about is to contrast the situations of two hypothetical families. Let's say that both households consist of married parents, in their thirties, with two young children.[2] Both families are low-income – that is, the total household income of each family is approximately the amount that the federal government has "declared" to be the poverty line for a family of four (with two children). In 1996, this figure was $15,911.

Brett and Samantha Jones (family 1) earned about $12,000 that year. Brett earned this income from his job at a local fast-food franchise (approximately two thousand hours at a rate of $6 per hour). He found himself employed at this low-wage job after being laid off from his relatively well-paid position as a sheet metal worker at a local manufacturing plant, which closed because of fierce competition from companies in Asia and Latin America. After six months of unemployment, the only work Brett could find was flipping burgers alongside teenagers from the local high school.

Fortunately for the Jones family, however, they owned their own home. Fifteen years earlier, when Brett graduated from high school, married Samantha, and landed his original job as a sheet metal worker, his parents had lent the newlyweds money out of their retirement nest egg that enabled Brett and Samantha to make a 10 percent down payment on a house. With Samantha's parents cosigning – backed by the value of their own home – the newlyweds took out a fifteen-year mortgage for the balance of the cost of their $30,000 home. Although money was tight in the beginning, they were nonetheless thrilled to have a

place of their own. During those initial, difficult years, an average of $209 of their $290.14 monthly mortgage payment was tax deductible as a home mortgage interest deduction. In addition, their annual property taxes of $800 were completely deductible, lowering their taxable income by a total of $3,308 per year. This more than offset the payments they were making to Brett's parents for the $3,000 they had borrowed for the down payment.

After four years, Brett and Samantha had paid back the $3,000 loan from his parents. At that point, the total of their combined mortgage payment ($290.14), monthly insurance premium ($50), and monthly property tax payment ($67), minus the tax savings from the deductions for mortgage interest and local property taxes, was less than the $350 that the Smiths (family 2) were paying to rent a unit the same size as the Joneses' house on the other side of town.

That other neighborhood, on the "bad" side of town, where David and Janet Smith lived, had worse schools and a higher crime rate and had just been chosen as a site for a waste disposal center. Most of the residents rented their housing units from absentee landlords who had no personal stake in the community other than profit. A few blocks from the Smiths' apartment was a row of public housing projects. Although they earned the same salaries and paid more or less the same monthly costs for housing as the Joneses did, the Smiths and their children experienced living conditions that were far inferior on every dimension, ranging from the aesthetic to the functional (buses ran less frequently, large supermarkets were nowhere to be found, and class size at the local school was well over thirty).

Like Brett Jones, David Smith had been employed as a sheet metal worker at the now-closed manufacturing plant. Unfortunately, the Smiths had not been able to buy a home when David was first hired at the plant. With little in the way of a down payment, they had looked for an affordable unit at the time, but the real estate agents they saw routinely claimed that there was just nothing available at the moment, although they promised to "be sure to call as soon as something comes up. . . ." The Smiths never heard back from the agents and eventually settled into a rental apartment.

David spent the first three months after the layoffs searching for work, drawing down the family's savings to supplement unemployment insurance – savings that were not significantly greater than those of the Joneses, since both families had more or less the same monthly expenses. After several months of searching, David managed to land a job. Unfortunately, it was of the same variety as the job Brett Jones found: working as a security guard at the local mall, for about $12,000 a year. Meanwhile, Janet Smith went to work part time, as a nurse's aide for a home health care agency, grossing about $4,000 annually.

After the layoffs, the Joneses experienced a couple of rough months, when they were forced to dip into their small cash savings. But they were able to pay off the last two installments of their mortgage, thus eliminating their single biggest living expense. So, although they had some trouble adjusting to their lower standard of living, they managed to get by, always hoping that another manufacturing job would become available or that another company would buy out the plant and reopen it. If worst came to worst, they felt that they could always sell their home and relocate in a less expensive locale or an area with a more promising labor market.

The Smiths were a different case entirely. As renters, they had no latitude in reducing their expenses to meet their new economic reality, and they could not afford their rent on David's reduced salary. The financial strain eventually proved too much for the Smiths, who fought over how to structure the family budget. After a particularly bad row when the last of their savings had been spent, they decided to take a break; both thought life would be easier and better for the children if Janet moved back in with her mother for a while, just until things turned around economically – that is, until David found a better-paying job. With no house to anchor them, this seemed to be the best course of action.

Several years later, David and Janet Smith divorced, and the children began to see less and less of their father, who stayed with a friend on a "temporary" basis. Even though together they had earned more than the Jones family (with total incomes of $16,000 and $12,000, respectively), the Smiths had a rougher financial, emotional, and family situation, which, we may infer, resulted from a lack of property ownership.

What this comparison of the two families illustrates is the inadequacy of relying on income alone to describe the economic and social circumstances of families at the lower end of the economic scale. With a $16,000 annual income, the Smiths were just above the poverty threshold. In other words, they were not defined as "poor," in contrast to the Joneses, who were.[3] Yet the Smiths were worse off than the Joneses, despite the fact that the U.S. government and most researchers would have classified the Jones family as the one who met the threshold of neediness, based on that family's lower income.

These income-based poverty thresholds differ by family size and are adjusted annually for changes in the average cost of living in the United States. In 1998, more than two dozen government programs – including food stamps, Head Start, and Medicaid – based their eligibility standards on the official poverty threshold. Additionally, more than a dozen states currently link their needs standard in some way to this poverty threshold. The example of the Joneses and the Smiths should tell us that something is gravely wrong with the way we are measuring economic hardship – poverty – in the United States. By ignoring assets, we not only give a distorted picture of life at the bottom of the income distribution but may even create perverse incentives.

Of course, we must be cautious and remember that the Smiths and the Joneses are hypothetically embellished examples that may exaggerate differences. Perhaps the Smiths would have divorced regardless of their economic circumstances. The hard evidence linking modest financial differences to a propensity toward marital dissolution is thin; however, a substantial body of research shows that financial issues are a major source of marital discord and relationship strain.[4] It is also possible that the Smiths, with nothing to lose in the form of assets, might have easily slid into the world of welfare dependency. A wide range of other factors, not included in our examples, affect a family's well-being and its trajectory. For example, the members of one family might have been healthier than those of the other, which would have had important economic consequences and could have affected family stability. Perhaps one family might have been especially savvy about using available resources and would have been able to take in boarders, do under-the-table work, or employ another strategy to better its standard of living. Nor do our examples address educational differences between the two households.

But I have chosen not to address all these confounding factors for the purpose of illustrating the importance of asset ownership *per se*. Of course, homeownership, savings behavior, and employment status all interact with a variety of other measurable and unmeasurable factors. This interaction, however, does not take away from the importance of property ownership itself.

The premise of this study is a relatively simple and straightforward one: in order to understand a family's well-being and the life chances of its children – in short, to understand its class position – we not only must consider income, education, and occupation but also must take into account accumulated wealth (that is, property, assets, or net worth – terms that I will use interchangeably throughout this study). While the importance of wealth is the starting point of

the study, its end point is the impact of the wealth distribution on racial inequality in America. As you might have guessed, an important detail is missing from the preceding description of the two families: the Smiths are black and have fewer assets than the Joneses, who are white.

At all income, occupational, and education levels, black families on average have drastically lower levels of wealth than similar white families. The situation of the Smiths may help us to understand the reason for this disparity of wealth between blacks and whites. For the Smiths, it was not discrimination in hiring or education that led to a family outcome vastly different from that of the Joneses; rather, it was a relative lack of assets from which they could draw. In contemporary America, race and property are intimately linked and form the nexus for the persistence of black–white inequality.

Let us look again at the Smith family, this time through the lens of race. Why did real estate agents tell the Smiths that nothing was available, thereby hindering their chances of finding a home to buy? This well-documented practice is called "steering," in which agents do not disclose properties on the market to qualified African American home seekers, in order to preserve the racial makeup of white communities – with an eye to maintaining the property values in those neighborhoods. Even if the Smiths had managed to locate a home in a predominantly African American neighborhood, they might well have encountered difficulty in obtaining a home mortgage because of "redlining," the procedure by which banks code such neighborhoods "red" – the lowest rating – on their loan evaluations, thereby making it next to impossible to get a mortgage for a home in these districts. Finally, and perhaps most important, the Smiths' parents were more likely to have been poor and without assets themselves (being black and having been born early in the century), meaning that it would have been harder for them to amass enough money to loan their children a down payment or to cosign a loan for them. The result is that while poor whites manage to have, on average, net worths of over $10,000, impoverished blacks have essentially no assets whatsoever.[5]

Since wealth accumulation depends heavily on intergenerational support issues such as gifts, informal loans, and inheritances, net worth has the ability to pick up both the current dynamics of race and the legacy of past inequalities that may be obscured in simple measures of income, occupation, or education. This thesis has been suggested by the work of sociologists Melvin Oliver and Thomas Shapiro in their recent book *Black Wealth/White Wealth*.[6] They claim that wealth is central to the nature of black-white inequality and that wealth – as opposed to income, occupation, or education – represents the "sedimentation" of both a legacy of racial inequality as well as contemporary, continuing inequities. Oliver and Shapiro provide a textured description of the divergence of black–white asset holdings. They touch on some of the causal factors leading to this growing gap, such as differential mortgage interest rates paid by black and white borrowers. However, because they use a "snapshot" of families as their primary source of information – that is, cross-sectional data collected at one point in time (the 1984 Survey of Income and Program Participation) – they are limited in the scope of their investigation of the causes and consequences of black–white wealth differentials over time.

I hope to build on the work of Oliver and Shapiro by developing a formal model for the inclusion of assets into statistical models of socioeconomic attainment and family processes, thereby mapping out the role that wealth inequities play in the larger context of a cycle of racial inequality. Specifically, it is the hypothesis of this study that certain tenacious racial differences – such as deficits in education, employment, wages, and even wealth itself among African Americans – will turn out to be indirect effects, mediated by class differences. In other words, it is not race *per se* that matters directly; instead, what matters are the wealth levels and class positions that are associated with race in America. In this manner, racial differences in income and asset levels have come to play a prominent role in the perpetuation of black–white inequality in the United States.

This is not to say that race does not matter; rather, it maps very well onto class inequality, which in turn affects a whole host of other life outcomes. In fact, when class is taken into consideration, African Americans demonstrate significant net *advantages* over whites on a variety of indicators (such as rates of high school graduation, for instance). In this fact lies the paradox of race and class in contemporary America – and the reason that both sides of the affirmative action debate can point to evidence to support their positions.

The Race–Class Debate

A brief review of the discourse on racial inequality may help to put the thesis of this book in historical perspective. The concept of equality most often used in public discourse was inherited from the French Revolution: *equality of opportunity*. Under this concept, equality would be achieved if each individual in a society enjoyed the right to compete in a contest unimpaired by discrimination of any kind. This form of equality would clearly be incompatible with an active, "color-aware" form of racial oppression such as the refusal to serve someone at a lunch counter or the denial of a job to an individual based on his or her physiognomy. Further, this concept fits very well with the game-like image many Americans have of the capitalist system. If the game is fair, our whole society is bettered by it. By contrast, if the rules are stacked in favor of one group, society is not making maximal use of its human resources. For example, if African Americans are barred from higher education, society as a whole may be deprived of the skills of a great surgeon or engineer who could not attend a university because of skin color. With this premise, arguments for equality of opportunity can often be made on the basis of efficiency rather than equity.

Because of this ideological safety valve, equality of opportunity is perhaps the least threatening type of equality to many in the white majority, who see a place for all at the starting gate as an underlying premise of the capitalist system. Lingering conscious or unconscious ideas of white superiority may have additionally blunted fears. According to this logic, whites would not have much to lose by allowing blacks into the economic game; if whites are inherently superior, why should they fear the entry of blacks into the contest? The belief in white superiority that had formed part of the public discourse since the early days of Western imperialism, we can speculate, may have provided a sense of security to some of the more privileged whites who did not fear for their class position, particularly during the period of rapid economic growth after World War II.

For these reasons, equality of opportunity served as the underlying philosophy and rallying cry that drove the liberal political triumphs of the 1950s and early 1960s, capped by the 1964 Civil Rights Act and the Voting Rights Act of 1965. With such legislation, equality of opportunity – in name at least – had been achieved. In theory, after 1965, discrimination in hiring, housing, and other aspects of life was illegal. It was at this point, according to sociologist William Julius Wilson[7] and others, that an overt phase of racial oppression ended in the United States and was replaced by economic subordination.

While legal equality of opportunity might have been established and some income gains made, institutionalized racism persisted nonetheless, and the scars of centuries of overt repression remained. A second type of equality had yet to be realized: *equality of condition* – more progressive and less ideologically acceptable to the American public than equality of opportunity. According to political scientist Jennifer Hochschild, "Three-fourths or more of both races agree that all people warrant equal respect, that skill rather than need should determine wages, that 'America should promote equal opportunity for all' rather than 'equal outcomes.' " She adds that most Americans think that everyone should attempt to amount to more than their parents and that "trying to get ahead is very important in making someone a true American."[8] Clearly, upward mobility and socioeconomic success are fundamental to at least the rhetoric of what it means to be American. By such a definition, African Americans may, in fact, be the most American of all, for by some socioeconomic indicators, they have made incredible progress since the passage of civil rights legislation. By other measures, however, they are not so "American" – that is, for whatever reason, upward mobility has been more difficult.

Although as a group African Americans have made progress in a number of socioeconomic areas, the base from which they were starting in the 1960s was dismally low. For instance, in 1964, only 9.4 percent of blacks held professional or managerial positions, compared to 24.7 percent of whites.[9] The median family income in the black community was less than half that in the white community. By the end of the decade (1969), 41.2 percent of black children still lived in poverty, compared to only 9.9 percent of white children.[10] Even when we compare blacks and whites with similar educational credentials, African Americans suffered from lower incomes and worked in less prestigious occupations than their white counterparts.[11] Statistics aside, the televised ghetto riots of the late 1960s may have been evidence enough for many American observers that substantial racial inequities remained in the United States.

Overall, conditions were worse for blacks than for whites across America. In addition, the mechanism by which inequality was transferred from generation to generation was different in the African American community. In their classic 1967 study, *The American Occupational Structure*, sociologists

Peter Blau and Otis Dudley Duncan observed that the relationship between the occupations of black fathers and the occupations of their sons was weaker than the similar relationship among whites: regardless of class origin, African American individuals seemed destined to end up in the lower, manual sector of the economy. Blau and Duncan called this condition "perverse equality." In the same vein, the higher an African American attempted to rise in the occupational hierarchy, the more discrimination the individual faced. "In short," wrote Blau and Duncan, "better educated Negroes fare even worse relative to whites than uneducated Negroes."[12]

Despite a lack of equality of condition, many sociologists and historians agree that the period of the 1950s and 1960s was a time of important gains for African Americans. For instance, between 1949 and 1969, the median income (adjusted for family size) increased by 173 percent among African Americans, in contrast to a 110 percent increase for whites. (Keep in mind, however, that blacks were starting from a base income that was slightly more than a third that of whites in 1949.)[13] Additionally, between 1940 and the early 1970s, the black middle class grew at a faster rate than the white middle class. Based on a definition of "middle class" as having a family income twice the poverty line (note the income-based conception of class), the percentage of African American households in this group rose from a minuscule 1 percent in 1940 to 39 percent in 1970.

The period since 1970 – the era of "economic subordination," according to Wilson – has been difficult to interpret in terms of race. Some of the positive trends continue for middle-class African Americans; other statistics, however, tell a different tale, a story of poor African Americans getting poorer. In deciphering the current state of race in America, it may help to view racial inequality in the context of the life course, starting with birth. Black infants, for example, are much more likely than white infants to be born with a low (under 2,500 grams) or a very low (under 1,500 grams) birth weight. In 1994, medical complications associated with low birth weight were the primary cause of death among black infants and the third leading cause for white infants. Correspondingly, the mortality rate among black infants that year (15.8 per thousand) was well over twice that among white and Hispanic babies (6.6 and 6.5 per thousand, respectively).[14]

Looking beyond infancy, we find that over half of all African American children under the age of six live in poverty, three times greater than the proportion in the white community.[15] When we move up the age ladder, the news gets better before it gets worse again. In examining educational statistics, we find that the high school completion rates for blacks and whites are essentially the same among younger adults (ages twenty-five to thirty-four, the group for whom civil rights advances should have had an effect), with 85 percent of African Americans attaining at least a high school education, compared to 88 percent of whites. Even more encouraging is that the proportion of adults in this same age group who receive some college education (not necessarily a degree) is higher for blacks than for whites (32 and 28 percent, respectively). When we examine college completion rates, however, we find that African Americans are only about half as likely as whites to complete a bachelor's degree (14 and 28 percent, respectively). The college attrition rate for black students has become a major problem on American campuses.[16]

When we move out of school and into the labor market, the situation deteriorates. The black–white wage ratio has begun to widen slightly for all education levels since the 1980s.[17] Labor force participation and unemployment differentials have also increased.[18] For example, in 1994, the unemployment rate for blacks was 13.9 percent, whereas it was only 6.2 percent for non-Hispanic whites. The black unemployment rate has only rarely dipped below double digits since the dawn of the civil rights era, and it surpassed 20 percent during the 1982–3 recession. Even when African Americans are able to land a job, it is likely to be a less desirable position. In 1997, only 16 percent of employed African Americans held professional or managerial jobs, compared to 31 percent of employed whites. By contrast, black workers were overrepresented in the service sector, with its lower wages: 26 percent of employed African Americans worked in service industries in 1997, while only 15 percent of their white counterparts held jobs in this sector.[19]

Income trends reflect the occupational position of black workers. In 1997, the median income for black families was 55 percent that of white families ($26,522 compared to $47,023). In this same year, 26 percent of black families lived under the poverty line, whereas only 6 percent of white families did so. Educational differences do not explain these income gaps. For instance, among individuals who are high school graduates (but have not completed additional education), median incomes are $14,881 and $18,446 for blacks and whites, respectively. When we consider only men, the disparity widens. Black male high school graduates earned a median income of $18,898 in 1997 compared to $26,028 for white males. In other words, in 1997, African American male high school graduates earned 73 cents to the dollar earned by white male high school graduates. For more educated groups, wage ratios are not much better.[20]

The labor market difficulties that African American men continue to face have repercussions further up the age ladder. As mentioned earlier, the black–white wealth gap is even wider than the income difference. Other areas of life are affected as well. For instance, in 1997, only 46 percent of black families consisted of a married couple (with or without children). This figure is 56 percent of that for whites (81 percent).[21] Some argue that this dearth of marriage in the African American community is partly a

result of a shortage of marriageable (read: well-employed) black men.[22] There seems to be a causal loop in the logic of the current discourse on race in the United States: if black families have two full-time workers, they can maintain economic equity with whites, but blacks face economic obstacles in getting and staying married. Race, family, and life chances seem to be inextricably linked in a vicious circle of inequality over the life course.

Given all these trends, it is understandable why liberals and conservatives are constantly at odds on issues such as the impact and continuing value of affirmative action or the reasons for persistent gaps in socioeconomic attainment between blacks and whites. Both sides can point to statistics to support their arguments, and the debate reaches a stalemate.[23]

The most provocative thesis regarding the state of racial equality today remains that issued by William Julius Wilson back in 1978 in his book *The Declining Significance of Race*, which was championed and attacked by a variety of scholars from both sides of the political debate. Wilson argued that the civil rights victories of the 1960s led to a situation in which overt racial oppression is largely a thing of the past (equality of opportunity), but in which the socioeconomic (read: class) differences between blacks and whites disadvantage African Americans relative to their white counterparts in terms of their chances for success in life. In its most distilled form, his argument is simply that class has eclipsed race as the most important factor determining the life chances of African Americans. As Wilson himself puts it in the first sentence of his classic work: "Race relations in America have undergone fundamental changes in recent years, so much so that now the life chances of individual blacks have more to do with their economic class position than with their day-to-day encounters with whites."[24]

Understandably, Wilson's controversial argument about the declining significance of race has come under careful scrutiny.

Many researchers have tested his hypothesis that class is more determinant than race of the life chances of black Americans. Support has been found for his claim in terms of occupational mobility both within and across generations,[25] although race still remains salient in predicting earnings for given education levels[26] and net worth.[27] Furthermore, many scholars have documented the continued importance of race in both the economic and the symbolic realms for many black Americans.[28] There is some disagreement about the exact mechanism by which race affects the life chances of black Americans: some claim that it has a direct impact net of socioeconomic background characteristics; others argue that it does not. Most are in agreement that race influences the way socioeconomic background (class) affects the outcomes of individuals (a sort of compromise in the race–class debate). In other words, a consensus seems to be emerging that blacks who come from middle-class backgrounds are doing better than ever before while poor, predominantly inner-city blacks are being left further and further behind. In other words, there is an "interaction" between race and class background.

The race–class debate is far from settled, however. At the time Wilson penned that provocative statement (1978), it had not even been fifteen years since the end of the era of overt, legally tolerated racial oppression. If class has eclipsed race for any group, it would have done so for those born since the 1960s. In this study, I hope to push the race–class debate further by examining this post-1960s cohort and by revising how we think about class by adding net worth to the measurement of socioeconomic status.

What is Social Class?

In the jargon of social theory, the concept of "class" implies fundamental economic cleavages in a society, such as those between laborers and capitalists, managers and workers, manual and nonmanual employees, skilled and unskilled workers, or even blue-collar and white-collar workers. In the practice of social research, however, categorical class measures such as these usually prove inferior in their predictive power to a more gradated approach such as measuring socioeconomic status (SES). Researchers generally use indicators of SES to gauge the influence of social background on a variety of outcomes. The three measures that usually constitute socioeconomic status are education, occupation, and income.

There are many theoretical and empirical reasons why these three measures have been used. Put simply, they work – that is, in combination, they explain a significant amount of variation in socioeconomic outcomes across and within generations. They are also fairly easy to measure. Education is usually measured as years of formal schooling or highest degree attained (high school, college, and so forth). Occupation is scored in terms of its social prestige (for instance, being a doctor is more prestigious than being a salesperson, which in turn is more prestigious than being a ditch digger). Income is fairly straightforward: the more one has, the better off one is. (Chapter Two [of original publication] provides a more thorough discussion of these variables.) What these three measures have in common is that they fit nicely with our image of a fair society in which everyone gets a shot to succeed according to his or her own merits. Educational attainment may be at least partly related to innate cognitive ability as measured by IQ; educational success often translates into a prestigious occupation, which may in turn yield a high income.

By contrast, wealth, which has been left out of empirical analysis thus far, has other connotations, such as inheritance. Wealth is much more stable within families and across generations than is income, occupation, or education. In short, we are less likely to have earned it and more likely to have inherited it or received it as a gift. Therefore, wealth does not fit neatly into our vision of the ideal, meritocratic society.[29] Yet, for this very reason, it is critical to consider wealth when addressing issues of intergenerational inequality. At the same time, the social prestige that accompanies the ownership of assets is often the end to which education, occupation, and income all serve as the means. In both these ways, wealth forms an important part of social class.

The University of California sociologists who authored the recent work *Inequality by Design: Cracking the Bell Curve Myth* offer a good summary of the importance of wealth to a sense of economic security and social class. "Being prosperous," they write, "may mean owning a vacation home, purchasing private security services, and having whatever medical care one wants; being squeezed may mean having one modest but heavily mortgaged house, depending on 911 when danger lurks, and delaying medical care because of the expense of copayments." They highlight the important interaction of assets, income, and class by stating that for average, middle-income Americans, "one missed mortgage payment or one chronic injury might be enough to push them into the class that has been left behind."[30]

These authors employ the image of a ladder to illustrate two conceptually separate questions of inequality that are worth investigating. Who ends up on which rung is one question (issues of opportunity); the other is how far apart the rungs are (issues of equity/distribution of rewards). Wealth in its most tangible form represents the rungs to which many aspire; however, its importance in the transmission of inequality reveals that how far apart the rungs are placed is not independent of the factors that determine who ends up on which rung. Thus, we must consider that wealth both represents class and determines class.

Through this dual nature, assets can serve to create or reinforce class identity. One mechanism by which property may help to cement a status group stems from its consumptive and conspicuous nature. For example, a status group might be unified on the basis of its common ownership of summer residences in a "selective" area. Expensive luxury cars might also signal status through what Thorstein Veblen called "conspicuous consumption," in his book *The Theory of the Leisure Class.*[31] Identity through consumption is not limited to elites, however, as Veblen may have implied in 1899, when he wrote; consumption has become (or may have always been) a realm of expression for the middle classes as well. In 1970, sociologist Edward Shils wrote about consumption under the rubric of "lifestyle," claiming that it is a basis for social standing that follows a different conceptual logic than the prestige hierarchy located within the labor market (that is, the doctor/ditch digger differential). He argued that "lifestyle is one of the most important bases of prestige because, like occupational role, it is among the most continuous and observable of the various deference entitlements."[32] In this manner, each investment decision – which house to buy, which securities to own – is a lifestyle judgment that creates a group status affiliation for the owner. This dynamic may be most apparent with visible investments – illiquid assets such as homes, vehicles, and businesses. "In its permanence," writes Charles Abrams of the family home, "the owner sees the stabilization of his own values; in the firmness of its foundation he follows his own roots into the community . . . in its ownership, he sees release from the fears and uncertainties of life."[33]

While wealth can create symbolic affiliations in the realm of lifestyle differentiation, it also has the effect of determining group alliances within the purely economic realm. At various times during the industrial history of the West, it may have made sense to speak of occupational categories as the prime, if not sole, locus of class identity. The union–management dichotomy at one time served as the contested field for group interactions within both the economic and the political spheres, and group identity largely followed this dichotomy. As Richard Sennett and Jonathan Cobb wrote in *The*

Hidden Injuries of Class, "The essential character of money power for most manual workers is that it comes to them not individually, but collectively, through union action. . . . The labor negotiator is fighting for categories of work to be rewarded, not for individuals to be singled out."[34] In the case of union contracts, the wages of co-workers (for instance, the two sheet metal workers described earlier) directly affect each other since co-workers often find themselves together in a collective bargaining situation.

Today, however, this is less often the case. Unionization rates have hit a low of 11 percent in the U.S. private sector. One is no longer tied to co-workers in the labor market to the same extent as yesteryear; rather, one is in direct competition with co-workers in an economy that relies increasingly on temporary and nonunionized labor. Skill differentiation has become more finely graduated within the work force even as its variance has increased (as is inevitable with the ceaseless division of labor); each worker is more an individual entrepreneur trying to protect his or her tenuous position through constant cultivation of "human capital." No longer – in a global, postindustrial economy – can workers stand united on the basis of occupational roles that are themselves in flux. Thus, we can speculate that class identity resulting from common economic interests may solidify less frequently in the labor market and increasingly in other areas of life.

The realm where one's own economic interest may remain directly tied to that of one's fellow humans is in the world of property relations. Property values offer a prepackaged measure of social worth. In a sense, asset values serve as a quantification of social structure defined through the law. For example, the price of a rare painting, a misprinted U.S. stamp, gold, or any security is determined collectively through the market and is "artificially" (by human action) propped up in the marketplace. The value of a Renoir, ten thousand shares of IBM stock, or a pork belly futures contract

is wholly determined by the fact that these items are socially desired within the society. In this sense, property values are where culture meets economics.

Nowhere can this be seen more clearly than in the realm of housing, the most common form of property accumulation in America. While it matters little what wages one's next-door neighbors earn, it matters dearly how the neighbors want to decorate the outside of their house. The value of the neighbors' property directly affects one's own economic fortunes – manifested in the price of one's own home. If the neighbors choose to decorate their home garishly (as defined by the tastes of the collectivity through the market) or to let it deteriorate, their action will lower not only their own property values but also the property values of other homes in the neighborhood by making the entire block a less "desirable" spot to live. In this manner, housing property merges – in a very visible way – symbolic status interests with direct economic ones. The results of this marriage range from strict zoning laws and school redistricting to "white flight" and the converse phenomenon of "gentrification." In all these ways, inequality is mapped by ownership for this generation and the next.

NOTES

1 Data from the Panel Study of Income Dynamics (PSID), 1994 Wealth Supplement. The PSID is an ongoing study conducted by the Survey Research Center, Institute for Social Research, at the University of Michigan; see the PSID Web site at *www.isr.umich.edu/src/psid*. For further statistics on median and mean net worth at various income levels, see Table A2.1 in the Appendix [of original publication].

2 These family descriptions were extrapolated from profiles of specific families who were interviewed for this study. The age, racial, income, family size, wealth, housing tenure, and divorce descriptions of these families come directly from cases 4348 and 1586 of

the PSID 1984 wave (inflation-adjusted to 1996 dollars). The names and other details are fictitious but are in line with previous research that would suggest such profiles.

3   Neither family received health insurance from an employer. Since the Smiths' income was under 185 percent of the poverty line, their children were eligible for Medicaid. (In most states, the Joneses' children would also have been eligible for Medicaid since that family's wealth was in the form of a home, which is excluded from the asset limits of many states.)

4   See, e.g., G. Levinger and O. Moles, eds., *Divorce and Separation: Contexts, Causes, and Consequences* (New York: Basic Books, 1979); and R. Conger, G. H. Elder, et al., "Linking Economic Hardship to Marital Quality and Instability," *Journal of Marriage and the Family* 52 (1990): 643–56.

5   Throughout this book, the terms "black" and "African American" are used interchangeably, as are the terms "Hispanic" and "Latino." Black people of Caribbean origin make up a negligible portion of the data sample.

6   M. Oliver and T. Shapiro, *Black Wealth/White Wealth: A New Perspective on Racial Inequality* (New York: Routledge, 1995)

7   W. J. Wilson, *The Declining Significance of Race: Blacks and Changing American Institutions* (Chicago: University of Chicago Press, 1978).

8   J. L. Hochschild, *Facing Up to the American Dream: Race, Class, and the Soul of the Nation* (Princeton, N.J.: Princeton University Press, 1995), p. 55.

9   Ibid.

10 S. Danziger and P. Gottschalk, *America Unequal* (New York and Cambridge: Russell Sage Foundation and Harvard University Press, 1995), p. 90.

11 P. Blau and O. D. Duncan, *The American Occupational Structure* (New York: Free Press, 1967).

12 Ibid., p. 239.

13 Much of this betterment can be traced to geographic mobility. In fact, the major explanation for black socioeconomic advancement during the 1940s and 1950s was the movement of African Americans from the rural South to the industrial North with its higher wages. See, e.g., M. A. Fosset,

O. R. Galle, and J. A. Burr, "Racial Occupational Inequality, 1940–1980: A Research Note on the Impact of Changing Regional Distribution of the Black Population," *Social Forces* 68 (1989): 415–27.

14 S. J. Ventura, J. A. Martin, S. C. Curtin, and T. J. Mathews, "Report of Final Natality Statistics, 1996," *Monthly Vital Statistics Report* 46 (1997): suppl. 2.

15 See National Center for Children in Poverty, *One in Four: America's Youngest Poor* (New York: Columbia University School of Public Health, 1995).

16 Statistics are from K. DeBarros and C. Bennett, "The Black Population in the United States: March 1997 (Update)," *Current Population Reports*, Series P-20, No. 508 (Washington, D.C.: U.S. Government Printing Office, 1998).

17 See, e.g., J. Bound and R. B. Freeman, "What Went Wrong? The Erosion of the Relative Earnings and Employment of Young Black Men in the 1980s," *Quarterly Journal of Economics* 107 (1992): 201–32; P. Moss and C. Tilly, "A Turn for the Worse: Why Black Men's Labour Market Fortunes Have Declined in the United States," *Sage Race Relations Abstracts* 18 (1993): 5–45.

18 C. Jencks, "Is the American Underclass Growing?" in *The Urban Underclass*, ed. C. Jencks and P. Peterson (Washington, D.C.: Brookings Institution, 1991).

19 DeBarros and Bennett, "The Black Population in the United States: March 1997."

20 Ibid.

21 Ibid.

22 W. J. Wilson, *The Truly Disadvantaged: The Inner City, the Underclass, and Public Policy* (Chicago: University of Chicago Press, 1987).

23 See, e.g., S. Thernstrom and A. Thernstrom, *America in Black and White: One Nation, Indivisible* (New York: Simon and Schuster, 1997).

24 Wilson, *Declining Significance of Race*, p. 1.

25 M. Hout, "Occupational Mobility of Black Men: 1962 to 1973," *American Sociological Review* 49 (1984): 308–22; I. S. Son, S. W. Model, and G. A. Fisher, "Polarization and Progress in the Black Community: Earnings and Status Gains for Young Black Males in the Era of Affirmative Action," *Sociological Forum* 4, no. 3 (1989): 309–27.

26 See two articles by C. Link, E. Ratledge, and K. Lewis: "Black–White Differences in Returns to Schooling: Some New Evidence," *American Economic Review* 66 (1976): 221–3; and "The Quality of Education and Cohort Variation in Black–White Earnings Differentials: Reply," *American Economic Review* 70 (1980): 196–203.

27 J. C. Henretta, "Race Differences in Middle-Class Lifestyle: The Role of Home Ownership," *Social Science Research* 8 (1979): 63–78.

28 J. Feagin and H. Vera, *White Racism: The Basics* (New York: Routledge, 1995); C. West, *Race Matters* (New York: Vintage, 1994).

29 Influential authors K. Davis and W. E. Moore acknowledged as much in their 1945 article "Some Principles of Stratification" (*American Sociological Review* 10 [1945]: 242–9).

30 C. Fischer, M. Hout, M. Sanchez-Jankowski, S. R. Lucas, A. Swidler, and K. Voss, *Inequality by Design: Cracking the Bell Curve Myth* (Princeton, N.J.: Princeton University Press, 1996), p. 3.

31 T. Veblen, *The Theory of the Leisure Class* (New York: Penguin, 1979).

32 Shils paraphrased in M. E. Sobel, "Lifestyle Differentiation and Stratification in Contemporary U.S. Society," *Research in Social Stratification and Mobility* 2 (1983): 116. Also see the original article: E. Shils, "Deference," in *The Logic of Social Hierarchies*, ed. E. O. Laumann, P. M. Siegal, and R. M. Hodge (Chicago: Markham, 1970), pp. 420–48.

33 Abrams cited in D. L. Kirp, J. P. Dwyer, and L. A. Rosenthal, *Our Town: Race, Housing, and the Soul of Suburbia* (New Brunswick, N.J.: Rutgers University Press, 1995), p. 83.

34 R. Sennett and J. Cobb, *The Hidden Injuries of Class* (New York: Basic Books, 1972), p. 36.

9

Black Picket Fences: Privilege and Peril among the Black Middle Class

Mary Pattillo-McCoy

Mary Pattillo-McCoy is Associate Professor of Sociology and African American Studies and a Faculty Fellow of the Institute for Policy Research at Northwestern University. Pattillo-McCoy's areas of interest include race and ethnicity, urban sociology, culture and qualitative methods. In her book, *Black Picket Fences* (University of Chicago Press, 1999), Pattillo-McCoy investigates the economic, spatial, and cultural forces that affect child-rearing and youth socialization in a black middle-class neighborhood on Chicago's South Side. Her most recent project is a three-year ethnography examining the simultaneous processes of low-income housing construction and gentrification in a black Chicago neighborhood, as well as a comparative study of the transformation of public housing in Chicago. Other research projects include an analysis of racial differences in the class composition of extended families, a study of educational outcomes among black and white middle-class youth, and a study of the rise of "team ethnography."

There is a paucity of contemporary studies on the black middle class, making it necessary to define *who* belongs in the black middle class, *when* such a group emerged, and *where* many middle-class African Americans live. The answers to these questions collectively indicate that progress in the immediate post-World War II period led social scientists to prematurely assume that the black middle class was secure, when in fact, deep racial disparities have persisted. Germane to my focus on the neighborhood context, the answer to the *where* question emphasizes the fact that black middle-class out-migration from inner-city areas has been greatly misunderstood. Middle-class African Americans have become more segregated from poor African Americans, but I argue that the increased *size* of the black middle class – not, as some suggest, its increased propensity to move away from poor blacks – has caused these observed changes in the configuration of black communities. In the end, the black middle class continues to live near and with the black poor. These facts influence and circumscribe social processes in Groveland.

What is Middle Class?

"Middle class" is a notoriously elusive category based on a combination of socioeconomic factors (mostly income, occupation, and education) and normative judgments (ranging from where people live, to what churches or clubs they belong to, to whether they plant flowers in their gardens). Among African Americans, where there has historically been less income and occupational diversity, the question of middle-class position becomes even more murky. Just as social scientists wrestle with these issues, so do the residents of Groveland. Charisse Baker, a teenager in the neighborhood, gave her explanation of how class divisions exist within a racial hierarchy.

> Me personally, I don't see rich black people on a regular basis, except on [the television show] *Fresh Prince of Bel Air*. I mean, I know it's black people that are doctors, that are lawyers. But because I don't see them every day, I don't think that we're as divided.

Mr. Simms, a Groveland resident fifty years Charisse's senior, also commented on the compressed nature of the black class structure:

> I guess that there are classes divided on how much money you possess. For black people those are more artificial than real because we don't have where there's a very large upper class. But there are classes. And some are divided on the basis of what they *think* they have, and what they *think* you don't have.

Conversations with Groveland residents like Charisse and Mr. Simms underscore the fluid and complex nature of class categories among African Americans. Although most Groveland residents settle on a label somewhere between "lower middle class" and "middle class" to describe their own class position, the intermediate descriptors are plentiful. Some classification schemes focus on inequality. One resident resolved that there are the "rich," and everyone else falls into the categories of "poor, poorer, and poorest." Other words, like *ghetto, bourgie* (the shortened version of *bourgeois*), and *uppity* are normative terms that Grovelandites use to describe the intersection of standard socioeconomic measures and normative judgments of lifestyles and attitudes. Still other people talk about class in geographic terms, delineating a hierarchy of places rather than of incomes or occupations.

Without wading into either the social-scientific or layman's debates over class categories (which are quite extensive), I apply the "middle class" label to Groveland because it meets many of the standard criteria for such a designation. A majority of Groveland residents qualify as middle class by any of the commonly used income-based definitions. For example, economists use a measure called the *income-to-needs ratio* to identify class categories. The income-to-needs ratio divides total family income by the federal poverty level based on the family's size. The lower bound of the income-to-needs ratio for middle-class status is frequently set at two; that is, if a family earns two times a poverty-level income, they are middle class. Almost three-fourths of Groveland's families have an income-to-needs ratio of greater than two, qualifying them as middle class.[1]

Sociological conceptions of class include occupation and education along with measures of income (Blau and Duncan 1967; Vanneman and Cannon 1987). Studies of the black middle class in particular have used white-collar employment as the marker of middle-class position (Blackwell 1985; Kronus 1971; Landry 1987; Oliver and Shapiro 1995; Wilson 1978; Wilson 1995). In Groveland, 65 percent of the working residents are employed in white-collar jobs, again making it majority middle class. The most strict definition of middle class (for both blacks and whites) includes only those with a college degree. Twenty percent of Groveland's adults have graduated from college. Although not a majority, this is a much larger proportion than the

12 percent (in 1990) of African American adults overall with a college degree.

Finally, aside from these more objective class measures, "typical" middle-class behaviors are readily apparent in Groveland. People mow their lawns, go to church, marry, vote (they *really* vote), work, own property, and so on and so on. While the blanket term *middle class* obscures the particularities of being *black* and middle class (which is the focus of this book), Groveland's residents labor diligently to maintain their families, their investments, and their neighborhood, and to further their achievements.

Having established Groveland as a middle-class neighborhood using contemporary standards, reviewing the history of stratification in the black community illustrates the changing axes upon which class standing has been defined. A historical perspective also highlights the recency of a sizable black middle-class cohort, and the processes by which neighborhoods like Groveland were established. Because most African Americans were economically poor until relatively recently, blacks have used changing criteria to make status distinctions. The identity of the black middle class (the *who*) changes *as* and *when* the general position of African Americans changes. Also, the ways in which social scientists have evaluated such changes in the black class structure have in some ways dictated the amount of attention given to various segments of the African American community.

The Evolution of the Black Middle Class

American slavery inhibited the creation of a complete stratification system based on occupation, income, and/or education in the black community. Yet even within the enslaved population, distinctions did emerge that were primarily motivated by the racial hierarchy on which slavery was based. Blacks with lighter skin had particular advantages over their darker kin because of their position in the slave economy. One of the most important divisions was between household or skilled servants and field hands, which confounded "occupation" and skin-tone variation (Frazier 1939). House servants' sustained and close contact with the white upper class allowed for direct experiential knowledge of white lifestyles. These "mulatto" house and skilled slaves, along with a disproportionately mixed-race group of free Negroes, constituted the "old black elite" after emancipation and through Reconstruction (Keith and Herring 1991; Landry 1987). This first black middle class was defined by its phenotypical, spatial, and cultural proximity to the white upper class (Frazier 1939).

The situation changed with the northward migration and urbanization of African Americans in the early twentieth century. The First World War halted European immigration and carried away white workers to fight, spurring the Great Migration of southern blacks to northern cities. Northern industrial jobs beckoned blacks from the failing and oppressive rural economy of the South. Taking an expanded chronological view of the migration, six and a half million southern African Americans migrated northward between 1910 and 1970, altering the spatial configuration of race relations in the North (Farley and Alien 1987; Lemann 1991). Whereas there had been a relatively high degree of residential integration of blacks and whites prior to the flood of black migrants to the North, with the migration, whites began to leave integrated neighborhoods. The physical color line hardened. By 1920, former patterns of residential racial integration had all but disappeared in northern urban centers, creating all-black ghettos, which subsequently required a different kind of black middle class (Drake and Cayton [1945] 1993; Du Bois [1899] 1996; Kusmer 1976; Osofsky 1966; Spear 1967; Trotter 1985).

Aside from a small black intelligentsia, the old black elite earned its living through service to whites. Its status was imperiled, however, as whites moved farther away from black settlements, and increasing European immigration after World War I created a pool of white ethnic competition to black services. The old black elite also exhibited an air of superiority over "common" blacks. As a result, the old black elite did not take advantage of new opportunities that the black ghetto produced – namely, service to the black masses. The new racial ghetto formed the foundation upon which a new black middle class could flourish, one composed of "ghetto entrepreneurs" (Landry 1987). While the African American class structure still did not represent the full diversity of occupations, the "institutional ghetto" (Spear 1967) provided a captive clientele for African American entrepreneurs and professionals. Socioeconomic characteristics became more important indicators of class status. The importance of subjective indices such as skin color and occupational and social association with whites did not disappear, but did subside.

During this time between the two world wars, the black middle class comprised three major segments – small capitalists, professionals, and clerical and sales workers (Landry 1987). Black enterprises were clustered in local personal services – barbershops and beauty shops, cleaners, restaurants, grocery stores, and tailors. Black doctors, dentists, and especially lawyers were restricted to working in the black community. Even though their incomes placed them atop the black class hierarchy, the impact of racial segregation on their incomes was still severe. In the 1920s, a black doctor's income averaged $2,500 per year, while white doctors averaged over $8,500 (Landry 1987). Black clerical and sales workers made the least progress of all during this period. In the South, the prospect of blacks selling to and interacting with a white clientele went against the racial moral order. In the North, there were more opportunities for such service, but among Cleveland's working women in the 1930s, for example, only 3 percent of black females were in clerical or sales positions, compared to almost half of native white females, and 20 percent of foreign-born white women (Landry 1987; also see Cunningham and Zalokar 1992). Clearly, the black middle class continued to differ substantially from the white middle class in that it was anchored by professionals and business people, whereas the white middle class had a sizable contingent of (especially female) clerical and sales workers. In addition to compositional differences in the middle-class populations, the proportion of blacks who were middle class did not top 10 percent until 1960, whereas the white middle class constituted more than 20 percent of the total white population as early as 1910 (Landry 1987).

The unprecedented economic growth and prosperity after World War II, along with the social and political pressures of the civil rights movement, greatly expanded the black middle class in the 1950s and 1960s. The black class structure began to resemble the white class structure, with greater occupational diversity. Between 1960 and 1970, the percentage of black women in clerical jobs more than doubled (Landry 1987). Black women left domestic service jobs in which they had been trapped since slavery. In 1940, nearly 60 percent of employed black women were domestics. That figure declined to 6 percent by 1980 (Cunningham and Zalokar 1992). Between 1940 and 1970, black male professionals and technical workers went from 2 percent to 7 percent of employed black males; black proprietors, managers, and officials increased from 1 percent to 3 percent; and clerical and sales workers from 2 percent to 10 percent of all employed black men (Wilson 1978).[2] The period from 1945 to the early 1970s was extraordinary in terms of opening opportunities for African Americans. Predominantly white educational institutions were admitting black students in large numbers, businesses were recruiting at black colleges, and unions yielded to the pressure of their formerly excluded black coworkers.[3]

The growth of the black middle class piqued the interest of social scientists. In the mid-1950s, sociologist E. Franklin Frazier (1957) incited debate with his unfavorable account of the social life and individual psychology of the black middle class. One of Frazier's students, Nathan Hare (1965), repeated Frazier's opinions in the mid-1960s. Both Frazier and Hare argued that the black middle class imitated the white upper class. Because of this foolish imitation, along with the rejection of and disdain for black folk culture, Frazier (1957, 98) claimed that members of the black middle class "live in a cultural vacuum and their lives are devoted largely to fatuities."

This thesis of a soulless, apathetic, and frivolous black middle class was put forth just at the time when African Americans were launching the fight for civil rights, and as more African Americans from working-class and poor backgrounds were moving up the class ladder. While some of these descriptions may have characterized a segment of the old black elite, they were less applicable to the black middle class of the postwar period. Subsequent studies that looked specifically at the social and cultural life of middle-class African Americans found that while they did stress the importance of owning a home, and involvement in insular, family-centered activities, civic and church involvements were also central to black middle-class identity (Barnes 1985; Bell 1983; Kronus 1971; Sampson and Milam 1975). Upwardly mobile African Americans displayed a commitment to improving the situation of the black poor, and to civil rights more generally. In direct challenge to Frazier's contentions, William Sampson and Vera Milam (1975, 164) wrote that "middle-class blacks are conscious of their blackness, seem to feel an obligation to the race due to their more 'privileged' position, and express a strong sense of group solidarity."

A study of a black middle-class Chicago neighborhood not too far from Groveland was also an explicit test of Frazier's propositions (Kronus 1971). There were not the patterns of frivolous partying, card playing, and conspicuous consumption that Frazier recorded. Politically (a sphere Frazier thought nonexistent for middle-class blacks), the study's author considered 60 percent of the neighborhood residents that he interviewed to be "militant." That is, they responded affirmatively to the following assertion: "In seeking to end racial discrimination, Negro Americans need to stop talking so much and start more economic boycotts and other direct action." During this period of sweeping changes, there were continued ties between the black poor and the black middle class, despite the latter's new homes in nearby neighborhoods. Being middle class did not annul the fact of being black.

Recent studies continue to find allegiances across classes within the black community. Michael Dawson (1994) notes that despite heterogeneity, African Americans are surprisingly united in their political views. Jennifer Hochschild (1995) does find class differences among blacks, but argues that blacks who have made it are actually "enjoying it less" because they continue to feel the constraints of racism, while poor African Americans maintain some faith in the American Dream. In institutions, other scholars show that the black middle class participates in churches and civic organizations that make giving assistance to less fortunate African Americans a priority (Billingsley 1992; Pattillo-McCoy 1998; Thompson 1986).

Yet despite continuing social and political ties, the reality of class schisms cannot be ignored. In *The Declining Significance of Race* (1978), William Julius Wilson argued that the African American community was splitting in two, with middle-class blacks improving their position relative to whites, and poor blacks becoming ever more marginalized. Civil rights legislation, especially affirmative action, worked well for African Americans poised to take advantage of educational and employment opportunities. The unsolved problem was what to do about

African Americans in poverty. They were doing poorly not primarily because they were black, Wilson argued, but because they were unskilled and because the structure of the labor market had changed around them. Grounded in the conviction that social structure influences the nature of race relations, Wilson saw the growth in high-wage employment and the rise of political liberalism as fueling the diminution of race as a factor in the stratification process. The life chances of blacks were becoming more dependent on their class position. African Americans with a college education were positioned to take advantage of jobs in a service-producing economy – jobs in trade and finance, public management, and social services. And because of affirmative action legislation, firms were motivated to hire these qualified blacks.[4]

At the same time, the situation for the black poor was stagnating, if not deteriorating. Black unemployment began to rise in the 1950s. There was not much difference in the unemployment rate for blacks and whites in 1930, but by the mid-1950s the ratio of black to white unemployment reached 2 to 1 (Farley 1985). These changes, Wilson and others argued, were the result of shifts in the mode of production. The number of well-paying manufacturing jobs in the central city had declined as a result of both technological changes and relocation. These changes permanently relegated unskilled blacks to low-wage, menial, and dead-end jobs, or pushed them out of the workforce altogether. Wilson's contribution was to direct attention to changes in the nature of production that disadvantaged unskilled blacks. His prognosis for the black middle class was relatively optimistic, a position for which he was criticized by other African American scholars. Wilson's critics rushed to prove him wrong and show that members of the new black middle class continued to face obstacles because of their race (Pinkney 1984; Willie 1979; Washington 1979, 1980; see Morris 1996 for a review).

Wilson responded to these criticisms with *The Truly Disadvantaged*. The title itself was insurance that readers would make no mistake about his true population of interest, which was not the black middle class. Wilson reiterated and refined his arguments about the declining fortunes of the black poor. He also added a spatial component. In addition to being left out of the labor market, poor blacks were also being further marginalized and isolated in deteriorating inner cities. The compelling story told in *The Truly Disadvantaged*, especially Wilson's thesis that the black middle class had "out-migrated" from the inner city, thoroughly moved interest away from the black middle and working classes. Attention landed squarely on the black poor. A research industry was born to test Wilson's ideas concerning this segment of the black community.[5] To be sure, the obstacles faced by poor blacks in a changing economy and the persistence of black poverty more generally are intolerable facts that merit considerable research and government resources. However, the research pendulum swung to the extreme, virtually ignoring the majority of African Americans who are not poor.

The irony in the timing of Wilson's work and the subsequent lack of interest in the condition of nonpoor African Americans is that, just as attentions were turning away from the black middle class, the initial grounds for optimism were undercut by the economic crises of the mid-1970s. The economy came to a screeching halt, and the black middle class experienced its share of skid marks. Studies in the 1970s found that class background for African Americans was becoming more important in determining occupational status, just as Wilson had posited (Featherman and Hauser 1976; Hout 1984). These trends did not extend into the 1980s, however, when racial differences in the ability to pass on one's privileged class status, or improve the position of one's children, became more pronounced. Data from the late 1980s showed that 60 percent of whites but only 36 percent of

African Americans from upper-white-collar backgrounds were able to maintain their parents' occupational status. Whites were also more likely to improve on their parents' occupational status; more than half of whites from lower-white-collar backgrounds moved into upper-white-collar jobs, compared to only 30 percent of blacks. Downward mobility – across generations and within one's lifetime – was also more prevalent among African Americans (Duncan, Smeeding, and Rogers 1993; Oliver and Shapiro 1995; Davis 1995).

The steady and large increases in the percentage of blacks who were middle class waned in the 1970s and 1980s. The black male middle class grew by only 1 percent between 1970 and 1980. Black women continued to make headway in clerical and sales positions, but their gains were slowed in the professional sphere, and they lost ground in business ownership (Landry 1987). In income, the gap between what whites earn and what African Americans earn has not shown signs of narrowing since the early 1970s. For younger workers, the gap may in fact be increasing. The reversal of the trend toward earnings equality is especially pronounced among college-educated African Americans, partly because of their concentration in declining sectors of the economy and the weakened enforcement of equal employment policies in the 1980s.[6]

In the 1980s, the percentage of blacks in middle-class occupations grew from 40 to 45 percent (Wilson 1996). By 1995, the percentage had grown to half of all black workers, while 60 percent of whites had middle-class jobs (Smith and Horton 1997). However, the white middle class has historically contained more upper- (professionals, entrepreneurs, managers, and executives) than lower-middle-class workers (mostly sales and clerical jobs), while the opposite is true among African Americans. The different occupational distributions partly account for continuing earnings disparities. Despite fanfare over the gains of black professionals and executives, most black middle-class families contain combinations of teachers, foremen, government bureaucrats, office assistants, entrepreneurs, firefighters, receptionists, and so on. When discussed in historical terms, then, the growth of the black middle class since World War II has been impressive. Yet viewed from a comparative perspective, African Americans continue to lag behind whites.

What this social and demographic history indicates is that the declining interest in the status of nonpoor blacks was premature. The African American community was in a short time transformed from a population almost uniform in its poverty to one with a nascent middle class – this as recently as the 1950s. But racial disparities in occupation, income, and intergenerational mobility were not eradicated by the few years of progress. The brief period of growth spawned a kind of dismissive optimism, but the economic and social purse strings were once again pulled tight, stalling the advances made by some African Americans. The continuing inequalities between middle-class whites and African Americans attest to the persistence of racism and discrimination, albeit in quite different forms than in the Jim Crow era (Bobo, Kluegel, and Smith 1997). In the next section we see that the same stages that characterize the socioeconomic past and present of African American – overwhelming disadvantage, followed by progress and optimism, followed by stagnation and retrenchment – are mirrored in the spatial history (the *where*) of the black middle class.

A Middle-Class Promised Land?

George Hicks, one of the Mississippi migrants to Chicago whose story is told in Nicholas Lemann's book *The Promised Land* (1991), epitomizes the moving patterns of many of Chicago's middle-class black families, including those in Groveland. George Hicks graduated from Alcorn State University, a historically black school in Mississippi. In 1960, utterly frustrated with the racism in the South, he moved to Chicago. Hicks first moved to the Woodlawn neighborhood, which was at that time at the southern tip of Chicago's established black community. When the black community expanded, Hicks moved further south into the Englewood neighborhood, which was the destination of many upwardly mobile African Americans looking for more space and newer housing. When he was promoted to the administrative ranks of the Chicago Housing Authority, he changed residences once more, again moving farther south. Along with him moved other African American families, many of whom were middle class, and all of whom were following the exodus of middle-class whites. This was George Hicks's last move, and the site of Lemann's interview with him. The neighborhood was still all black, and still predominantly middle class. However, Lemann (1991, 278) took care to note that "the parlous state of the black slums in Chicago is a constant looming presence in the consciousness of the black middle class." George Hicks's story illustrates how African Americans, like other groups, have always tried to translate upward class mobility into geographic mobility, but remain physically and psychically close to the poorer neighborhoods they leave behind.

During the period from the Great Depression until the end of World War II, just before George Hicks arrived in Chicago, the boundaries of black ghettos in northern cities solidified. Despite the fact that black enclaves were swelling with southern migrants, black residential options were limited by the lack of new housing construction, and especially the organized and legally inscribed white resistance to integration (Farley and Allen 1987; Sugrue 1996). Single-family homes in the "Black Belts" of major cities were partitioned into ever smaller apartments, kitchenettes, and boarding rooms. Diseases became plagues in such crowded conditions, as did fires, rats, and generally unhealthy conditions (Hirsch 1983). Figuratively, the Black Belt fastened

around an obese black community. In fact, the reason that many Groveland residents gave for moving their families into the neighborhood in the 1960s was that they simply wanted more space.

Home-building resumed after World War II, increasing the residential options of blacks who could afford to move (Farley 1996). The congested conditions in the Black Belt, the postwar availability of new housing for whites in the suburbs, and the improving economic means of blacks all contributed to the growth of the Black Belt into previously all-white neighborhoods. This "out-migration" of the black middle class has been a popular explanation for the decline of inner cities. In the 1940s and 1950s, so this argument goes, black neighborhoods were vertically integrated; that is, black middle-, working-, and lower-class families all lived together. Then in the 1960s and 1970s, increasing educational and occupational opportunities translated into residential mobility, and black middle-class families moved up and out of communities that once housed a diversity of classes. They took with them their income, their work ethic, their financial commitment to community institutions, and their example of legitimate success (Wilson 1987). The outcome is the isolation of poor African Americans in the neighborhoods abandoned by middle-class blacks.

However, this out-migration *suggestion* without sufficient consideration of out-migration *outcomes* gives the erroneous impression that the black middle class had escaped the strictures of racial segregation. Little attention is given to where this stabilizing population is moving.[7] The inference is that nonpoor blacks are integrating white neighborhoods, but mostly their exact destinations are left unclear. Wherever they might be moving, goes this popular wisdom, they no longer reside in "ghetto neighborhoods" or "inner-city communities." With these assumptions, and the confidence that the black middle class was on its way to parity with similarly positioned whites, all attentions turned toward the black poor stranded in deteriorating inner cities.

Again, the optimistic projections for the black middle class have not been realized. At the end of the 1960s, the early period of black suburbanization, observers found that "patterns of residential segregation by race within suburbs are emerging which are similar to those found within central cities" (Farley 1970, 512). When African Americans moved to white suburbs, many whites moved out. In general, black suburbs are located near city limits (Galster 1991) and are often the result of the "spillover" of black urban enclaves into suburban munici- palities. In other cases, black "suburbs" are actually older and declining manufacturing cities that surround larger cities. East St. Louis, which is one of the poorest cities in the country, is situated in the St. Louis metro- politan area and is therefore a suburb of the city of St. Louis, although it manifests few of the positive attributes of suburbs. In the South, blacks living in rural areas have been redefined as suburbanites as the administra- tive boundaries of the nearest metropolitan area have enveloped them (Massey and Denton 1993). These classifications can be misleading when simply enumerating increases in the black suburban population.[8]

While some black families *have* integrated white neighborhoods as many commenta- tors had predicted, the black middle class overall remains as segregated from whites as the black poor (Farley 1991). This means that the search for better neighborhoods has taken place *within* a segregated housing market. As a result, black middle-class neighborhoods are often located next to pre- dominantly black areas with much higher poverty rates. Blacks of all socioeconomic statuses tend to be confined to a limited geo- graphic space, which is formally designated by the discriminatory practices of banks, insurance companies, and urban planners, and symbolically identified by the formation of cultural and social institutions. Thus, while the size of the Black Belt has increased, extending beyond the adminis-

trative boundaries of cities and into adjacent suburbs, it remains effective in strapping-in the black community.

Researchers at the Rockefeller Institute of Government at the State University of New York at Albany illustrate this point using census data for nine major metropolitan areas, Chicago being one of them. They report that 78 percent of Chicago's African Americans live in majority-black tracts. (Black tracts are defined as more than 50 percent black.) In all nine primary metropolitan statistical areas (PMSAs), including Atlanta, Baltimore, Chicago, Detroit, Houston, Los Angeles, New York, Philadelphia, and Washington, D.C., 68 per- cent of African Americans live in majority- black tracts. The experience of living in a predominantly black neighborhood holds for middle-class African Americans as well. Sixty percent of black households with annual earnings over $45,000, and 58 percent of black households making over $75,000, live in majority-black census tracts. Although the incidence of living in such tracts declines with household income, these are already high earnings thresholds, encompassing only about 20 percent of all black households.

Viewed from another perspective, 61 percent of black Chicagoans who live in these majority-black census tracts (and 67 percent of African Americans over the nine PMSAs) live in "moderate" – or "middle" – income tracts where the median household income is .5 to 1.5 times that of the PMSA. Groveland falls into this grouping of census tracts. Thus, Grovelandites are not unique in their residential situation. A majority of African Americans in large cities live in predominantly black neighborhoods, and a majority of these neighborhoods are moderate to middle income, not poor. Hence, the experiences of Groveland resi- dents are important for understanding the neighborhood processes that affect many African Americans.

Within these segregated black commu- nities there is an internal, class-based organization that has existed since their for- mation. The attempts of the most educated and best paid African Americans to move out of very poor neighborhoods are not new phenomena. In the 1920s, E. Franklin Frazier (1939) identified seven zones (each about one square mile) within Chicago's South Side Black Belt. Using a unique set of variables to delineate the class status of each zone, Frazier found sizable compositional differences. The black middle class of that era was clustered in the seventh, southern- most zone. From the first zone (closest to the central business district, and the oldest part of the Black Belt) to the seventh zone, the percentage of southern-born heads of households decreased, illiteracy rates dropped, and the proportion of mulat- tos rose. Most objectively, the percentage of white-collar male workers rose from 5.8 percent in zone 1 to 34.2 percent in zone 7. The black middle class was very small, but nonetheless attempted to carve out a black middle-class residential space, even at the beginning of the century.

St. Clair Drake and Horace Cayton ([1945] 1993, 658–9) followed in the tradi- tion of Frazier, writing about the effects of segregation on the residential choices of middle-class blacks in Chicago's Black Belt in the 1930s and early 1940s. Their descrip- tion is still relevant:

> Out of the search for better neigh- borhoods has arisen the ecological pattern of the Black Belt . . . with its "best," "worst," and "mixed areas." . . . Negroes are unable to keep their communities "middle-class" because the Black Ghetto is too small to accommodate its population and the less well-to-do must *filter into* these "best" areas. [Emphasis added.]

Drake and Cayton described an ongoing "sifting and sorting" of economic classes within the segregated Black Belt. The black middle class pushed southward (and west- ward) against the borders of the Black Belt, with low-income blacks following their

initial forays. In a later edition of *Black Metropolis*, Drake and Cayton ([1945] 1993, 827) noted the particular expansion of black middle-class enclaves in the 1960s: "The South Side ghetto has become more 'gilded' as a large amount of property in good condition has been turned over to middle-class   Negroes."   Segregation, however, remained pervasive.

Even William Julius Wilson, a leading proponent of the out-migration argument, recognized early efforts of middle-class blacks to segregate themselves. Describing the pre-1960s black community, Wilson (1987, 7) wrote, "lower-class, working- class, and middle-class black families all lived more or less in the same *communities* (albeit in different *neighborhoods*)" (emphasis added). This pattern of a large black com- munity with a diversity of black neighbor- hoods within it – some very poor, some diverse, and others solidly middle class – survives today. The Black Belt has *core* and *periphery* areas (Jargowsky and Bane 1991; Morenoff and Sampson 1997) created by the constraints of racial segregation, but also by a desire to live among other blacks. Middle-class African Americans have at- tempted to leave behind their poor neigh- bors in core ghetto areas – only to relocate to peripheral areas abutting their previous residences. In the contemporary African American ghetto there are still the best, mixed, and worst areas. This situation is the result of both the continuous out-migration of middle-class blacks and the racially segregated housing market they encounter in their attempts to move.[9]

Hence, a rereading of historic and con- temporary black residential patterns sug- gests the following. African Americans have long attempted to translate socioeconomic success into residential mobility, making them similar to other ethnic groups (Massey and Denton 1985). They desire to purchase better homes, safer neighborhoods, higher quality schools, and more amenities with their increased earnings. Out-migration has been a constant process. The black middle class has *always* attempted to leave poor neighborhoods, but has never been able to get very far. However, when the relative *size* of the black middle class grew, the size of its residential enclaves grew as well. *The increase in the number of black middle-class persons has led to growth in the size of black middle-class enclaves, which in turn increases the spatial distance between poor and middle-class African Americans. This greater physical separation within a segregated black community accounts for the popular belief that black middle-class out-migration is a recent and alarming trend.*

The raw number of blacks in the middle class has increased dramatically. In 1960, only 385,586 black men and women in the entire country were professionals or semi-professionals, business owners, managers, or officials. By 1980, that number had grown to well over one million (1,317,080). Similar increases took place in the category of sales and clerical workers, which increased from 391,927 blacks in 1960 to well over two million such workers in 1980. By 1995, nearly seven million African Americans were employed in middle-class occupations (Smith and Horton 1997). All of these new social workers and receptionists, insurance salespeople and government bureaucrats would have to be housed somewhere.

The key dimension of black middle-class out-migration, then, is not that it has increased. There has been steady movement of black families who could afford to move. The difference is that the black middle class is now a much larger proportion of the black community than it has ever been. In the 1930s, there were only two small census tracts at the southern tip of Chicago's Black Belt that were majority middle class. The black middle class was not substantial enough to numerically predominate in any one neighborhood. By contrast, in the 1990s version of Chicago's South Side Black Belt, there is a band of contiguous community areas with a total population of more than a quarter million that could be described as a black middle-class enclave within Chicago's larger black South Side.[10] Over 95 percent of the residents of this stretch of neighborhoods are black, over 60 percent work in white-collar jobs, and the median family income is above the Chicago median. This middle-class area – nearly seven miles long and seven miles wide at the extreme tips – is full of African Americans who "are determined to maintain what America generally regards as 'the middle-class way of life'" (Drake and Cayton [1945] 1993, 518).

While the black middle-class area in contemporary Chicago is sizable, it by no means totally separates blacks of different classes. Residential interclass interaction is most likely in the transitional, or "mixed," areas. These neighborhoods might well be considered vertically integrated.[11] But even the predominantly middle-class areas remain tied to the core ghetto. Administrative boundaries have no regard for the neighborhoods established by the black middle class. High schools service neighborhoods with a diversity of residents. Police districts are responsible for the residents of housing projects as well as those who live in owner-occupied single-family homes. Supermarkets, parks, nightclubs, scout troops, churches, and beaches all service a heterogeneous black population. Also, the poverty rates of the neighborhoods that make up Chicago's black middle-class expanse range from a low of 7 percent to a high of 17 percent. The middle-class way of life is in constant jeopardy in black middle-class neighborhoods because of the unique nature of their composition and location.[12]

The geography and demographic makeup of Groveland are illustrative of its status as a part of Chicago's black middle-class South Side. All but one of the neighborhoods bordering Groveland have lower median family incomes and higher poverty rates than Groveland. The Treelawn community, which is one community removed from Groveland, has a median family income of under $19,000 – not even half the median family income in Groveland. Its poverty rate of over 30 percent is almost triple that of Groveland. All of these contiguous neighborhoods are over 90 percent black, illustrating the hypersegregation of Chicago (Massey and Denton 1993). Finally, using a measure of the most violent kind of crime, homicide, there are clear perils associated with living in a black middle-class neighborhood. All but two of the neighborhoods adjacent to Groveland have higher homicide rates. Homicide rates in predominantly white communities in Chicago barely overlap with the levels of violence in the Groveland area. Thus, while there is a concentration of black middle-class community areas, their internal diversity, higher crime rates, and island-like character affect the experiences of the residents who live in them.

The situation in Chicago and Groveland is duplicated across the country. After comparing census tracts in all cities with a population of over 100,000, Robert Sampson and William Julius Wilson (1995, 42) concluded that the " 'worst' urban contexts in which whites reside are considerably better than the average context of black communities." The residential returns to being middle class for blacks are far smaller than for middle-class whites. In Philadelphia, Douglas Massey, Gretchen Condran, and Nancy Denton found that African Americans with college educations had a more than 20 percent chance of coming in contact in their neighborhood with someone receiving welfare, whereas college-educated whites had only an 8 percent chance of such contact. This pattern was repeated for interaction with blue-collar workers, high school dropouts, and the unemployed. Massey and Denton (1993, 153) later concluded that for blacks, "high incomes do not buy entrée to residential circumstances that can serve as springboards for future socioeconomic mobility."[13] In terms of exposure to crime, middle-class blacks are again at a disadvantage, even when they move to the suburbs. Echoing the

comments of other researchers, one study found that "even the most affluent blacks are not able to escape from crime, for they reside in communities as crime-prone as those housing the poorest whites" (Alba, Logan, and Bellair 1994, 427).

These comparisons are not meant to suggest that middle-class white neighborhoods are without problems similar to those faced by middle-class blacks. Studies of the fragility of middle-class whites (Danziger and Gottschalk 1995; Newman 1989, 1993); the wayward leanings of some middle-class white suburban youth (Gaines 1991; Monti 1994); and the struggle by middle-class whites to hold on to neighborhood investments (Camacho and Joravsky 1989) all indicate that middle-class status is a precarious standing for many Americans, regardless of race. However, the spatial immediacy of the threats of crime and drugs for many middle-class black neighborhoods differentiates them from similar white neighborhoods.

The problems confronting middle-class African Americans are not solved by simply moving away from a low-income black family and next door to a middle-class white family. The fact that a neighborhood's racial makeup is frequently a proxy for the things that really count – quality of schools, security, appreciation of property values, political clout, and availability of desirable amenities – attests to the ways in which larger processes of discrimination penalize blacks at the neighborhood level. Racial inequalities perpetuate the higher poverty rate among blacks and ensure that segregated black communities will bear nearly the full burden of such inequality. The argument for residential integration is not to allow the black middle class to easily abandon black neighborhoods. Instead, more strict desegregation laws would also open the door for low-income blacks to move to predominantly white neighborhoods, where jobs and resources are unfairly clustered. Yet we need not wait for whites to accept blacks into their neighborhoods, and think of integration as the panacea for current problems. Aggressive measures must be taken to improve the socioeconomic conditions of African Americans *where they are*. By highlighting *where* the black middle class lives, it becomes apparent that concentrated urban poverty has repercussions not only for poor African Americans, but for middle-class blacks as well, while a majority of middle-class whites move farther into the hinterlands. A comprehensive antipoverty agenda would have positive benefits for African Americans as a group, and therefore for the residential environs of the black middle class – although it leaves unchallenged the desire of many blacks and even more whites to live with others of the same race.[14]

NOTES

1   There is less agreement on the upper bound of the income-to-needs ratio that distinguishes the middle from the upper class (Danziger and Gottschalk 1995; Duncan, Boisjoly, and Smeeding 1996). Other income-based class definitions include persons living in families with incomes that fall between the 20th and 80th or 90th percentiles of all family incomes (Duncan, Smeeding, and Rogers 1993), or those whose family incomes fall within a fixed income range, such as $25,000–$50,000 (Oliver and Shapiro 1995). The advantage of an income-based definition is that it provides mutually exclusive categories of "middle class" and "poor." Defining someone as middle class based on occupation or education does not rule out the possibility that the person is poor.

2   For other chartings of occupational changes among African Americans, see Blackwell 1985; Farley 1985; Farley and Allen 1987; and Jaynes and Williams 1989.

3   Both Freeman (1976) and Wilson (1978) present data that indicate the premium placed on African American college graduates in the 1960s. Wilson (1978, 101), for example, charts the increase in corporate

recruiting visits to black colleges and universities. Autobiographical accounts, such as Lorene Cary's *Black Ice* (1991) and Jake Lamar's *Bourgeois Blues* (1991), give personal renderings of experiences with integrated institutions during this time, while Zweigenhaft and Domhoff (1991) provide an analysis of the early graduates of a special program that placed African Americans in elite private schools.

On unions, Bracey, Meier, and Rudwick (1971) give a general overview of the incorporation of blacks into unions, while Dickerson (1986) offers a more focused discussion of this process in the steel mills in Pennsylvania. Although the beginnings of black unionization predated the postwar period, greater strides were made during the 1950s and 1960s.

4   There are two important caveats to Wilson's focus on class. First, Wilson noted in both his first book. *Power, Racism, and Privilege* (1973), and in *The Declining Significance of Race* (1978) that "any sudden shift in the nation's economy that would throw whites into greater competition with blacks for, say, housing and jobs could create and intensify racial tension and, at least for the whites who feel threatened by black advancement, reverse the trend toward increasing racial tolerance" (1973, 141). Therefore, he did not see the fluid competitive race relations of the postwar period as a static state, and allowed for the possibility that trends could be reversed. Second, Wilson (1978, 2) specified that race continued to be a structuring category in the social and political arenas. Wilson's point was that race was declining in significance with regard to the occupational and economic life chances of blacks, not that it was less important in the realm of housing, or education, or interracial interaction.

5   In their fourth year of conducting citation analysis to determine the most often cited African American social scientists, the *Journal of Blacks in Higher Education* (1997, 18) reported, "The winner and still champion is William Julius Wilson." Wilson was the only African American scholar on a list of the fifty top-selling books in sociology (Gans 1997). *The Declining Significance of*

Race was named by *Contemporary Sociology* (1996) as one of the "Ten Most Influential Books of the Past Twenty-Five Years." In a footnote to his most recent book, Wilson himself noted (1996, 276): "Following the publication of *The Truly Disadvantaged* in 1987, an unprecedented number of social scientists began to conduct research on various aspects of ghetto poverty – many of them devoted to testing the theoretical assumptions I had raised in the book."

6   Companion papers by Bound and Dresser (1998) and Bound and Freeman (1992) investigate racial earnings gaps for men and women separately. Black college graduates and midwesterners lost the most ground toward earnings equality with similar whites. These findings are similar to those of other studies that highlight the impact of the 1970s economic downturn on those who had most benefited from the economic growth of the 1950s and 1960s (Blau and Beller 1992; Cancio, Evans, and Maume 1996; Corcoran and Parrott 1998; Harrison and Gorham 1992; Smith and Welch 1989).

7   Wilson (1987) made intermittent references to "higher-income neighborhoods" and "the suburbs" as the destinations of nonpoor blacks. He writes (143): "The exodus of black middle-class professionals from the inner city has been increasingly accompanied by a movement of stable working-class blacks to higher-income neighborhoods in other parts of the city and to the suburbs." Although this thesis is associated with Wilson in the academic world, it shares wide popularity outside of the academy.

8   On black suburbanization see Clay 1979; Massey and Denton 1988; Galster 1991; Taeuber and Taeuber 1965; Logan and Alba 1995; Logan, Alba, and Leung 1996; Schnore, Andre, and Sharp 1976.

9   Since *The Truly Disadvantaged*, Wilson has recognized that the black middle class remains a part of the segregated ghetto. In an appendix to his later book *When Work Disappears*, Wilson reviews some of the studies on racial segregation. He concludes (1996, 242):

> Thus, the black middle-class outmigration from mixed-income areas that then became ghettos did not result in a significant decrease in black migrants' contact with poorer blacks, for the areas to which they relocated were at the same time being abandoned by nonpoor whites, a process that increased the spread of segregation and poverty during the 1970s.

This reality remains obscured, however, by continuing emphasis on the isolation of the black poor.

10 Seventy-five "community areas" were defined in the 1930s by social scientists at the University of Chicago. They attempted to take into account an area's history, local definitions, natural boundaries, and trade and institutional membership patterns. The census tract grid for Chicago was created such that community areas fully contained a collection of census tracts, making census data easily aggregated to the community area level (Chicago Fact Book Consortium 1995). The black middle-class area discussed here refers to eight neighboring community areas.

11 Jargowsky (1997, chap. 2) defines census tracts with poverty rates from 20 to 40 percent as "borderline neighborhoods," noting their propensity to tip into being high-poverty areas by the subsequent census year. He also finds that previously nonpoor tracts became borderline in the 1980s.

12 The patterns described in Chicago inform the finding of increasing class segregation among African Americans (Massey and Eggers 1990; Jargowsky 1996). Class segregation is commonly measured at the census tract level. The index of dissimilarity (D) describes the extent to which census tracts mirror the metropolitan distribution of black incomes. It is practically interpreted as the percentage of blacks of a certain class who would have to move to a different census tract in order to reproduce the black income distribution of the urban area (James and Taeuber 1985). The proximity measure (P*) is another segregation indicator. P* tells the probability that a middle-class black person, for example, will live in a census tract with someone of a different

class group (e.g., someone on welfare). Both D and P* are tract-level measurements.

If by its sheer *numbers* the black middle class is more able to predominate in certain census tracts (and those tracts combine into neighborhoods, and those neighborhoods aggregate into communities), then inter-class segregation indices will reflect these tract-level changes. A higher proportion of blacks of a specified class would have to move to a different census tract in order to replicate the metropolitan black income distribution (D). Also, middle-class blacks will be less likely to come in contact with poor blacks in their census tract, and more likely to live with other middle-class blacks (P*). The increased size of the black middle-class population, then, improves its ability to establish homogeneous tracts, and results in the finding of increased class segregation among African Americans.

The fact that blacks of different classes are more likely to live in different census tracts does not, however, take account of space. Neither D nor P* says anything about the proximity of black middle-class tracts to black poor tracts. These measures do not capture processes of clustering, or "the tendency for black areas to adhere together within one large agglomeration" (Massey and Denton 1993, 75). Sixteen of the thirty cities studied by Massey and Denton (1993) exhibited notable clustering patterns. Therefore, while the black middle class has created somewhat separate census tracts, these areas are clustered with low-income black tracts in the same way described by Drake and Cayton in the 1930s.

Finally, class segregation measures are based on the overall distribution of incomes. The higher overall poverty rate among blacks translates into more poverty in the neighborhoods inhabited by the black middle class (Erbe 1975; Farley 1991). Consider, for example, a metropolitan area with a black poverty rate of 30 percent and a white poverty rate of 10 percent, which is quite a realistic hypothetical. If there were no class segregation for either race and complete racial segregation, all African Americans (including the middle class) would live in census tracts with a 30 percent poverty rate, while whites would live in tracts

that are only 10 percent poor. This simulation is similar to those done by Massey and Denton (1993), except here the focus is on the impact on the black middle class rather than on how segregation disadvantages the black poor. Because the index of dissimilarity is based on the metropolitan distribution of black incomes, the low overall socioeconomic status of African Americans is replicated in each census tract in a situation of no class segregation. The reality is that there is moderate class segregation among blacks and high racial segregation between blacks and whites. Therefore, segregated black communities bear almost all the full burden of disproportionate poverty among blacks. The black middle class alleviates some of this burden by establishing black middle-class neighborhoods, but its residential situation continues to differ from that of the white middle class. See Pattillo-McCoy 1998 for a fuller discussion of these issues.

13   These disparities have been documented in numerous other studies (Darden 1987; Erbe 1975; Fainstein and Nesbitt 1996; Farley 1991; Landry 1987; Massey, Gross, and Shibuya 1994; Villemez 1980).

14   Farley, Steeh, Krysan, Jackson, and Reeves (1994) investigate the residential preferences of African Americans and whites in Detroit. They find, "Most African-Americans preferred areas where there already was a substantial representation of blacks. The ideal neighborhood was one in which blacks comprised at least one-half the residents" (1994, 762). Racial residential instability arises because a majority of whites say they would not feel comfortable in such a neighborhood. Whites report that they would try to move out of a neighborhood where half the residents were black, and they would not be willing to move in. Thus the compositional thresholds vary by racial group and inhibit the formation of stable, mixed areas.

REFERENCES

Alba, Richard D., John R. Logan, and Paul E. Bellair. 1994. "Living with Crime: The Implications of Racial/Ethnic Differences in Suburban Location." *Social Forces* 73: 395–434.

Barnes, Annie S. 1985. *The Black Middle Class Family: A Study of Black Subsociety, Neighborhood, and Home in Interaction.* Bristol, Ind.: Wyndham Hall Press.

Bell, Michael J. 1983. *The World from Brown's Lounge: An Ethnography of Black Middle-Class Play.* Urbana, Ill.: University of Illinois Press.

Billingsley, Andrew. 1992. *Climbing Jacob's Ladder: The Enduring Legacy of African American Families.* New York: Simon & Schuster.

Blackwell, James E. 1985. *The Black Community: Diversity and Unity.* 2d edition. New York: Harper & Row.

Blau, Francine D., and Andrea H. Beller. 1992. "Black-White Earnings over the 1970s and 1980s: Gender Differences in Trends." *Review of Economic Statistics* 74: 276–86.

Blau, Peter, and Otis D. Duncan. 1967. *The American Occupational Structure.* New York: The Free Press.

Bobo, Lawrence, James R. Kluegel, and Ryan A. Smith. 1997. "Laissez-Faire Racism: The Crystallization of a Kinder, Gentler Antiblack Ideology." Pp. 15–42 in *Racial Attitudes in the 1990s.* Steven A. Tuch and Jack K. Martin, eds. Westport, Conn.: Praeger.

Bound, John, and Laura Dresser. 1998. "The Erosion of the Relative Earnings and Employment of Young African American Women during the 1980s." In *African American and Latina Women at Work: Race, Gender, and Economic Inequality.* New York: Russell Sage.

Bracey, John H., Jr., August Meier, and Elliott Rudwick, eds. 1971. *Black Workers and Organized Labor.* Belmont, Calif.: Wadsworth.

Camacho, Eduardo, and Ben Joravsky. 1989. *Against the Tide: The Middle Class in Chicago.* Chicago: Community Renewal Society.

Cancio, A. Silvia, T. David Evans, and David Maume, Jr. 1996. "Reconsidering the Declining Significance of Race: Racial Differences in Early Career Wages." *American Sociological Review* 61: 541–56.

Cary, Lorene. 1991. *Black Ice.* New York: Knopf.

Chicago Fact Book Consortium, eds. 1995. *Local Community Fact Book, Chicago Metropolitan Area, 1990.* Chicago: University of Illinois.

Clay, Phillip L. 1979. "The Process of Black Suburbanization." *Urban Affairs Quarterly* 14: 405–24.

Contemporary Sociology. 1996. "Ten Most Influential Books of the Past 25 Years." *Contemporary Sociology* 25, 3.

Corcoran, Mary, and Sharon Parrott. 1998. "African American Women's Economic Progress." In *African American and Latina Women at Work: Race, Gender, and Economic Inequality.* New York: Russell Sage.

Cunningham, James S., and Nadja Zalokar 1992. "The Economic Progress of Black Women, 1940–1980: Occupational Distribution and Relative Wages." *Industrial and Labor Relations Review* 45: 540–55.

Danziger, Sheldon, and Peter Gottschalk. 1995. *America Unequal.* New York: Russell Sage.

Darden, Joe T. 1987. "Socioeconomic Status and Racial Residential Segregation: Blacks and Hispanics in Chicago." *International Journal of Comparative Sociology* 28: 1–13.

Davis, Theodore J., Jr. 1995. "The Occupational Mobility of Black Men Revisited: Does Race Matter?" *Social Science Journal* 32: 121–35.

Dawson, Michael C. 1994. *Behind the Mule: Race and Class in African-American Politics.* Princeton, N.J.: Princeton University Press.

Dickerson, Dennis C. 1986. *Out of the Crucible: Black Steelworkers in Western Pennsylvania, 1875–1980.* Albany: State University of New York Press.

Drake, St. Clair, and Horace Cayton. [1945] 1993. *Black Metropolis: A Study of Negro Life in a Northern City.* Revised and enlarged edition. Chicago: University of Chicago Press.

Du Bois, W. E. B. [1899] 1996. *The Philadelphia Negro: A Social Study.* Philadelphia: University of Pennsylvania Press.

Duncan, Greg, Timothy Smeeding, and Willard Rogers. 1993. "W(h)ither the Middle Class? A Dynamic View." Pp. 240–71 in *Poverty and Prosperity in the USA in the Late Twentieth Century.* Dimitri B. Papadimitriou and Edward N. Wolff, eds. New York: St. Martin's Press.

Duncan, Greg, Johanne Boisjoly, and Timothy Smeeding. 1996. "Economic Mobility of Young Workers in the 1970s and 1980s." *Demography* 33: 497–509.

Erbe, Brigitte Mach. 1975. "Race and Socioeconomic Segregation." *American Sociological Review* 40: 801–12.

Fainstein, Norman, and Susan Nesbitt. 1996. "Did the Black Ghetto Have a Golden Age? Class Structure and Class Segregation in New York City, 1949–1970, with Initial Evidence for 1990." *Journal of Urban History* 23: 3–28.

Farley, Reynolds. 1970. "The Changing Distribution of Negroes within Metropolitan Areas: The Emergence of Black Suburbs." *American Journal of Sociology* 75: 512–29.

———. 1985. "Three Steps Forward and Two Back? Recent Changes in the Social and Economic Status of Blacks." *Ethnic and Racial Studies* 8: 4–28.

———. 1991. "Residential Segregation of Social and Economic Groups among Blacks, 1970–80." Pp. 274–98 in *The Urban Underclass*. Christopher Jencks and Paul E. Peterson, eds. Washington, D.C.: Brookings Institution.

———. 1996. "Black-White Residential Segregation: The Views of Myrdal in the 1940s and Trends of the 1980s." Pp. 45–75 in *An American Dilemma Revisited*. Obie Clayton, Jr., ed. New York: Russell Sage.

Farley, Reynolds, and Walter R. Allen. 1987. *The Color Line and the Quality of American Life*. New York: Russell Sage Foundation.

Farley, Reynolds, Charlotte Steeh, Maria Kyrsan, Tara Jackson, and Keith Reeves. 1994. "Stereotypes and Segregation: Neighborhoods in the Detroit Area." *American Journal of Sociology* 100: 750–80.

Featherman, David, and Robert Hauser. 1976. "Changes in the Socioeconomic Stratification of the Races, 1962–73." *American Journal of Sociology* 82: 621–51.

Frazier, E. Franklin. 1939. *The Negro Family in the United States*. Chicago: University of Chicago Press.

———. 1957. *The Black Bourgeoisie*. New York: Free Press.

Freeman, Richard B. 1976. *Black Elite: The New Market for Highly Educated Black Americans*. New York: McGraw-Hill.

Gaines, Donna. 1991. *Teenage Wasteland: Suburbia's Dead End Kids*. New York: Pantheon Books.

Galster, George C. 1991. "Black Suburbanization: Has It Changed the Relative Location of Races? *Urban Affairs Quarterly* 26: 621–8.

Gans, Herbert J. 1997. "Best-Sellers by Sociologists: An Exploratory Study." *Contemporary Sociology* 26: 131–5.

Hare, Nathan. 1965. *The Black Anglo Saxons*. New York: Marzani & Mansell.

Harrison, Bennett, and Lucy Gorham. 1992. "What Happened to African-American Wages in the 1980s?" Pp. 39–55 in *The Metropolis in Black and White*. George Galster and Edward Hill, eds. New Brunswick, N.J.: Center for Urban Policy Research.

Hirsch, Arnold R. 1983. *Making the Second Ghetto: Race and Housing in Chicago*. New York: Cambridge University Press.

Hochschild, Jennifer L. 1995. *Facing Up to the American Dream: Race, Class, and the Soul of the Nation*. Princeton, N.J.: Princeton University Press.

Hout, Michael. 1984. "Occupational Mobility of Black Men: 1962 to 1973." *American Sociological Review* 49: 308–22.

James, David E., and Karl E. Taeuber, 1985. "Measures of Segregation." Pp. 1–32 in *Sociological Methodology*. Nancy Brandon Tuma, ed. San Francisco: Jossey-Bass.

Jargowsky, Paul. 1996. "Take the Money and Run: Economic Segregation in U.S. Metropolitan Areas." *American Sociological Review* 61: 984–98.

———. 1997. *Poverty and Place: Ghettos, Barrios, and the American City*. New York: Russell Sage.

Jargowsky, Paul, and Mary Jo Bane. 1991. "Ghetto Poverty in the United States, 1970–1980." Pp. 235–73 in *The Urban Underclass*. Christopher Jencks and Paul E. Peterson, eds. Washington, D.C.: Brookings Institution.

Jaynes, Gerald, and Robin Williams, eds. 1989. *A Common Destiny: Blacks and American Society*. Washington, D.C.: National Research Council.

Journal of Blacks in Higher Education. Summer 1997. "The Most Highly Cited Black Scholars of 1996." *Journal of Blacks in Higher Education* 16: 18–19.

Keith, Verna, and Cedric Herring. 1991. "Skin Tone Stratification in the Black Community." *American Journal of Sociology* 97: 760–78.

Kronus, Sidney. 1971. *The Black Middle Class*. Columbus, Ohio: Merrill.

Kusmer, Kenneth L. 1976. *A Ghetto Takes Shape: Black Cleveland, 1870–1930*. Chicago: University of Illinois Press.

Lamar, Jake. 1991. *Bourgeois Blues: An American Memoir*. New York: Summit Books.

Landry, Bart. 1987. *The New Black Middle Class*. Berkeley: University of California Press.

Lemann, Nicholas. 1991. *The Promised Land: The*

Great Black Migration and How It Changed America. New York: Vintage Books.

Logan, John R., and Richard Alba. 1995. "Who Lives in Affluent Suburbs? Racial Differences in Eleven Metropolitan Regions." *Sociological Focus* 28: 353–64.

Massey, Douglas, and Nancy Denton. 1985. "Spatial Assimilation as a Socioeconomic Outcome." *American Sociological Review* 50: 94–106.

——. 1988. "Suburbanization and Segregation in U.S. Metropolitan Areas." *American Journal of Sociology* 94: 592–626.

——. 1993. *American Apartheid: Segregation and the Making of the Underclass*. Cambridge: Harvard University Press.

Massey, Douglas, and Mitchell Eggers. 1990. "The Ecology of Inequality: Minorities and the Concentration of Poverty, 1970–1980." *American Journal of Sociology* 95: 1153–88.

Massey, Douglas, Andrew Gross, and Kumiko Shibuya. 1994. "Migration, Segregation and the Concentration of Poverty." *American Sociological Review* 59: 425–45.

Monti, Daniel. 1994. *Wannabe: Gangs in Suburbs and Schools*. Cambridge, Mass.: Blackwell.

Morenoff, Jeffrey D., and Robert J. Sampson. 1997. "Violent Crime and the Spatial Dynamics of Neighborhood Transition: Chicago, 1970–1990." *Social Forces* 76: 31–64.

Morris, Aldon. 1996. "What's Race Got to Do with It?" *Contemporary Sociology* 25: 309–13.

Newman, Katherine S. 1989. *Falling from Grace: The Experience of Downward Mobility in the American Middle Class*. New York: Vintage Books.

——. 1993. *Declining Fortunes: The Withering of the American Dream*. New York: Basic Books.

Oliver, Melvin L., and Thomas M. Shapiro. 1995. *Black Wealth/White Wealth: A New Perspective on Racial Inequality*. New York: Routledge.

Osofsky, Gilbert 1966. *Harlem: The Making of a Ghetto*. New York: Harper & Row.

Pattillo-McCoy, Mary. 1998. "The Invisible Black Middle Class." Paper presented at the annual meeting of the American Sociological Association, San Francisco, Calif.

Pinkney, Alphonso. 1984. *The Myth of Black Progress*. New York: Cambridge University Press.

Sampson, Robert J., and William Julius Wilson. 1995. "Toward a Theory of Race, Crime and Urban Inequality." Pp. 37–54 in *Crime and Inequality*. John Hagan and Ruth D. Peterson, eds. Stanford: Stanford University Press.

Sampson, William A., and Vera Milam. 1975. "The Intraracial Attitudes of the Black Middle Class: Have They Changed?" *Social Problems* 23: 153–65.

Schnore, Leo F., Carolyn D. Andre, and Harry Sharp. 1976. "Black Suburbanization, 1930–1970." *The Changing Face of the Suburbs*. Barry Schwartz, ed. Chicago: University of Chicago Press.

Smith, James, and Finis Welch. 1989. "Black Economic Progress After Myrdal." *Journal of Economic Literature* 27: 519–64.

Smith, Jessie Carney, and Carrell Horton, eds. 1997. *Statistical Record of Black America*. 4th edition. Detroit: Gale Research Press.

Spear, Allan H. 1967. *Black Chicago: The Making of a Negro Ghetto: 1890–1920*. Chicago: University of Chicago Press.

Sugrue, Thomas. 1996. *The Origins of the Urban Crisis: Race and Inequality in Postwar Detroit*. Princeton, N.J.: Princeton University Press.

Taeuber, Karl, and Elaine Taeuber. 1965. *Negroes in Cities*. Chicago: Aldine Publishers.

Thompson, Daniel C. 1986. *A Black Elite: A Profile of Graduates of UNCF Colleges*. New York: Greenwood Press.

Trotter, Joe William. 1985. *Black Milwaukee: The Making of an Industrial Proletariat, 1915-45*. Urbana: University of Illinois Press.

Vanneman, Reeve, and Lynn Weber Canon. 1987. *The American Perception of Class*. Philadelphia: Temple University Press.

Villemez, Wayne. 1980. "Race, Class, and Neighborhood: Differences in the Residential Return on Individual Resources." *Social Forces* 59: 414–30.

Washington, Joseph R., ed. 1979. *The Declining Significance of Race: A Dialogue among Black and White Social Scientists*. Philadelphia: University of Pennsylvania Afro-American Studies Program.

——, ed. 1980. *Dilemmas of the New Black Middle Class*. Philadelphia: University of Pennsylvania Afro-American Studied Program.

Willie, Charles Vert. 1979. *The Caste and Class Controversy*. Bayside, N.Y.: General Hall.

Wilson, Frank. 1995. "Rising Tide or Ebb Tide? Recent Changes in the Black Middle Class in the U.S., 1980–1990." *Research in Race and Ethnic Relations* 8: 21–55.

Wilson, William Julius. 1973. *Power, Racism, and Privilege: Race Relations in Theoretical and Socio-historical Perspectives*. New York: The Free Press.

——. 1978. *The Declining Significance of Race: Blacks and Changing American Institutions*. Chicago: University of Chicago Press.

——. 1987. *The Truly Disadvantaged: The Inner City, the Underclass and Public Policy*. Chicago: University of Chicago Press.

——. 1996. *When Work Disappears: The World of the New Urban Poor*. New York: Knopf.

Zweigenhaft, Richard L., and G. William Domhoff. 1991. *Blacks in the White Establishment? A Study of Race and Class in America*. New Haven: Yale University Press.

10

Ain't No Making It:
Aspirations and Attainment in
a Low-Income Neighborhood

Jay MacLeod

As an undergraduate, MacLeod wrote *Ain't No Makin' It: Aspirations and Attainment in a Low-Income Neighborhood*, a sociology textbook based on his work with inner-city youth. After studying in England as a Rhodes Scholar, he worked as a community organizer in rural Mississippi, where he collaborated with teenagers to produce the film *Minds Stayed on Freedom: The Civil Rights Struggle in the Rural South, An Oral History* in 1991. Now an Anglican priest in Mossley, a mill town in Lancashire, England, MacLeod holds degrees in social studies and theology.

"Any child can grow up to be president." So says the achievement ideology, the reigning social perspective that sees American society as open and fair and full of opportunity. In this view, success is based on merit, and economic inequality is due to differences in ambition and ability. Individuals do not inherit their social status; they attain it on their own. Since education ensures equality of opportunity, the ladder of social mobility is there for all to climb. A favorite Hollywood theme, the rags-to-riches story resonates in the psyche of the American people. We never tire of hearing about Andrew Carnegie, for his experience validates much that we hold dear about America, the land of opportunity. Horatio Alger's accounts of the spectacular mobility achieved by men of humble origins through their own unremitting efforts occupy a treasured place in our national folklore. The American Dream is held out as a genuine prospect for anyone with the drive to achieve it.

"I ain't goin' to college. Who wants to go to college? I'd just end up gettin' a shitty job anyway." So says Freddie Piniella,[1] an intelligent eleven-year-old boy from Clarendon Heights, a low-income housing development in a northeastern city. This statement, pronounced with certitude and feeling, completely contradicts our achievement ideology. Freddie is pessimistic about his prospects for social mobility and disputes schooling's capacity to "deliver the goods." Such a view offends our sensibilities and seems a rationalization. But Freddie has a point. What of Carnegie's grammar school classmates who labored in factories or pumped gas? For every Andrew Carnegie there are thousands of able and intelligent workers who were left behind to occupy positions in the class structure not much different from those held by their parents.

What about the static, nearly permanent element in the working class, whose members consider the chances for mobility remote and thus despair of all hope? These people are shunned, hidden, forgotten – and for good reason – because just as the self-made individual is a testament to certain American ideals, so the very existence of an "underclass" in American society is a living contradiction to those ideals.

Utter hopelessness is the most striking aspect of Freddie's outlook. Erik H. Erikson writes that hope is the basic ingredient of all vitality;[2] stripped of hope, there is little left to lose. How is it that in contemporary America a boy of eleven can feel bereft of a future worth embracing? This is not what the United States is supposed to be. The United States is the nation of hopes and dreams and opportunity. As Ronald Reagan remarked in his 1985 State of the Union Address, citing the accomplishments of a young Vietnamese immigrant, "Anything is possible in America if we have the faith, the will, and the heart."[3] But to Freddie Piniella and many other Clarendon Heights young people who grow up in households where their parents and older siblings are undereducated, unemployed, or imprisoned, Reagan's words ring hollow. For them the American Dream, far from being a genuine prospect, is not even a dream. It is a hallucination.

I first met Freddie Piniella in the summer of 1981 when as a student at a nearby university I worked as a counselor in a youth enrichment program in Clarendon Heights. For ten weeks I lived a few blocks from the housing project and worked intensively with nine boys, aged eleven to thirteen. While engaging them in recreational and educational activities, I was surprised by the modesty of their aspirations. The world of middle-class work was entirely alien to them; they spoke about employment in construction, factories, the armed forces, or, predictably, professional athletics. In an ostensibly open society, they were a group of boys whose occupational aspirations did not even cut across class lines.

The depressed aspirations of Clarendon Heights youngsters are telling. There is a strong relationship between aspirations and occupational outcomes; if individuals do not even aspire to middle-class jobs, then they are unlikely to achieve them. In effect, such individuals disqualify themselves from attaining the American definition of success – the achievement of a prestigious, highly remunerative occupation – before embarking on the quest. Do leveled aspirations represent a quitter's cop-out? Or does this disqualifying mechanism suggest that people of working-class origin encounter significant obstacles to social mobility?

Several decades of quantitative sociological research have demonstrated that the social class into which one is born has a massive influence on where one will end up. Although mobility between classes does take place, the overall structure of class relations from one generation to the next remains largely unchanged. Quantitative mobility studies can establish the extent of this pattern of social reproduction, but they have difficulty demonstrating *how* the pattern comes into being or is sustained. This is an issue of immense complexity and difficulty, and an enduring one in the field of sociology, but it seems to me that we can learn a great deal about this pattern from youngsters like Freddie. Leveled aspirations are a powerful mechanism by which class inequality is reproduced from one generation to the next.

In many ways, the world of these youths is defined by the physical boundaries of the housing development. Like most old "projects" (as low-income public housing developments are known to their residents), Clarendon Heights is architecturally a world unto itself. Although smaller and less dilapidated than many urban housing developments, its plain brick buildings testify that cost efficiency was the overriding consideration in its construction. Walking through Clarendon Heights for the first time in spring 1981, I was struck by the contrast between the project and the sprawling lawns and elegant buildings of the college quadrangle I had left only a half hour earlier. It is little more than a mile from the university to Clarendon Heights, but the transformation that occurs in the course of this mile is startling. Large oak trees, green yards, and impressive family homes give way to ramshackle tenement buildings and closely packed, triple decker, wooden frame dwellings; the ice cream parlors and bookshops are replaced gradually by pawn shops and liquor stores; book-toting students and businesspeople with briefcases in hand are supplanted by tired, middle-aged women lugging bags of laundry and by clusters of elderly, immigrant men loitering on street corners. Even within this typical working-class neighborhood, however, Clarendon Heights is physically and socially set off by itself.

Bordered on two sides by residential neighborhoods and on the other two by a shoe factory, a junkyard, and a large plot of industrial wasteland, Clarendon Heights consists of six large, squat, three-story buildings and one high rise. The architecture is imposing and severe; only the five chimneys atop each building break the harsh symmetry of the structures. Three mornings a week the incinerators in each of the twenty-two entryways burn, spewing thick smoke and ash out of the chimneys. The smoke envelops the stained brick buildings, ash falling on the black macadam that serves as communal front yard, backyard, and courtyard for the project's two hundred families. (A subsequent landscaping effort did result in the planting of grass and trees, the erection of little wire fences to protect the greenery, and the appearance of flower boxes lodged under windows.) Before its renovation, a condemned high-rise building, its doors and windows boarded up, invested the entire project with an ambiance of decay and neglect.

Even at its worst, however, Clarendon Heights is not a bad place to live compared to many inner-city housing projects. This relatively small development, set in a working-class neighborhood, should not be confused with the massive, scarred projects of the nation's largest cities. Nevertheless, the social fabric of Clarendon Heights is marked by problems generally associated with low-income housing developments. Approximately 65 percent of Clarendon Heights' residents are white, 25 percent are black,[4] and 10 percent are other minorities. Few adult males live in Clarendon Heights; approximately 85 percent of the families are headed by single women. Although no precise figures are available, it is acknowledged by the City Housing Authority that significant numbers of tenants are second- and third-generation public housing residents. Social workers estimate that almost 70 percent of the families are on some additional form of public assistance. Overcrowding, unemployment, alcoholism, drug abuse, crime, and racism plague the community.

Clarendon Heights is well known to the city's inhabitants. The site of two riots in the early and mid-1970s and most recently of a gunfight in which two policemen and their assailant were shot, the project is considered a no-go area by most of the public. Even residents of the surrounding Italian and Portuguese neighborhoods tend to shun Clarendon Heights. Social workers consider it a notoriously difficult place in which to work; state and county prison officials are familiar with the project as a source for a disproportionately high number of their inmates. Indeed, considering its relatively small size, Clarendon Heights has acquired quite a reputation.

This notoriety is not entirely deserved, but it is keenly felt by the project's tenants. Subject to the stigma associated with residence in public housing, they are particularly sensitive to the image Clarendon Heights conjures up in the minds of outsiders. When Clarendon Heights residents are asked for their address at a bank, store, or office, their reply often is met with a quick glance of curiosity, pity, superiority, suspicion, or fear. In the United States, residence in public housing is often an emblem of failure, shame, and humiliation.

To many outsiders, Freddie's depressed aspirations are either an indication of laziness or a realistic assessment of his natural assets and attributes (or both). A more sympathetic or penetrating observer would cite the insularity of the project and the limited horizons of its youth as reasons for Freddie's outlook. But to an insider, one who has come of age in Clarendon Heights or at least has access to the thoughts and feelings of those who have, the situation is not so simple. This study, very simply, attempts to understand the aspirations of older boys from Clarendon Heights. It introduces the reader not to modern-day Andrew Carnegies, but to Freddie Piniella's role models, teenage boys from the neighborhood whose stories are less often told and much less heard. These boys provide a poignant account of what the social structure looks like from the bottom. If we let them speak to us and strive to understand them on their own terms, the story that we hear is deeply disturbing. We shall come to see Freddie's outlook not as incomprehensible self-defeatism, but as a perceptive response to the plight in which he finds himself.

Although the general picture that emerges is dreary, its texture is richly varied. The male teenage world of Clarendon Heights is populated by two divergent peer groups. The first group, dubbed the Hallway Hangers because of the group's propensity for "hanging" in a particular hallway in the project, consists predominantly of white boys. Their characteristics and attitudes stand in marked contrast to the second group, which is composed almost exclusively of black youths who call themselves the Brothers. Surprisingly, the Brothers speak with relative optimism about their futures, while the Hallway Hangers are despondent about their prospects for social mobility. This dichotomy is illustrated graphically by the responses of Juan (a Brother) and Frankie (a Hallway Hanger) to my query about what their lives will be like in twenty years.

JUAN: I'll have a regular house, y'know, with a yard and everything. I'll have a steady job, a good job. I'll be living the good life, the easy life.

FRANKIE: I don't fucking know. Twenty years. I may be fucking dead. I live a day at a time. I'll probably be in the fucking pen.

Because aspirations mediate what an individual desires and what society can offer, the hopes of these boys are linked inextricably with their assessment of the opportunities available to them. The Hallway Hangers, for example, seem to view equality of opportunity in much the same light as did R. H. Tawney in 1938 – that is, as "a heartless jest . . . the impertinent courtesy of an invitation offered to unwelcome guests, in the certainty that circumstances will prevent them from accepting it."[5]

SLICK: Out here, there's not the opportunity to make money. That's how you get into stealin' and all that shit. . . . All right, to get a job, first of all, this is a handicap, out here. If you say you're from the projects or anywhere in this area, that can hurt you. Right off the bat: reputation.

The Brothers, in contrast, consistently affirm the actuality of equality of opportunity.

DEREK: If you put your mind to it, if you want to make a future for yourself, there's no reason why you can't. It's a question of attitude.

The optimism of the Brothers and the pessimism of the Hallway Hangers stem, at least in part, from their different appraisals of the openness of American society. Slick's belief that "the younger kids have nothing to hope for" obviously influences his own aspirations. Conversely, some of the Brothers aspire to middle-class occupations partly because they do not see significant societal barriers to upward mobility.

To understand the occupational hopes of the Brothers and the Hallway Hangers – and the divergence between them – we must first gauge the forces against which lower-class individuals must struggle in their pursuit of economic and social advancement. Toward this end, we should consider social reproduction theory, which is a tradition of sociological literature that strives to illuminate the specific mechanisms and processes that contribute to the intergenerational transmission of social inequality. Put simply, reproduction theory attempts to show how and why the United States can be depicted more accurately as the place where "the rich get richer and the poor stay poor" than as "the land of opportunity." Social reproduction theory identifies the barriers to social mobility, barriers that constrain without completely blocking lower- and working-class individuals' efforts to break into the upper reaches of the class structure.

Structure Versus Agency: "No One to Blame but Me"

Every individual in this study holds himself acountable for his condition. The Brothers blamed themselves for their academic mediocrity. The Hallway Hangers were less self-critical but still reproached themselves for screwing up in school. Eight years later, for both groups, the verdict is similar. The Brothers variously chastised themselves for being lazy, unmotivated, indecisive, unrealistic, overly opportunistic, fickle, and generally inept. Juan is straightforward: "I really screwed up." Super is equally succinct: "I just fucked everything up." The Hallway Hangers, it turns out, are also hard on themselves.

(*all in separate interviews*)

JINKS: I could kick myself in the ass, because if I stayed in school, I'd probably have a better job, and I'd be doing better in life right now.

CHRIS: I fucked up. I regret everything. I feel real bad about my mom. I just fucked up, man, fucked everything up. I'd like to regain back the trust of my family. Man, I wouldn't wish this situation on anyone.

STONEY: I was doing good for a while. Running this pizza place over in Medway. He gave me the keys, the boss did. I was running it, doing a good job, too. The money wasn't great but still. I ended up fucking the guy over. He vouched for me when I was in the pre-release center. I burned that bridge. About two months after I got out I said, "Here, here's the key, I'm fuckin' through, I'm sick of this." Shoulda stayed. Shoulda stuck it out. He might've given me more money, who knows? My judgment sucks sometimes.

FRANKIE: I know today I wasted a lot of my life. I had a lotta fun but I wasted a lot of it. Lotta guys went to jail, lotta guys were just fucked up, man. And I was fucked up in my own way.

BOO-BOO: I should never have got into drugs. I dunno, if I could do one thing, start all over again, I'd just go right back to school, I'd do my thing, wouldn't get tied up in all this bullshit I got tied up in.

STEVE: I've been fucking up big time, Jay, no lie. Going away [to jail] too much, man. Fighting with my girl. I left her, and she called up and said I was doing drugs and drinkin' and all that other shit. Which I was. Called my probation officer and ratted me right out. . . . I dunno, dude, I guess I've got no one to blame but me.

Both the Brothers and the Hallway Hangers hold themselves responsible for their plight. Like most Americans, they point to personal vices and individual shortcomings to account for their subordinate position in the class structure.

But this is not the whole story. We have already seen that, apart from Mike and Derek, the Brothers blame not only themselves but also the socioeconomic order for their failure to get ahead. James argues most forcefully that the economic system is also to blame. He acknowledges constraints on economic opportunity, holds the government accountable, and sympathizes with those who turn to illegal activity. But James also contends that lower-class culture prevents people from developing proper ambition.

JM: What do you think about the white kids at Clarendon Heights? Steve, Slick, Frankie, Jinks?

JAMES: They, er, gee, what can I say about that? They reached a certain level in their life and then they just stayed at that level. They just said, "Oh well, this is my life. This is what my life's gonna be." But it's all attitude, it's all if you wanna go farther than you are. They're gonna be in the Heights all their life. It's like back to, if you grow up in a certain environment, then that's what you gonna live. That's what you're gonna live all your life. That's what you're used to. And that's how their life is. It's the same as the Coopers next door. The Coopers next door are always gonna be the same. They're never gonna change. Fifty years from now a new set of Coopers will be the same exact as these Coopers. Because they've reached a certain level, and they're always gonna be at that level. I'm not down on them, that's all they know. They're gonna just say, "I stopped at that level." But you can't say that. You have to want more for your kids and for your grandkids.

The idea that the intergenerational transmission of poverty is due, at least in part, to cultural attitudes and behavior is also implied by Slick. Like James, Slick points to macroeconomic constraints on opportunity, cultural deficiencies of the community, and individual shortcomings.

SLICK: I feel like I was robbed. I look at people and I say, y'know, I could be doin' what this guy's doing. If I had a college degree or something. But how was I gonna go to college? Know what I'm sayin'? I couldn't afford to go back to Latin Academy. My par——, my mother couldn't, because we moved into this city. So that robbed me of that deal, know

what I mean? You've just got to deal with it the best way you fucking can. Believe me, I was pissed off about it, and I still think about it to this day. I shouldn't be this dirty. Look at how filthy I am, working with my hands, blisters all over me and shit. I should be working at an office with a tie and nice suit on.

JM: So what do you say to the rich guy who listens to this story and says, "Wait a minute. He wasn't robbed. That was him. He could've, when he came to Lincoln High, he could've made it. It was the people he hung out with, or . . ."

SLICK: Nope.

JM: What do you say to him?

SLICK: What I say to him is, "Come down and learn for yourself, come down and see for yourself what it's like." Because you take it – I was a perfect A student all through my school years til I got yanked out of Latin Academy. When I moved here it was like, I ain't never got beat up before. I was into school. I was into sports and shit. I come here, get picked on, get my ass kicked all the fucking time. Finally, I went from being an A student to being, you know, you gotta defend yourself. What are you gonna study, you can't read a book on how to, on how to act like these people do. Y'know, you gotta treat an animal like a fucking animal. That's how it goes.

In the next breath, Slick places the corrosive influence of Clarendon Heights culture within a broader context of class inequality. Slick challenges the apparent superiority of the rich who, he claims, would be lost in Clarendon Heights without the props and symbols of their social status.

SLICK: Tell a person like that to come on down. I'll let 'em stay at my mother's house. The rich people you're talking about. Let 'em stay there with the cockroaches and the junkies shooting up outside and see how they react to it. Without their little Porsches and their little Saabs. Y'know, let them survive for a little while.

Slick's passing reference to roaches touches on an important dimension of lower-class life often missed by outside observers: what Wacquant calls the "demoralization effects" of life in intense poverty and permanent material insecurity. Living in places like Clarendon Heights tends to eat away at a person's energy and insides over time.[6] Slick knows it is different elsewhere and begins to articulate a critique of class privilege. But like the others, he holds himself responsible for his condition.

SLICK: I personally should've finished high school, then went on to some sort of college, any kinda college. Then looked over my options and *planned* on what I was doing. *Planned* on having children. *Planned* on my career. Instead of things just happening.

Like social theorists, both the Brothers and the Hallway Hangers wrestle with the roles of structure, culture, and agency in the reproduction of social inequality.

It should be obvious from this study that all three levels of analysis – the individual, the cultural, and the structural – play their part in the reproduction of social inequality. Had Slick been born into a middle-class family, he probably *would* be sitting in an office with a suit and tie on. Had his peer group been into Shakespeare and square roots rather than beer balls and bong hits, Slick might not be so blistered and dirty. Finally, Slick would be in better shape had he made different choices himself. Although all three levels have explanatory power, the structural one is primary because it reaches down into culture and individual agency. The culture of Clarendon Heights – with its violence, racism, and other self-destructive features (as well as its resilience, vitality, and informal networks of mutual support) – is largely a response to class exploitation in a highly stratified society. Similarly, Slick's individual strategies have developed not in a social vacuum but in the context of chronic social immobility and persistent poverty. To be sure, individual agency is important.

Causality runs in both directions in a reflexive relationship between structure and agency. Structural constraints on opportunity lead to leveled aspirations, and leveled aspirations in turn affect job prospects. Contrary to popular belief, structure is still the source of inequality.

Most Americans tend to ignore the link between individual behavior and cultural patterns on the one hand and economic inequality on the other, but neither Jinks nor Frankie fall into this trap. Both contextualize their peer group in a nexus of class injustice.

JM: When you look back on the heyday, back in high school as teenagers and the closeness you guys had, what d'you think brought you together that way, compared to other people?

JINKS: Probably because we all grew up together, we were all the same age. We all went to school together. We were spendin' most of our times together as a unit, most of the time in the day. We were spendin' more time together, all of us, than we were with our families. We went through the good and the bad together. Most of the times were bad. I mean, in the projects, it's not everybody's happy-go-lucky. Nine times out of ten you're strugglin' to get what you want. So it makes your friendships bond tighter. Because you gotta rely on other people to help you through whatever it is you need. We didn't have money. So we had to get by with whatever we could. And how I look at it, what we used to get by with was our friendship.

JM: What would you say to those people who drive by and look over and see us. You can almost see it in their eyes, in . . .

JINKS: Yeah, they're stereotyping right away: "Yeah, these kids are no good." But they should try to take the time out to understand us instead of right away, "He's a hoodlum because he lives in a project." I mean, there are a lot of people out here who are just like me – hard-workin'. They'll do anything for anybody.

All they want is to be treated the way they treat people, y'know, with respect and kindness. They're not out there to screw anybody, but there are a lot of people, "Areas like this bring trouble."

Frankie also refers to class prejudice and, like Jinks, sees their peer group as rooted in the experience of growing up poor in a hostile dominant culture.

FRANKIE: Well back then, y'know, back then we were cool. We hung tight because, I know today, because we were looked down on our whole lives, man. From the projects. I believe, in my opinion, we were never invited anywhere. When we were places, y'know, people always knew: "Those are the kids from the projects." I would say we stuck together just, for a fact that, just, just to prove these people right. "You're right." We were from the fucking projects, and you didn't invite us to your party so we're gonna come anyways, just to fuck it up. And it was the generation before us, the generation before us, when my brothers and them were growing up . . . it was just our values, man: Stick tight. We were taught that you had to stick together, just from generation to generation . . . I grew up thinking I was a bad fucking kid. And I liked that. I liked being known as a bad kid. I look back there – there aren't any bad kids – there's a lotta kids that just had a fucking tough life.

Bad kids or bad circumstances? Frankie leads us right back to the theoretical impasse between structure and agency. To what extent are the Hallway Hangers and Brothers victims of a limited opportunity structure, and to what extent are they victims of their own flawed choices?

Is Super, for example, forced to deal drugs because he was born at the bottom of a class society that glorifies conspicuous consumption while denying the poor real opportunity? Or does Super simply choose to deal drugs because he can't be bothered to work his way up legitimately like everybody else?

In short, to paraphrase the title of Diego Gambetta's book, was he pushed or did he jump?[7] Is Super *pushed* into crime by the forces of social reproduction? Or does he *jump* as a matter of individual choice? Certainly Super is *pushed from behind* by forces of which he is largely unaware. Super was handicapped in school by the effects of cultural capital, tracking, and teacher expectations. On the job market, Super's alternatives are limited by the sectoral shift from manufacturing jobs to poorly paid service positions and then squeezed further by racial discrimination embedded in the labor market. Thus, Super is pushed from behind by structural forces acting "behind his back" that propel him into the street economy. In addition, Super is *pulled from the front*, as it were, by structural forces that he sees and with which he wittingly struggles. Super is aware, for example, that the economy's recessionary plunge means fewer legitimate jobs are available and that his high school diploma is far less helpful than he imagined. He also believes that cocaine capitalism proffers more of a career structure than do legitimate jobs in the new postindustrial economy. Pushed from behind and pulled from the front by structural forces, Super's entry into the informal economy is nevertheless his own decision individually taken. Super *jumps* into the cocaine trade because he wants to. Super wants "to be someone, make fast money, have respect," and his decision is intentional and even rational. And yet the decision cannot be understood apart from the structural limitations on his options. In the end, perhaps the fairest account is that Super was *pushed into jumping*.

Structure and agency are inseparable. Individual agents like Super are always structurally situated, and thus human agency is itself socially structured. Social structures reach into the minds and even the hearts of individuals to shape their attitudes, motivations, and worldviews. Structural determination is thus inscribed in the very core of human agency.[8] Bourdieu's concept of habitus captures the interpenetration of structure and agency, but habitus is more a label for a site than an explanation of what goes on within it. Bourdieu neglects the actual process whereby external forces and internal consciousness wrestle with each other. Rather, he seems to imply that agents are unwittingly and unconsciously disposed to adjust their dispositions and practices to the external constraints that bear upon them. In Bourdieu's view, all this happens behind the backs of agents in the sense that it unfolds beneath the level of rationality, conscious deliberation, and intentional choice. And yet while pushed from behind by structural constraints of which they are unaware, the Brothers and Hallway Hangers are also pulled by forces that they actively and consciously manipulate. Although he claims otherwise, Bourdieu's notion of habitus fails to allow space for this kind of conscious, calculative decisionmaking. Habitus is an ingenious concept, and Bourdieu is surely correct to insist on a dialectical relationship between objective structures and internal subjectivities. However, Bourdieu never makes clear *how* the habitus engenders thought and action, and so his resolution of the agency – structure dualism seems more a sidestep than a solution.[9]

Still, by insisting on the inseparability of structure and agency, Bourdieu reminds us not only that structure is at the heart of agency but also that agency can reach to the heart of structure. The social universe people inhabit isn't simply received as a given from without; rather, it is produced and constructed anew by agents. As Wacquant explains, "The structures of society that seem to stand over and against agents as external objects are but the 'congealed' outcome of the innumerable acts of cognitive assembly guiding their past and present actions."[10] Structures are not fixed, binding, nor unalterable, yet they often appear so. Bourdieu unravels and picks apart the symbolic power that cloaks exploitative and oppressive relationships

with an aura of inevitability and renders them fair, natural, and normal.

Now we begin to see why the Brothers and Hallway Hangers give no indication that they might be able to alter the structures that constrain them. Among them there is very little political or collective energy, or even a sense that change is possible. Of the Brothers, for example, James is critical of the economic system and government policy but never suggests an alternative to the policy he criticizes, much less an alternative to the economic system. Neither do the Hallway Hangers envisage the possibility of substantive change. Jinks complains about class injustice in his workplace but feels politically impotent.

JINKS: . . . He's a complete moron, and he can do as he pleases because his father's the boss. Because he's got money it makes everything he does right, y'know, whether it be wrong or right. He can't do no wrong. I see it at my job and everywhere else, and it's just all over the world.

JM: But apart from just recognizing that, it doesn't seem to make you that angry.

JINKS: It does and it don't. At times it does, but there's a lot of things in this world that make me angry. If I was to let every little thing that makes me angry bother me, I would be upset twenty-four hours a day. I would hate the world. I just try to have a few beers, smoke a few joints, and laugh at the world. It's so fucked up, it ain't even funny any more. That's why I try gettin' the philosophy, Hooray for me, and fuck everybody else. Cuz no matter how hard you try, you're not gonna change it. I cannot worry about every little thing in life, okay, because there's too much out there to piss me off. And no matter what I do, if anything I try, it's not gonna change it. It's not gonna make it a better place for anybody.

JM: Most people say, y'know, this is the United States, it's a democracy. Is it impossible that we could vote into office people that would change things for the better?

JINKS: That's my philosophy. I don't even vote because all politicians are crooks. The only thing they can agree on is to give themselves a raise. What about the poor folk? I mean, how many people are out on the streets homeless? They cannot put money aside to help feed them and support them, right, but they can give themselves a ten, twenty thousand dollar a year raise. . . . We're in a state of recession, right? Fine, the cost of living goes up. How come our paychecks don't go up? It's just, I look at it at times, the whole world's fucked. No matter what you do, you gotta come out losin'. You can try and try and try and never get anywhere.

These last comments highlight the deeply felt sense of powerlessness amongst residents of Clarendon Heights. In 1983 Jinks was adamant that personal ambition was pointless: "I think you're kiddin' yourself to have any [aspirations]. We're just gonna take whatever we can get." Now his pessimism extends to aspirations for social change as well. "No matter what you do, you gotta come out losin'. You can try and try and try and never get anywhere."

This is pretty depressing stuff. We might expect those who are suspicious of the chances for individual upward mobility to be disposed toward collective political action to transform society. But when political *and* personal efficacy is judged illusory, then resignation and despair are liable to take over. The human psyche, however, resists hopelessness, and the Hallway Hangers are cast back on individual aspirations to sustain them. Slick is angling to be a supervisor on his roofing crew. Frankie wants to qualify as a mechanical contractor and supervise a building. Boo-Boo still hopes to be a mechanic; and Stoney, to own a pizza parlor. Shorty's aspirations are untempered by reality.

SHORTY: I'm s'posed to be getting my settlement soon, for gettin' stabbed. It's called victim of a violent crime, y'know. And I'm s'posed to get like probably forty grand.

I'm gonna give my mother some money, help her out with some of her bills, and I'm gonna go halfs with my brother. We're gonna buy a two-family house and rent it out, the whole thing, and I still live with my mother, y'know. We'll see how that goes, and if it goes good we'll gonna buy another one and then another one, and just keep buyin' real estate, that's the thing to get into. . . . I will make money one of these days. Like to buy a nice fucking condo on Palm Beach. Next to the Kennedys' (*laughter*). No, I'm serious. I'm gonna make some money.

As implausible as Shorty's vision may be, his aspirations help to keep him going. Whereas the Hallway Hangers previously drew sustenance from their peer group, today they rely on their own individual hopes. The Hallway Hangers have slid into the system alongside the Brothers. Without their tight clique and its own definitions of success, the Hallway Hangers have become much more incorporated into mainstream culture. Far from celebrating their outcast status, they see retrospectively in 1991 that their youthful resistance dug them deeper into marginality.

Frankie articulates this point most clearly. Today, he wants and needs to see opportunity. His recovery program from drug and alcohol abuse is predicated on a sense of personal efficacy, on a can-do mentality that emphasizes control over one's destiny. Given his own recovery, Frankie is preoccupied with the toll that substance abuse has taken on the Hallway Hangers.

FRANKIE: There's a lot of sickness there and I see it. I see it today, y'know. Two years ago I was part of it, y'know, and today I'm not, and I can see. For once I'm on the outside lookin' in. It's changes and it's drugs – there's no other way to put it. That's the bottom line. And I just know that from experience.

JM: Do you see any causes even beneath the drugs? Like, I'm hearin' you say that a lot of your problems during that time and individuals' problems now is the drinking, is the drugs. Are there things, are there other things that have kept people back?

FRANKIE: The economy sucks. It's just bad, a lotta people just don't see a lotta opportunity, y'know? They just don't see opportunity in life, man.

JM: Is it that they don't see it, or is it that the opportunity's not there?

FRANKIE: (*After a long pause*) Back then, I would say it's, y'know, they'd probably think it's not there. I, I, some days I still don't think it's there, but it's there, man. Y'know, you only feel when you stop tryin'. My whole problem is I never began to try, y'know? And I'm sure maybe that's some of their problems, y'know? You gotta be willing to try.

JM: It's interesting to hear you say, y'know, that you gotta try, cuz I remember back then you would look at the black kids from around the Heights – the Dereks and Mokey and . . .

FRANKIE: Your buddies.

JM: Yeah, right. You said they were chumps because they did try, because they tried in school and they were convinced that they would make it.

PRANKIE: Well, I look today, and if anyone shoulda had a chance to make it, it's fuckin', it's black people. . . . But no, I look at it today, y'know, they were probably doing the right thing, y'know? But my motives were different then, you hafta realize. I know I realize that. My motives were fucked up back then.

JM: Has it paid off for them?

FRANKIE: I dunno. I don't see them. I dunno what the fuck they're doin'. I don't care (*laughs*). But I dunno. I haven't seen them. I know I wasted quite a bit of my life.

Here Frankie cuts to the crux of the matter. His confession that "my motives were fucked up back then" sounds like an admission that the Hallway Hangers' resistance ultimately proved counterproductive. Caught in the game and convinced that the rules are beyond changing, Frankie's only sensible option is to commit himself to the competition. Frankie wants to believe that the future is in his own hands, only "you gotta be willing to try." Otherwise, what is left to hang on to? But the Brothers have always tried, and unbeknownst to Frankie, they have failed to make it. And what does Frankie himself have to show for all his aspiration and application, his job counseling and vocational training, his sobriety and disabled status? Frankie is unemployed. But he is absolutely right to make the effort and seize what little opportunity may arise. What other choice does he have? As Rickey, a street hustler from the ghetto of Chicago's South Side, relates: "You know, like I said, it's a goo' feelin' sayin,' 'Hey, you can't make it but you try.'"[11] For Frankie, as for the Brothers, Hallway Hangers, and countless Rickeys across the country, hope flies in the face of crushing odds. The American Dream may be but a mirage. Still, it provides a vision toward which the thirsty may stumble.

NOTES

1   All names of neighborhoods and individuals have been changed to protect the anonymity of the study's subjects.

2   Erik H. Erikson, *Gandhi's Truth* (New York: Norton, 1969), p. 154.

3   Ronald Reagan, "State of the Union Address to Congress," *New York Times*, 6 February 1985, p. 17.

4   Part One, written in 1984, refers to African Americans as "blacks."

5   R. H. Tawney, *Equality* (London: Allen and Unwin, 1938), p. 110.

6   Loïc J. D. Wacquant, "The Ghetto, the State, and the New Capitalist Economy," *Dissent* (Fall 1989):508–20.

7   Diego Gambetta, *Were They Pushed or Did They Jump?* (Cambridge: Cambridge University Press, 1987). These schemes – of being pushed from behind and pulled from the front – are borrowed from Gambetta but take on a somewhat different meaning in the present context.

8   Loïc J. D. Wacquant, "On the Tracks of Symbolic Power," *Theory, Culture, and Society* 10 (August 1993):3–4.

9   To be fair, Bourdieu reckons that the structure-agency dilemma is improperly framed and leads to a theoretical cul-de-sac. It would be harsh to fault him for failing to resolve this dilemma, if it were not claimed by others that he succeeds in dissolving and transcending the structure-agency dualism.

10   Wacquant, "On the Tracks of Symbolic Power," p. 3.

11   Loïc J. D. Wacquant, " 'The Zone': Le métier de 'hustler' dans ie ghetto noir américain," *Actes de la recherche en science sociales* 93 (June 1992):58.

Part III

Lifestyles of the Rich and Famous

11

From *Democracy in America*

Alexis de Tocqueville (1805–1859)

De Tocqueville studied law in Paris and worked as a substitute judge in Versailles before coming to the United States in 1831 (at age 25). Upon his return to France, he was active in politics and was elected to the French Chamber of Deputies in 1839. He later served in the Constituent Assembly, the Legislative Assembly, and as minister of foreign affairs. He is most famously known for *Democracy in America*, a two-volume study of the American people and their political institutions (Volume I, 1835; Volume II, 1940). The book addresses social issues such as religion, the press, money, class structure, racism, the role of the state, and the judicial system. *Democracy in America* continues to be immensely popular and remains widely cited. He is also author of *The U.S. Penitentiary System and its Application in France* with Gustave de Beaumont (1833); *The Old Regime and the Revolution* (1856); *Recollections* (1893, published posthumously).

The Taste for Physical Comfort in America

In America the taste for physical well-being is not always exclusive, but it is general; and though all do not feel it in the same manner, yet it is felt by all. Everyone is preoccupied caring for the slightest needs of the body and the trivial conveniences of life.

Something of the same sort is more and more conspicuous in Europe.

Among the causes responsible for these similar results in the New and Old Worlds there are some so germane to my subject that they should be mentioned.

When wealth is fixed by heredity in the same families, one finds many people in the enjoyment of the comforts of life without their developing an exclusive taste for them.

That which most vividly stirs the human heart is certainly not the quiet possession of something precious but rather the imperfectly satisfied desire to have it and the continual fear of losing it again.

The rich in aristocratic societies, having never experienced a lot different from their own, have no fear of changing it; they can hardly imagine anything different. The comforts of life are by no means the aim of their existence; they are just a way of living. They take them as part of existence and enjoy them without thinking about them.

The universal, natural, and instinctive human taste for comfort being thus satisfied without trouble or anxiety, their faculties turn elsewhere and become involved in some grander and more difficult undertaking that inspires and engrosses them.

That is why aristocrats often show a haughty contempt for the physical comforts they are actually enjoying and show singular powers of endurance when ultimately deprived of them. Every revolution which has shaken or overthrown an aristocracy has proved how easily people accustomed to superfluity can manage without necessities, whereas those who have laboriously attained comfort can hardly survive when they have lost it.

Turning from the upper classes to the lower, I can discern analogous effects from different causes.

In nations where an aristocracy dominates society, the people finally get used to their poverty just as the rich do to their opulence. The latter are not preoccupied with physical comfort, enjoying it without trouble; the former do not think about it at all because they despair of getting it and because they do not know enough about it to want it.

In societies of that sort the poor are driven to dwell in imagination on the next world; it is closed in by the wretchedness of the actual world but escapes therefrom and seeks for joys beyond.

But when distinctions of rank are blurred and privileges abolished, when patrimonies are divided up and education and freedom spread, the poor conceive an eager desire to acquire comfort, and the rich think of the danger of losing it. A lot of middling fortunes are established. Their owners have enough physical enjoyments to get a taste for them, but not enough to content them. They never win them without effort or indulge in them without anxiety.

They are therefore continually engaged in pursuing or striving to retain these precious, incomplete, and fugitive delights.

If one tries to think what passion is most natural to men both stimulated and hemmed in by the obscurity of their birth and the mediocrity of their fortune, nothing seems to suit them better than the taste for comfort. The passion for physical comfort is essentially a middle-class affair; it grows and spreads with that class and becomes preponderant with it. Thence it works upward into the higher ranks of society and thence spreads downward to the people.

In America I never met a citizen too poor to cast a glance of hope and envy toward the pleasures of the rich or whose imagination did not snatch in anticipation good things that fate obstinately refused to him.

On the other hand, I never found among the wealthy Americans that lofty disdain for physical comfort which can sometimes be seen among even the most opulent and dissolute aristocracies.

Most of these rich men were once poor; they had felt the spur of need; they had long striven against hostile fate, and now that they had won their victory, the passions that accompanied the struggle survived. They seemed drunk on the petty delights it had taken forty years to gain.

Not but that in the United States, as elsewhere, there are a fairly large number of rich men who, having inherited their property, effortlessly possess a wealth they have not gained. But even these people appear to be no less attached to the delights of the material world. Love of comfort has become the dominant national taste. The main current of human passions running in that direction sweeps everything along with it.

Particular Effects of the Love of Physical Pleasures in Democratic Times

It might be supposed, from what has just been said, that the love of physical pleasures would continually lead the Americans into moral irregularities, disturb the peace of families, and finally threaten the stability of society itself.

But it does not happen like that. The passion for physical pleasures produces in democracies effects very different from those it occasions in aristocratic societies.

It sometimes happens that boredom with public affairs, excess of wealth, decay of belief, and national decadence little by little seduce an aristocracy to pursue nothing but sensual delights. At other times the power of a prince or the weakness of a people, without depriving the nobility of their wealth, forces them to avoid positions of power, and shutting the road to great undertakings, leaves them abandoned to restless desires. Then with heavy hearts they fall back on their own resources and seek in sensual joys oblivion of their former greatness.

When the members of an aristocratic society thus turn exclusively to sensual pleasures they usually force into that one direction all the energy accumulated by long experience of power.

Just to seek comfort is not enough for such men. What they require is sumptuous depravity and startling corruption. They worship material things magnificently and seem eager to excel in the art of besotting themselves.

The stronger, more glorious, and free an aristocracy once was, the more depraved will it appear, and whatever may have been the splendor of its virtues, I dare predict that its vices will always be more startling.

But love of physical pleasures never leads democratic peoples to such excesses. Among them love of comfort appears as a tenacious, exclusive, and universal passion, but always a restrained one. There is no question of building vast palaces, of conquering or excelling nature, or sucking the world dry to satisfy one man's greed. It is more a question of adding a few acres to one's fields, planting an orchard, enlarging a house, making life ever easier and more comfortable, keeping irritations away, and satisfying one's slightest needs without trouble and almost without expense. These are petty aims, but the soul cleaves to them; it dwells on them every day and in great detail; in the end they shut out the rest of the world and sometimes come between the soul and God.

This, it may be said, can only apply to men of middling fortune; the rich will display tastes akin to those which flourished in aristocratic periods. I contest that suggestion.

Where physical pleasures are concerned, the opulent citizens of a democracy do not display tastes very different from those of the people, either because, themselves originating from the people, they really do share them or because they think they ought to accept their standards. In democratic societies public sensuality has adopted a moderate and tranquil shape to which all are expected to conform. It is as hard for vices as for virtues to slip through the net of common standards.

Wealthy men living in democracies therefore think more of satisfying their slightest needs than seeking extraordinary delights. They indulge a quantity of little wants but do not let themselves give rein to any great disorderly passion. They are more prone to become enervated than debauched.

So in democracies the taste for physical pleasures takes special forms which are not opposed by their nature to good order; indeed they often require good order for their satisfaction. Nor is it hostile to moral regularity, for sound morals are good for public tranquillity and encourage industry. It may even, not infrequently, combine with a type of religious morality; people want to do as well as possible in this world without giving up their chances in the next.

Some physical delights cannot be indulged without crime; from these they abstain strictly. There are others allowed by religion and morality; the heart, imagination, and life itself are given up to these without reserve, until, snatching at these, men lose sight of those more precious goods which constitute the greatness and the glory of mankind.

I do not reproach equality for leading men astray with forbidden delights, but I do complain that it absorbs them in the quest of those permitted completely.

By such means a kind of decent materialism may come to be established on earth, which will not corrupt souls but soften and imperceptibly loosen the springs of action.

Why the Americans are Often so Restless in the Midst of their Prosperity

In certain remote corners of the Old World you may sometimes stumble upon little places which seem to have been forgotten among the general tumult and which have stayed still while all around them moves. The inhabitants are mostly very ignorant and very poor; they take no part in affairs of government, and often governments oppress them. But yet they seem serene and often have a jovial disposition.

In America I have seen the freest and best educated of men in circumstances the happiest to be found in the world; yet it seemed to me that a cloud habitually hung on their brow, and they seemed serious and almost sad even in their pleasures.

The chief reason for this is that the former do not give a moment's thought to the ills they endure, whereas the latter never stop thinking of the good things they have not got.

It is odd to watch with what feverish ardor the Americans pursue prosperity and how they are ever tormented by the shadowy suspicion that they may not have chosen the shortest route to get it.

Americans cleave to the things of this world as if assured that they will never die, and yet are in such a rush to snatch any that come within their reach, as if expecting to stop living before they have relished them. They clutch everything but hold nothing fast, and so lose grip as they hurry after some new delight.

An American will build a house in which to pass his old age and sell it before the roof is on; he will plant a garden and rent it just as the trees are coming into bearing; he will clear a field and leave others to reap the harvest; he will take up a profession and leave it, settle in one place and soon go off elsewhere with his changing desires. If his private business allows him a moment's relaxation, he will plunge at once into the whirlpool of politics. Then, if at the end of a year crammed with work he has a little spare leisure, his restless curiosity goes with him traveling up and down the vast territories of the United States. Thus he will travel five hundred miles in a few days as a distraction from his happiness.

Death steps in in the end and stops him before he has grown tired of this futile pursuit of that complete felicity which always escapes him.

At first sight there is something astonishing in this spectacle of so many lucky men restless in the midst of abundance. But it is a spectacle as old as the world; all that is new is to see a whole people performing in it.

The taste for physical pleasures must be regarded as the first cause of this secret restlessness betrayed by the actions of the Americans, and of the inconstancy of which they give daily examples.

A man who has set his heart on nothing but the good things of this world is always in a hurry, for he has only a limited time in which to find them, get them, and enjoy them. Remembrance of the shortness of life continually goads him on. Apart from the goods he has, he thinks of a thousand others which death will prevent him from tasting if he does not hurry. This thought fills him with distress, fear, and regret and keeps his mind continually in agitation, so that he is always changing his plans and his abode.

Add to this taste for prosperity a social state in which neither law nor custom holds anyone in one place, and that is a great further stimulus to this restlessness of temper. One will then find people continually changing path for fear of missing the shortest cut leading to happiness.

It is, however, easy to understand that although those whose passions are bent on physical pleasures are eager in their desires, they are also easily discouraged. For as their ultimate object is enjoyment, the means to it must be prompt and easy, for otherwise the trouble of getting the pleasure would be greater than the pleasure when won. Hence the prevailing temper is at the same time ardent and soft, violent and enervated. Men are often less afraid of death than of enduring effort toward one goal.

Equality leads by a still shorter path to the various effects I have just described.

When all prerogatives of birth and fortune are abolished, when all professions are open to all and a man's own energies may bring him to the top of any of them, an ambitious man may think it easy to launch on a great career and feel that he is called to no common destiny. But that is a delusion which experience quickly corrects. The same equality which allows each man to entertain vast hopes makes each man by himself weak. His power is limited on every side, though his longings may wander where they will.

Not only are men powerless by themselves, but at every step they find immense obstacles which they had not at first noticed.

They have abolished the troublesome privileges of some of their fellows, but they come up against the competition of all. The barrier has changed shape rather than place. When men are more or less equal and are following the same path, it is very difficult for any of them to walk faster and get out beyond the uniform crowd surrounding and hemming them in.

This constant strife between the desires inspired by equality and the means it supplies to satisfy them harasses and wearies the mind.

One can imagine men who have found a degree of liberty completely satisfactory to them. In that case they will enjoy their independence without anxiety or excitement.

But men will never establish an equality which will content them.

No matter how a people strives for it, all the conditions of life can never be perfectly equal. Even if, by misfortune, such an absolute dead level were attained, there would still be inequalities of intelligence which, coming directly from God, will ever escape the laws of man.

No matter, therefore, how democratic the social condition and political constitution of a people may be, one can be sure that each and every citizen will be aware of dominating positions near him, and it is a safe guess that he will always be looking doggedly just in that direction. When inequality is the general rule in society, the greatest inequalities attract no attention. When everything is more or less level, the slightest variation is noticed. Hence the more equal men are, the more insatiable will be their longing for equality.

Among democratic peoples men easily obtain a certain equality, but they will never get the sort of equality they long for. That is a quality which ever retreats before them without getting quite out of sight, and as it retreats it beckons them on to pursue. Every instant they think they will catch it, and each time it slips through their fingers. They see it close enough to know its charms, but they do not get near enough to enjoy it, and they will be dead before they have fully relished its delights.

That is the reason for the strange melancholy often haunting inhabitants of democracies in the midst of abundance, and of that disgust with life sometimes gripping them in calm and easy circumstances.

In France we are worried about the increasing rate of suicides; in America suicide is rare, but I am told that madness is commoner than anywhere else.

Those are different symptoms of the same malady.

The Americans do not kill themselves, however distressed they may be, because their religion forbids them to do so and because materialist philosophy is practically unknown to them, although the passion for prosperity is general.

Their will resists, but reason frequently gives way.

In democratic times enjoyments are more lively than in times of aristocracy, and more especially, immeasurably greater numbers taste them. But, on the other hand, one must admit that hopes and desires are much more often disappointed, minds are more anxious and on edge, and trouble is felt more keenly.

12

The Miser and the Spendthrift

Georg Simmel (1858–1918)

Georg Simmel was one of the leading theorists to emerge in German social philosophy around the turn of the last century. Simmel did much to establish the German sociological tradition. His was a sociology of "forms" and "numbers," and Simmel can be considered the grandfather of contemporary network theory. He achieved his greatest notoriety posthumously for essays based on his lectures, addressing topics as diverse as "the metropolis and mental life" to "the dyad and the triad" to "the miser and the spendthrift." He wrote fifteen major works in the fields of philosophy, ethics, sociology, and cultural criticism, and another five or six less significant works. His two major early works, *The Problems of the Philosophy of History* and the two volumes of the *Introduction to the Science of Ethics*, were published in 1892–3; these were followed in 1900 by his seminal work, *The Philosophy of Money*, a book on the border between philosophy and sociology. Simmel produced several other major works, including, *Sociology: Investigations on the Forms of Sociation* (1908); *Fundamental Questions of Sociology* (1917); *Philosophische Kultur* (1911); *Goethe* (1913); *Rembrandt* (1916); *Hauptprobleme der Philosophie* (1910); and *Lebensanschauung* (1918).

The miser [is one who] finds bliss in the sheer possession of money, without proceeding to the acquisition and enjoyment of particular objects. His sense of power is therefore more profound and more precious to him than dominion over specific objects could ever be. As we have seen, the possession of concrete objects is inherently circumscribed; the greedy soul who ceaselessly seeks satisfaction and penetration to the ultimate, innermost absolute nature of objects is painfully rebuffed by them. They are and remain separate, resisting incorporation into the self and thus terminating even the most passionate possession in frustration. The possession of money is free of this contradiction latent in all other kinds of possession. At the cost of not obtaining things and of renouncing all the specific satisfactions that are tied to particulars, money can provide a sense of power far enough removed from actual empirical objects that it is not subject to the limitations imposed by possession of them. Money alone do we own completely and without limitations. It alone can be completely incorporated into the use which we plan for it.

The pleasures of the miser are almost aesthetic. For aesthetic pleasures likewise lie beyond the impermeable reality of the world and depend on its appearance and luster, which are fully accessible to the mind and can be penetrated by it without resistance. The phenomena associated with money are only the clearest and most transparent instances of a series of phenomena in which the same principle is realized in other contexts. I once met a man who, though no longer young and a well-to-do family man, spent all his time learning every skill he could – languages, which he never employed, superb dancing, which he never pursued; accomplishments of every sort, which he never made use of and did not even want to use. This characteristic is precisely that of the miser: satisfaction in the complete possession of a potentiality with no thought whatsoever about its realization. At the same time, it exemplifies an attraction akin to the aesthetic, the mastery of both the pure form and the ideal of objects or of behavior, in respect to which every step toward reality – with its unavoidable obstacles, setbacks, and frustrations – could only be a deterioration, and would necessarily constrain the feeling that objects are potentially absolutely to be mastered.

Aesthetic contemplation, which is possible for any object and only especially easy for the beautiful, most thoroughly closes the gap between the self and the object. It allows as easy, effortless, and harmonious formation of the image of the object as if this image were determined only by the nature of the self. Hence the sense of liberation which accompanies an aesthetic mood; it is characterized by emancipation from the stuffy dull pressure of life, and the expansion of the self with joy and freedom into the objects whose reality would otherwise violate it. Such is the psychological tone of joy in the mere possession of money. The strange coalescing, abstraction, and anticipation of ownership of property which constitutes the meaning of money is like aesthetic pleasure in permitting consciousness a free play, a portentous extension into an unresisting medium, and the incorporation of all possibilities without violation or deterioration by reality. If one defines beauty as *une promesse de bonheur* ["a promise of happiness"], this definition is yet another indicator of the similarity between aesthetic attraction and the attraction of money, because the latter lies in the promise of the joys money makes possible.

There have been attempts to combine the attraction of as yet formless value with the attraction of forming; this is one of the meanings of jewelry and trinkets. Their owner appears as the representative and master of a possibly very great sum which symbolizes his coalesced power; but also in jewelry the absolute liquidity and sheer potentiality of money has been shaped into some measure of definiteness of form and of specific qualities. Especially striking is the following instance of such an attempt at combination (of liquidity and definite form): In India it was long the custom to keep and especially to save money in the form of jewelry. That is, one had the rupees melted and made into jewelry (with only a very small loss of value), and stored it to be given out as silver should the need arise. Apparently value in the form of jewelry is both more condensed and richer in quality. This combination permits value to appear more closely linked to the person in that it becomes more individualistic and temporarily loses its atomized nature. So convincing is this appearance that since Solomon's day royal treasuring of precious metals in the form of utensils has been based on the treacherous belief (or delusion) that the treasure is closest to the family and safest from the grasp of enemies in this form. The direct use of coins as jewelry often is done to keep the fortune about one's person, under constant supervision. Jewelry, which is an ornament for the person, is also a symbol of its bearer, and it is hence essential that it be valuable; both this ideal purpose of jewelry and the previously mentioned practical purpose depend on the close association of jewelry with the self. In the Orient the most important requirement of all wealth is that one can flee with it, that is, that it be absolutely obedient to the owner and his fate.

It should also be noted that joy in the possession of money also doubtlessly contains an idealistic moment whose importance only appears paradoxical because on the one hand, the means to obtain it are necessarily diminished in the process of obtaining it and on the other hand because this feeling of joy is usually expressed by the individual in a nonidealistic form. This should not obscure the fact that joy in the sheer possession of money is one of the abstract joys, one of the furthest removed from sensuous immediacy, and one of those mediated most exclusively by the process of thinking and fantasy. In this respect it is similar to the joy of victory, which is so strong in some individuals that they simply do not ask what they really gain by winning. . . .

The spendthrift is far more similar to the miser than their apparent polarization would seem to indicate. Let us note that in primitive economies the miserly conservation of valuables is not consistent with the nature of these valuables, that is, with the very limited storage time of agricultural products. Therefore, when their conversion into indefinitely storable money is not practical or is at any rate not a matter of course, one only rarely finds miserly hoarding. Where agricultural products are produced and consumed immediately there usually exists a certain liberality, especially toward guests and the needy. Money is much more inviting to collect and therefore makes such liberality much less likely. Thus Petrus Martyr praises the cocoa-bags which served the ancient Mexicans as money, because they cannot be long hoarded or cached and therefore cannot engender miserliness. Similarly, natural conditions limit the feasibility and attractiveness of prodigality.

Prodigal consumption and foolish squandering (except for senseless destruction) are limited by the capacity of household members and outsiders to consume.

But the most important fact is that the waste of money has a different meaning and a new nuance that completely distinguish it from the waste of concrete objects. The latter means that value for any reasonable purposes of the individual is simply destroyed, whereas in the former case it has been purposelessly converted into other values. The wastrel in the money economy (who alone is significant for a philosophy of money) is not someone who senselessly gives his money to the world but one who uses it for senseless purchases, that is, for purchases that are not appropriate to his circumstances. The pleasure of waste must be distinguished from pleasure in the fleeting enjoyment of objects, from ostentation, and from the excitement of the alteration of acquisition and consumption. The pleasure of waste depends simply on the instant of the expenditure of money for no-matter-what objects. For the spendthrift, the attraction of the instant overshadows the rational evaluation either of money or of commodities.

At this point the position of the spendthrift in the instrumental nexus becomes clear. The goal of enjoying the possession of an object is preceded by two steps – first, the possession of money and, second, the expenditure of money for the desired object. For the miser, the first of these grows to be a pleasurable end in itself; for the spendthrift, the second. Money is almost as important to the spendthrift as to the miser, only not in the form of possessing it, but in its expenditure. His appreciation of its worth swells at the instant that money is transformed into other values; the intensity of this feeling is so great that he purchases the enjoyment of this moment at the cost of dissipating all more concrete values.

It is therefore clear to the observer that the indifference about the value of money which constitutes the essence and the charm of prodigality is possible only because money is actually treasured and assumed to be special. For the indifferent man's throwing away of his money would itself be done with indifference. The following case is typical of the enormous waste of the ancien régime: when a lady returned the 4,000–5,000 franc diamond that Prince Conti had sent her, he had it shattered and used the fragments as blotting sand for the note in which he informed her of the incident. Taine adds the following remark about the attitudes of that age: one is the more a man of the world the less one is concerned about money. But precisely herein lies the self-delusion. For as in a dialectic, the conscious and strongly negative stance toward money has the opposite sentiment as its basis, which alone provides it with meaning and attraction.

The same is true of those shops that may be found in the metropolis which, in direct contrast to stores that advertise bargains, smugly boast that they have the *highest* prices. Thus they imply that their customers are the Best People – those who do not ask about prices. But the noteworthy fact is that they do not emphasize what really matters – the quality of their merchandise. Thus they unconsciously do place money above all else, albeit with a reversal of value. Because of its close association with money, a spendthrift's lust easily grows to a monstrous extent and robs its victim of all reasonable sense of proportion. For money lacks the regulation that human capacity imposes on concrete objects. This is exactly the same immoderation that characterizes miserly avarice. The pure potentiality which it seeks instead of the enjoyment of real objects tends toward the infinite. Unlike the latter, it has no inherent or external reasons for restraint. When avarice lacks positive external constraints and limitations, it tends to become completely amorphous and increasingly passionate. This is the reason for the peculiar immoderation and bitterness of inheritance disputes. Since neither effort nor objective

apportionment determines one's own claim, no one is inclined a priori to recognize the claims of others. One's own claims, therefore, lack all restraint and any encroachment upon them is perceived as a particularly unreasonable injustice. This inherent lack of a relationship between the wish and any assessment of its object, which in inheritance disputes stems from the personal relations involved in the inheritance situation, in the case of avarice arises from the nature of the object. A coinage rebellion in Braunschweig in 1499 is an excellent illustration of the lack of principle which is encouraged by the nature of money and which prevents the limitation of demands. The government wanted only the good coinage to be valid, whereas previously bad coinage had also existed. And thereupon the same persons who had taken only good coinage for their goods and labor revolted violently because their payments in bad coinage were no longer accepted! The frequent coexistence of good and bad coinage provides the fullest opportunities for the immoderation of avarice, compared to which the most intense other passions seem to have only a partial hold over the emotions. Even in China there have been revolutions because the government paid in bad coinage but collected taxes in good coinage.

This tendency to immoderation inherent in the pure interest in money as such is also, I should like to hypothesize, the hidden source of a peculiar phenomenon found in stock exchanges. The small grain speculators, known in English as the *Outsiders*, almost without exception assume a bull market. I believe that the logically undeniable, if practically irrelevant, fact that the gain of bear market speculation is potentially limited whereas that of a bull market speculation is not provides the emotional attraction for this behavior. The large-scale grain speculators whose goal is the actual delivery of merchandise calculate the probabilities for both market trends, but for the pure money speculation such as is found in gambling in futures, any trend is adequate as long as the trend is potentially infinite.

Such a trend, which constitutes the inner motivational structure of an interest in money, is still more evident as the basis of the following events.

The German agricultural economy in the period from 1830 to 1880 provided constantly rising returns. This led to the illusion that the boom would continue forever. Consequently, farms were no longer bought at their current value, but at that which they were expected to acquire at current rates of increase. This is the cause of the present plight of the agricultural economy. It is the monetary nature of the returns that produces the wrong conception of value: When [returns] are based only on "utility value," on an immediate concrete amount, the idea of increase is cautiously limited; but the potentiality and anticipation of monetary value is unbounded.

This is the basis of the nature of miserliness and prodigality. Both reject on principle that calculation of value which alone can stop and limit the instrumental nexus: a calculation based on the consummatory enjoyment of the object. The spendthrift – who is not to be confused with the epicure and the merely frivolous, although all these elements can be blended in a given case – becomes indifferent to the object once he possesses it. For this reason his enjoyment of it is marred by the curse of restlessness and transience. The moment of its beginning is also that of its undoing. The life of the spendthrift is marked by the same demonic formula as that of the miser: every pleasure attained arouses the desire for further pleasure, which can never be satisfied. Satisfaction can never be gained because it is being sought in a form that from the beginning foregoes its ends and is confined to means and to the moment before fulfillment. The miser is the more abstract of the two; *his* goal is reached even earlier than the usual goal. The spendthrift gets somewhat closer to real objects. He abandons the movement toward a rational goal at a later point [than the miser], at which he stops as though it were the real goal. This formal identity of the two types despite the diametrical opposition of their visible behaviors – and the lack of a regulating substantive aim which suggests a capricious interplay between the two equally senseless tendencies – explain why miserliness and prodigality are often found in the same person, sometimes in different areas of interest and sometimes in connection with different moods. Constricting or expansive moods are expressed in miserliness or prodigality, as though the impulse were the same and merely the valence differed.

13

The Very Rich

C. Wright Mills

C. Wright Mills was one of the leading public intellectuals of twentieth-century America and a pioneering social scientist. From his position at Columbia University, he left a legacy of interdisciplinary work including two books that changed the way many people viewed their lives and the structure of power in the United States: *White Collar* (1951) and *The Power Elite* (1956). Mills persistently challenged the status quo both within his profession (see, e.g., *The Sociological Imagination* [1959]) and in society as a whole, until his untimely death in 1962. Most recently his work has appeared in *C. Wright Mills: Letters and Autobiographical Writings*, edited by Kathryn Mills with Pamela Mills, published by the University of California Press (2001).

Many Americans now feel that the great American fortunes are something that were made before World War I, or at least that they were broken up for good by the crash of 1929. Except perhaps in Texas, it is felt, there are no very rich anymore, and, even if there are, they are simply elderly inheritors about to die, leaving their millions to tax collectors and favorite charities. Once upon a time in America there were the fabulously rich; now that time is past and everyone is only middle class.

Such notions are not quite accurate. As a machine for producing millionaires, American capitalism is in better shape than such unsound pessimism would indicate. The fabulously rich, as well as the mere millionaires, are still very much among us; moreover, since the organization of the United States for World War II, new types of

'rich men' with new types of power and prerogative have joined their ranks. Together they form the corporate rich of America, whose wealth and power is today comparable with those of any stratum, anywhere or anytime in world history.

1

It is somewhat amusing to observe how the scholarly world has changed its views of the big-business circles of which the very rich are a part. When the great moguls were first discovered in print, the muckrakers of journalism had their counterparts in the academic journals and books; during the 'thirties, The Robber Barons clawed and bit their way to infamy, as Gustavus Myers's neglected work became a Modern Library best-seller and Matthew Josephson and Ferdinand

Lundberg were the men to quote. Just now, with the conservative postwar trend, the robber barons are being transformed into the industrial statesmen. The great corporations, full of publicity consciousness, are having their scholarly histories written, and the colorful image of the great mogul is becoming the image of a constructive economic hero from whose great achievement all have benefited and from whose character the corporate executive borrows his right to rule and his good, solid, justified feelings about doing so. It is as if the historians could not hold in their heads a hundred-year stretch of history but saw all of it carefully through the political lens of each and every administration.

Two general explanations for the fact of the very rich – now and in the past – are widely available. The first, of muckraker origin, was best stated by Gustavus Myers, whose work is a gigantic gloss in pedantic detail upon Balzac's assertion that behind every great fortune there lies a crime. The robber barons, as the tycoons of the post-Civil-War era came to be called, descended upon the investing public much as a swarm of women might descend into a bargain basement on Saturday morning. They exploited national resources, waged economic wars among themselves, entered into combinations, made private capital out of the public domain, and used any and every method to achieve their ends. They made agreements with railroads for rebates; they purchased newspapers and bought editors; they killed off competing and independent businesses, and employed lawyers of skill and statesmen of repute to sustain their rights and secure their privileges. There *is* something demonic about these lords of creation; it is not merely rhetoric to call them robber barons. Perhaps there is no straightforward economic way to accumulate $100 million for private use; although, of course, along the way the unstraightforward ways can be delegated and the appropriator's hands kept clean. If all the big money is not easy money, all the

easy money that is safe is big. It is better, so the image runs, to take one dime from each of ten million people at the point of a corporation than $100,000 from each of ten banks at the point of a gun. It is also safer.

Such harsh images of the big rich have been frequently challenged, not so much on the grounds of any error in the facts advanced, as on the grounds that they result from estimations from the point of view of legality, morality, and personality, and that the more appropriate view would consider the economic function that the propertied moguls have performed in their time and place. According to this view, which has been most ably summed up by Joseph Schumpeter, the propertied giants are seen as men who stand at the focal points of the 'perennial gale of innovations' that sweeps through the heyday of capitalism. By their personal acumen and supernormal effort, they create and combine private enterprises in which are embodied new technical and financial techniques or new uses for old ones. These techniques and the social forms they have assumed are the very motors of the capitalist advance, and the great moguls who create and command them are the pacesetters of the capitalist motion itself. In this way, Schumpeter combines a theory of capitalist progress with a theory of social stratification to explain, and indeed to celebrate, the 'creative destruction' of the great entrepreneurs.[1]

These contrasting images – of the robber and of the innovator – are not necessarily contradictory: much of both could be true, for they differ mainly in the context in which those who hold them choose to view the accumulators of great fortune. Myers is more interested in legal conditions and violations, and in the more brutal psychological traits of the men; Schumpeter is more interested in their role in the technological and economic mechanics of various phases of capitalism, although he, too, is rather free and easy with his moral evaluations, believing that only men of superior acumen and energy in each generation are lifted to the top by the mechanics they are assumed to create and to focus.

The problem of the very rich is one example of the larger problem of how individual men are related to institutions, and, in turn, of how both particular institutions and individual men are related to the social structure in which they perform their roles. Although men sometimes shape institutions, institutions always select and form men. In any given period, we must balance the weight of the character or will or intelligence of individual men with the objective institutional structure which allows them to exercise these traits.

It is not possible to solve such problems by referring anecdotally either to the guile or the sagacity, the dogmatism or the determination, the native intelligence or the magical luck, the fanaticism or the superhuman energy of the very rich as individuals. These are but differing vocabularies, carrying different moral judgments, with which the activities of the accumulators may be described. Neither the ruthlessness and illegality, with which Gustavus Myers tends to rest content, nor the far-sighted, industrial statesmanship, with which many historians now seem happier, are *explanations* – they are merely accusation or apology. That is why modem social psychologists are not content to explain the rise of any social and economic stratum by moral reference to the personal traits of its members.

The more useful key, and one which rests easier within the modern mind, is provided by more objective circumstances. We must understand the objective structure of opportunities as well as the personal traits which allow and encourage given men to exploit these objective opportunities which economic history provides them. Now, it is perfectly obvious that the personal traits required for rising and for holding one's place among waterfront gangsters will be different from those required for success

among peaceful sheepherders. Within American capitalism, it is equally obvious that different qualities were required for men who would rise in 1870 than for men who would rise eight decades later. It seems therefore rather beside the point to seek the key to the very rich in the secret springs of their personalities and mannerisms.

Moreover, explanations of the rich as a social fact by reference to their personal traits as individuals are usually tautological. The test of 'ability,' for example, in a society in which money is a sovereign value is widely taken to be money-making: 'If you are so smart, why aren't you rich?' And since the criterion of ability is the making of money, of course ability is graded according to wealth and the very rich have the greatest ability. But if that is so, then ability cannot be used in explanation of the rich; to use the acquisition of wealth as a sign of ability and then to use ability as an explanation of wealth is merely to play with two words for the same fact: the existence of the very rich.

The shape of the economy at the time of Carnegie's adolescence was more important to his chances than the fact that he had a practical mother. No matter how 'ruthless' Commodore Vanderbilt might have been, he would have accomplished little in appropriating railroads had the political system not been utterly corruptible. And suppose the Sherman Act had been enforced in such a way as to break up the legal buttress of the great corporation.[2] Where would the very rich in America – no matter what their psychological traits – now be? To understand the very rich in America, it is more important to understand the geographical distribution of oil and the structure of taxation than the psychological traits of Haroldson L. Hunt; more important to understand the legal framework of American capitalism and the corruptibility of its agents than the early childhood of John D. Rockefeller; more important to understand the technological progression of the capitalist mechanism than the boundless energy of Henry Ford, more important to understand the effects of war upon the need for oil and the tax loophole of depletion than Sid Richardson's undoubted sagacity; more important to understand the rise of a system of national distribution and of the mass market than the frugality of F. W. Woolworth. Perhaps J. P. Morgan did as a child have very severe feelings of inadequacy, perhaps his father did believe that he would not amount to anything; perhaps this did effect in him an inordinate drive for power for power's sake. But all this would be quite irrelevant had he been living in a peasant village in India in 1890. If we would understand the very rich we must first understand the economic and political structure of the nation in which they become the very rich.

It requires many types of men and vast quantities of national endowment to run capitalism as a productive apparatus and a money-making machine. No type of man could have accumulated the big fortunes had there not been certain conditions of economic, material, and political sort. The great American fortunes are aspects of a particular kind of industrialization which has gone on in a particular country. This kind of industrialization, involving very private enterprise, has made it possible for men to occupy such strategic positions that they can dominate the fabulous means of man's production; link the powers of science and labor; control man's relation to nature – and make millions out of it. It is not hindsight that makes us sure of this; we can easily predict it of nations not yet industrialized, and we can confirm it by observing other ways of industrialization.

The industrialization of Soviet Russia has now revealed clearly to the world that it is possible to carry through a rapidly advancing industrialization without the services of a private stratum of multimillionaires. That the Soviet Union has done so at the cost of political freedom does not alter the *fact* of the industrialization. The private corporation – and its attendant multimillionaire accumu-

lations – is only one way, not the only way, to industrialize a nation. But in America it has been the way in which a vast rural continent has been turned into a great industrial grid. And it has been a way that has involved and allowed the great accumulators to appropriate their fortunes from the industrial process.

The opportunities to appropriate great fortunes out of the industrialization of America have included many facts and forces which were not and could not be contingent upon what manner of men the very rich have been, or upon anything they have done or did not do.

The basic facts of the case are rather simple. Here was a continental domain full of untapped natural resources. Into it there migrated millions of people. As the population steadily increased, the value of the land continuously rose. As the population increased, it formed at once a growing market for produce and goods and a growing labor supply. Since the agricultural sector of the population was growing, the industrialist did not have to depend upon his own laborers in factory and mine for his market.

Such facts of population and resources do not of themselves lead to great accumulations. For that, a compliant political authority is needed. It is not necessary to retail anecdotes about the legal illegalities and the plainer illegalities which the very rich of each of our three generations have successfully practiced, for they are well known. It is not possible to judge quantitatively the effects of these practices upon the accumulations of great fortunes, for we lack the necessary information. The general facts, however, are clear: the very rich have used existing laws, they have circumvented and violated existing laws, and they have had laws created and enforced for their direct benefit.

The state guaranteed the right of private property; it made legal the existence of the corporation, and by further laws, interpretations of laws, and lack of reinforcement made possible its elaboration. Accordingly, the very rich could use the device of the corporation to juggle many ventures at once and to speculate with other people's money. As the 'trust' was outlawed, the holding company law made it legal by other means for one corporation to own stock in another. Soon 'the formation and financing of holding companies offered the easiest way to get rich quickly that had ever legally existed in the United States.'[3] In the later years of higher taxes, a combination of 'tax write-offs' and capital gains has helped the accumulation of private fortunes before they have been incorporated.

Many modern theories of industrial development stress technological developments, but the number of inventors among the very rich is so small as to be unappreciable. It is, as a matter of fact, not the far-seeing inventor or the captain of industry but the general of finance who becomes one of the very rich. That is one of the errors in Schumpeter's idea of the 'gale of innovations': he systematically confuses technological gain with financial manipulation. What is needed, as Frederick Lewis Allen once remarked, is 'not specialized knowledge, but persuasive salesmanship, coupled with the ability to command the millions and the investment-sales machinery of a large banking house, and to command also the services of astute corporation lawyers and stock-market operators.'[4]

In understanding the private appropriations of the very rich, we must also bear in mind that the private industrial development of the United States has been much underwritten by outright gifts out of the people's domain. State, local, and federal governments have given land free to railroads, paid for the cost of shipbuilding, for the transportation of important mail. Much more free land has been given to businesses than to small, independent homesteaders. Coal and iron have been legally determined not to be covered by the 'mineral' rights held by the government on the land it leased. The government has subsidized private industry

by maintaining high tariff rates, and if the taxpayers of the United States had not paid, out of their own labor, for a paved road system, Henry Ford's astuteness and thrift would not have enabled him to become a billionaire out of the automobile industry.[5]

In capitalistic economies, wars have led to many opportunities for the private appropriation of fortune and power. But the complex facts of World War II make previous appropriations seem puny indeed. Between 1940 and 1944, some $175 billion worth of prime supply contracts – the key to control of the nation's means of production – were given to private corporations. A full two-thirds of this went to the top one hundred corporations – in fact, almost one-third went to ten private corporations. These companies then made money by selling what they had produced to the government. They were granted priorities and allotments for materials and parts; they decided how much of these were to be passed down to sub-contractors, as well as who and how many sub-contractors there should be. They were allowed to expand their own facilities under extremely favorable amortization (20 per cent a year) and tax privileges. Instead of the normal twenty or thirty years, they could write off the cost in five. These were also generally the same corporations which operated most of the government-owned facilities, and obtained the most favorable options to 'buy' them after the war.

It had cost some $40 billion to build all the manufacturing facilities existing in the United States in 1939. By 1945, an additional $26 billion worth of high-quality new plant and equipment had been added – two thirds of it paid for directly from government funds. Some 20 of this $26 billion worth was usable for producing peacetime products. If to the $40 billion existing, we add this $20 billion, we have a $60 billion productive plan usable in the post-war period. The top 250 corporations owned in 1939 about 65 per cent of the facilities then existing, operated during the war 79 per cent of all new privately operated facilities built with government money, and held 78 per cent of all active prime war supply contracts as of September 1944.[6] No wonder that in World War II, little fortunes became big and many new little ones were created.

2

Before the Civil War, only a handful of wealthy men, notably Astor and Vanderbilt, were multimillionaires on a truly American scale. Few of the great fortunes exceeded $1,000,000; in fact, George Washington, who in 1799 left an estate valued at $530,000, was judged to be one of the richest Americans of his time. By the 1840's, in New York City and all of Massachusetts, there were only thirty-nine millionaires. The word 'millionaire,' in fact, was coined only in 1843, when, upon the death of Peter Lorillard (snuff, banking, real estate), the newspapers needed a term to denote great affluence.[7]

After the Civil War, these men of earlier wealth were to be recognized as Family Founders, the social shadow of their earlier wealth was to affect the status struggle within the metropolitan 400, and in due course their fortunes were to become part of the higher corporate world of the American economy. But the first really great American fortunes were developed during the economic transformation of the Civil War era, and out of the decisive corruptions that seem to be part of all American wars. A rural, commercial capitalism was then transformed into an industrial economy, within the legal framework of the tariff, the National Banking Act of 1863 and, in 1868, the Fourteenth Amendment, which by later interpretations sanctified the corporate revolution. During this shift in political framework and economic base, the first generation of the very rich came to possess units of wealth that dwarfed any that had previously been appropriated. Not only were the peaks of the money pyramid higher, but the base of the upper levels was apparently broader. By 1892, one survey revealed the existence of at least 4,046 American millionaires.[8]

In our own era of slump and war, there is debate about the number and the security – and even the very existence – of great American fortunes. But about the latter nineteenth century all historians seem agreed: between the Civil War and World War I, great captains of enormous wealth rose speedily to pre-eminence.

We shall take this generation, which came to full maturity in the 'nineties, as the first generation of the very rich. But we shall use it merely as a bench mark for the two following generations, the second coming to maturity about 1925, and the third, in the middle years of the twentieth century. Moreover, we shall not study merely the six or seven best-known men upon whom textbook historians and anecdotal biographers have based their criticisms and their adulations. For each of these last three generations, we have gathered information about the richest ninety or so individuals. In all, our study of these three lists enables us to expand our view of the American rich to include 275 American men and women, each of whom has possessed a minimum of about $30 million.[9]*

Among the very rich one can find men born poor and men born rich, men who were – and are – as flamboyant in their exercise of the power of money as they were in accumulating it, and others as miserly in their lives as harsh in their acquisitions. Here is John D. Rockefeller – the pious son of a Baptist peddler – who created literally scores of multimillionaire descendants. But here is Henry O. Havemeyer whose grandfather left him three million, and Henrietta Green who as a child was taught to study the financial pages of the paper and died at age eighty-two leaving 100 million. And we must not forget George F. Baker, Jr., a Harvard graduate and inheritor of the presidency of the First National Bank of

* See this note for a statement of the procedures used in selecting the very rich.

New York, who bathed and shaved and dressed each morning on his speed cruiser coming into Wall Street from Long Island, and who, in 1929, with six other bankers, mobilized a quarter of a billion dollars in a futile effort to stabilize the crash.[10]

The big rich are not all of the past nor are they all from Texas. It is true that five of the richest *ten* among us today are of the Texas crop, but of the 90 richest men and women of 1950 of whom we have adequate knowledge, only 10 per cent are Texans.

Popular literature now offers many glimpses of fabulously rich individuals in various postures – august and ridiculous; of various origins – humble and elevated; of different styles of life – gay, sad, lonely, convivial. But what do all these glimpses mean? Some started poor, some were born rich – but which is the *typical* fact? And what are the keys to their success? To find out we must go beyond the six or seven tycoons in each generation about whom social historians and biographers have provided endless anecdotes. We must study a large enough number of individuals to feel that we have a representative group.

The 275 people about whom we have gathered information represent the bulk of those individuals who are known to historians, biographers, and journalists as the richest people living in the United States since the Civil War – the 90 richest of 1900, the 95 of 1925, and the 90 of 1950. Only by examining such groups are we able to ask and to answer, with some accuracy, the deceptively simple questions that interest us about the origins and careers of the very rich.

At the top of the 1900 group is John D. Rockefeller with his billion dollars; at the top in 1925 is Henry Ford I with his billion; and, in 1950, it is reported (although it is not so certain as in other periods) that H. L. Hunt is worth 'one or two billions.' The fortune of another Texan, Hugh Roy Cullen, has also been reputed of late to come to a billion.[11] These three or four men are probably the richest of the rich Americans; they are the only billionaires of which financial biographers are fairly certain.*

3

In none of the latest three generations has a majority of the very rich been composed of men who have risen.

During the course of American history since the Civil War, the proportion of the very rich whose fathers worked as small farmers or storekeepers, as white-collar employees or wage workers has steadily decreased. Only 9 per cent of the very rich of our own time originated in lower-class families – in families with only enough money to provide essential needs and sometimes minor comforts.

The history of the middle-class contribution to the very rich is a fairly stable one: in the 1900 generation, it provided two out of ten; in 1925, three; and in 1950 again two. But the upper-class and the lower-class

* The same amount of money of course has had different value at different periods. But we have not allowed this fact to modify our listings. We are *not* here interested in the question of whether $15 million in 1900 was worth $30 or $40 million in 1950 values. Our sole interest is in *the richest* at each of these periods, regardless of how rich that may be compared with the rich of other periods, or compared with the income and property of the population at large. The wealth of each generation, accordingly, is presented here in the dollar value of the time each generation reached the mature age of about 60.

Because of the unknown factor of inflation, it is necessary to use extreme caution in interpreting such facts as the following: of the 1950 generation, including billionaire Hunt, some six people are estimated to own more than $300 million, compared with no more than three such people in 1900 or 1925. Farther down the pyramid from these exalted levels, the distribution according to size of fortune is rather similar in each of the three generations. Roughly, about 20 per cent of each group are in the 100 million or more bracket; the remaining being rather equally divided between the $50–99 million and the $30–49 million levels.

contributions have quite steadily reversed themselves. Even in the famous nineteenth-century generation, which scholarly historians usually discuss with the anecdotal details of the self-making myth, as many of the very rich derived from the upper class (39 per cent) as from the lower. Still, it is a fact that in that generation, 39 per cent of the very rich were sons of lower-class people. In the 1925 generation, the proportion had shrunk to 12 per cent, and by 1950, as we have seen, to 9 per cent. The upper classes, on the other hand, contributed 56 per cent in 1925; and in 1950, 68 per cent.

The reality and the trend are clearly the upper-class recruitment of the truly upper class of properties wealth. Wealth not only tends to perpetuate itself, but as we shall see, tends also to monopolize new opportunities for getting 'great wealth.' Seven out of ten of the very rich among us today were born into distinctly upper-class homes, two out of ten on the level of middle-class comfort, and only one in lower-class milieu.

Occupationally, 'upper class' among these very rich has meant the big businessman. At no time has the entire business stratum in America, big and little, been greater than 8 or 9 per cent of the working population at large; but in these three generations of the very rich as a whole, seven out of ten of the fathers have been urban entrepreneurs; one has been a professional man, one has been a farmer, and one has been a white-collar employee or wage worker. Across the generations these proportions have been quite stable. The very rich – of 1900 as of 1950 – have come out of the entrepreneurial strata; and, as we shall see, in a rather curious way, on their higher levels, many of them have continued to be active in an 'entrepreneurial' manner.

About 10 per cent of those who have possessed the great American fortunes have been born in foreign lands, although only 6 per cent grew up outside the United States, immigrating after they were adult. Of the

late nineteenth-century generation which reached full maturity by 1900, of course, more were foreign-born than in 1950. About 13 per cent of the 1900 rich were foreign-born, compared with about 24 per cent of the adult male U.S. population who were at that time foreign-born. By 1950, only 2 per cent of the very rich were foreign-born (compared with 7 per cent of the white 1950 population).[12]

The eastern seaboard has, of course, been the historical locale of the very rich: in all, some eight out of ten of those who grew up in America have done so in this region. There were as many from the East in 1925 (82 per cent) as in 1900 (80 per cent). By 1950, however, the proportions from the East – as among the population in the country as a whole – had dropped (to 68 per cent), a direct result of the emergence of the southwestern multimillionaires, who make up some 10 per cent of the very rich of 1950, compared with only about 1 per cent in 1900 and in 1925. The proportions who grew up in the Chicago–Detroit–Cleveland area have remained rather constant over the three historical epochs, 16 per cent in 1900 to 19 per cent in 1950.

The very rich come from the cities, especially from the larger cities of the East. Even in 1900, a full 65 per cent of the general American population lived in rural areas,[13] and many more than that had grown up on the farm; but only 25 per cent of the very rich of 1900 came from rural areas. And, since 1925 more than six out of ten of the very rich have grown up in metropolitan areas.

American-born, city-bred, eastern-originated, the very rich have been from families of higher class status, and, like other members of the new and old upper classes of local society and metropolitan 400, they have been Protestants. Moreover, about half have been Episcopalians, and a fourth, Presbyterians.[14]

With such facts before us, we would expect, and we do find, that the very rich have always been more highly educated than the common run of the population: even in 1900, 31 per cent of the very rich had graduated from college; by 1925, 57 per cent had done so; and by 1950, 68 per cent of the holders of great American fortunes were college graduates. That educational advantages are generally a result of family advantages is made clear by the fact that within each generation those from higher class levels are better educated than those from lower – in 1900, 46 per cent of those of upper-class levels, but only 17 per cent of those from lower, had graduated from college. But, by the third generation considered here – the very rich of 1950 – the difference in the amount of education according to class origin decreased: 60 per cent of the very rich who had originated on lower or middle-class levels graduated from college, compared with 71 per cent of those from the upper classes.

Half of all those among the very rich who attended any college attended those of the Ivy League; in fact, almost a third went either to Harvard or to Yale, the rest being scattered among Princeton, Columbia, Cornell, Dartmouth, and Pennsylvania. An additional 10 per cent attended other famous eastern colleges, such as Amherst, Brown, Lafayette, Williams, Bowdoin, and another 10 per cent were students at one of a handful of well-known technical schools. The remaining 30 per cent went to colleges and universities scattered all over the United States.

The preponderance of Ivy League colleges is, of course, a direct result of the higher class origin of the very rich: as the proportions of very rich from the upper classes increases, so do the proportions who attend the Ivy League schools. Of those who were college educated, 37 per cent of the 1900 generation, 47 per cent of 1925, and 60 per cent of 1950 very rich attended such schools.

Back in 1900, when only 39 per cent of the very rich were children of upper-class parents, 88 per cent of those originating in such upper-class families are known to have inherited fortunes of a half a million dollars or more – usually much more. By 1950, some 93 per cent of the very rich from the upper classes were inheritors. It is frequently said that taxes now make it impossible for the very rich to leave outright a fortune of $90 or $100 million to their children, and this is, in a simple legal sense, true. Yet, the 1950 very rich are very much a continuation of the very rich of 1925; in fact, more of a continuation than those of 1925 were of the 1900 generation. While 56 per cent of the very rich of 1925 originated in the upper classes, only 33 per cent had relatives among the very rich of 1900. But 68 per cent of the 1950 very rich originated in the upper classes and 62 per cent had relatives among the very rich of the earlier generations.

Moreover, by the middle years of the twentieth century, it is, in some ways easier to transfer position and power to one's children than it was in 1900 or 1925, for then the lines of power and position were not so elaborately organized, buttressed, and entrenched in well-established circles, and the transfer of power and position seemed to be firmly assured only by means of huge personal fortunes. Among the very rich of 1950, however, there are many ways, as we shall have occasion to see, to pass on to children strategic positions in the apparatus of appropriation that constitutes the higher corporate level of American free, private enterprise.

4

The very rich in America are not dominantly an idle rich and never have been. The proportions among them that are rentiers and not much else, have, of course, increased significantly: in 1900, some 14 per cent; in 1925, some 17 per cent; and by 1950, 26 per cent. By virtue of how they spend their time, about one-fourth of the very richest people can now be called members of a leisure class.

Yet neither the idea of the very rich as miserly coupon clippers nor as flamboyant playboys is the representative fact. The idle miser as well as the busy spendthrift are represented among the very rich of America, but, in the history of the great American fortunes, the misers have not all been *mere* coupon clippers; they have usually 'worked' in some way to increase the value of the coupons they would have to clip – or at least pretended to do so while having others to manage for them.* And the spendthrifts have not all been merely that: some have gambled a million and often come up with two or three more; for their spendthrift activities have often been in the realm of appropriative speculation.

The men among the idle rich of 1900 were either third- or fourth-generation Astors or third-generation Vanderbilts: on their estates they relaxed with their horses, or on beaches with their yachts offshore, while their wives played often frantic and always expensive social games. By 1925,

there were only a few more rentiers among the very rich but many more of them were women. They lived as expensively as did those of 1900, but now they were more scattered over the United States and they were given less publicity in the emerging world of the celebrity. Having beyond any doubt 'arrived' socially, these very rich women often became engaged by 'the arts' instead of 'society,' or busily pretended to be.[15] And in fact, some of them were spending more time in philanthropy than in social amusements or personal splendor, a fact that was in part due to the sober, Puritan beliefs of John D. Rockefeller from whose accumulations much of their money derived.

In the 1950 generation, both the proportion of rentiers (which we have seen to be 26 per cent) and the proportions of women among them (70 per cent) have increased, but they do not seem to form any one social type. There are the modern playgirls – Doris Duke and Barbara Hutton now expertly and

---

* The supposed shamefulness of labor, on which many of Veblen's conceptions of the upper classes rest, does not square very well with the Puritan work ethic so characteristic of much of American life, including many upper-class elements. I suppose that in his book on the leisure class, Veblen is speaking only of upper, not middle, classes – certainly he is not writing of wealthy Puritan middle classes. He did not want to call what the higher businessman does 'work,' much less productive work. The very term, leisure class, became for him synonymous with upper class, but there has been and there is a *working* upper class – in fact, a class of prodigiously active men. That Veblen did not approve of their work, and in fact refused to give it that term – work being one of his positive words – is irrelevant. Moreover, in this case it obscures and distorts our understanding of the upper classes as a social formation. Yet for Veblen fully to have admitted this simple fact would have destroyed (or forced the much greater sophistication of) his whole perspective and indeed one of the chief moral bases of his criticism.

From one rather formal viewpoint, it should be noted that Veblen was a profoundly conserva-

tive critic of America: he wholeheartedly accepted one of the few unambiguous, all-American values: the value of efficiency, of utility, of pragmatic simplicity. His criticism of institutions and the personnel of American society was based without exception on his belief that they did not adequately fulfill this American value. If he was, as I believe, a Socratic figure, he was in his own way as American as Socrates in his was Athenian. As a critic, Veblen was effective precisely because he used the American value of efficiency to criticize American reality. He merely took this value seriously and used it with devastatingly systematic rigor. It was a strange perspective for an American critic in the nineteenth century, or in our own. One looked down from Mont St. Michel, like Henry Adams, or across from England, like Henry James. With Veblen perhaps the whole character of American social criticism shifted. The figure of the last-generation American faded and the figure of the first-generation American – the Norwegian immigrant's son, the New York Jew teaching English literature in a midwestern university, the southerner come north to crash New York – was installed as the genuine, if no longer 100-per-cent-American, critic.

expensively trying to conserve their youth; but there are also those who live, as did Mrs. Anita McCormick Blaine, an active life of spending money and time on philanthropy and education, taking little active part in social affairs. And there was Hetty Sylvia H. Green Wilks, the modern version of the miserly coupon clipper, who, as a child, had spent her summers 'in a barred and shuttered house and had to go to bed at 7:30 p.m. for no lights burned in the Green house after that hour.'[16]

The history of the very rich in America is, in the main, a patriarchal history: men have always held from 80 to 90 per cent of great American fortunes. The increase, over the generations, in the proportions of the very rich who are recruited from inheritors of great wealth has not meant that all the rich have become 'idle.' We have seen that 62 per cent of the very rich of 1950 were born into families connected with earlier generations of very rich; but that only 26 per cent of the 1950 very rich are in their life-ways an idle rich. And many of the very rich who have inherited their wealth have spent their lives working to keep it or to increase it. The game that has interested them most has been the game of the big money.

Yet some 26 per cent of the very rich of today are rentiers and more or less economically idle; and another 39 per cent occupy high positions in firms owned or controlled by their families.[17] The rentiers and the family-managers thus account for 65 per cent of the very rich of our time. What of the 35 per cent remaining who *rose* to very rich status?

5

If many of those who were born into the very rich have spent their lives working, it is obvious that those who rose into it from middle and lower class levels are not likely to have been idle. The rise into the very rich stratum seems to involve an economic career which has two pivotal features: the big jump and the accumulation of advantages.

I   No man, to my knowledge has ever entered the ranks of the great American fortunes merely by saving a surplus from his salary or wages. In one way or another, he has to come into command of a strategic position which allows him the chance to appropriate big money, and usually he has to have available a considerable sum of money in order to be able to parlay it into really big wealth. He may work and slowly accumulate up to this big jump, but at some point he must find himself in a position to take up the main chance for which he has been on the lookout. On a salary of two or three hundred thousand a year, even forgetting taxes, and living like a miser in a board shack, it has been mathematically impossible to save up a great American fortune.*

II   Once he has made the big jump, once he has negotiated the main chance, the man who is rising gets involved in the accumulation of advantages, which is merely another

---

* If you started at 20 years of age and worked until you were 50 or so, saving $200,000 a year, you would still have, at a rate of 5 per cent compound interest, only $14 million, less than half of the lower limits we have taken for the great American fortunes.

But if you had bought only $9,900 worth of General Motors stock in 1913, and, rather than use your judgment, had gone into a coma – allowing the proceeds to pile up in General Motors – then, in 1953, you would have about $7 million.

And, if you had not even exercised the judgment of choosing General Motors, but merely put $10,000 into each of the total of 480 stocks listed in 1913 – a total investment of about $1 million – and then gone into a coma until 1953, you would have come out worth $10 million and have received in dividends and rights another $10 million. The increase in value would have amounted to about 899 per cent, the dividend return at 999 per cent. Once you have the million, advantages would accumulate – even for a man in a coma.[18]

way of saying that to him that hath shall be given. To parlay considerable money into the truly big money, he must be in a position to benefit from the accumulation advantages. The more he has, and the more strategic his economic position, the greater and the surer are his chances to gain more. The more he has, the greater his credit – his opportunities to use other people's money – and hence the less risk he need take in order to accumulate more. There comes a point in the accumulation of advantages, in fact, when the risk is no risk, but is as sure as the tax yield of the government itself.

The accumulation of advantages at the very top parallels the vicious cycle of poverty at the very bottom. For the cycle of advantages includes psychological readiness as well as objective opportunities: just as the limitations of lower class and status position produce a lack of interest and a lack of self-confidence, so do objective opportunities of class and status produce interest in advancement and self-confidence. The confident feeling that one can of course get what one desires tends to arise out of and to feed back into the objective opportunities to do so. Energetic aspiration lives off a series of successes; and continual, petty failure cuts the nerve of the will to succeed.[19]

Most of the 1950 very rich who are related to the very rich of earlier generations have been born with the big jump already made for them and the accumulation of advantages already firmly in operation. The 39 per cent of the very rich of 1900 who originated from the upper classes inherited the big jump; and a few of them, notably the Vanderbilts and Astors, also inherited the positions involving the accumulation of advantages. J. P. Morgan's father left him $5 million and set him up as a partner in a banking firm connected with financial concerns in both Europe and America. That was his big jump. But the accumulation of advantages came later when, in his capacity as financier and broker, J. P. Morgan could lend other people's money to promote the sale of stocks and bonds in new companies, or the consolidation of existing companies, and receive as his commission enough stock to eventually enable his firm to control the new corporation.[20]

After experience and profit in a lumber business, with his millionaire father's financial support, Andrew Mellon went into his father's bank and expanded it to national scale. He then became involved in the accumulation of advantages by lending the bank's money to young businesses – particularly in 1888, when the owners of patents for the refining of aluminum sold a share of their Pittsburgh Reduction Company to the Mellons in return for $250,000 which they used to construct a mill. Andrew saw to it that this aluminum company remained a monopoly, and that the Mellons came out the controlling power.[21]

No man, to my knowledge, has ever entered the ranks of the great American fortunes merely by a slow bureaucratic crawl up the corporate hierarchies. 'Many of the top executives in some of our largest corporations,' Benjamin F. Fairless, Chairman of the Board of U. S. Steel, said in 1953, 'have spent a lifetime in the field of industrial management without ever having been able to accumulate as much as a million dollars. And I know that to be fact because I happen to be one of them myself.'[22] That statement is not true in the sense that the heads of the larger corporations do not typically become millionaires: they do. But it is true in the sense that they do not become millionaires because they are 'experts' in the field of industrial management; and it is true in that it is not by industry but by finance, not by management but by promotion and speculation that they typically become enriched. Those who have risen into the very rich have been economic politicians and members of important cliques who have been in positions permitting them to appropriate for personal uses out of the accumulation of advantages.

Very few of those who have risen to great wealth have spent the major portions of their working lives steadily advancing from one position to another within and between the corporate hierarchies. Such a long crawl was made by only 6 per cent of the very rich in 1900, and 14 per cent in 1950. But even these, who apparently did move slowly up the corporate hierarchy, seem rarely to have made the grade because of talents in business management. More often such talents as they possessed were the talents of the lawyer or – very infrequently – those of the industrial inventor.

The long crawl comes to a pay-off only if it is transformed into an accumulation of advantages; this transformation is often a result of a merger of companies. Usually such a merger takes place when the companies are relatively small and often it is cemented by marriage – as when the du Ponts bought out Laflin and Rand, their largest competitor, and Charles Copeland – assistant to the president of Laflin and Rand – became assistant treasurer of du Pont and married Luisa D'Anbelot du Pont.[23]

The slow movement through a sequence of corporate positions may also mean that one has accumulated enough inside information and enough friendship to be able, with less risk or with no risk, to speculate in the promotion or manipulation of securities. That is why the generation of 1925 contains the largest proportions of the very rich making the long crawl; then the market was open for such profits and the rules of speculation were not so difficult as they were later to become.

Whatever type of venture it is that enables the rich man to parlay his stake into a great appropriation, at one point or another the 'bureaucratic' men have usually been as much 'entrepreneurs' as were the classic founders of fortunes after the Civil War. Many of them, in fact – like Charles W. Nash[24] – broke out on their own to found their own companies. Once the crawl was made, many of these men, especially of the 1925 set, took on all the gambling spirit and even some of the magnificence usually associated with the robber barons of the late nineteenth century.

The economic careers of the very rich are neither 'entrepreneurial' nor 'bureaucratic.' Moreover, among them, many of those who take on the management of their families' firms are just as 'entrepreneurial' or as 'bureaucratic' as those who have not enjoyed such inheritance. 'Entrepreneur' and 'bureaucrat' are middle-class words with middle-class associations and they cannot be stretched to contain the career junctures of the higher economic life in America.

The misleading term 'entrepreneur' does not have the same meaning when applied to small businessmen as it does when applied to those men who have come to possess the great American fortunes. The sober bourgeois founding of a business, the gradual expanding of this business under careful guidance until it becomes a great American corporation is not an adequate picture of the fortune founders at the higher levels.

The entrepreneur, in the classic image, was supposed to have taken a risk, not only with his money but with his very career; but once the founder of a business has made the big jump he does not usually take serious risks as he comes to enjoy the accumulation of advantages that lead him into great fortune. If there is any risk, someone else is usually taking it. Of late, that someone else, as during World War II and in the Dixon-Yates attempt, has been the government of the United States. If a middle-class businessman is in debt for $50,000, he may well be in trouble. But if a man manages to get into debt for $2 million, his creditors, if they can, may well find it convenient to produce chances for his making money in order to repay them.[25]

The robber barons of the late nineteenth century usually founded or organized companies which became springboards for the financial accumulations that placed them among the very rich. In fact, 55 per cent of the very rich of 1900 made the first step to great fortune by the big jump of promoting or organizing their own companies. By 1925, however, and again in 1950, only 22 per cent of the very rich made such a jump.

Very rarely have the men of any of these generations become very rich merely by the energetic tutelage of one big firm. The accumulation of advantages has usually required the merging of other businesses with the first one founded – a financial operation – until a large 'trust' is formed. The manipulation of securities and fast legal footwork are the major keys to the success of such higher entrepreneurs. For by such manipulation and footwork they attained positions involved in the accumulation of advantages.

The major economic fact about the very rich is the fact of the accumulation of advantages: those who have great wealth are in a dozen strategic positions to make it yield further wealth. Sixty-five per cent of the very richest people in America today are involved in enterprises which their families have passed on to them or are simply living as rentiers on the huge returns from such properties. The remaining 35 per cent are playing the higher economic game more actively, if no more daringly, than those who used to be called entrepreneurs but who in later day capitalism are more accurately called the economic politicians of the corporate world.

There are several ways to become rich. By the middle of the twentieth century in the United States, it has become increasingly difficult to earn and to keep enough money so as to accumulate your way to the top. Marriage involving money is at all times a delicate matter, and when it involves big money, it is often inconvenient and sometimes insecure. Stealing, if you do not already have much money, is a perilous undertaking. If you are really gambling for money, and do so long enough, your capital

will, in the end, balance out; if the game is fixed, you are really earning it or stealing it, or both, depending on which side of the table you sit. It is not usual, and it never has been the dominant fact, to create a great American fortune merely by nursing a little business into a big one. It is not usual and never has been the dominant fact carefully to accumulate your way to the top in a slow, bureaucratic crawl. It is difficult to climb to the top, and many who try fall by the way. It is easier and much safer to be born there.

6

In earlier generations the main chance, usually with other people's money, was the key; in later generations the accumulation of corporate advantages, based on grandfathers' and father's position, replaces the main chance. Over the last three generations, the trend is quite unmistakable: today, only 9 per cent of the very rich came from the bottom; only 23 per cent are of middle-class origin; 68 per cent came from the upper classes.

The incorporation of the United States economy occurred on a continent abundantly supplied with natural resources, rapidly peopled by migrants, within a legal and political framework willing and able to permit private men to do the job. They did it. And in fulfilling their historical task of organizing for profit the industrialization and the incorporation, they acquired for their private use the great American fortunes. Within the private corporate system, they became the very rich.

In realizing the power of property and in acquiring instruments for its protection, the very rich have become involved, and now they are deeply entrenched, in the higher corporate world of the twentieth-century American economy. Not great fortunes, but great corporations are the important units of wealth, to which individuals of property are variously attached. The corporation is the source of wealth, and the basis of the continued power and privilege of wealth. All the men and the families of great wealth are now identified with large corporations in which their property is seated.

Economically, as we have seen, neither the inheritors nor the accumulators have become an idle rich class of leisurely and cultivated persons. There are such among them, but almost three-fourths of the very rich of our day have continued to be more or less, and in one way or another, economically active. Their economic activities are, of course, corporation activities: promoting and managing, directing and speculating.

Moreover, as the propertied family has entered the corporate economy, it has been joined in the corporate world by the managers of these properties, who, as we shall presently see, are not themselves exactly unpropertied, and who, in fact, are not an entirely distinct economic species from the very rich. The organizing center of the propertied classes has, of course, shifted to include other powers than those held by the big propertied families. The property system, of which rich men form so key a part, has been strengthened by its managerial reorganization, and it has been supplemented by the executive stratum, within and between the great corporations, which works energetically for the common interests of the corporate rich.

Socially, the men and women of the great American fortunes have taken their places as leaders of the several metropolitan 400's. Of the ninety members of the 1900 very rich, only nine were included in Ward McAllister's 1892 list, but roughly half of the families in our 1900 listing have descendants who in 1940 were listed in the Social Registers of Philadelphia, Boston, Chicago, or New York. The very rich are leading members of the metropolitan 400. They belong to its clubs, and many of them, and almost all of their children, went to Groton and then to Harvard, or to other such schools. Twelve of the fifteen sons (who lived to be of college age) of the ten men out of the 1900 very rich whom Frederick Lewis Allen selected as the leading financiers of

1905, went to either Harvard or Yale; the other three to Amherst, Brown, and Columbia.[26]

The very rich do not reign alone on top of visible and simple hierarchies. But that they have been supplemented by agents and by hierarchies in the corporate structure of the economy and of the state does not mean that they have been displaced. Economically and socially, the very rich have not declined. After the crash and after the New Deal, the very rich have had to operate with skilled, legal technicians (both in and out of governments) whose services are essential in the fields of taxes and government regulations, corporate reorganization and merger, war contracts and public relations. They have also adopted every conceivable type of protective coloration for the essentially irresponsible nature of their power, creating the image of the small-town boy who made good, the 'industrial statesman,' the great inventor who 'provides jobs,' but who, withal, remains just an average guy.

What has happened is that the very rich are not so visible as they once seemed, to observers of the muckraker age, for example – who provided the last really public view of the top of American society. The absence of systematic information and the distraction of 'human-interest' trivia tend to make us suppose that they do not really matter and even that they do not really exist. But they are still very much among us – even though many are hidden, as it were, in the impersonal organizations in which their power, their wealth, and their privileges are anchored.

NOTES

1   Cf. Joseph A. Schumpeter, *Capitalism, Socialism and Democracy* 3rd ed. (New York: Harper, 1950), pp. 81 ff.

2   For a careful and revealing analysis of the attitudes and connections of the Presidents and the commissioners involved in antitrust action during the crucial Progressive

Era, see Meyer H. Fishbein, *Bureau of Corporations: An Agency of the Progressive Era* (MA
thesis, American University, 1954), esp. pp.
19–29, 100–19.

3   Frederick Lewis Allen, *The Lords of Creation*
(New York: Harper, 1935), pp. 9–10.

4   Ibid. p. 12.

5   Cf. *Time*, 10 August 1953, p. 82.

6   Report of the Smaller War Plants Corpora-
tion to the Special Committee to Study
Problems of American Small Business, U.S.
Senate, *Economic Concentration and World
War II*, 79th Congress, 2nd Session, Senate
Committee Print No. 6 (Washington, D.C.:
U.S. Government Printing Office, 1946), pp.
37, 39, 40.

7   On wealth in Colonial America, see Dixon
Wecter, *The Saga of American Society* (New
York: Scribner's, 1937), chap. 2; and
Gustavus Myers, *History of the Great Ameri-
can Fortunes*, 1907 (revised Modern Library
edition, 1936), pp. 55–6, 59, 85. On the
estate of George Washington, see ibid. p. 49.
On the multi-millionaires in the early
1840's, see A. Forbes and J. W. Greene, *The
Rich Men of Massachusetts* (Boston: Fetridge
& Co., 1851); Moses Yale Beach, *Wealth and
Pedigree of the Wealthy Citizens of New York
City* (New York: Compiled with much care
and published at the Sun Office, 1842), 4th
ed.; and 'Wealth and Biography of the
Wealthy Citizens of Philadelphia,' by a
Member of the Philadelphia Bar, 1845. On
the New York multi-millionaires in the
middle 1850's, see Moses Yale Beach, 'The
Wealthy Citizens of the City of New York,'
12th ed. (New York: Published at the
Sun Office, 1855). On the coinage of the
word 'millionaire,' see Wecter, *The Saga of
American Society*, p. 113.

8   See The New York Tribune, *Tribune Monthly*,
June 1892. Sidney Ratner has recently
edited a book, *New Light on the History
of Great American Fortunes* (New York:
Augustus M. Kelley, 1953), which reprints
two listings of American millionaires – from
the *Tribune Monthly*, June 1892 and the
World Almanac, 1902. These lists are of little
use in the attempt to list the very rich (see
note 9 below) since only rarely is an estimate
of the exact size of the fortune given; examination of this list shows that hundreds of
'mere millionaires' appear alongside John D.
Rockefeller and Andrew Carnegie.

9   In a country which, as Ferdinand Lundberg
once remarked, 'literally flaunts a chaos of
statistics about subjects of little general
interest,' there are no precise figures on the
great fortunes. To list the names of the
richest people of three generations, I have
had to do the best that I could with such
unsystematic sources as are available. I
have, of course, availed myself of all the histories of great fortunes in the United States,
as well as the biographies of those who possessed them. Twice in the twentieth century
– 1924 and 1938 – rather systematic information has been published on large incomes
or big properties (see below); and there
is an intermittent stream of information
and myth appearing in newspapers and
magazines, the facts of a probated will,
the tax scandal, the anecdote about rich
individuals.

I began with a list of all persons mentioned in the books listed below who were
born after 1799 and who were stated to
have ever possessed $30 million or more.
In many cases, the size of the fortune was
not estimated in the source of the name;
but taking note of all possible names, we
searched all the sources at hand for estimations of the size of fortune. The general criterion of $30 million is mainly a matter of
convenience. We found that such a criterion
will yield 371 names; since it was necessary
to compile detailed information about the
fortune and the career of each of these individuals, our resources did not permit us to
handle a larger list. Here are the sources
used:

(I) Gustavus Myers, *History of the Great
American Fortunes*, 1907 (revised Modern
Library edition, 1936). (II) Gustavus Myers,
The Ending of Hereditary Fortunes (New York:
Julian Messner, 1939). (III) Matthew
Josephson, *The Robber Barons* (New York:
Harcourt, Brace, 1934). (IV) Frederick Lewis
Allen, *The Lords of Creation* (New York:
Harper, 1935). (V) Ferdinand Lundberg,
America's 60 Families, 1937 (New York: The
Citadel Press, 1946) – our cautious use of
this book is discussed below in (XI). (VI)
Dixon Wecter, The *Saga of American Society*
(New York: Scribner's, 1937). (VII) 'Richest
U.S. Women,' *Fortune*, November 1936.
(VIII) Stewart H. Holbrook, *The Age of the
Moguls* (New York: Doubleday, 1953). Based

in considerable detail upon Myers' work and those of other historians, this work is mainly a popularization of earlier work. (ix) 'Noted Americans of the Past: American Industrial Leaders, Financiers and Merchants,' *World Almanac*, 1952, p. 381, and 1953, p. 783. Does not include estimates of fortunes. (x) Cleveland Amory, *The Last Resorts* (New York: Harper, 1952). There are naturally many duplications of people mentioned in these sources; but each one of them has yielded information unmentioned by all the others.

Three further sources require more detailed discussion:

(xi) In 1924 and again in 1925, a temporary law allowed the release of information on the size of income-tax payments made on incomes for 1923 and 1924. Journalists were admitted to various offices of the Bureau of Internal Revenue and there copied names with the taxes paid by each. The release of this data was so administratively sloppy that one paper published data about a man whom another paper ignored, some errors were printed, and in some cases all journalists missed the names of people who were known to have paid large taxes. (There were, of course, some wealthy people whose entire income was tax free.) Selecting the 1924 income tax list for study, we took everyone who had paid $200,000 or more in taxes as listed in either or in both *The New York Times* or *The New York Herald Tribune*, 2 to 15 September 1925.

The average tax at this time and at these levels resulted in a payment of about 40 per cent of the gross income; so a payment of $200,000 reveals an annual income during 1924 of about $500,000. Since most such high incomes are derived from investments, an overall figure of 5 per cent return on investment would mean that for one to obtain a half million dollars from investments, the capital owned would have to be about $10 million. It has been presumed that only about one-third of most entire fortunes were at that time in taxable sources; hence, the over-all fortune owned would be three times larger than the taxable fortune. (These are the calculations Ferdinand Lundberg made on the 1924 returns in his book cited above. He comments that 'in individual instances the multiplication by three of the net fortune upon whose income a tax was paid may result in some distortion, but this appears to be the only way in which to obtain a general approximation; and as the method gives generally accurate results, the picture as a whole is not overdrawn. Rather it is very conservative.' (p. 25.) I think this is so.) By these calculations, then, a tax of $200,000 indicates an income of $500,000, a taxable fortune of 10 million, and an entire fortune of 30 million.

Most evidence from those estates that were probated shortly after 1924 shows that these calculations are reasonably accurate. For instance, according to these calculations, the $434,000 tax payment of Richard Teller Crane, Jr., indicated a total fortune of $64.8 million; he died in 1931 leaving an estate of 50 million. Ogden Mills' tax payment of $372,000 would indicate a fortune of 55.5 million in 1924; he died in 1929 leaving 41 million. There are, of course, cases in which people's estates were much less, but they usually were known to have *lost* their money (such as grain speculator Arthur W. Cutten who was wiped out in the 1929 crash) or given it away before their death. I included such people as long as they were at any one time in possession of $30 million.

I know of no systematic use of these names. Ferdinand Lundberg, in 1937, compiled a list of '60 families' which, in fact, are not all families and which number – as 'families' – not 60, but about 74. But he does not analyze them systematically. By 'systematic' I understand that similar information is compiled for each person on the list and generalizations made therefrom.

What Lundberg does is (1) generalize blood relations – sometimes cousinhood only – into power and financial cliques. We do not wish to confuse the two. In addition (2), we cannot go along with the list he has abstracted from *The New York Times*, which is not uniformly made up of families or individuals or companies but is a miscellany.

Of the so-called 60 families, there are 37 'families' represented by more than one member's tax payments. There are eight unrelated men included along with the Morgans; and there is another group of seven families forming his 38th 'family' (this is the 'Standard Oil Group'). The list is filled out with 22 individuals paying 1924 taxes ranging from $188,608 to $791,851. Thus, if 'family' is to mean a blood tie, there are many more than 60 families on his list; but the list is not even a full account of these families, since only those paying a tax under the *family name* were included. Moreover, there are a number of people (e.g. J. H. Brewer, L. L. Cooke) who paid much higher taxes in 1924 than many of the people named by Lundberg but who are not included in his listing of '60 families.' Some, but not all, of these are not listed in *The New York Times*, but are in *The New York Herald Tribune*, which Mr. Lundberg seems to have ignored.

More importantly for the purpose of obtaining a list of the top richest *persons* is the fact that some of the families in Lundberg's list of the top 60 do not even appear among the very rich when individuals are concerned. The Deerings, for instance: Lundberg uses three Deerings; the tax payment of all three adds up to $315,701. We do not include the Deerings on our list of the 'very rich' since James Deering paid a tax of only $179,896; Charles, only $139,341; the third Deering, some $7,000. The same type of procedure holds for the Tafts, Lehmans, and deForests. They are all undoubtedly rich people, but not to the same degree as the people in whom we are interested.

(XII) A more recent systematic source of information regarding size of private fortunes is the Temporary National Economic Committee's Monograph No. 29: 'The Distribution of Ownership in the 200 Largest Non-Financial Corporations' (Washington: U.S. Government Printing Office, 1940). This monograph gives the 20 largest stockholders of record in each of the 200 largest non-financial corporations, along with the stockholdings of the directors and officers of these corporations, as of 1937 or 1938. Although it does contain most of the well-known fortunes that are based upon industrial ownership, the list is not complete: it does not cover money held in government or local bonds, in real estate or in financial houses. Moreover, in a number of instances

ownership even of industrial corporations is disguised by the practice of recording the ownership of a block of stock under various investment houses which do not divulge the names of the actual owners. Nevertheless, this TNEC list represents the best we have found for the later period. Compared with the scattered case studies available for the nineteenth century, the wealthy it discloses are a rather stable set of men.

From this source I have taken each person for whom the total value of all shares owned in all companies listed was equal to $10 million or more in 1937 or 1938. Multiplying this figure by three (assuming again that the taxable wealth represents only one-third of the total fortune owned), gives us all those people owning $30 million or more in the late 'thirties.

(XIII) None of the sources above provide really up-to-date information about the very rich. Many of the people named in the various books, and in the 1924 and 1938 lists, are, of course, still alive; and we have found living heirs to people now dead – through obituaries, we tried to trace the fortunes of all names selected, and included in our list all those heirs whom we have found to have inherited $30 million or more.

(XIV) In order to obtain information about people now alive, the following agencies and government bureaus were contacted – various officials in each of them gave us such information as they could, none of it 'official,' and none of much use to us: the Federal Reserve Board of New York; the Securities Exchange Commission; U.S. Department of Commerce, Bureau of Domestic Commerce; and the Bureau of Internal Revenue's Statistical Division and Information Division. Individuals were also contacted in the following private organizations: Dun & Bradstreet; The National Industrial Conference Board's Division of Business Economics; *The Wall Street Journal*; *Barron's*; *Fortune*; The Russell Sage Foundation; *U.S. News and World Report*; Brookings Institution; Bureau of National Affairs, Federal Savings and Loan; and two private investment houses. People seen in these organizations could only refer us to sources of which we were already aware. Some had never thought much about the problem, others seemed slightly shocked at the idea of 'finding out' about the top wealthy people, others were enchanted with the idea but helpless as to sources. I am grateful to Professor Fred Blum for making most of these contacts for us, and for his helpful comments on this whole problem.

(xv) During the post-World War II years, I have been searching current papers and periodicals for any mention of other multi-millionaires. From magazines such as *Business Week*, *Look* and *Life* and *Time* and from *The New York Times*, I have picked up additional names, mainly of the new crop of Texans. In this search for additional names, I have had the benefit of about two dozen interested students and friends.

Because of the necessarily miscellaneous character of the collection of names, we cannot be certain, and I do not claim, that the list includes *all* the richest people in America over the last 100 years; nor that all the people whom we have included in our list have, in proven fact, possessed at one time or another, $30 million.

Two things, however, can be said with reasonable surety: (1) There is fairly good evidence for the accuracy of the $30 million figure. In cases of people who have died, I have checked by probate of will and found that these estimations seem quite accurate. (2) Even though the list cannot be proved to exhaust the richest – including every single person who has owned the prescribed amounts – all of these people are undoubtedly among the richest people in the United States by any reasonable definition. Undoubtedly in our listing we have missed some who should have been included, and have included others who should not have been. But we have included all those people about whom printed information is available to us, and it is our opinion that such errors as might occur do not materially affect the picture. In short, no exact and proven list seems to us possible; this list seems to us a quite reasonable approximation of the most prominent very rich people in America over the last one hundred years.

The foregoing outline of procedure, along with a preliminary listing of the names selected, and a secondary listing of

people we had designated as being of lesser wealth, were sent, for suggestions and criticisms to the following: Dr. John M. Blair of the Bureau of Industrial Economics, Federal Trade Commission; Professor Thomas Cochran of the University of Pennsylvania; Professor Shepard Clough of Columbia University; Professors Arthur Cole, Leland H. Jenks, and Sigmund O. Diamond of the Research Center of Entrepreneurial History at Harvard University; Professors Joseph Dorfman and Robert S. Lynd of Columbia University; Professor Frank Freidel of Stanford University; Frank Fogarty of *Business Week*; Ernest Dale of the School of Business, Columbia University; and Max Lerner of the *New York Post* and Brandeis University. I wish to thank these people for their time, consideration and help on this problem, although they are in no way responsible for any errors of fact or judgement.

Of the 371 names, I was unable to find, from a search of biographical sources, the books mentioned above, and newspaper files, any information about the life of 69 of them. More than half of these names came from the 1924 tax lists where we had only the last name and first initials to go by. The speculative nature of many large incomes during the 'twenties would lead me to believe that the chances were high that many of these incomes did not represent durable great fortunes; and our concern with the 'most prominent' very rich in America makes it feasible to omit these 69 people from the Very Rich. At any rate it was necessary.

In an effort to make some allowance for the variance in the value of the dollar over the periods in which we are interested, I ranked the members of each of our three generations by the estimated sizes of their fortunes. Economic historians whom I consulted have indicated that they 'do not know of any satisfactory device for reducing a given amount of money to purchasing power equivalents over a long period of time' (Letter to the author from Sigmund O. Diamond and Leland H. Jenks, 30 March 1954). Of course, when one gets into the multi-million-dollar categories, the cost of living – which is usually the purpose of establishing relative purchasing power – is not a matter of concern.

For each generation I took the 90 richest people. We are thus considering the 90 or so *most prominent* and rich*est* in each of the three historical epochs. This gives us a total of 275 cases for concentrated analysis, which is the upper 74 per cent of the 371 cases mentioned by all sources known to us.

Of the 90 cases selected as Group I, the median year of birth in 1841; the median years of death, 1912. The year when the median age is 60 is therefore 1901; hereafter Group I is identified as the 1900 generation.

Of the 95 cases selected from Group II, the median year of birth is 1867; the median year of death, 1936. The year when the median age is 60 is therefore 1927; Group II thus consists of the 1925 generation.

Of the 90 cases in Group III, the median year of birth is 1887; and most of these were still alive in 1954. On the average they were 60 in 1947; Group III is thus the 1950 generation.

10 On John D. Rockefeller, see Wecter, op. cit. pp. 141–2, 482; Frederick Lewis Allen, *The Lords of Creation* pp. 4–7; *The New York Times*, 24 May 1937 and 6 June 1937; and, for further references, John T. Flynn, *God's Gold* (New York: Harcourt, Brace, 1932). On Henry O. Havemeyer, see *Dictionary of American Biography*; Myers, *History of the Great American Fortunes*, pp 697 ff.; and *The New York Times*, 5 December 1907. On Henrietta Green, see *Dictionary of American Biography*; *The New York Times*, 4 July 1916, p. 1 and 9 July 1916, magazine section; and Boyden Sparkes and Samuel Taylor Moore, *The Witch of Wall Street; Hetty Green* (Garden City, N.Y.: Doubleday Doran, 1935). On George F. Baker, Jr., see *Who Was Who, 1897–1942*; and *The New York Times*, 31 May 1937.

11 On Hunt and Cullen, see *The New York Times*, 21 November 1952 and the magazine section of 8 March 1953; *The Washington Post*, 15 through 19 February 1954; and other reports of the United Press Survey such as those of Preston McGraw in the *Long Island Star-Journal*, 4 and 5 August 1954 and Gene Patterson, 'World's Richest Man is a Texan,' *Pacific Coast Business and Shipping Register*, 16 August 1954.

12 The figure on the proportion of foreign-born adult U.S. males in 1900 was calculated from the U.S. Department of Commerce, *Historical Statistics of the U.S., 1789–1945*, p. 32. On the foreign-born white population in the United States in 1950, cf. *The World Almanac, 1954*, p. 266.

13 See *Historical Statistics of the U.S., 1789–1945*, p. 29.

14 The general figures on religion cannot be given with more precision for religious faith is unknown for a good many of the very rich. The censuses are likewise inaccurate on religious denominations for most periods of U.S. history, thus also prohibiting comparison of any one group with the general population.

15 For instance, Eleanor Rice, who was the daughter of William L. Elkins and at one time the wife of George D. Widener, gave millions to a variety of artistic and educational organizations and her last husband was a physician and geographer who was famed for expeditions to South America to study tropical diseases and native tribes. See *The New York Herald Tribune*, 5 October 1951. At her palatial home in California, Mary Virginia McCormick had a permanent staff of musicians and imported entire symphony orchestras for parties and concerts. See *The New York Times*, 26 May 1951.

16 On Anita McCormick Blaine, see *The New York Times*, 13 February 1954; on Hetty Sylvia Green Wilks, see *The New York Times*, 6 February 1951, p. 27.

17 Even in 1900, when only 39 per cent of the very rich were recruited from the upper classes, some 25 per cent of the very rich were economic men of this family-manager type. William Henry Vanderbilt, son of the Commodore and dead by 1900, became a conservative manager of the Vanderbilt enterprises, and, in fact, was head of them when they reached their financial high point. It is, of course, difficult to know whether this was a result of his management – which was neither speculative nor extravagant – or a result of objective changes resulting in the increased value of railroad securities. The indolence of his sons, who spent more time in Europe

playing a game of fashion, was perhaps less a cause of the relative decline of the Vanderbilt fortune than the down-swing of the railroad economy. Cf. Wayne Andrews, *The Vanderbilt Legend*, New York: Harcourt, Brace, 1941. George D. Widener, son of P. A. B. Widener, became a stockholder in 23 companies and was president and director of 18. He was an active type of economic man in that he was involved in 1902 in a suit for fraud for praising a weak company so that he could sell his stock in it and get out before it failed. Cf. *Philadelphia Public Ledger*, 2 April 1912 and *Philadelphia Press*, 23 September 1902.

Of the modern-day family managers there is, for instance, Vincent Astor – the great-grandson of John Jacob Astor – who may be an enthusiast for yachting and automobile racing, but he disappointed society editors in their search for the idle life of scandal when, at the death of his father, he quit Harvard and, at the age of 21, began to improve the value of the Astor land in New York City. Young Vincent changed the management policy by abolishing many tenements and attempting to bring middle and upper-class clientele to Astor land, thus, of course, increasing its value to him. Cf. Harvey O'Connor, *The Astors*, New York: Knopf, 1941, p. 336. And the daily decisions of John D. Rockefeller III involve the disposition of millions of dollars; he has a full-time job for which he was trained: philanthropic work on an international scope. Moreover, he has been active as a director in many American corporations, including the New York Life Insurance Company and the Chase National Bank.

18   See *The New York Times*, 1 August 1954, pp. 1, 7.
19   On the vicious circle of poverty and the withdrawal from success, see Mills, *White Collar* (New York: Oxford University Press, 1951), pp. 259 ff.
20   See Myers, *History of the Great American Fortunes*, pp. 634 ff.; Lewis Corey, *The House of Morgan* (New York: G. Howard Watt, 1930); and John K. Winkler, *Morgan the Magnificent* (New York: The Vanguard Press, 1930).
21   See Harvey O'Connor, *How Mellon Got Rich* (New York: International Pamphlets, 1933) and *Mellon's Millions* (New York: John Day, 1933); Frank R. Denton, *The Mellons of Pittsburgh* (New York: Newcomen Society of England, American Branch, 1948); and *The New York Times*, 30 August 1937, p. 16.
22   Quoted in *Time*, 1 June 1953, p. 38.
23   See *The New York Times*, 2 February 1944, p. 15.
24   See *The New York Times*, 7 June 1948, p. 19.
25   See Wallace Davis, *Corduroy Road* (Houston: Anson Jones Press, 1951).

See also the testimony of James D. Stietenroth, former chief financial officer of the Mississippi Power & Light Co., in regard to the Dixon-Yates contract, reported in the Interim Report of the Subcommittee of the Committee on the Judiciary on Antitrust and Monopoly on Investigation Into Monopoly in the Power Industry, *Monopoly in the Power Industry*, U.S. Senate, 83d Congress, 2nd Session (Washington, D.C., U.S. Government Printing Office, 1955), pp. 12 ff.

26   Cf. Frederick Lewis Allen, *The Lords of Creation*, p. 85.

14

Bobos in Paradise: The New Upper Class and How They Got There

David Brooks

David Brooks is a senior editor at the *Weekly Standard*, a contributing editor at *Newsweek*, a correspondent for the *Atlantic Monthly* and a commentator on National Public Radio and the *NewsHour with Jim Lehrer*. He was formerly a reporter and editor at the *Wall Street Journal*. He writes often about the intersection of culture and economics in American life and is the author of the book *Bobos in Paradise: The New Upper Class and How They Got There*.

Without much fuss or public discussion, the admissions officers wrecked the WASP establishment. The story at Harvard, told by Richard Herrnstein and Charles Murray in the relatively uncontroversial first chapter of *The Bell Curve*, epitomizes the tale. In 1952 most freshmen at Harvard were products of the same WASP bastions that popped up on the *Times* weddings page: the prep schools in New England (Andover and Exeter alone contributed 10 percent of the class), the East Side of Manhattan, the Main Line of Philadelphia, Shaker Heights in Ohio, the Gold Coast of Chicago, Grosse Pointe of Detroit, Nob Hill in San Francisco, and so on. Two-thirds of all applicants were admitted. Applicants whose fathers had gone to Harvard had a 90 percent admission rate. The average verbal SAT score for the incoming men was 583, good but not stratospheric. The average score across the Ivy League was closer to 500 at the time.

Then came the change. By 1960 the average verbal SAT score for incoming freshmen at Harvard was 678, and the math score was 695 – these are stratospheric scores. The average Harvard freshman in 1952 would have placed in the bottom 10 percent of the Harvard freshman class of 1960. Moreover, the 1960 class was drawn from a much wider socioeconomic pool. Smart kids from Queens or Iowa or California, who wouldn't have thought of applying to Harvard a decade earlier, were applying and getting accepted. Harvard had transformed itself from a school catering mostly to the northeastern social elite to a high-powered school reaching more of the brightest kids around the country. And this transformation was replicated in almost all elite schools. At Princeton in 1962, for example, only 10 members of the 62-man football team had attended private prep schools. Three decades earlier every member of the Princeton team was a prep school boy.

Why did this happen? Nicholas Lemann provides the guts of the answer in his book *The Big Test*. It's a remarkable story, because in many ways the WASP elite destroyed itself, and did so for the highest of motives. James Bryant Conant was president of Harvard after World War II, and so sat at the pinnacle of the Protestant Establishment. Nonetheless, Conant was alarmed by the thought that America might develop a hereditary aristocracy consisting of exactly the sort of well-bred young men he was training in Cambridge. Conant dreamed of replacing this elite with a new elite, which would be based on merit. He didn't envision a broad educated populace making democratic decisions. Rather, he hoped to select out a small class of Platonic guardians who would be trained at elite universities and who would then devote themselves selflessly to public service.

To help find these new guardians, Conant enlisted Henry Chauncey, a graduate of Groton and Harvard, an Episcopalian, a descendant of Puritan stock. Chauncey didn't have Conant's grand vision of what society should look like, but he did have a more distilled passion – for standardized tests and the glorious promise of social science. Chauncey was an enthusiast for tests the way other technoenthusiasts have fallen in love with the railroad, or nuclear power, or the Internet. He believed tests were a magnificent tool that would enable experts to measure people's abilities and manage society on a more just and rational basis. Chauncey went on to become the head of the Educational Testing Service, which created the Scholastic Aptitude Test. And so to a degree rare among social engineers, he was actually able to put his enthusiasm into practice. As Lemann observes, we are now living in a world created by Conant and Chauncey's campaign to replace their own elite with an elite based on merit, at least as measured by aptitude tests.

Conant and Chauncey came along during an era uniquely receptive to their message. The American intellectual class has probably never been so sure of itself, before or since. Sociologists, psychologists, and macro-economists thought they had discovered the tools to solve personal and social problems. Freud's writings, which promised to explain the inner workings of the human mind, were at the peak of their influence. The McCarthy controversy mobilized segments of the intellectual class. The launching of Sputnik made educational rigor seem vital to the national interest. Finally, John F. Kennedy brought intellectuals into the White House, elevating intellectuals into the social stratosphere (at least many of them thought so).

Conant and Chauncey were not the only academics who rose up to assert intellectual values against those of the WASP Establishment. In 1956 C. Wright Mills wrote *The Power Elite*, a direct assault on the establishment if ever there was one. In 1959 Jacques Barzun wrote *The House of Intellect*. In 1963 Richard Hofstadter wrote *Anti-Intellectualism in American Life*, a sprawling, confident broadside by an academic superstar against the "practical" classes, both rich and poor. In 1964 Digby Baltzell, of the University of Pennsylvania, wrote *The Protestant Establishment*, a book that introduced the term WASP and detailed the establishment's intellectual and moral failings. Though largely sympathetic to WASP ideals, he argued that the WASP elite had become a self-satisfied caste that was unwilling to bring in enough new talent to replenish the ranks. By and large, these academics wanted the universities to serve as meritocratic and intellectual hothouses, not as finishing schools for the social elite. Faculty members demanded that admissions officers look at the legacy applications more critically.

The WASPs had fended off challenges to their cultural hegemony before, either by simply ignoring them or by counterattacking. The first half of the century brought what historian Michael Knox Beran calls the "risorgimento of the well-to-do." Families like the Roosevelts adopted a tough, manly ethos in order to restore vigor and self-confidence to the East Coast elite and so preserve its place atop the power structure. In the 1920s, sensing a threat to the "character" of their institutions, Ivy League administrators tightened their official or unofficial Jewish quotas. Nicholas Murray Butler at Columbia reduced the proportion of Jews at his school from 40 to 20 percent in two years. At Harvard, President A. Lawrence Lowell diagnosed a "Jewish Problem" and also enforced quotas to help solve it. But by the late fifties and early sixties, the WASPs could no longer justify such discrimination to others or to themselves. John F. Kennedy's chief of protocol, Angier Biddle Duke, was forced to resign from his favorite men's club, the Metropolitan Club in Washington, because it was restricted.

History, as Pareto once remarked, is the graveyard of aristocracies, and by the late fifties and early sixties the WASP Establishment had no faith in the code – and the social restrictions – that had sustained it. Maybe its members just lost the will to fight for their privileges. As the writer David Frum theorizes, it had been half a century since the last great age of fortune making. The great families were into at least their third genteel generation. Perhaps by then there wasn't much vigor left. Or perhaps it was the Holocaust that altered the landscape by discrediting the sort of racial restrictions that the Protestant Establishment was built on.

In any case, in 1964 Digby Baltzell astutely perceived the crucial trends. "What seems to be happening," he wrote in *The Protestant Establishment*, "is that a scholarly hierarchy of campus communities governed by the values of admissions committees is gradually supplanting the class hierarchies of local communities which are still governed by the values of parents. . . . Just as the hierarchy of the Church was the main avenue of advancement for the talented and ambitious youth from the lower orders during the medieval period, and just as the business enterprise was responsible for the nineteenth century rags-to-riches dream (when we were predominantly an Anglo-Saxon country), so the campus community has now become the principal guardian of our traditional opportunitarian ideals."

The campus gates were thus thrown open on the basis of brains rather than blood, and within a few short years the university landscape was transformed. Harvard, as we've seen, was changed from a school for the well-connected to a school for brainy strivers. The remaining top schools eliminated their Jewish quotas and eventually dropped their restrictions on women. Furthermore, the sheer numbers of educated Americans exploded. The portion of Americans going to college had been rising steadily throughout the 20th century, but between 1955 and 1974 the growth rate was off the charts. Many of the new students were women. Between 1950 and 1960 the number of female students increased by 47 percent. It then jumped by an additional 168 percent between 1960 and 1970. Over the following decades the student population kept growing and growing. In 1960 there were about 2,000 institutions of higher learning. By 1980 there were 3,200. In 1960 there were 235,000 professors in the United States. By 1980 there were 685,000.

Before this period, in other words, the WASP elites dominated prestige education and made up a significant chunk of all the college-educated population. By the end of this period, the well-bred WASPs no longer dominated the prestige schools and they made up just an infinitesimal slice of the educated class. The elite schools had preserved their status. The proportion of Ivy League graduates in *Who's Who* has remained virtually constant throughout the past 40 years. But the schools maintained their dominance by throwing over the mediocrities from the old WASP families and bringing in less well connected meritocrats.

The rapid expansion of the educated class was bound to have as profound an impact on America as rapid urbanization has had on other countries at other moments in history. By the mid-1960s the middle-aged WASPs still wielded some authority in the corporate world. They still possessed enormous social and political prestige, not to mention financial capital. But on campus they had been overrun. Imagine now you are a young meritocrat, the child of, say, a pharmacist and an elementary school teacher, accepted to a prestigious university in the mid-sixties. You are part of a huge cohort of education arrivistes. Your campus still has some of the aristocratic trappings of the WASP culture, though it is by now a little embarrassed by them. And as you look out into the world, you see the last generation of the Old Guard – still holding key jobs and social authority. They are in the positions of power and prestige you hope to occupy. But they are still living by an ethos you consider obsolete, stifling, and prejudiced. Among other things, that ethos, which emphasizes birth and connections, blocks your ascent. Naturally, you and your many peers, even if you do not think about it deliberately, are going to try to finish off the old regime. You are going to try to destroy what is left of the WASP ethos and replace it with your own ethos, which is based on individual merit.

More broadly, you are going to try to change the social character of the nation. The rise of the meritocrats produced a classic revolution of rising expectations. Tocqueville's principle of revolutions proved true: as social success seems more possible for a rising group, the remaining hindrances seem more and more intolerable. The social revolution of the late sixties was not a miracle or a natural disaster, the way it is sometimes treated by writers on the left and right. It was a logical response to the trends of the crucial years between 1955 and 1965. The components of elite status were due to change. The culture of upscale America was due for a revolution.

The Sixties

"How's our award-winning scholar?" one of the overbearing adults asks the Dustin Hoffman character, Ben, as he comes downstairs in the first scene in *The Graduate*. Mike Nichols's movie, which was the top money-making film of 1968, is about an introspective college graduate who has just come back to a rich white suburb in California after finishing a lavishly successful stint at an East Coast school. He realizes, to his horror, the immense cultural gulf between his parents and himself. As Baltzell had anticipated, campus values displaced parental values. In that famous first scene, Ben is cooed over and passed around like a conquering hero by a group of gladhanding, loud-talking WASP elders. Hoffman's face is an oasis of calm amid a riot of Dale Carnegie bonhomie. There's plenty of cocktail party jollity. His mother starts reading out his college accomplishments from the class yearbook. And one of the smug moguls pulls him out to the pool, extends a cloak of self-importance, and tells him that the future is in plastics – a scene that brutally exemplifies the cultural decay of the old order. Millionaire moviemakers tend to be merciless when depicting millionaire businessmen and lawyers, and *The Graduate* casts an unpitying eye on the life of the Protestant elite: the lavish wet bars, the monogrammed golf clothes, the gold watches, the white furniture against white walls, the shallowness and hypocrisy, and in the form of Mrs. Robinson, their lives of cocktail-soaked desperation. Ben doesn't know what he wants out of life, but he is certain he doesn't want *that*.

In Charles Webb's original novel, the character of Ben Braddock is a six-foot-tall, blue-eyed blond. Mike Nichols first imagined Robert Redford in the role. That casting would have better explained why Mrs. Robinson is sexually attracted to Ben, but it probably would have ruined the picture's prospects. Who wants to identify with a mopey, blue-eyed, blond Adonis? But Hoffman is a sensitive soul, not an Aryan Dick Diver type. So he perfectly represented all the new ethnic strivers who were suddenly pouring through the colleges, facing life in the affluent suburbs, and finding it arid and stifling.

The educated-class rebellion we call "the sixties" was about many things, some of them important and related to the Civil Rights movement and Vietnam, some of them entirely silly, and others, like the sexual revolution, overblown (actual sexual behavior was affected far more by the world wars than by the Woodstock era). But at its core the cultural radicalism of the sixties was a challenge to conventional notions of success. It was not only a political effort to dislodge the establishment from the seats of power. It was a cultural effort by the rising members of the privileged classes to destroy whatever prestige still attached to the WASP lifestyle and the WASP moral code, and to replace the old order with a new social code that would celebrate spiritual and intellectual ideals. The sixties radicals rejected the prevailing definition of accomplishment, the desire to keep up with the Joneses, the prevailing idea of social respectability, the idea that a successful life could be measured by income, manners, and possessions. The educated baby boomers of the 1960s wanted to take the things the Protestant elite regarded as high status and make them low status. The demographic shifts of the 1950s led to the cultural conflicts of the 1960s. Or, as the endlessly impressive Digby Baltzell prophesied in *The Protestant Establishment*: "The economic reforms of one generation tend to produce status conflicts in the next."

What exactly would the sixties student leaders hate about the *New York Times* weddings page of 1959? It's worth making a short list here because the habits of thought that were established when the educated class was in its radical stage continue to influence its thinking now in its hour of supremacy. The student radicals would have detested the couples displayed on the weddings page for what was *perceived* to be their conformity, their formality, their traditionalism, their carefully defined gender roles, their ancestor worship, their privilege, their

unabashed elitism, their unreflective lives, their self-satisfaction, their reticence, their contented affluence, their coldness.

We'll go into greater detail about all these cultural shifts in the pages that follow, but to put it bluntly, the radicals of the 1960s favored bohemian self-expression and despised the earlier elite for its arid self-control. And their effort to tear down the old customs and habits of the previous elite was not achieved without social cost. Old authorities and restraints were delegitimized. There was a real, and to millions of people catastrophic, breakdown in social order, which can be measured in the stunning rise in divorce, crime, drug use, and illegitimacy rates.

And Then Comes Money

The hardest of the hard-core sixties radicals believed the only honest way out was to reject the notion of success altogether: drop out of the rat race, retreat to small communities where real human relationships would flourish. But that sort of utopianism was never going to be very popular, especially among college grads. Members of the educated class prize human relationships and social equality, but as for so many generations of Americans before them, achievement was really at the core of the sixties grads' value system. They were meritocrats, after all, and so tended to define themselves by their accomplishments. Most of them were never going to drop out or sit around in communes smelling flowers, raising pigs, and contemplating poetry. Moreover, as time went by, they discovered that the riches of the universe were lying at their feet.

At first, when the great hump of baby boom college graduates entered the workforce, having a college degree brought few financial rewards or dramatic life changes. As late as 1976, the labor economist Richard Freeman could write a book called *The Overeducated American*, arguing that higher education didn't seem to be paying off in the marketplace. But the information age kicked in, and the rewards for education grew and grew. In 1980, according to labor market specialist Kevin Murphy of the University of Chicago, college graduates earned roughly 35 percent more than high school graduates. But by the mid-1990s, college graduates were earning 70 percent more than high school graduates, and those with graduate degrees were earning 90 percent more. The wage value of a college degree had doubled in 15 years.

The rewards for intellectual capital have increased while the rewards for physical capital have not. That means that even liberal arts majors can wake up one day and find themselves suddenly members of the top-income brackets. A full professor at Yale who renounced the capitalist rat race finds himself making, as of 1999, $113,100, while a professor at Rutgers pulls in $103,700 and superstar professors, who become the object of academic bidding wars, now can rake in more than $300,000 a year. Congressional and presidential staffers top out at $125,000 (before quintupling that when they enter the private sector), and the journalists at national publications can now count on six-figure salaries when they hit middle age, not including lecture fees. Philosophy and math majors head for Wall Street and can make tens of millions of dollars from their quantitative models. America has always had a lot of lawyers, and now the median income for that burgeoning group is $72,500, while income for the big-city legal grinds can reach seven figures. And super-students still flood into medicine – three-quarters of private practitioners net more than $100,000. Meanwhile, in Silicon Valley there are more millionaires than people. In Hollywood television scriptwriters make $11,000 to $13,000 a week. And in New York top magazine editors, like Anna Wintour of *Vogue*, make $1 million a year, which is slightly more than the head of the Ford Foundation. And these dazzling incomes flow not only to the baby boomers, who might still find them surprising, but to all the subsequent generations of college graduates as well, most of whom have never known a world without $4 million artists' lofts, $350-a-night edgy hotels, avant-garde summer homes, and the rest of the accoutrements of the countercultural plutocracy.

The information age has produced entirely new job categories, some of which seem like practical jokes, though you wouldn't know it from the salaries: creativity officer, chief knowledge officer, team spirit coordinator. Then there are the jobs that nobody dreamed of in high school: Web page designer, patent agent, continuity writer, foundation program officer, talk show booker, and on and on. The economy in this era is such that oddballs like Oliver Stone become multimillionaire moguls and slouchy dropouts like Bill Gates get to run the world. Needless to say, there are still gypsy scholars scraping by while looking for a tenure-track position, and there are still poor saps in the publishing industry parlaying their intelligence into obscenely small paychecks. But the whole thrust of the information age has been to reward education and widen the income gap between the educated and the uneducated. Moreover, the upper middle class has grown from a small appendage of the middle class into a distinct demographic hump populated largely by people with fancy degrees. Within a few years, barring a severe economic downturn, there will be 10 million American households with incomes over $100,000 a year, up from only 2 million in 1982. Consider the cultural and financial capital of that large group, and you begin to appreciate the social power of the upper middle class. Many of the members of the educated elite didn't go out hungry for money. But money found them. And subtly, against their will, it began to work its way into their mentality.

The members of the educated elite find they must change their entire attitude first toward money itself. When they were poor students, money was a solid. It came in a chunk with every paycheck, and they would gradually chip little bits off to pay the bills.

They could sort of feel how much money they had in their bank account, the way you can feel a pile of change in your pocket. But as they became more affluent, money turned into a liquid. It flows into the bank account in a prodigious stream. And it flows out just as quickly. The earner is reduced to spectator status and is vaguely horrified by how quickly the money is flowing through. He or she may try to stem the outward flow in order to do more saving. But it's hard to know where to erect the dam. The money just flows on its own. And after a while one's ability to stay afloat through all the ebbs and flows becomes a sign of accomplishment in itself. The big money stream is another aptitude test. Far from being a source of corruption, money turns into a sign of mastery. It begins to seem deserved, natural. So even former student radicals begin to twist the old left-wing slogan so that it becomes: From each according to his abilities, to each according to his abilities.

The educated elites not only earn far more money than they ever thought they would but now occupy positions of enormous responsibility. We're by now all familiar with modern-day executives who have moved from SDS to CEO, from LSD to IPO. Indeed, sometimes you get the impression the Free Speech movement produced more corporate executives than Harvard Business School.

What's more amazing is the growth of lucrative industries in which everybody involved is a member of the educated class. Only about 20 percent of the adult population of America possesses a college degree, but in many large cities and suburban office parks, you can walk from office to office, for mile upon mile, and almost everybody in the place will have a sheepskin in the drawer. Educated elites have taken over much of the power that used to accrue to sedate old WASPs with dominating chins. Economists at the International Monetary Fund jet around the world reshaping macroeconomic policies. Brainiacs at McKinsey & Company swoop down on corporate offices run by former college quarterbacks and issue reports on how to merge or restructure.

The educated elites have even taken over professions that used to be working class. The days of the hard-drinking blue-collar journalist, for example, are gone forever. Now if you cast your eye down a row at a Washington press conference, it's: Yale, Yale, Stanford, Emory, Yale, and Harvard. Political parties, which were once run by immigrant hacks, are now dominated by communications analysts with Ph.D.s. If you drive around the old suburbs and follow the collarless-shirt bohemians home from their organic fruit stands, you notice they have literally moved into the houses of the old stockbroker elite. They are sleeping in the old elite's beds. They are swamping the old elite's institutions. As the novelist Louis Auchincloss summarized it, "The old society has given way to the society of accomplishment." Dumb good-looking people with great parents have been displaced by smart, ambitious, educated, and antiestablishment people with scuffed shoes.

The Anxieties of Abundance

Over the past 30 years, in short, the educated class has gone from triumph to triumph. They have crushed the old WASP elite culture, thrived in an economy that lavishly rewards their particular skills, and now sit atop many of the same institutions they once railed against. But all this has created a gnawing problem. How do they make sure they haven't themselves become self-satisfied replicas of the WASP elite they still so forcefully denounce?

Those who want to win educated-class approval must confront the anxieties of abundance: how to show – not least to themselves – that even while climbing toward the top of the ladder they have not become all the things they still profess to hold in contempt. How to navigate the shoals between their affluence and their self-respect. How to reconcile their success with their spirituality, their elite status with their egalitarian ideals. Socially enlightened members of the educated elite tend to be disturbed by the widening gap between rich and poor and are therefore made somewhat uncomfortable by the fact that their own family income now tops $80,000. Some of them dream of social justice yet went to a college where the tuition costs could feed an entire village in Rwanda for a year. Some once had "Question Authority" bumper stickers on their cars but now find themselves heading start-up software companies with 200 people reporting to them. The sociologists they read in college taught that consumerism is a disease, and yet now they find themselves shopping for $3,000 refrigerators. They took to heart the lessons of *Death of a Salesman*, yet now find themselves directing a sales force. They laughed at the plastics scene in *The Graduate* but now they work for a company that manufactures . . . plastic. Suddenly they find themselves moving into a suburban house with a pool and uncomfortable about admitting it to their bohemian friends still living downtown.

Though they admire art and intellect, they find themselves living amidst commerce, or at least in that weird hybrid zone where creativity and commerce intersect. This class is responsible for more yards of built-in bookshelf space than any group in history. And yet sometimes you look at their shelves and notice deluxe leather-bound editions of all those books arguing that success and affluence is a sham: *Babbitt*, *The Great Gatsby*, *The Power Elite*, *The Theory of the Leisure Class*. This is an elite that has been raised to oppose elites. They are affluent yet opposed to materialism. They may spend their lives selling yet worry about selling out. They are by instinct antiestablishmentarian yet somehow sense they have become a new establishment.

The members of this class are divided against themselves, and one is struck by how much of their time is spent earnestly wrestling with the conflict between their reality and their ideals. They grapple with the trade-offs between equality and privilege ("I believe in public schooling, but the private school just seems better for my kids"), between convenience and social responsibility ("These disposable diapers are an incredible waste of resources, but they are so easy"), between rebellion and convention ("I know I did plenty of drugs in high school, but I tell my kids to Just Say No").

But the biggest tension, to put it in the grandest terms, is between worldly success and inner virtue. How do you move ahead in life without letting ambition wither your soul? How do you accumulate the resources you need to do the things you want without becoming a slave to material things? How do you build a comfortable and stable life for your family without getting bogged down in stultifying routine? How do you live at the top of society without becoming an insufferable snob?

The Reconcilers

These educated elites don't despair in the face of such challenges. They are the Résumé Gods. They're the ones who aced their SATs and succeeded in giving up Merlot during pregnancy. If they are not well equipped to handle the big challenges, no one is. When faced with a tension between competing values, they do what any smart privileged person bursting with cultural capital would do. They find a way to have both. They reconcile opposites.

The grand achievement of the educated elites in the 1990s was to create a way of living that lets you be an affluent success and at the same time a free-spirit rebel. Founding design firms, they find a way to be an artist and still qualify for stock options. Building gourmet companies like Ben & Jerry's or Nantucket Nectars, they've found a way to be dippy hippies and multinational corporate fat cats. Using William S. Burroughs in ads for Nike sneakers and incorporating Rolling Stones anthems into their marketing campaigns, they've reconciled the antiestablishment style with the corporate imperative. Listening to management gurus who tell them to thrive on chaos and unleash their creative potential, they've reconciled the spirit of the imagination with service to the bottom line. Turning university towns like Princeton and Palo Alto into entrepreneurial centers, they have reconciled the highbrow with the high tax bracket. Dressing like Bill Gates in worn chinos on his way to a stockholders' meeting, they've reconciled undergraduate fashion with upper-crust occupations. Going on eco-adventure vacations, they've reconciled aristocratic thrill-seeking with social concern. Shopping at Benetton or the Body Shop, they've brought together consciousness-raising and cost control.

When you are amidst the educated upscalers, you can never be sure if you're living in a world of hippies or stockbrokers. In reality you have entered the hybrid world in which everybody is a little of both.

Marx told us that classes inevitably conflict, but sometimes they just blur. The values of the bourgeois mainstream culture and the values of the 1960s counterculture have merged. That culture war has ended, at least within the educated class. In its place that class has created a third culture, which is a reconciliation between the previous two. The educated elites didn't set out to create this reconciliation. It is the product of millions of individual efforts to have things both ways. But it is now the dominant tone of our age. In the resolution between the culture and the counterculture, it is impossible to tell who co-opted whom, because in reality the bohemians and the bourgeois co-opted each other. They emerge from this process as bourgeois bohemians, or Bobos.

The New Pecking Order

So when the Protestant Establishment collapsed, it is not as if America became a magical place without elites, without hier-

archies, without etiquette and social distinctions. That may have been true during the age of transition. In the 1970s and through part of the 1980s, it really was difficult to pick out a coherent social order. But that fluidity couldn't last – and it's probably a good thing too. Countries need to achieve new states of social equilibrium, and that has now happened to America. New codes are in place that are different from the old codes but serve many of the same social functions of giving order and coherence to life.

American social life, for example, is just as hierarchical as it was in the 1950s, maybe more so. Hierarchies based on connections have given way. Under the code of the meritocrats, people are more likely to be judged by their posts. Invitations to Renaissance weekends, Aspen Institute seminars, Esther Dyson technology conferences, and exclusive private dinners are all determined by what job you have. If you have a prestigious position, your social life is secure. You will find constant validation by surrounding yourself with people as accomplished as or even more accomplished than you are, and you will come to relish what might be called the joy of summits. If you do not, your social life will always have those awkward moments when someone next to you at dinner turns and asks, "What do you do?"

If you are a visiting name professor from Yale freshly arrived on a small campus to give a guest lecture, you will be taken to dinner at the finest restaurant the town has to offer. But if you are a faculty member at Colgate invited to be a guest lecturer, you'll be dining at the home of your host with her kids. If you are an undersecretary in the Justice Department, you will be the keynote lunchtime speaker at various bar association conferences, but if you move on to some lucrative law firm, you will be lucky to serve on one of the end-of-the-day panel discussions. According to the *New York Observer*, former *New Yorker* editor Tina Brown used to throw parties at which top-rank writers and editors were invited to arrive at eight and lower-ranked writers and editors were told to show up at nine-thirty.

Of course, this does not mean those with the biggest offices automatically earn the highest rank. Your career choice has to reflect the twisting demands of the Bobo ethos. In the 1950s the best kind of money to have was inherited money. Today in the Bobo establishment the best kind of money is incidental money. It's the kind of money you just happen to earn while you are pursuing your creative vision. That means the most prestigious professions involve artistic self-expression as well as big bucks. A novelist who makes $1 million a year is far more prestigious than a banker who makes $50 million. A software designer who has stock options in the millions is more prestigious than a real estate developer with holdings in the tens of millions. A newspaper columnist who makes $150,000 a year will get his calls returned more quickly than a lawyer who makes six times that. A restaurant owner with one successful nightspot will be on the receiving end of more cocktail party fawning than a shopping center owner with six huge malls.

This is the age of discretionary income. People are supposed to forgo earnings opportunities in order to lead richer lives. If you have not forgone any earnings, you just can't expect your status to be very high, no matter how much money you've got in the bank. Professors who are good-looking enough to have become newscasters but chose not to are admired and envied more than professors who had no alternative but to go into the academy. People who have made $100 million with purportedly anti-commercial independent movies are more prestigious than people who have made $150 million studio movies. A rock star who goes platinum with a sensitive acoustic album is more admired (and in the long run therefore more bankable) than a rock star who goes double platinum with a regular headbanging album. Media people like Christiane Amanpour and James Rubin will have their wedding featured at the top spot

of the *New York Times* weddings page, whereas ordinary financial analysts will be reduced to paragraph status down below. The guy who dropped out of Harvard to start a software company is asked to give the dinner speech at a grand affair, and sitting next to him will be the Vanderbilt heir who eagerly solicits his attention and has to pay for the dinner.

To calculate a person's status, you take his net worth and multiply it by his antimaterialistic attitudes. A zero in either column means no prestige, but high numbers in both rocket you to the top of the heap. Thus, to be treated well in this world, not only do you have to show some income results; you have to perform a series of feints to show how little your worldly success means to you. You always want to dress one notch lower than those around you. You may want to wear a tattoo or drive a pickup truck or somehow perform some other socially approved act of antistatus deviance. You will devote your conversational time to mocking your own success in a manner that simultaneously displays your accomplishments and your ironic distance from them. You will ceaselessly bash yuppies in order to show that you yourself have not become one. You will talk about your nanny as if she were your close personal friend, as if it were just a weird triviality that you happen to live in a $900,000 Santa Monica house and she takes the bus two hours each day to the barrio. You will want to perfect a code to subtly downplay your academic credentials. If asked where you went to school, you will reply "Harvard?" with a little upward lilt at the end of your pronunciation, as if to imply, "Have you ever heard of it?" When referring to your stint as a Rhodes scholar, you will say, "While I was in England on a program . . ." In Washington I once asked a transplanted Englishman where he went to school and he replied, "A little school near Slough," The village of Slough is a modest little place west of London. The next town over is called Eton.

Class Rank

Nor is it true that the decline of the old WASP code of morality has left America in a moral vacuum. Some people see the decline of the old Protestant Establishment and mourn our losses: no more chivalry, no more of that keen sense of duty and public service, no more gravitas and deference to authority, no more reticence and self-effacement, no more chastity or decorum, no more gentlemen, no more ladies, no more honor and valor. They see the codes and rules that have fallen away and too quickly assume that we have entered a nihilistic age.

In fact, our morals have followed the same cycle of decay and regeneration as our manners. The old Protestant Establishment and its ethical system faded. There was a period of anarchy. But more recently the new educated establishment has imposed its own set of rules. And it is not clear, especially at first glance, which moral framework is more restrictive, the old WASP ethos or the new Bobo one.

These topics are all in front of us. Suffice it to say, this has got to be one of the most anxious social elites ever. We Bobos are not anxious because there is an angry mob outside the gates threatening to send us to the guillotine. There isn't. The educated elite is anxious because its members are torn between their drive to succeed and their fear of turning into sellouts. Furthermore, we are anxious because we do not award ourselves status sinecures. Previous establishments erected social institutions that would give their members security. In the first part of the 20th century, once your family made it into the upper echelons of society, it was relatively easy to stay there. You were invited on the basis of your connections to the right affairs. You were admitted, nearly automatically, to the right schools and considered appropriate for the right spouses. The pertinent question in those circles was not what do you do, but who are you. Once you were established as a Biddle or an Auchincloss or a Venderlip, your way was clear. But members of today's educated class can never be secure about their own future. A career crash could be just around the corner. In the educated class even social life is a series of aptitude tests; we all must perpetually perform in accordance with the shifting norms of propriety, ever advancing signals of cultivation. Reputations can be destroyed by a disgraceful sentence, a lewd act, a run of bad press, or a terrible speech at the financial summit at Davos.

And more important, members of the educated class can never be secure about their children's future. The kids have some domestic and educational advantages – all those tutors and developmental toys – but they still have to work through school and ace the SATs just to achieve the same social rank as their parents. Compared to past elites, little is guaranteed.

The irony is that all this status insecurity only makes the educated class stronger. Its members and their children must constantly be alert, working and achieving. Moreover, the educated class is in no danger of becoming a self-contained caste. Anybody with the right degree, job, and cultural competencies can join. Marx warned that "the more a ruling class is able to assimilate the most prominent men [or women] of the dominated classes, the more stable and dangerous its rule." And in truth it is hard to see how the rule of the meritocrats could ever come to an end. The WASP Establishment fell pretty easily in the 1960s. It surrendered almost without a shot. But the meritocratic Bobo class is rich with the spirit of self-criticism. It is flexible and amorphous enough to co-opt that which it does not already command. The Bobo meritocracy will not be easily toppled, even if some group of people were to rise up and conclude that it should be.

15

The Case of Pullman, Illinois

Michael Walzer

Michael Walzer has written about a wide variety of topics in political theory and moral philosophy: political obligation, just and unjust war, nationalism and ethnicity, economic justice and the welfare state. He has played a part in the revival of a practical, issue-focused ethics and in the development of a pluralist approach to political and moral life. He is currently working on the toleration and accommodation of "difference" in all its forms and also on a (collaborative) project focused on the history of Jewish political thought. He has written over a dozen books, including, *The Revolution of the Saints: A Study in the Origins of Radical Politics* (Harvard University Press, 1965); *Just and Unjust Wars* (Basic Books, 1977); *Spheres of Justice* (Basic Books, 1983); *What It Means to be an American* (Marsillio, 1992); and *On Toleration* (Yale University Press, 1997).

George Pullman was one of the most successful entrepreneurs of late nineteenth century America. His sleeping, dining, and parlor cars made train travel a great deal more comfortable than it had been, and only somewhat more expensive; and on this difference of degree, Pullman established a company and a fortune. When he decided to build a new set of factories and a town around them, he insisted that this was only another business venture. But he clearly had larger hopes: he dreamed of a community without political or economic unrest — happy workers and a strike-free plant.[1] He clearly belongs, then, to the great tradition of the political founder, even though, unlike Solon of Athens, he didn't enact his plans and then go off to Egypt, but stayed on to run the town he had designed. What else could he do, given that he owned the town?

Pullman, Illinois, was built on a little over four thousand acres of land along Lake Calumet just south of Chicago, purchased (in seventy-five individual transactions) at a cost of eight hundred thousand dollars. The town was founded in 1880 and substantially completed, according to a single unified design, within two years. Pullman (the owner) didn't just put up factories and dormitories, as had been done in Lowell, Massachusetts, some fifty years earlier. He built private homes, row houses, and tenements for some seven to eight thousand people, shops and offices (in an elaborate arcade), schools, stables, playgrounds, a market, a hotel, a library, a theater, even a church: in short, a model town, a planned community. And every bit of it belonged to him.

> A stranger arriving at Pullman puts up at a hotel managed by one of Mr. Pullman's employees, visits a theater where all the attendants are in Mr. Pullman's service, drinks water and burns gas which Mr. Pullman's water and gas works supply, hires one of his outfits from the manager of Mr. Pullman's livery stable, visits a school in which the children of Mr. Pullman's employees are taught by other employees, gets a bill charged at Mr. Pullman's bank, is unable to make a purchase of any kind save from some tenant of Mr. Pullman's, and at night he is guarded by a fire department every member of which from the chief down is in Mr. Pullman's service.[2]

This account is from an article in the *New York Sun* (the model town attracted a lot of attention), and it is entirely accurate except for the line about the school. In fact, the schools of Pullman were at least nominally run by the elected school board of Hyde Park Township. The town was also subject to the political jurisdiction of Cook County and the State of Illinois. But there was no municipal government. Asked by a visiting journalist how he "governed" the people of Pullman, Pullman replied, "We govern them in the same way a man governs his house, his store, or his workshop. It is all simple enough."[3] Government was, in his conception, a property right; and despite the editorial "we," this was a right singly held and singly exercised. In his town, Pullman was an autocrat. He had a firm sense of how its inhabitants should live, and he never doubted his right to give that sense practical force. His concern, I should stress, was with the appearance and the behavior of the people, not with their beliefs. "No one was required to subscribe to any set of ideals before moving to [Pullman]." Once there,

however, they were required to live in a certain way. Newcomers might be seen "lounging on their doorsteps, the husband in his shirtsleeves, smoking a pipe, his untidy wife darning, and half-dressed children playing about them." They were soon made aware that this sort of thing was unacceptable. And if they did not mend their ways, "company inspectors visited to threaten fines."[4]

Pullman refused to sell either land or houses – so as to maintain "the harmony of the town's design" and also, presumably, his control over the inhabitants. Everyone who lived in Pullman (Illinois) was a tenant of Pullman (George). Home renovation was strictly controlled; leases were terminable on ten days' notice. Pullman even refused to allow Catholics and Swedish Lutherans to build churches of their own, not because he opposed their worship (they were permitted to rent rooms), but because his conception of the town called for one rather splendid church, whose rent only the Presbyterians could afford. For somewhat different reasons, though with a similar zeal for order, liquor was available only in the town's one hotel, at a rather splendid bar, where ordinary workers were unlikely to feel comfortable.

I have stressed Pullman's autocracy; I could also stress his benevolence. The housing he provided was considerably better than that generally available to American workers in the 1880s; rents were not unreasonable (his profit margins were in fact quite low); the buildings were kept in repair; and so on. But the crucial point is that all decisions, benevolent or not, rested with a man, governor as well as owner, who had not been chosen by the people he governed. Richard Ely, who visited the town in 1885 and wrote an article about it for *Harper's Monthly*, called it "unAmerican . . . benevolent, well-wishing feudalism."[5] But that description wasn't quite accurate, for the men and women of Pullman were entirely free to come and go. They were also free to live outside the town and commute to work in its factories, though in hard times Pullman's tenants were apparently the last to be laid off. These tenants are best regarded as the subjects of a capitalist enterprise that has simply extended itself from manufacturing to real estate and duplicated in the town the discipline of the shop. What's wrong with that?

I mean the question to be rhetorical, but it is perhaps worthwhile spelling out the answer. The inhabitants of Pullman were guest workers, and that is not a status compatible with democratic politics. George Pullman hired himself a metic population in a political community where self-respect was closely tied to citizenship and where decisions about destinations and risks, even (or especially) local destinations and risks, were supposed to be shared. He was, then, more like a dictator than a feudal lord; he ruled by force. The badgering of the townspeople by his inspectors was intrusive and tyrannical and can hardly have been experienced in any other way.

Ely argued that Pullman's ownership of the town made its inhabitants into something less than American citizens: "One feels that one is mingling with a dependent, servile people." Apparently, Ely caught no intimations of the great strike of 1894 or of the courage and discipline of the strikers.[6] He wrote his article early on in the history of the town; perhaps the people needed time to settle in and learn to trust one another before they dared oppose themselves to Pullman's power. But when they did strike, it was as much against his factory power as against his town power. Indeed, Pullman's foremen were even more tyrannical than his agents and inspectors. It seems odd to study the duplicated discipline of the model town and condemn only one half of it. Yet this was the conventional understanding of the time. When the Illinois Supreme Court in 1898 ordered the Pullman Company (George Pullman had died a year earlier) to divest itself of all property not used for manufacturing purposes, it argued that the ownership of a town, but not of a company, "was incompatible with the theory and spirit of our institutions."[7] The town had to be governed democratically – not so much because ownership made the inhabitants servile, but because it forced them to fight for rights they already possessed as American citizens.

It is true that the struggle for rights in the factory was a newer struggle, if only because factories were newer institutions than cities and towns. I want to argue, however, that with regard to political power democratic distributions can't stop at the factory gates. The deep principles are the same for both sorts of institution. This identity is the moral basis of the labor movement – not of "business unionism," which has another basis, but of every demand for progress toward industrial democracy. It doesn't follow from these demands that factories can't be owned; nor did opponents of feudalism say that land couldn't be owned. It's even conceivable that all the inhabitants of a (small) town might pay rent, but not homage, to the same landlord. The issue in all these cases is not the existence but the entailments of property. What democracy requires is that property should have no political currency, that it shouldn't convert into anything like sovereignty, authoritative command, sustained control over men and women. After 1894, at least, most observers seem to have agreed that Pullman's ownership of the town was undemocratic. But was his ownership of the company any different? The unusual juxtaposition of the two makes for a nice comparison.

They are not different because of the entrepreneurial vision, energy, inventiveness, and so on that went into the making of Pullman sleepers, diners, and parlor cars. For these same qualities went into the making of the town. This, indeed, was Pullman's boast: that his "'system' which had succeeded in railroad travel, was now being applied to the problems of labor and housing."[8] And if the application does not give rise to political power in the one case, why should it do so in the other?*

Nor are the two different because of the investment of private capital in the company. Pullman invested in the town, too, without thereby acquiring the right to govern its inhabitants. The case is the same with men and women who buy municipal bonds: they don't come to own the municipality. Unless they live and vote in the town, they cannot even share in decisions about how their money is to be spent. They have no political rights; whereas residents do have rights, whether they are investors or not. There seems no reason not to make the same distinction in economic associations, marking off investors from participants, a just return from political power.

Finally, the factory and the town are not different because men and women come willingly to work in the factory with full knowledge of its rules and regulations. They also come willingly to live in the town, and in neither case do they have full knowledge of the rules until they have some experience of them. Anyway, residence does not constitute an agreement to despotic rules even if the rules are known in advance; nor is prompt departure the only way of expressing opposition. There are, in fact, some associations for which these last propositions might plausibly be reversed. A man who joins a monastic order requiring strict and unquestioning obedience, for example,

seems to be choosing a way of life rather than a place to live (or a place to work). We would not pay him proper respect if we refused to recognize the efficacy of his choice. Its purpose and its moral effect are precisely to authorize his superior's decisions, and he can't withdraw that authority without himself withdrawing from the common life it makes possible. But the same thing can't be said of a man or a woman who joins a company or comes to work in a factory. Here the common life is not so all-encompassing and it does not require the unquestioning acceptance of authority. We respect the new worker only if we assume that he has not sought out political subjection. Of course, he encounters foremen and company police, as he knew he would; and it may be that the success of the enterprise requires his obedience, just as the success of a city or a town requires that citizens obey public officials. But in neither case would we want to say (what we might say to the novice monk): if you don't like these officials and the orders they give, you can always leave. It's important that there be options short of leaving, connected with the appointment of the officials and the making of the rules they enforce.

Other sorts of organizations raise more difficult questions. Consider an example that Marx used in the third volume of *Capital* to illustrate the nature of authority in a communist factory. Cooperative labor requires, he wrote, "one commanding will," and he compared this will to that of an orchestra conductor.[9] The conductor presides over a harmony of sounds and also, Marx seems to have thought, over a harmony of musicians. It is a disturbing comparison, for conductors have often been despots. Should their will be commanding? Perhaps it should, since an orchestra must express a single interpretation of the music it plays. But patterns of work in a factory are more readily negotiated. Nor is it the case that the members of an orchestra must yield to the conductor with regard to every aspect of the life they

* But perhaps it was Pullman's expertise, not his vision, energy, and so on, that justified his autocratic rule. Perhaps factories should be assimilated to the category of disciplinary institutions and run by scientific managers. But the same argument might be made for towns. Indeed, professional managers are often hired by town councils; they are subject, however, to the authority of the elected councilors. Factory managers are subject, though often ineffectively, to the authority of owners. And so the question remains: Why owners rather than workers (or their elected representatives)?

share. They might claim a considerable voice in the orchestra's affairs, even if they accept when they play the conductor's commanding will.

But the members of an orchestra, like the workers in a factory, while they spend a great deal of time with one another, don't live with one another. Perhaps the line between politics and economics has to do with the difference between residence and work. Pullman brought the two together, submitted residents and workers to the same rule. Is it enough if residents rule themselves while only workers are submitted to the power of property, if the residents are citizens and the workers metics? Certainly the self-rule of residents is commonly thought to be a matter of the first importance. That's why a landlord has so much less power over his tenants than a factory owner over his workers. Men and women must collectively control the place where they live in order to be safe in their own homes. *A man's home is his castle.* I will assume that this ancient maxim expresses a genuine moral imperative. But what the maxim requires is not political self-rule so much as the legal protection of the domestic sphere – and not only from economic but also from political interventions. We need a space for withdrawal, rest, intimacy, and (sometimes) solitude. As a feudal baron retired to his castle to brood over public slights, so I retire to my home. But the political community is not a collection of brooding places, or not only that. It is also a common enterprise, a public place where we argue together over the public interest, where we decide on goals and debate acceptable risks. All this was missing in Pullman's model town, until the American Railway Union provided a forum for workers and residents alike.

From this perspective, an economic enterprise seems very much like a town, even though – or, in part, because – it is so unlike a home. It is a place not of rest and intimacy but of cooperative action. It is a place not of withdrawal but of decision. If landlords possessing political power are likely to be intrusive on families, so owners possessing political power are likely to be coercive of individuals. Conceivably the first of these is worse than the second, but this comparison doesn't distinguish the two in any fundamental way; it merely grades them. Intrusiveness and coercion are alike made possible by a deeper reality – the usurpation of a common enterprise, the displacement of collective decision making, by the power of property. And for this, none of the standard justifications seems adequate. Pullman exposed their weaknesses by claiming to rule the town he owned exactly as he ruled the factories he owned. Indeed, the two sorts of rule are similar to one another, and both of them resemble what we commonly understand as authoritarian politics. The right to impose fines does the work of taxation; the right to evict tenants or discharge workers does (some of) the work of punishment. Rules are issued and enforced without public debate by appointed rather than by elected officials. There are no established judicial procedures, no legitimate forms of opposition, no channels for participation or even for protest. If this sort of thing is wrong for towns, then it is wrong for companies and factories, too.

Imagine now a decision by Pullman or his heirs to relocate their factory/town. Having paid off the initial investment, they see richer ground elsewhere; or, they are taken with a new design, a better model for a model town, and want to try it out. The decision, they claim, is theirs alone since the factory/town is theirs alone; neither the inhabitants nor the workers have anything to say. But how can this be right? Surely to uproot a community, to require large-scale migration, to deprive people of homes they have lived in for many years; these are political acts, and acts of a rather extreme sort. The decision is an exercise of power; and were the townspeople simply to submit, we would think they were not self-respecting citizens. What about the workers?

What political arrangements should the workers seek? Political rule implies a certain degree of autonomy, but it's not clear that autonomy is possible in a single factory or even in a group of factories. The citizens of a town are also the consumers of the goods and services the town provides; and except for occasional visitors, they are the only consumers. But workers in a factory are producers of goods and services; they are only sometimes consumers, and they are never the only consumers. Moreover, they are locked into close economic relationships with other factories that they supply or on whose products they depend. Private owners relate to one another through the market. In theory, economic decisions are non-political, and they are coordinated without the interventions of authority. Insofar as this theory is true, worker cooperatives would simply locate themselves within the network of market relations. In fact, however, the theory misses both the collusions of owners among themselves and their collective ability to call upon the support of state officials. Now the appropriate replacement is an industrial democracy organized at national as well as local levels. But how, precisely, can power be distributed so as to take into account both the necessary autonomy and the practical linkage of companies and factories? The question is often raised and variously answered in the literature on workers' control. I shall not attempt to answer it again, nor do I mean to deny its difficulties; I only want to insist that the sorts of arrangements required in an industrial democracy are not all that different from those required in a political democracy. Unless they are independent states, cities and towns are never fully autonomous; they have no absolute authority even over the goods and services they produce for internal consumption. In the United States today, we enmesh them in a federal structure and regulate what they can do in the areas of education, criminal justice, environmental use, and so on. Factories and companies would have to be similarly enmeshed and similarly regulated (and they would also be taxed). In a developed economy, as in a

developed polity, different decisions would be made by different groups of people at different levels of organization. The division of power in both these cases is only partly a matter of principle; it is also a matter of circumstance and expediency.

The argument is similar with regard to the constitutional arrangements within factories and companies. There will be many difficulties working these out; there will be false starts and failed experiments exactly as there have been in the history of cities and towns. Nor should we expect to find a single appropriate arrangement. Direct democracy, proportional representation, single-member constituencies, mandated and independent representatives, bicameral and unicameral legislatures, city managers, regulatory commissions, public corporations – political decision making is organized and will continue to be organized in many different ways. What is important is that we know it to be political, the exercise of power, not the free use of property.

Today, there are many men and women who preside over enterprises in which hundreds and thousands of their fellow citizens are involved, who direct and control the working lives of their fellows, and who explain themselves exactly as George Pullman did. I govern these people, they say, in the same way a man governs the things he owns. People who talk this way are wrong. They misunderstand the prerogatives of ownership (and of foundation, investment, and risk taking). They claim a kind of power to which they have no right.

To say this is not to deny the importance of entrepreneurial activity. In both companies and towns, one looks for people like Pullman, full of energy and ideas, willing to innovate and take risks, capable of organizing large projects. It would be foolish to create a system that did not bring them forward. They are of no use to us if they just brood in their castles. But there is nothing they do that gives them a right to rule over the rest of us, unless they can win our agreement. At a certain point in the development of an enterprise, then, it must pass out of entrepreneurial control; it must be organized or reorganized in some political way, according to the prevailing (democratic) conception of how power ought to be distributed. It is often said that economic entrepreneurs won't come forward if they cannot hope to own the companies they found. But this is like saying that no one would seek divine grace or knowledge who did not hope to come into hereditary possession of a church or "holy commonwealth," or that no one would found new hospitals or experimental schools who did not intend to pass them on to his children, or that no one would sponsor political innovation and reform unless it were possible to own the state. But ownership is not the goal of political or religious life, and there are still attractive and even compelling goals. Indeed, had Pullman founded a better town, he might have earned for himself the sort of public honor that men and women have sometimes taken as the highest end of human action. If he wanted power as well, he should have run for mayor.

NOTES

1   Stanley Buder, *Pullman: An Experiment in Industrial Order and Community Planning, 1880–1930* (New York, 1967).

2   Ibid., pp. 98–9.

3   Ibid., p. 107.

4   Ibid., p. 95; see also William M. Carwardine, *The Pullman Strike*, intro. Virgil J. Vogel, (Chicago, 1973), chaps. 8, 9, 10.

5   Richard Ely, quoted in Buder, *Pullman* [17], p. 103.

6   Ibid.; see also Carwardine, *Pullman Strike* [20], chap. 4.

7   Carwardine, *Pullman Strike* [20], p. xxxiii.

8   Buder, *Pullman* [17], p. 44.

9   Karl Marx, *Capital* (New York, 1967), vol. III, pp. 383, 386. Lenin repeats the argument, suggesting "the mild leadership of a conductor of an orchestra" as an example of communist authority; see "The Immediate Tasks of the Soviet Government," in *Selected Works* (New York, n.d.), vol. VII, p. 342.

Part IV

Lifestyles of the Poor and Anonymous

16

Swapping

Carol Stack

Carol Stack is a professor of education at the University of California at Berkeley; she uses an anthropological perspective to research rural and urban poverty, child and family policy, gender, work and identity, and migration. She is most notably the author of *All Our Kin: Strategies for Survival in a Black Community*. She teaches in the Women's Studies Department and the Graduate School of Education and has served as the Chancellor's Assistant on the Status of Women, writing a report on pay and promotion differentials between male and female faculty members. She has been a Guggenheim Fellow and a Fellow of the Center for Advanced Study in the Behavioral Sciences. She is also working on a book about the labor force, entitled, *Why Work? The Meaning and Dignity of Work in the Lives of Minority Youth.*

Ruby Banks took a cab to visit Virginia Thomas, her baby's aunt, and they swapped some hot corn bread and greens for diapers and milk. In the cab going home Ruby said to me, "I don't believe in putting myself on nobody, but I know I need help every day. You can't get help just by sitting at home, laying around, house-nasty and everything. You got to get up and go out and meet people, because the very day you go out, that first person you meet may be the person that can help you get the things you want. I don't believe in begging, but I believe that people should help one another. I used to wish for lots of things like a living room suite, clothes, nice clothes, stylish clothes – I'm sick of wearing the same pieces. But I can't, I can't help myself because I have my children and I love them and I have my

mother and all our kin. Sometimes I don't have a damn dime in my pocket, not a crying penny to get a box of paper diapers, milk, a loaf of bread. But you have to have help from everybody and anybody, so don't turn no one down when they come round for help."

Black families living in The Flats need a steady source of cooperative support to survive. They share with one another because of the urgency of their needs. Alliances between individuals are created around the clock as kin and friends exchange and give and obligate one another. They trade food stamps, rent money, a TV, hats, dice, a car, a nickel here, a cigarette there, food, milk, grits, and children.

Few if any black families living on welfare for the second generation are able to accumulate a surplus of the basic necessities to be able to remove themselves from poverty or from the collective demands of kin. Without the help of kin, fluctuations in the meager flow of available goods could easily destroy a family's ability to survive (Lombardi 1973). Kin and close friends who fall into similar economic crises know that they may share the food, dwelling, and even the few scarce luxuries of those individuals in their kin network. Despite the relatively high cost of rent and food in urban black communities, the collective power within kin-based exchange networks keeps people from going hungry.

As low-skilled workers, the urban poor in The Flats cannot earn sufficient wages and cannot produce goods. Consequently, they cannot legitimately draw desired scarce goods into the community. Welfare benefits which barely provide the necessities of life – a bed, rent, and food – are allocated to households of women and children and are channeled into domestic networks of men, women, and children. All essential resources flow from families into kin networks.

Whether one's source of income is a welfare check or wages from labor, people in The Flats borrow and trade with others in order to obtain daily necessities. The most important form of distribution and exchange of the limited resources available to the poor in The Flats is by means of trading, or what people usually call "swapping." As people swap, the limited supply of finished material goods in the community is perpetually redistributed among networks of kinsmen and throughout the community.

The resources, possessions, and services exchanged between individuals residing in The Flats are intricately interwoven. People exchange various objects generously: new things, treasured items, furniture, cars, goods that are perishable, and services which are exchanged for child care, residence, or shared meals. Individuals enlarge their web of social relations through repetitive and seemingly habitual instances of swapping. Lily Jones, a resident in The Flats, had this to say about swapping, "That's just everyday life, swapping. You not really getting ahead of nobody, you just get better things as they go back and forth."

The Obligation to Give

"Trading" in The Flats generally refers to any object or service offered with the intent of obligating. An object given or traded represents a possession, a pledge, a loan, a trust, a bank account – given on the condition that something will be returned, that the giver can draw on the account, and that the initiator of the trade gains prerogatives in taking what he or she needs from the receiver.

Mauss's (1954) classic interpretation of gift exchange in primitive societies stresses the essence of obligation in gift giving, receiving, and repaying. A gift received is not owned and sometimes can be reclaimed by the initiator of the swap. A person who gives something which the receiver needs or desires, gives under a voluntary guise. But the offering is essentially obligatory, and in The Flats, the obligation to repay carries kin and community sanctions.

An individual's reputation as a potential partner in exchange is created by the opinions others have about him (Bailey 1971). Individuals who fail to reciprocate in swapping relationships are judged harshly. Julia Rose, a twenty-five-year-old mother of three, critically evaluated her cousin Mae's reputation, "If someone who takes things from me ain't giving me anything in return, she can't get nothing else. When someone like that, like my cousin Mae, comes to my house and says, 'Ooo, you should give me that chair, honey. I can use it in my living room, and my old man would just love to sit on it,' well, if she's like my cousin, you don't care what her old man wants, you satisfied with what yours wants. Some people like my cousin don't mind borrowing from anybody, but she don't loan you no money, her clothes, nothing. Well, she ain't shit. She don't believe in helping nobody and lots of folks gossip about her. I'll never give her nothing again. One time I went over there after I had given her all these things and I asked her, 'How about loaning me an outfit to wear?' She told me, 'Girl, I ain't got nothing. I ain't got nothing clean. I just put my clothes in the cleaners, and what I do have you can't wear 'cause it's too small for you.' Well, lots of people talks about someone who acts that way."

Degrees of entanglement among kinsmen and friends involved in networks of exchange differ in kind from casual swapping. Those actively involved in domestic networks swap goods and services on a daily, practically an hourly, basis. Ruby Banks, Magnolia Waters' twenty-three-year-old daughter, portrays her powerful sense of obligation to her mother in her words, "She's my mother and I don't want to turn her down." Ruby has a conflicting sense of obligation and of sacrifice toward her mother and her kinsmen.

"I swap back and forth with my mother's family. She wouldn't want nobody else to know how much I'm doing for her, but hell, that's money out of my pocket. We swap back and forth, food stamps, kids, clothes, money, and everything else. Last month the AFDC people had sent me forty dollars to get a couch. Instead of me getting a couch, I took my money over to Mama's and divided with her. I gave her fifteen dollars of it and went on to wash because my kids didn't have a piece clean. I was washing with my hands and a bar of face soap before the money come. I took all the clothes I had, most of the dirty ones I could find, and washed them. It ran me up to six dollars and something with the cab that my sister took back home. I was sitting over at the laundry worrying that Mama didn't have nothing to eat. I took a cab over there and gave her ten more dollars. All I had left to my name was ten dollars to pay on my couch, get food, wash, and everything. But I ignored my problems and gave Mama the money I had. She didn't really

have nothing after she paid some bills. She was over there black and blue from not eating – stomach growling. The craziest thing was that she wouldn't touch the rent money. I gave the last five dollars out of the rent money. She paid her sister her five and gave me five to get the kids something to eat. I said, 'What about my other ten?', but she put me off. She paid everybody else and I'm the one who's helping her the most. I could have most everything I needed if I didn't have to divide with my people. But they be just as poor as me, and I don't want to turn them down."

Close kin who have relied upon one another over the years often complain about the sacrifices they have made and the deprivation they have endured for one another. Statements similar to Ruby's were made by men and women describing the sense of obligation and sacrifice they feel toward female kin: their mothers, grandmothers, or "mamas." Commitment to mutual aid among close kin is sometimes characterized as if they were practically "possessed" or controlled by the relationship. Eloise, captured by the incessant demands of her mother, says, "A mother should realize that you have your own life to lead and your own family. You can't come when she calls all the time, although you might want to and feel bad if you can't. I'm all worn out from running from my house to her house like a pinball machine. That's the way I do. I'm doing it 'cause she's my mother and 'cause I don't want to hurt her. Yet, she's killing me."

When Magnolia and Calvin Waters inherited a sum of money, the information spread quickly to every member of their domestic network. Within a month and a half all of the money was absorbed by participants in their network whose demands and needs could not be refused.

The ebb and flow of goods and services among kinsmen is illustrated in the following example of economic and social transactions during one month in 1970 between participants in a kin-based cooperative network in The Flats. As I wrote in my field notes:

> Cecil (35) lives in The Flats with his mother Willie Mae, his oldest sister and her two children, and his younger brother. Cecil's younger sister Lily lives with their mother's sister Bessie. Bessie has three children and Lily has two. Cecil and his mother have part-time jobs in a café and Lily's children are on aid. In July of 1970 Cecil and his mother had just put together enough money to cover their rent. Lily paid her utilities, but she did not have enough money to buy food stamps for herself and her children. Cecil and Willie Mae knew that after they paid their rent they would not have any money for food for the family. They helped out Lily by buying her food stamps, and then the two households shared meals together until Willie Mae was paid two weeks later. A week later Lily received her second ADC check and Bessie got some spending money from her boyfriend. They gave some of this money to Cecil and Willie Mae to pay their rent, and gave Willie Mae money to cover her insurance and pay a small sum on a living room suite at the local furniture store. Willie Mae reciprocated later on by buying dresses for Bessie and Lily's daughters and by caring for all the children when Bessie got a temporary job.

The people living in The Flats cannot keep their resources and their needs a secret. Everyone knows who is working, when welfare checks arrive, and when additional resources are available. Members of the middle class in America can cherish privacy concerning their income and resources, but the daily intimacy created by exchange transactions in The Flats insures that any change in a poor family's resources becomes "news." If a participant in an exchange network acquires a new car, new clothes, or a sum of money, this information is imme-

diately circulated through gossip. People are able to calculate on a weekly basis the total sum of money available to their kin network. This information is necessary to their own solvency and stability.

Social relationships between kin who have consistently traded material and cultural support over the years reveal feelings of both generosity and martyrdom. Long-term social interactions, especially between female kin, sometimes become highly competitive and aggressive. At family gatherings or at a family picnic it is not unusual to see an exaggerated performance by someone, bragging about how much he has done for a particular relative, or boasting that he provided all the food and labor for the picnic himself. The performer often combines statements of his generosity with great claims of sacrifice. In the presence of other kin the performer displays loyalty and superiority to others. Even though these routines come to be expected from some individuals, they cause hurt feelings and prolonged arguments. Everyone wants to create the impression that he is generous and manipulative, but no one wants to admit how much he depends upon others.

The trading of goods and services among the poor in complex industrial societies bears a striking resemblance to patterns of exchange organized around reciprocal gift giving in non-Western societies. The famous examples of reciprocal gift giving first described by Malinowski (1922), Mauss (1925), and Lévi-Strauss (1969) provided a basis for comparison. Patterns of exchange among people living in poverty and reciprocal exchanges in cultures lacking a political state are both embedded in well-defined kinship obligations. In each type of social system strategic resources are distributed from a family base to domestic groups, and exchange transactions pervade the whole social-economic life of participants. Neither industrial poor nor participants in non-industrial economies have the opportunity to control their environment or to acquire a surplus of scarce goods (Dalton 1961;

Harris 1971; Lee 1969; Sahlins 1965). In both of these systems a limited supply of goods is perpetually redistributed through the community.

The themes expressed by boasting female performers and gossiping kin and friends resemble themes which have emerged from black myth, fiction, and lore (Abrahams 1963; Dorson 1956, 1958). Conflicting values of trust and distrust, exploitation and friendship, the "trickster" and the "fool," have typically characterized patterns of social interaction between Blacks and Whites; notions of trust and distrust also suffuse interpersonal relations within the black community. These themes become daily utterances between cooperating kinsmen who find themselves trapped in a web of obligations. But the feelings of distrust are more conspicuous among friends than among kin.

Many students of social relations within the black community have concluded that friendships are embedded in an atmosphere of distrust. However, intense exchange behavior would not be possible if distrust predominated over all other attitudes toward personal relations. Distrust is offset by improvisation: an adaptive style of behavior acquired by persons using each situation to control, manipulate, and exploit others. Wherever there are friendships, exploitation possibilities exist (Abrahams 1970, p. 125). Friends exploit one another in the game of swapping, and they expect to be exploited in return. There is a precarious line between acceptable and unacceptable returns on a swap. Individuals risk trusting others because they want to change their lives. Swapping offers a variety of goods and something to anticipate. Michael Lee, a twenty-eight-year-old Flats resident, talks about his need to trust others, "They say you shouldn't trust nobody, but that's wrong. You have to try to trust somebody, and somebody has to try to trust you, 'cause everybody need help in this world."

A person who gives and obligates a large number of individuals stands a better chance of receiving returns than a person who limits his circle of friends. In addition, repayments from a large number of individuals are returned intermittently: people can anticipate receiving a more-or-less continuous flow of goods. From this perspective, swapping involves both calculation and planning.

Obtaining returns on a trade necessarily takes time. During this process, stable friendships are formed. Individuals attempt to surpass one another's displays of generosity; the extent to which these acts are mutually satisfying determines the duration of friendship bonds. Non-kin who live up to one another's expectations express elaborate vows of friendship and conduct their social relations within the idiom of kinship. Exchange behavior between those friends "going for kin" is identical to exchange behavior between close kin.

The Rhythm of Exchange

"These days you ain't got nothing to be really giving, only to your true friends, but most people trade," Ruby Banks told me. "Trading is a part of everybody's life. When I'm over at a girl friend's house, and I see something I want, I say, 'You gotta give me this; you don't need it no way.' I act the fool with them. If they say no, I need that, then they keep it and give me something else. Whatever I see that I want I usually get. If a friend lets me wear something of theirs, I let them wear something of mine. I even let some of my new clothes out. If my friend has on a new dress that I want, she might tell me to wait till she wear it first and then she'll give it to me, or she might say, well take it on." Exchange transactions are easily formed and create special bonds between friends. They initiate a social relationship and agreed upon reciprocal obligations (Gouldner 1960; Foster 1963; Sahlins 1965).[1]

Reciprocal obligations last as long as both participants are mutually satisfied. Individuals remain involved in exchange relationships by adequately drawing upon the credit they accumulate with others through swapping. Ruby Banks' description of the swapping relationship that developed between us illustrates this notion. "When I first met you, I didn't know you, did I? But I liked what you had on about the second time you seen me, and you gave it to me. All right, that started us swapping back and forth. You ain't really giving nothing away because everything that goes round comes round in my book. It's just like at stores where people give you credit. They have to trust you to pay them back, and if you pay them you can get more things."

Since an object swapped is offered with the intent of obligating the receiver over a period of time, two individuals rarely simultaneously exchange things. Little or no premium is placed upon immediate compensation; time has to pass before a counter-gift or a series of gifts can be repaid. While waiting for repayments, participants in exchange are compelled to trust one another. As the need arises, reciprocity occurs. Opal Jones described the powerful obligation to give that pervades interpersonal relationships. "My girl friend Alice gave me a dress about a month ago, and last time I went over to her house, she gave me sheets and towels for the kids, 'cause she knew I needed them. Every time I go over there, she always gives me something. When she comes over to my house, I give her whatever she asks for. We might not see each other in two or three months. But if she comes over after that, and I got something, I give it to her if she want it. If I go over to her house and she got something, I take it – canned goods, food, milk – it don't make no difference.

"My TV's been over to my cousin's house for seven or eight months now. I had a fine couch that she wanted and I gave it to her too. It don't make no difference with me what it is or what I have. I feel free knowing that I done my part in this world. I don't ever expect nothing back right away, but when I've given something to kin or friend, whenever they think about me they'll bring something on around. Even if we don't see each other for two or three months. Soon enough they'll come around and say, 'Come over my house, I got something to give you.' When I get over there and they say, 'You want this?', if I don't want it my kin will say, 'Well, find something else you like and take it on.'"

When people in The Flats swap goods, a value is placed upon the goods given away, but the value is not determined by the price or market value of the object. Some goods have been acquired through stealing rings, or previous trades, and they cost very little compared to their monetary value. The value of an object given away is based upon its retaining power over the receiver; that is, how much and over how long a time period the giver can expect returns of the gift. The value of commodities in systems of reciprocal gift giving is characterized by Lévi-Strauss (1969, p. 54), "Goods are not only economic commodities, but vehicles and instruments for realities of another order, such as power, influence, sympathy, status and emotion. . . ."

Gifts exchanged through swapping in The Flats are exchanged at irregular intervals, although sometimes the gifts exchanged are of exactly the same kind. Despite the necessity to exchange, on the average no one is significantly better off. Ruby Banks captured the pendulous rhythm of exchange when she said, "You ain't really giving nothing away because everything that goes round comes round in my book."

These cooperating networks share many goals constituting a group identity – goals so interrelated that the gains and losses of any of them are felt by all participants. The folk model of reciprocity is characterized by recognized and urgent reciprocal dependencies and mutual needs. These dependencies are recognized collectively and carry collective sanctions. Members of second-generation welfare families have calculated the risk of giving. As people say, "The poorer you are, the more likely you are to pay back." This criterion often determines which kin and friends are actively recruited into exchange networks.

Gift exchange is a style of interpersonal relationship by which local coalitions of cooperating kinsmen distinguish themselves from other Blacks – those low-income or working-class Blacks who have access to steady employment. In contrast to the middle-class ethic of individualism and competition, the poor living in The Flats do not turn anyone down when they need help. The cooperative lifestyle and the bonds created by the vast mass of moment-to-moment exchanges constitute an underlying element of black identity in The Flats. This powerful obligation to exchange is a profoundly creative adaptation to poverty.

Social Networks

The most typical way people involve others in their daily domestic lives is by entering with them into an exchange relationship. Through exchange transactions, an individual personally mobilizes others as participants in his social network. Those engaged in reciprocal gift giving are recruited primarily from relatives and from those friends who come to be defined as kin. The process of exchange joins individuals in personal relationships (Boissevain 1966). These interpersonal links effectively define the web of social relationships in The Flats.

Kinsmen and others activated into one another's networks share reciprocal obligations toward one another. They are referred to as "essential kin" in this study.[2] Strings of exchanges which actively link participants in an individual's network define that individual's personal kindred. The personal kindreds described in Chapter 4 [of original publication] are ego-centered networks. Even the personal kindreds of half siblings differ slightly; each half sibling shares some kin, but relates uniquely to others. Personal kindreds are not a category from which

individuals are recruited, but a selection of individuals mobilized for specific ends (Goodenough 1970; Keesing 1966).

In the process of exchange, people become immersed in a domestic web of a large number of kinfolk who can be called upon for help and who can bring others into the network. Domestic networks comprise the network of cooperating kinsmen activated from participants' overlapping personal kindreds. Domestic networks are not ego-centered; several participants in the network can recruit kin and friends to participate in domestic exchanges. Similar to personal kindreds, domestic networks are a selection of individuals mobilized for specific ends and they can be mobilized for extended periods of time.

Many descriptions of black American domestic life by both Blacks and Whites (Frazier 1939; Drake and Cayton 1945; Abrahams 1963; Moynihan 1965; Rainwater 1966) have overlooked the interdependence and cooperation of kinsmen in black communities. The underlying assumptions of these studies seem to imply that female-headed households and illegitimacy are symptomatic of broken homes and family disorganization. These studies fail to account for the great variety of domestic strategies in urban black communities. Whitten and Wolfe (1972, p. 41) suggest that one of the advantages of network analysis is that the researcher can avoid mere categorizing of social systems as "disorganized." The network model can explain a particular web of social relations from several points of view. Throughout this study a network perspective is used to interpret the basis of interpersonal links between those individuals mobilized to solve daily domestic problems.

NOTES

1   Foster's (1963) model of the dyadic contract includes two types of dyadic contractual ties: colleague ties between individuals of

approximately equal socio-economic positions and patron-client ties between individu-als of unequal social position. The underlying principles of exchange transactions discussed in this chapter approximate features of the dyadic model of colleague ties. According to Foster's model, colleague ties are expressed by repeated exchanges; they are informal and exist as long as participants are satisfied; they are usually of long duration; and exact or perfectly balanced reciprocity between partners is never achieved.

2   "Essential kin" refers to members of the culturally specific system of kinship categories and others who activate and validate their jural rights by helping one another, thereby creating reciprocal obligations toward one another. Firth (1970) distinguishes between "effective kin" (those kin with whom one maintains social contact) and "intimate kin" (those kin with whom contact is purposeful, close, and frequent – members of the immediate family circle).

REFERENCES

Abrahams, Roger. 1963. *Deep Down in the Jungle: Negro Narrative Folklore from the Streets of Philadelphia.* Hatboro, Pa.: Folklore Associates.

——. 1970. *Positively Black.* Englewood Cliffs, N. J.: Prentice-Hall.

Bailey, F. G. 1971. *Gifts and Poison: The Politics of Reputation.* New York: Schocken Books.

Boissevain, Jeremy. 1966. "Patronage in Sicily." *Man*, Journal of the Royal Anthropological Institute of Great Britain and Ireland 1(1): 18–33.

Dalton, George, 1961. "Economic Theory and Primitive Society." *American Anthropologist* 63: 1–25.

Dorson, Richard. 1956. *Negro Folktales in Michigan.* Cambridge, Mass.: Harvard University Press.

——. 1958. *Negro Tales from Pine Bluff, Arkansas, and Calvin, Michigan.* Bloomington: Indiana University Press.

Drake, St. Clair, and Cayton, Horace R. 1945. *Black Metropolis: A Study of Negro Life in a Northern City.* New York: Harcourt, Brace.

Firth, Raymond; Hubert, Jane; and Forge, Anthony. 1970. *Families and Their Relatives: Kinship in a Middle-Class Sector of London.* New York: Humanities Press.

Foster, George. 1963. "The Dyadic Contract in Tzintzuntzan II: Patron–Client Relationships." *American Anthropologist* 65: 1280–94.

Frazier, E. Franklin. 1939. *The Negro Family in the United States.* Chicago: University of Chicago Press.

Goodenough, Ward H. 1970. *Description and Comparison in Cultural Anthropology.* Chicago: Aldine Publishing Company.

Gouldner, Alvin W. 1960. "The Norm of Reciprocity: A Preliminary Statement." *American Sociological Review* 25: 161–78.

Harris, Marvin. 1971. *Culture, Man, and Nature: An Introduction to General Anthropology.* New York: Thomas Y. Crowell.

Keesing, Roger M. 1966. "Kwaio Kindreds." *Southwestern Journal of Anthropology* 22: 346–55.

Lee, Richard B. 1969. "!Kung Bushman Subsistence: An Input–Output Analysis." In *Environment and Culture Behavior: Ecological Studies in Cultural Anthropology*, ed. A. P. Vayda, pp. 47–79. New York: Natural History Press.

Lévi-Strauss, Claude. 1969. *The Elementary Structures of Kinship.* Boston: Beacon Press (first published 1949).

Lombardi, John R. 1973. "Exchange and Survival." Preprint. Boston: Boston University.

Malinowski, Bronislaw. 1922. *Argonauts of the Western Pacific.* New York: Dutton.

Mauss, Marcel. 1925. "Essai sur le don: Forme et raison de l'échange dans les sociétés archaïques." *Année Sociologique*, n.s., I: 30–186.

——. 1954. *The Gift.* New York: The Free Press.

Moynihan, Daniel Patrick. 1965. "The Negro Family: The Case for National Action." Washington, D.C.: U.S. Government Printing Office. Prepared for the Office of Policy Planning and Research of the Department of Labor.

Rainwater, Lee. 1966. "Crucible of Identity: The Negro Lower-Class Family." *Daedalus* 95(2): 172–216.

Sahlins, Marshall D. 1965. "On the Sociology of Primitive Exchange." In *The Relevance of Models for Social Anthropology*, ed. Michael Banton. A.S.A. Monograph I. London: Tavistock Publications; New York: Praeger.

Whitten, N. E., and Wolfe, Alvin W. 1973. "Network Analysis." In *The Handbook of Social and Cultural Anthropology*, ed. John J. Honigmann. Chicago: Rand-McNally.

17

The Code of the Streets

Elijah Anderson

Elijah Anderson is the Charles and William L. Day Distinguished Professor of the Social Sciences at the University of Pennsylvania. An expert on the sociology of black America, he is the author of the widely regarded sociological work, *A Place on the Corner: A Study of Black Street Corner Men* (1978) and numerous articles on the black experience, including "Of Old Heads and Young Boys: Notes on the Urban Black Experience" (1986), "Sex Codes and Family Life among Inner-City Youth" (1989), and "The Code of the Streets," which was the cover story in the May 1994 issue of *The Atlantic Monthly*. For his ethnographic study *Streetwise: Race, Class and Change in an Urban Community* (1990), he was honored with the Robert E. Park Award of the American Sociological Association. Dr. Anderson authored the "Introduction" to the republication of *The Philadelphia Negro* by W. E. B. Du Bois (1996), and his expanded version of the *Atlanic* piece, *The Code of the Street: Decency, Violence, and the Moral Life of the Inner City* was published by W. W. Norton in 1999.

Of all the problems besetting the poor inner-city black community, none is more pressing than that of interpersonal violence and aggression. It wreaks havoc daily with the lives of community residents and increasingly spills over into downtown and residential middle-class areas. Muggings, burglaries, carjackings, and drug-related shootings, all of which may leave their victims or innocent bystanders dead, are now common enough to concern all urban and many suburban residents. The inclination to violence springs from the circumstances of life among the ghetto poor – the lack of jobs that pay a living wage, the stigma of race, the fallout from rampant drug use and drug trafficking, and the resulting alienation and lack of hope for the future.

Simply living in such an environment places young people at special risk of falling victim to aggressive behavior. Although there are often forces in the community which can counteract the negative influences, by far the most powerful being a strong, loving, "decent" (as inner-city residents put it) family committed to middle-class values, the despair is pervasive enough to have spawned an oppositional culture, that of "the streets," whose norms are often consciously opposed to those of mainstream society. These two orientations –

decent and street – socially organize the community, and their coexistence has important consequences for residents, particularly children growing up in the inner city. Above all, this environment means that even youngsters whose home lives reflect mainstream values – and the majority of homes in the community do – must be able to handle themselves in a street-oriented environment.

This is because the street culture has evolved what may be called a code of the streets, which amounts to a set of informal rules governing interpersonal public behavior, including violence. The rules prescribe both a proper comportment and a proper way to respond if challenged. They regulate the use of violence and so allow those who are inclined to aggression to precipitate violent encounters in an approved way. The rules have been established and are enforced mainly by the street-oriented, but on the streets the distinction between street and decent is often irrelevant; everybody knows that if the rules are violated, there are penalties. Knowledge of the code is thus largely defensive; it is literally necessary for operating in public. Therefore, even though families with a decency orientation are usually opposed to the values of the code, they often reluctantly encourage their children's familiarity with it to enable them to negotiate the inner-city environment.

At the heart of the code is the issue of respect – loosely defined as being treated "right," or granted the deference one deserves. However, in the troublesome public environment of the inner city, as people increasingly feel buffeted by forces beyond their control, what one deserves in the way of respect becomes more and more problematic and uncertain. This in turn further opens the issue of respect to sometimes intense interpersonal negotiation. In the street culture, especially among young people, respect is viewed as almost an external entity that is hard-won but easily lost, and so must constantly be guarded. The rules of the code in fact provide a framework for negotiating respect. The person whose very appearance – including his clothing, demeanor, and way of moving – deters transgressions feels that he possesses, and may be considered by others to possess, a measure of respect. With the right amount of respect, for instance, he can avoid "being bothered" in public. If he is bothered, not only may he be in physical danger but he has been disgraced or "dissed" (disrespected). Many of the forms that dissing can take might seem petty to middle-class people (maintaining eye contact for too long, for example), but to those invested in the street code, these actions become serious indications of the other person's intentions. Consequently, such people become very sensitive to advances and slights, which could well serve as warnings of imminent physical confrontation.

This hard reality can be traced to the profound sense of alienation from mainstream society and its institutions felt by many poor inner-city black people, particularly the young. The code of the streets is actually a cultural adaptation to a profound lack of faith in the police and the judicial system. The police are most often seen as representing the dominant white society and not caring to protect inner-city residents. When called, they may not respond, which is one reason many residents feel they must be prepared to take extraordinary measures to defend themselves and their loved ones against those who are inclined to aggression. Lack of police accountability has in fact been incorporated into the status system: the person who is believed capable of "taking care of himself" is accorded a certain deference, which translates into a sense of physical and psychological control. Thus the street code emerges where the influence of the police ends and personal responsibility for one's safety is felt to begin. Exacerbated by the proliferation of drugs and easy access to guns, this volatile situation results in the ability of the street oriented minority (or those who effectively "go for bad") to dominate the public spaces.

Decent and Street Families

Although almost everyone in poor inner-city neighborhoods is struggling financially and therefore feels a certain distance from the rest of America, the decent and the street family in a real sense represent two poles of value orientation, two contrasting conceptual categories. The labels "decent" and "street," which the residents themselves use, amount to evaluative judgments that confer status on local residents. The labeling is often the result of a social contest among individuals and families of the neighborhood. Individuals of the two orientations often coexist in the same extended family. Decent residents judge themselves to be so while judging others to be of the street, and street individuals often present themselves as decent, drawing distinctions between themselves and other people. In addition, there is quite a bit of circumstantial behavior – that is, one person may at different times exhibit both decent and street orientations, depending on the circumstances. Although these designations result from so much social jockeying, there do exist concrete features that define each conceptual category.

Generally, so-called decent families tend to accept mainstream values more fully and attempt to instill them in their children. Whether married couples with children or single-parent (usually female) households, they are generally "working poor" and so tend to be better off financially than their street-oriented neighbors. They value hard work and self-reliance and are willing to sacrifice for their children. Because they have a certain amount of faith in mainstream society, they harbor hopes for a better future for their children, if not for themselves. Many of them go to church and take a strong interest in their children's schooling. Rather than dwelling on the real hardships and inequities facing them, many such decent people, particularly the increasing number of grandmothers raising grandchildren, see their difficult situation as a test from God and derive great support from their faith and from the church community.

Extremely aware of the problematic and often dangerous environment in which they reside, decent parents tend to be strict in their child-rearing practices, encouraging children to respect authority and walk a straight moral line. They have an almost obsessive concern about trouble of any kind and remind their children to be on the lookout for people and situations that might lead to it. At the same time, they are themselves polite and considerate of others, and teach their children to be the same way. At home, at work, and in church, they strive hard to maintain a positive mental attitude and a spirit of cooperation.

So-called street parents, in contrast, often show a lack of consideration for other people and have a rather superficial sense of family and community. Though they may love their children, many of them are unable to cope with the physical and emotional demands of parenthood, and find it difficult to reconcile their needs with those of their children. These families, who are more fully invested in the code of the streets than the decent people are, may aggressively socialize their children into it in a normative way. They believe in the code and judge themselves and others according to its values.

In fact the overwhelming majority of families in the inner-city community try to approximate the decent-family model, but there are many others who clearly represent the worst fears of the decent family. Not only are their financial resources extremely limited, but what little they have may easily be misused. The lives of the street-oriented are often marked by disorganization. In the most desperate circumstances people frequently have a limited understanding of priorities and consequences, and so frustrations mount over bills, food, and, at times, drink, cigarettes, and drugs. Some tend toward self-destructive behavior; many street-oriented women are crack-addicted ("on the pipe"), alcoholic, or involved in complicated relationships with men who abuse them. In addition, the seeming intractability of their situation, caused in large part by the lack of well-paying jobs and the persistence of racial discrimination, has engendered deep-seated bitterness and anger in many of the most desperate and poorest blacks, especially young people. The need both to exercise a measure of control and to lash out at somebody is often reflected in the adults' relations with their children. At the least, the frustrations of persistent poverty shorten the fuse in such people – contributing to a lack of patience with anyone, child or adult, who irritates them.

In these circumstances a woman – or a man, although men are less consistently present in children's lives – can be quite aggressive with children, yelling at and striking them for the least little infraction of the rules she has set down. Often little if any serious explanation follows the verbal and physical punishment. This response teaches children a particular lesson. They learn that to solve any kind of interpersonal problem one must quickly resort to hitting or other violent behavior. Actual peace and quiet, and also the appearance of calm, respectful children conveyed to her neighbors and friends, are often what the young mother most desires, but at times she will be very aggressive in trying to get them. Thus she may be quick to beat her children, especially if they defy her law, not because she hates them but because this is the way she knows to control them. In fact, many street-oriented women love their children dearly. Many mothers in the community subscribe to the notion that there is a "devil in the boy" that must be beaten out of him or that socially "fast girls need to be whupped." Thus much of what borders on child abuse in the view of social authorities is acceptable parental punishment in the view of these mothers.

Many street-oriented women are sporadic mothers whose children learn to fend for themselves when necessary, foraging for food and money any way they can get it. The children are sometimes employed by drug dealers or become addicted themselves. These children of the street, growing up with little supervision, are said to "come up hard." They often learn to fight at an early age, sometimes using short-tempered adults around them as role models. The street-oriented home may be fraught with anger, verbal disputes, physical aggression, and even mayhem. The children observe these goings-on, learning the lesson that might makes right. They quickly learn to hit those who cross them, and the dog-eat-dog mentality prevails. In order to survive, to protect oneself, it is necessary to marshal inner resources and be ready to deal with adversity in a hands-on way. In these circumstances physical prowess takes on great significance.

In some of the most desperate cases, a street-oriented mother may simply leave her young children alone and unattended while she goes out. The most irresponsible women can be found at local bars and crack houses, getting high and socializing with other adults. Sometimes a troubled woman will leave very young children alone for days at a time. Reports of crack addicts abandoning their children have become common in drug infested inner-city communities. Neighbors or relatives discover the abandoned children, often hungry and distraught over the absence of their mother. After repeated absences, a friend or relative, particularly a grandmother, will often step in to care for the young children, sometimes petitioning the authorities to send her, as guardian of the children, the mother's welfare check, if the mother gets one. By this time, however, the children may well have learned the first lesson of the streets: survival itself, let alone respect, cannot be taken for granted; you have to fight for your place in the world.

Campaigning for Respect

These realities of inner-city life are largely absorbed on the streets. At an early age, often even before they start school, children from street-oriented homes gravitate to the streets, where they "hang" – socialize with their peers. Children from these generally permissive homes have a great deal of latitude and are allowed to "rip and run" up and down the street. They often come home from school, put their books down, and go right back out the door. On school nights eight- and nine-year-olds remain out until nine or ten o'clock (and teenagers typically come in whenever they want to). On the streets they play in groups that often become the source of their primary social bonds. Children from decent homes tend to be more carefully supervised and are thus likely to have curfews and to be taught how to stay out of trouble.

When decent and street kids come together, a kind of social shuffle occurs in which children have a chance to go either way. Tension builds as a child comes to realize that he must choose an orientation. The kind of home he comes from influences but does not determine the way he will ultimately turn out – although it is unlikely that a child from a thoroughly street oriented family will easily absorb decent values on the streets. Youths who emerge from street-oriented families but develop a decency orientation almost always learn those values in another setting – in school, in a youth group, in church. Often it is the result of their involvement with a caring "old head" (adult role model).

In the street, through their play, children pour their individual life experiences into a common knowledge pool, affirming, confirming, and elaborating on what they have observed in the home and matching their skills against those of others. And they learn to fight. Even small children test one another, pushing and shoving, and are ready to hit other children over circumstances not to their liking. In turn, they are readily hit by other children, and the child who is toughest prevails. Thus the violent resolution of disputes, the hitting and cursing, gains social reinforcement.

The child in effect is initiated into a system that is really a way of campaigning for respect.

In addition, younger children witness the disputes of older children, which are often resolved through cursing and abusive talk, if not aggression or outright violence. They see that one child succumbs to the greater physical and mental abilities of the other. They are also alert and attentive witnesses to the verbal and physical fights of adults, after which they compare notes and share their interpretations of the event. In almost every case the victor is the person who physically won the altercation, and this person often enjoys the esteem and respect of onlookers. These experiences reinforce the lessons the children have learned at home: might makes right, and toughness is a virtue, while humility is not. In effect they learn the social meaning of fighting. When it is left virtually unchallenged, this understanding becomes an ever more important part of the child's working conception of the world. Over time the code of the streets becomes refined.

Those street-oriented adults with whom children come in contact – including mothers, fathers, brothers, sisters, boyfriends, cousins, neighbors, and friends – help them along in forming this understanding by verbalizing the messages they are getting through experience: "Watch your back." "Protect yourself." "Don't punk out." "If somebody messes with you, you got to pay them back." "If someone disses you, you got to straighten them out." Many parents actually impose sanctions if a child is not sufficiently aggressive. For example, if a child loses a fight and comes home upset, the parent might respond, "Don't you come in here crying that somebody beat you up; you better get back out there and whup his ass. I didn't raise no punks! Get back out there and whup his ass. If you don't whup his ass, I'll whup your ass when you come home." Thus the child obtains reinforcement for being tough and showing nerve.

While fighting, some children cry as though they are doing something they are ambivalent about. The fight may be against their wishes, yet they may feel constrained to fight or face the consequences – not just from peers but also from caretakers or parents, who may administer another beating if they back down. Some adults recall receiving such lessons from their own parents and justify repeating them to their children as a way to toughen them up. Looking capable of taking care of oneself as a form of self-defense is a dominant theme among both street-oriented and decent adults who worry about the safety of their children. There is thus at times a convergence in their child-rearing practices, although the rationales behind them may differ.

Self-image Based on "Juice"

By the time they are teenagers, most youths have either internalized the code of the streets or at least learned the need to comport themselves in accordance with its rules, which chiefly have to do with interpersonal communication. The code revolves around the presentation of self. Its basic requirement is the display of a certain predisposition to violence. Accordingly, one's bearing must send the unmistakable if sometimes subtle message to "the next person" in public that one is capable of violence and mayhem when the situation requires it, that one can take care of oneself. The nature of this communication is largely determined by the demands of the circumstances but can include facial expressions, gait, and verbal expressions – all of which are geared mainly to deterring aggression. Physical appearance, including clothes, jewelry, and grooming, also plays an important part in how a person is viewed; to be respected, it is important to have the right look.

Even so, there are no guarantees against challenges, because there are always people around looking for a fight to increase their share of respect – or "juice," as it is sometimes called on the street. Moreover, if a person is assaulted, it is important, not only in the eyes of his opponent but also in the eyes of his "running buddies," for him to avenge himself. Otherwise he risks being "tried" (challenged) or "moved on" by any number of others. To maintain his honor he must show he is not someone to be "messed with" or "dissed." In general, the person must "keep himself straight" by managing his position of respect among others; this involves in part his self-image, which is shaped by what he thinks others are thinking of him in relation to his peers.

Objects play an important and complicated role in establishing self-image. Jackets, sneakers, gold jewelry, reflect not just a person's taste, which tends to be tightly regulated among adolescents of all social classes, but also a willingness to possess things that may require defending. A boy wearing a fashionable, expensive jacket, for example, is vulnerable to attack by another who covets the jacket and either cannot afford to buy one or wants the added satisfaction of depriving someone else of his. However, if the boy forgoes the desirable jacket and wears one that isn't "hip," he runs the risk of being teased and possibly even assaulted as an unworthy person. To be allowed to hang with certain prestigious crowds, a boy must wear a different set of expensive clothes – sneakers and athletic suit – every day. Not to be able to do so might make him appear socially deficient. The youth comes to covet such items – especially when he sees easy prey wearing them.

In acquiring valued things, therefore, a person shores up his identity – but since it is an identity based on having things, it is highly precarious. This very precariousness gives a heightened sense of urgency to staying even with peers, with whom the person is actually competing. Young men and women who are able to command respect through their presentation of self – by allowing their possessions and their body language to speak for them – may not have to campaign for regard but may, rather, gain it by the force of their manner. Those who are unable to command respect in this way must actively campaign for it – and are thus particularly alive to slights.

One way of campaigning for status is by taking the possessions of others. In this context, seemingly ordinary objects can become trophies imbued with symbolic value that far exceeds their monetary worth. Possession of the trophy can symbolize the ability to violate somebody – to "get in his face," to take something of value from him, to "dis" him, and thus to enhance one's own worth by stealing someone else's. The trophy does not have to be something material. It can be another person's sense of honor, snatched away with a derogatory remark. It can be the outcome of a fight. It can be the imposition of a certain standard, such as a girl's getting herself recognized as the most beautiful. Material things, however, fit easily into the pattern. Sneakers, a pistol, even somebody else's girlfriend, can become a trophy. When a person can take something from another and then flaunt it, he gains a certain regard by being the owner, or the controller, of that thing. But this display of ownership can then provoke other people to challenge him. This game of who controls what is thus constantly being played out on inner-city streets, and the trophy – extrinsic or intrinsic, tangible or intangible – identifies the current winner.

An important aspect of this often violent give-and-take is its zero-sum quality. That is, the extent to which one person can raise himself up depends on his ability to put another person down. This underscores the alienation that permeates the inner-city ghetto community. There is a generalized sense that very little respect is to be had, and therefore everyone competes to get what affirmation he can of the little that is available. The craving for respect that results gives people thin skins. Shows of deference by others can be highly soothing, contributing to a sense of security, comfort, self-

confidence, and self-respect. Transgressions by others which go unanswered diminish these feelings and are believed to encourage further transgressions. Hence one must be ever vigilant against the transgressions of others or even appearing as if transgressions will be tolerated. Among young people, whose sense of self-esteem is particularly vulnerable, there is an especially heightened concern with being disrespected. Many inner-city young men in particular crave respect to such a degree that they will risk their lives to attain and maintain it.

The issue of respect is thus closely tied to whether a person has an inclination to be violent, even as a victim. In the wider society people may not feel required to retaliate physically after an attack, even though they are aware that they have been degraded or taken advantage of. They may feel a great need to defend themselves during an attack, or to behave in such a way as to deter aggression (middle-class people certainly can and do become victims of street-oriented youths), but they are much more likely than street-oriented people to feel that they can walk away from a possible altercation with their self-esteem intact. Some people may even have the strength of character to flee, without any thought that their self-respect or esteem will be diminished.

In impoverished inner-city black communities, however, particularly among young males and perhaps increasingly among females, such flight would be extremely difficult. To run away would likely leave one's self-esteem in tatters. Hence people often feel constrained not only to stand up and at least attempt to resist during an assault but also to "pay back" – to seek revenge – after a successful assault on their person. This may include going to get a weapon or even getting relatives involved. Their very identity and self-respect, their honor, is often intricately tied up with the way they perform on the streets during and after such encounters. This outlook reflects the circumscribed opportunities of the inner-city poor. Generally people outside the ghetto have other ways of gaining status and regard, and thus do not feel so dependent on such physical displays.

By Trial of Manhood

On the street, among males these concerns about things and identity have come to be expressed in the concept of "manhood." Manhood in the inner city means taking the prerogatives of men with respect to strangers, other men, and women – being distinguished as a man. It implies physicality and a certain ruthlessness. Regard and respect are associated with this concept in large part because of its practical application: if others have little or no regard for a person's manhood, his very life and those of his loved ones could be in jeopardy. But there is a chicken-and-egg aspect to this situation: one's physical safety is more likely to be jeopardized in public because manhood is associated with respect. In other words, an existential link has been created between the idea of manhood and one's self-esteem, so that it has become hard to say which is primary. For many inner-city youths, manhood and respect are flip sides of the same coin; physical and psychological well-being are inseparable, and both require a sense of control, of being in charge.

The operating assumption is that a man, especially a real man, knows what other men know – the code of the streets. And if one is not a real man, one is somehow diminished as a person, and there are certain valued things one simply does not deserve. There is thus believed to be a certain justice to the code, since it is considered that everyone has the opportunity to know it. Implicit in this is that everybody is held responsible for being familiar with the code. If the victim of a mugging, for example, does not know the code and so responds "wrong," the perpetrator may feel justified even in killing him and may feel no remorse. He may think, "Too bad, but it's his fault. He should have known better."

So when a person ventures outside, he must adopt the code – a kind of shield, really – to prevent others from "messing with" him. In these circumstances it is easy for people to think they are being tried or tested by others even when this is not the case. For it is sensed that something extremely valuable is at stake in every interaction, and people are encouraged to rise to the occasion, particularly with strangers. For people who are unfamiliar with the code – generally people who live outside the inner city – the concern with respect in the most ordinary interactions can be frightening and incomprehensible. But for those who are invested in the code, the clear object of their demeanor is to discourage strangers from even thinking about testing their manhood. And the sense of power that attends the ability to deter others can be alluring even to those who know the code without being heavily invested in it – the decent inner-city youths. Thus a boy who has been leading a basically decent life can, in trying circumstances, suddenly resort to deadly force.

Central to the issue of manhood is the widespread belief that one of the most effective ways of gaining respect is to manifest "nerve." Nerve is shown when one takes another person's possessions (the more valuable the better), "messes with" someone's woman, throws the first punch, "gets in someone's face," or pulls a trigger. Its proper display helps on the spot to check others who would violate one's person and also helps to build a reputation that works to prevent future challenges. But since such a show of nerve is a forceful expression of disrespect toward the person on the receiving end, the victim may be greatly offended and seek to retaliate with equal or greater force. A display of nerve, therefore, can easily provoke a life-threatening response, and the background knowledge of that possibility has often been incorporated into the concept of nerve.

True nerve exposes a lack of fear of dying. Many feel that it is acceptable to risk dying over the principle of respect. In fact, among the hard-core street-oriented, the clear risk of violent death may be preferable to being "dissed" by another. The youths who have internalized this attitude and convincingly display it in their public bearing are among the most threatening people of all, for it is commonly assumed that they fear no man. As the people of the community say, "They are the baddest dudes on the street." They often lead an existential life that may acquire meaning only when they are faced with the possibility of imminent death. Not to be afraid to die is by implication to have few compunctions about taking another's life. Not to be afraid to die is the quid pro quo of being able to take somebody else's life – for the right reasons, if the situation demands it. When others believe this is one's position, it gives one a real sense of power on the streets. Such credibility is what many inner-city youths strive to achieve, whether they are decent or street-oriented, both because of its practical defensive value and because of the positive way it makes them feel about themselves. The difference between the decent and the street-oriented youth is often that the decent youth makes a conscious decision to appear tough and manly; in another setting – with teachers, say, or at his part-time job – he can be polite and deferential. The street-oriented youth, on the other hand, has made the concept of manhood a part of his very identity; he has difficulty manipulating it – it often controls him.

Girls and Boys

Increasingly, teenage girls are mimicking the boys and trying to have their own version of "manhood." Their goal is the same – to get respect, to be recognized as capable of setting or maintaining a certain standard. They try to achieve this end in the ways that have been established by the boys, including posturing, abusive language, and the use of violence to resolve disputes, but the issues for the girls are different. Although conflicts over turf and status exist

among the girls, the majority of disputes seem rooted in assessments of beauty (which girl in a group is "the cutest"), competition over boyfriends, and attempts to regulate other people's knowledge of and opinions about a girl's behavior or that of someone close to her, especially her mother.

A major cause of conflicts among girls is "he say, she say." This practice begins in the early school years and continues through high school. It occurs when "people," particularly girls, talk about others, thus putting their "business in the streets." Usually one girl will say something negative about another in the group, most often behind the person's back. The remark will then get back to the person talked about. She may retaliate or her friends may feel required to "take up for" her. In essence this is a form of group gossiping in which individuals are negatively assessed and evaluated. As with much gossip, the things said may or may not be true, but the point is that such imputations can cast aspersions on a person's good name. The accused is required to defend herself against the slander, which can result in arguments and fights, often over little of real substance. Here again is the problem of low self-esteem, which encourages youngsters to be highly sensitive to slights and to be vulnerable to feeling easily "dissed." To avenge the dissing, a fight is usually necessary. Because boys are believed to control violence, girls tend to defer to them in situations of conflict. Often if a girl is attacked or feels slighted, she will get a brother, uncle, or cousin to do her fighting for her. Increasingly, however, girls are doing their own fighting and are even asking their male relatives to teach them how to fight. Some girls form groups that attack other girls or take things from them. A hard-core segment of inner-city girls inclined toward violence seems to be developing. As one thirteen-year-old girl in a detention center for youths who have committed violent acts told me, "To get people to leave you alone, you gotta fight. Talking don't always get you out of stuff." One major difference between girls and boys: girls rarely use guns. Their fights are therefore not life-or-death struggles. Girls are not often willing to put their lives on the line for "manhood." The ultimate form of respect on the male-dominated inner-city street is thus reserved for men.

"Going for Bad"

In the most fearsome youths such a cavalier attitude toward death grows out of a very limited view of life. Many are uncertain about how long they are going to live and believe they could die violently at any time. They accept this fate; they live on the edge. Their manner conveys the message that nothing intimidates them; whatever turn the encounter takes, they maintain their attack – rather like a pit bull, whose spirit many such boys admire. The demonstration of such tenacity "shows heart" and earns their respect.

This fearlessness has implications for law enforcement. Many street-oriented boys are much more concerned about the threat of "justice" at the hands of a peer than at the hands of the police. Moreover, many feel not only that they have little to lose by going to prison but that they have something to gain. The toughening-up one experiences in prison can actually enhance one's reputation on the streets. Hence the system loses influence over the hard core who are without jobs, with little perceptible stake in the system. If mainstream society has done nothing for them, they counter by making sure it can do nothing to them.

At the same time, however, a competing view maintains that true nerve consists in backing down, walking away from a fight, and going on with one's business. One fights only in self-defense. This view emerges from the decent philosophy that life is precious, and it is an important part of the socialization process common in decent homes. It discourages violence as the primary means of resolving disputes and encourages

youngsters to accept nonviolence and talk as confrontational strategies. But "if the deal goes down," self-defense is greatly encouraged. When there is enough positive support for this orientation, either in the home or among one's peers, then nonviolence has a chance to prevail. But it prevails at the cost of relinquishing a claim to being bad and tough, and therefore sets a young person up as at the very least alienated from street-oriented peers and quite possibly a target of derision or even violence.

Although the nonviolent orientation rarely overcomes the impulse to strike back in an encounter, it does introduce a certain confusion and so can prompt a measure of soul-searching, or even profound ambivalence. Did the person back down with his respect intact or did he back down only to be judged a "punk" – a person lacking manhood? Should he or she have acted? Should he or she have hit the other person in the mouth? These questions beset many young men and women during public confrontations. What is the "right" thing to do? In the quest for honor, respect, and local status – which few young people are uninterested in – common sense most often prevails, which leads many to opt for the tough approach, enacting their own particular versions of the display of nerve. The presentation of oneself as rough and tough is very often quite acceptable until one is tested. And then that presentation may help the person pass the test, because it will cause fewer questions to be asked about what he did and why. It is hard for a person to explain why he lost the fight or why he backed down. Hence many will strive to appear to "go for bad," while hoping they will never be tested. But when they are tested, the outcome of the situation may quickly be out of their hands, as they become wrapped up in the circumstances of the moment.

An Oppositional Culture

The attitudes of the wider society are deeply implicated in the code of the streets. Most people in inner-city communities are not totally invested in the code, but the significant minority of hard-core street youths who are have to maintain the code in order to establish reputations, because they have – or feel they have – few other ways to assert themselves. For these young people the standards of the street code are the only game in town. The extent to which some children – particularly those who through upbringing have become most alienated and those lacking in strong and conventional social support – experience, feel, and internalize racist rejection and contempt from mainstream society may strongly encourage them to express contempt for the more conventional society in turn. In dealing with this contempt and rejection, some youngsters will consciously invest themselves and their considerable mental resources in what amounts to an oppositional culture to preserve themselves and their self-respect. Once they do, any respect they might be able to garner in the wider system pales in comparison with the respect available in the local system; thus they often lose interest in even attempting to negotiate the mainstream system.

At the same time, many less alienated young blacks have assumed a street-oriented demeanor as a way of expressing their blackness while really embracing a much more moderate way of life; they, too, want a nonviolent setting in which to live and raise a family. These decent people are trying hard to be part of the mainstream culture, but the racism, real and perceived, that they encounter helps to legitimate the oppositional culture. And so on occasion they adopt street behavior. In fact, depending on the demands of the situation, many people in the community slip back and forth between decent and street behavior.

A vicious cycle has thus been formed. The hopelessness and alienation many young inner-city black men and women feel, largely as a result of endemic joblessness and persistent racism, fuels the violence they engage in. This violence serves to confirm the negative feelings many whites and some middle-class blacks harbor toward the ghetto poor, further legitimating the oppositional culture and the code of the streets in the eyes of many poor young blacks. Unless this cycle is broken, attitudes on both sides will become increasingly entrenched, and the violence, which claims victims black and white, poor and affluent, will only escalate.

18

Sidewalk Sleeping and Crack Bingeing

Mitchell Duneier

Mitchell Duneier is Professor of Sociology at the University of California at Santa Barbara and at the University of Wisconsin at Madison. He has also taught at the City University of New York Graduate Center. Duneier's first book, *Slim's Table: Race, Respectability, and Masculinity* (1992) won the American Sociological Association Distinguished Scholarly Publication Award. *Slim's Table* examines the lives of older black and white men in a Chicago diner to show a side of race relations often ignored in studies of the inner city. His second volume, *Sidewalk* (1999), uses largely homeless, New York City street vendors as a lens through which to investigate issues of race, class, and urban politics. *Sidewalk* won the *Los Angeles Times* Book Prize and the Sorokin Award from the Society for the Study of Social Problems. He is currently working on a global ethnography of workers in the information processing industry.

In the early 1980s, residents of many American cities came to see their sidewalk life as a new kind of struggle. They perceived that conventional standards did not apply on streets like Sixth Avenue. Politicians responded by advancing programs for restoring order and reducing crime that seemed to be the exact opposite of Jacobs's "eyes upon the street." Jacobs wrote: "The first thing to understand is that the public peace – the sidewalk and street peace – of cities is not kept primarily by the police, necessary as police are. It is kept primarily by an intricate, almost unconscious, network of voluntary control and standards among the people themselves, and enforced by the people themselves."[1] For many city dwellers, informal social control was no longer enough, because the eyes upon the street were no longer conventional. The

Editor's Note: This selection from Mitchell Duneier's book *Sidewalk* was originally a chapter titled, "Sidewalk Sleeping." However, given that this piece is being presented in isolation from the rest of the text, the title was expanded to demonstrate that the author is speaking about a very specific group of homeless men in this section: crack cocaine users. Readers should be careful not to assume that the issues facing this subpopulation are generalizable to other individuals who are homeless or marginally housed. They are not. Other sections of *Sidewalk* elaborate on these distinctions.

police were essential to the maintenance of order and could no longer be the "or else" of social control.

The most prominent argument for using formal methods of social control was advanced by the social scientists James Q. Wilson and George Kelling in an article entitled "Broken Windows," which appeared in *The Atlantic Monthly* in March 1982. They grounded their argument in the 1969 report by social psychologist Philip Zimbardo, who had arranged to have automobiles without license plates parked with their hoods up in the Bronx and Palo Alto, California. In both places, according to Wilson and Kelling's summary of Zimbardo's study, vandalism occurred once passersby sensed that the cars were abandoned and "no one cared." In Palo Alto, it was middle-class white passersby who did the damage; in the South Bronx, it was poor minority ones. Using Zimbardo's experiment as an analogy, Wilson and Kelling went on to argue that the appearance of a single broken window in a neighborhood (not merely in an abandoned car) gives a sense that "no one cares." Once the "no one cares" threshold is met, they claimed, "serious crime will flourish." And even before crime increases, citizens will begin to feel the anxiety that comes from "a sense that the street is disorderly, a source of distasteful, worrisome encounters. . . . One unrepaired broken window is a signal that no one cares, . . . so breaking more windows costs nothing."[2]

Although for Jacobs disorder serves many positive functions and for Wilson and Kelling it does not, their approaches are only superficially different in other ways. Both ask what sorts of unintended consequences flow from particular sorts of publicly visible practices. Jacobs's argument, in part, is that public characters (who in her analysis are respectable figures) generate a sense of predictability by acting as eyes, and this generates social order, by creating a set of cultural meanings and expectations that "someone cares." Wilson and Kelling and those who advocate stronger police control believe that visible forms of disorder and disrepute have the unintended consequence of producing crime, by creating a set of cultural meanings or expectations that "no one cares."

Through what came to be called the "broken windows" theory, Wilson and Kelling laid the scholarly groundwork for a political combat plan that responded to the concerns of vast numbers of city dwellers who wanted to feel safer on their streets. In the 1980s and 1990s, these issues became the substance of two successive New York City mayoral elections. In 1989, Democratic Mayor David Dinkins initially tried to show tolerance for sidewalk vendors, scavengers, and panhandlers even as he hired William Bratton, a transit-police chief who vigorously applied Wilson and Kelling's ideas. In 1993, Dinkins went down to defeat to the Republican Rudolph Giuliani, who intensified the same policies (as he would later promote Bratton to the post of Police Commissioner) as he ran an unrelenting campaign against the forces that were said to be diminishing the "quality of life" for conventional members of the electorate. Since 1993, crime rates have dropped dramatically in New York City. Because crime rates have also dropped in cities where the "broken windows" theory has not been applied, the extent to which the dramatic drop in New York can be attributed to "broken windows"–style social control is a matter of fierce debate.

Having examined the way that the informal ties of the sidewalk help men as they struggle to live in accordance with standards of moral worth, I want to look now at the very acts that lead policymakers to classify these same persons as "broken windows." These are acts which seem not to be regulated by informal social controls among the vendors themselves, and which have made sidewalk life seem like a new kind of battleground for many conventional citizens. In what follows, I will focus on four apparently indecent behaviors: when some men working the sidewalks urinate in public, detain local residents in conversation, sell stolen goods, and sleep on the sidewalk. (I might have focused, say, on the sale of marijuana or crack, but during the time of my fieldwork such petty dealing was uncommon – only once did I see a man working with the vendors sell marijuana to a passerby – and also has been addressed in detail by other scholars.)[3]

Thus far, I have tried to show that what makes sidewalk life viable is an informal system of social control, maintained in part by people like Hakim, Marvin, and Jamaane. The question is this: If the informal system is so powerful, how and why do some men persist in these acts? And aren't the people who do these things the very people I claim are trying not to give up on basic standards? How is it that the same person who makes a conscious decision to "respect" society by scavenging trash or panhandling (instead of breaking into parked cars or selling drugs) turns around and urinates against the side of a building? How much respect does he really have for society if he engages in such behavior? In examining some of the hardest cases and the most contradictory evidence, I hope to address the limitations of informal modes of social control.

A Puzzle

On a late night in August, Ron came up to me and asked if I would hold sixty of the ninety dollars he had earned that day. Even if he asked for it later on that night, he told me, I shouldn't give it to him.

Marvin, Hakim, Jamaane, and Alice were also often asked to hold other people's money (mainly because they did not use drugs). By the end of my first summer working full-time on the block, I sometimes found myself holding someone's money as well.

What is the significance of a person's giving me fifty or sixty dollars to hold and insisting that I not give it back to him later on that night, even if he asks? It means he is

about to buy some five- or ten-dollar vials of crack cocaine ("nickel" or "dime" vials) and does not want to spend all of his money on drugs. A nickel in a crack stem is often referred to as a "good hit," a dime as two "good hits." The high from a nickel lasts for about five minutes, but can be made to last as long as fifteen minutes if the person has no more of the drug. Then a depression tends to set in, leading him to smoke more. A person with a hundred dollars can do a nickel every two or three minutes, going through a pocketful of money in less than an hour. Some smoke up to a hundred dollars in a night, usually extending their supply over a few hours. It is no wonder that a man might give someone else money to hold so as to have enough left over the next day to buy food, purchase merchandise to sell, or settle debts.

Sometimes when Ron asked me to hold his money, he returned at one or two in the morning and insisted on getting it back. Once, when I refused and reminded Ron what he had told me earlier, he said, My money is my money! Give it to me!

Okay, Ron, I'll give you twenty dollars, I responded, and did so.

An hour later, Ron laid his body down and went to sleep.

When I arrived on the block the next day, I noticed Ron sitting on a milk crate, evidently drunk. Rather than give him the rest of his money, I walked away before he saw me. A few days later, now sober, he expressed appreciation that I hadn't returned the money to him earlier. He then used it to buy some extra books from Joe Garbage, who had struck gold on a hunt. He also bought some food, and paid back a debt of ten dollars to Marvin.

Instead of having me hold his money, he might have used it to stay at the White House Hotel on the Bowery, which now charges ten dollars for a cubicle room, or at one of a number of other hotels. He could have gone and checked into the hotel *before* he smoked, a common practice of men who know they don't want to sleep outside after they get high. Or, like Conrad, another vendor of scavenged magazines on the block that night, who was (at that time) addicted to crack, he could have reserved three nights at the White House with a lump-sum payment.

When I told Hakim that I found this behavior puzzling, he said he could offer no explanation to help me out. But he offered to take the tape recorder and do an interview with Ron.

"Do the other guys that [are] out here know about the White House?"

"Yeah! But they [don't] want to spend that money. Ain't nobody gonna save up no eight dollars!"

"But, Ron!" exclaimed Hakim. "Eight dollars! Save up? You can make eight dollars out here in five minutes!"

"In one sale! "Ron laughed.

"You just made a sale for . . ."

"Fifteen dollars! "said Ron.

"That's two nights right there!" said Hakim.

"Yeah, that's two nights."

"It's warm?" asked Hakim. "It's clean?"

"Yeah, it's clean."

"It beats sleeping out here on the sidewalk?"

"Yeah, definitely."

"But you are saying these guys don't want to spend eight dollars a day, which out here is peanuts, to stay somewhere rather than the sidewalk?"

"Yeah. And you get a bed, towels for a shower, and soap. They have a big shower down in the basement."

The Logic of the Habitat

Approximately a third of the men working on Sixth Avenue sleep on these sidewalks, in the subway, or on nearby blocks. In his influential 1994 book, *The Homeless*, sociologist Christopher Jencks argues: "A bed in a New York or Chicago cubicle hotel currently costs about $8 a night. Most people who have enough money to buy substantial amounts of crack could therefore afford to rent a cubicle instead. A large fraction of the single adults in New York shelters who test positive for cocaine presumably think that a crack high, however brief, is worth more than a scuzzy cubicle." He goes on: "We badly need more reliable information on where the homeless get their money and how they spend it. But the only way to collect better information is to spend endless hours with the homeless, observing what they do instead of just asking them about such matters on surveys."[4]

In responding to Jencks's plea for more and better evidence, I did *not* find that these men spend every bit of additional money they have on drugs. Why, then, do they continue to sleep on the street?

As we have seen, the blocks are a place in which various survival elements can be networked together, making it a particularly good subsistence habitat for the street entrepreneur. A defining feature of un-housed persons on Sixth Avenue is that a complex social organization has arisen from the work they do to sustain themselves.[5] There are two basic reasons, rather than a lack of available housing or a lack of money, why embeddedness in a habitat leads a person to remain on the street. First, a man will sleep on the blocks as a function of the complementarity of the various habitat elements (such as food, basic shelter, and an opportunity to make a little money) coming together in one place. Second, he may sleep there because his friends are out there watching tables, which makes the habitat a place where he feels safe and even comfortable. He is there for the same reason that Jane Jacobs says a busy sidewalk life makes pedestrians feel safe: because those who are out know that eyes are upon the street.

Because resources are valuable in the setting by virtue of their contextual connections, people working the street use the sidewalks in accordance with a logic that derives from the complementarity of different elements. To understand the act of sleeping on the sidewalks, rather than assuming a person is making a trade-off between drugs and a room, it is always useful to consider a person's overall logic and how it is encouraged or structured by the existence of the habitat.

Why might a man choose to sleep on the sidewalk? Some common answers:

To save a vending space. "If you see the spot that Ishmael got, he want to be there all the time, twenty-four hours," Ron told me. "He don't want to leave the spot and have it be taken by somebody else when they get here in the morning. So he figure he just stay there."

Ishmael confirmed that he stays there because doing so maintains another resource, a space on the sidewalk from which to sell his magazines. We have, of course, already seen [in original publication] a variation on this theme: a person who earns his money as a table watcher may stay on the block all night to earn his pay.

To save money. Grady, a longtime drug user, now clean, who recently discovered that he is HIV-positive, sleeps on the sidewalk or in the dungeon of the subway because of the complex of other activities that exist within the habitat. He told me that someone is always getting on or off the train in the middle of the night, so that he usually feels safe and comfortable on the sidewalk or in the dungeon. His plan is to to sleep on the streets in the summer and fall, so that he can have enough money saved up for the winter, when it gets cold. Such a plan would not be possible unless the habitat provided a space for sleeping that Grady considered a safe and comfortable alternative to a hotel.

For a time, he went to a hotel on days that he spent with his girlfriend, Phyllis. But when she was locked up in the Riker's Island prison, a hotel hardly seemed worth it to him anymore. In one month he saved a thousand dollars for the winter and for a trip to see his mother in Florida. (I counted the money.)

Hakim interviewed Grady about his finances and sleeping. Grady explained that he was saving his money for the winter. He knows that, like other men, he could earn enough money in the winter to afford housing then, but this would force him to be working outside during the coldest months of the year as he tries to combat HIV. His choice is not between drugs and an apartment, but between an apartment in the warm weather and an apartment in the cold, or between an apartment when his girlfriend is with him and one when she is not.

To use crack. Even though there are many police officers around Sixth Avenue, a person who is using crack often prefers to be on the sidewalk, near those police, rather than in a hotel (presumably away from the police). Why? Because he knows that in a hotel the manager can call the precinct and say that something suspicious is going on in a particular room. "The police can get a key from the front desk and walk right on in," Ron told me. "You might be engaged in some kind of activity and you are busted. That's one of the reasons they say hotels is not safe."

Also, Ron, like other crack users, is paranoid about being in small, enclosed spaces when he is high. This might also help explain how crack use became associated with the rise in the number of unhoused persons. And, of course, the continuous stream of money that comes from the entrepreneurial activity of the sidewalk makes it possible for Ron to keep bingeing all night long – smoking or drinking until he passes out, or sitting in his chair at the table until he falls asleep.[6]

"Once You're Homeless, You're Always Homeless"

The person who sleeps on the blocks to save a space, to save money, or to use drugs is making use of the complementarity of the various subsistence elements available in one place.

In each case, the person who regularly makes the decision to remain on the sidewalk overnight has a vocabulary for expressing its acceptability to him. Hakim used my tape recorder to conduct an interview in which Mudrick made a number of statements that illustrate this point. Mudrick often sleeps on the steps of the church, on subway trains, or on the floor of a storage room in the building where he makes extra money taking out the trash. Here he keeps his clothes neatly folded.

"Once any man is homeless, he's always homeless," Mudrick told Hakim.

"In what respect?" asked Hakim.

"You got a bed, Hakim? You sleep in your bed, right?"

"I prefer to sleep in my bed," responded Hakim.

"I sleep on the floor." Mudrick continued. "Ask my daughter where I sleep when I go see Dyneisha. Me and my granddaughter go get a blanket and sleep on the floor. My daughter asked me why I can't sleep in the bed. I said, 'Listen. It's a long story. One day you might hear it . . .' She don't know what streets I live on. You see, I sleep on the sidewalk."

"Would you spend ten dollars a night to stay in the White House Hotel?"

"I can't afford it!"

"But, Mudrick, you making money!"

"What I'm gonna stay in the hotel for when the same thing as the hotel is sleeping in the street? What's the difference?"

"So, if tomorrow you won the lottery or you inherited an apartment on Tenth Street with a bed and furniture and everything, you gonna sleep on the floor?"

"That's right! I choose to be homeless."

"You choose to be homeless?"

"I choose to be! Where else I had to go when I come here? I didn't have no money. I came here to find a job and work. But that didn't work and my money ran out."

"If a man who sells magazines or books makes fifty to sixty dollars a day, what would stop him from taking ten dollars and going to the White House?"

"People who sleep in the street that make that kind of money want to do this."

"So you saying it's not a question of money?"

"Listen, a bed is made to sleep in. I don't sleep in it. I'm not used to it. I don't want to get used to it. I got a choice. I gonna stay in the street. I ain't going to go nowhere."

"No matter how much money you make?"

"No matter how much. Once you're homeless, you're always homeless."

In speaking of their own deep acceptance of their condition, men sometimes refer to their initial unhoused condition as a choice, sometimes blatantly contradicting biographical facts from the same interview or an earlier conversation. (In this case, Mudrick claims to be "homeless" by choice in the same sentence in which he recalls his inability to find a job that would put a roof over his head.) Once again we are reminded that interviewing does not necessarily produce a clear understanding of the men's personal choices, even if we do get to hear the vocabulary through which they explain their condition.

Two of the most common explanations for remaining on the street are "I can't afford a room" and "The hotel is not safe." Yet, when challenged on these claims, many men will state that sleeping in certain hotels (like the White House) is as safe as sleeping on the sidewalk, and few men will stick to their claim that they really can't find in their earnings the money for a hotel. "Safety" sometimes seems to refer to being free from police searches.

Mudrick's "Once you're homeless, you're always homeless," seems to be linked to his body's response to the social and physical experience of sleeping on a hard surface. His body seems to have grown to prefer a particular physical experience, which makes the social experience of homelessness acceptable in ways it would not be for the average person. For some of these men, sleeping in a bed no longer feels natural.

Although most Americans take sleeping in a bed as basic to decency, the conventional bed is not a physical necessity but a cultural artifact; many people of the world regard a bed as less healthy for sleeping than a hard surface.[7]

Ishmael hardly ever leaves the corner of Sixth Avenue and Eighth Street. Yet, when Hakim asked him if he considers himself homeless, he said, "No! I don't consider myself homeless. No. See, I don't sleep on the street. I don't lay out on the street. I don't act like I can't work."

"You say you don't sleep on the street. But I've seen you for quite some time in a chair on the sidewalk, asleep."

"On the sidewalk, sitting down, asleep. Okay? At a job, asleep. Okay? I'm at my job, asleep. It's not like I'm not at a job! I'm not stretched out on the ground."

So some men deny being homeless even as they demonstrate an acceptance of that condition in other terms. The "homeless" condition itself does not constitute the basic role through which these men define themselves. *The entrepreneurial activity* – more than the person's unhoused state – is central to personal identity. If you ask a person to tell you about himself, he'll likely say, "I'm a vendor," not, "I'm homeless." (Here recall Ron and Marvin's bargaining techniques, the way they sell their wares and "get over," producing self-respect and a sense that they are independent businessmen.)

Although passersby regard him as a "homeless" man, Ishmael's answers suggest that he sees his work as basic to who he is. Indeed, most aspects of Ishmael's day on Sixth Avenue are tightly scheduled in accordance with the demands of work and the principle of complementarity within a habitat. He knows that the police will walk the beat at certain times, and he *must* be present at his table during those periods if his belongings are not to be taken. He knows that trash is put out at certain times, so that he must be out "hunting" then. He knows that customers will purchase the most magazines at certain other times, so he must be

present on the block then. He knows it is good to be present on the block if he is to be there when a random person appears with a donation of magazines.

He may tell a researcher that he would choose to have a place to live, but not if that means he must give up the things that otherwise sustain him: yes, a place to sleep; but also free or cheap food, social networks, abundant trash, and, most important, a place to earn a living by selling what he takes from the trash. Into his presence on these blocks must be read more than the existence of "homelessness." We must see in the uses to which he puts the sidewalk an embeddedness in habitat, a series of complementary elements tied together in an encompassing manner that ultimately sustains. In networking together complementary sustaining elements, Ishmael chooses to sleep on the block – not because this is the best sleeping alternative he has, and not because he has spent all of his money on drugs, but because he is on the block first and foremost to work and, through that work, to live his life.

To speak about the little choices people make on a day-to-day basis is not to comprehend the circumstances that led them to the street. Nor does a close look at this population solve the problem of understanding other types of unhoused people whose sustenance activities have not led to complex forms of social organization.[8] We must not begin with the assumption that the unhoused on Sixth Avenue are the same as single mothers with their children walking the streets, unhoused families living in cars, individuals sleeping by themselves underneath bridges, or persons who cannot find a place to stay.[9] Research suggests, for example, that the destruction of New York City's Single Residence Occupancy (S.R.O.) housing stock was a primary contributing factor to the rise in visible big-city homelessness in the 1980s.[10]

Nevertheless, when people sleeping *on these blocks* decide to stay there, it becomes questionable to many passersby whether they are really struggling to live "decent" lives. The answer, I think, is that such acts pose no challenge to what we saw in the first three chapters of [the original publication]: each of these men is engaged in such a struggle. This is most evident in the way they choose to support themselves: through honest entrepreneurial activity. If they were using drugs, could not work for other people in a tolerable manner, had no marketable skills, and then robbed to support their habit, we might reasonably conclude that they had given up on the struggle to live in accordance with society's standards. In this case, the men have made clever use of a local ordinance to appropriate public space and avoid engaging in criminal activity that hurts others. As Ishmael sees his life, others can do the same thing with the space that he did, appropriating it from him. So he has to protect it by staying there, or at least he thinks he must.

Some argue that no matter how "degraded" or "victimized" a man is, he must be held up to the same standards as everyone else. Actually, a sociological analysis gains power when it takes up such a challenge, comparing the acts these men engage in with those of other members of society who are not viewed as "victims." Ishmael brings to mind people whom society considers respectable who, like him, choose to sleep where their jobs are. Owners of small retail businesses may have spent the first ten years of ownership sleeping in the attic. They are afraid that, if they are not present, things may get fouled up. Even once their store runs like clockwork, they seem to believe they mustn't be away from it.

It is tempting to believe that the difference between Ishmael and "decent" people is that the latter have solved problems of where to sleep in ways that fit in better with standard ways of doing things. To some extent, this is true. But when "decent" people have not done so, few people accuse them of being indecent. This is because they don't fit the delinquent stereotype and

aren't as public in their behavior. Few people actually see what they do.

There are, of course, many people in America and throughout the world who appropriate public space and sleep outside. In Santa Barbara, California, some people sleep in beat-up Volkswagen buses by the Amtrak station, sometimes for months at a time. There are many other people who appropriate the public lands with sleeping bags and camp out as they make their way up and down the coast. These people are white, and often come from middle-class families. That they use drugs while they do their camping seems of little concern to anyone. Fewer people question their decency.

If Ron is too paranoid to rent a room when he is high on crack, and if Grady is afraid of being outside in cold weather and wants to save his money, it is hard to argue in consequence that they have given up on the struggle to live a "decent" life.

It is important to note that of the sixteen men who have at one time regularly slept on these blocks, only five currently spend their nights out there. Like Ron, of the eleven men who left the blocks for a housed existence, *all* still work out on these or other sidewalks as vendors. At any given time on the blocks, someone is looking to take the money he has saved and get himself a place to live. As I write this, Grady has now secured an apartment and his partner Keith White has saved $1,000 to be able to afford a security deposit for an apartment in Brooklyn. The opportunities to vend ultimately do help many men to stabilize their lives.

But there are always some people who take sleeping on the blocks to an extreme. When I asked Hakim to account for the failure of people like himself, Marvin, and Jaamane to stop sidewalk sleeping altogether (in cases where it does not seem necessary), he said: "It's not as if, in the case of Ishmael, that we have not tried to talk to him and say, 'This is what we would like for you to do to move your life beyond sleeping on the sidewalk.' In the early days I was optimistic about it, but I came to the conclusion that he was not interested in creating a balance in his life beyond work, work, work. Once a guy gets used to living a certain way, it takes a long time to adjust to doing anything better."

The practical test of whether the informal controls have been a failure is whether a system of control brought in from the outside could do better. If informal mentoring does not discourage sidewalk sleeping on its own, could the government implement formal regulations that would work? For example, if the city were to assign spaces to vendors, it would be unnecessary for men to sleep on the sidewalk to maintain their rights. In theory, this would encourage some people who are living on the streets to go elsewhere at night. If a person had a property right to a particular sidewalk space, he or she would not feel a need to sleep there to maintain it.

Such a regulation might well lead to greater order on our sidewalks and among the people dwelling on them. But the evidence suggests that many of these particular unhoused people would not go to hotels anyway. Even if the right to vend at night were taken away, men who are out on the sidewalk because they are accustomed to hard surfaces would likely remain outside. And those who are there to make money for drug bingeing would also likely remain outside, panhandling or stealing the money, instead of vending. From what we know about these men and their lives, it is fair to speculate that the effort to reduce disorder through more formal regulation might even result in greater disorder; that eliminating vending and scavenging might result in more theft.

Informal mentoring and controls simply cannot contain all acts that go against common notions of decency, nor could we expect government to establish a policy that would do any better. The best alternative, of course, would be better drug treatment and

men who are willing to avail themselves of it. But even with the best programs in place, some people will choose to binge. Some of those will choose to earn their money honestly. And some of those will sleep on the sidewalk. The contribution of the informal system of social control inherent in sidewalk life is to encourage men to live "better" lives within the framework of their own and society's weaknesses.

NOTES

1 Jacobs, *The Death and Life of Great American Cities* (New York: Vintage, 1961), pp. 131–2.

2 Wilson had done empirical research in the 1970s arguing that the crime rate goes down when police focus on minor crimes such as citing for moving violations. These results were confirmed with more sophisticated statistical techniques by Robert Sampson and Jacqueline Cohen, who concluded: "Proactive policing has been shown to have significant and relatively strong inverse effects on robbery, especially adult robbery by both blacks and whites. . . . Hence, on strict empirical grounds the results suggest that cities . . . with higher levels of proactive police strategies directed at public disorders also generate significantly lower robbery rates." (Robert J. Sampson and Jacqueline Cohen, "Deterrent Effects of the Police on Crime: A Replication and Theoretical Extension," *Law and Society Review* 22, no. 1 [1988]: 163–89, 184–5.)

3 See, for example, Philippe Bourgeois, *In Search of Respect* (Cambridge: Cambridge University Press, 1995).

4 Jencks, *The Homeless* (Cambridge, MA: Harvard University Press, 1994), p. 44.

5 In considering the distinctiveness of these unhoused persons, I will pay attention to four concepts – population, (social) organization, environment, and technology, POET – the very concepts that Otis Dudley Duncan once described as essential to territorial demography or human ecology. (See Otis Dudley Duncan, "Human Ecology and Population Studies," in Philip M. Hauser

and Otis Dudley Duncan, eds., *The Study of Population* [Chicago: University of Chicago Press, 1959], pp. 678–716.) This population has four characteristics that make it distinctive. First, its individuals constitute a population unit in a particular space with a character different from any of the men as individuals. This unit enables men who could not survive on their own to "make it" as a group. Second, the population unit exists in an environment and remains there by acting on the environment despite the environment's best efforts to act on it. Third, the population unit develops particular techniques and technologies in order to gain sustenance from the environment. And fourth, an intricate social organization arises from those sustenance-producing activities. In developing the framework, I am building on the earlier work of Kim Hopper, "Economies of Makeshift," *Urban Anthropology*, vol. 14 (1985): 1–3, which argued for the importance of understanding "the particular way homelessness meshes with other subsistence activities" (p. 214).

6   Morgan and Zimmer, "The Social Pharmacology of Smokeable Cocaine," p. 145.

7   Galen Cranz, *The Chair* (New York: W. W. Norton, 1998).

8   For a wider view, see Jim Baumohl, ed., *Homelessness in America* (Phoenix: Oryx Press, 1996).

9   In looking at Sixth Avenue, therefore, my purpose is not to make generalizations about homelessness that could be sustained only with different methods or with comparisons to populations I don't know, but to understand the uses to which the sidewalks of Greenwich Village are being put today. In the process, though, we may learn something about the types of questions that could be asked about other homeless street people – that is, what it is about a particular environment that makes it a sustainable habitat for this person or group of people. After all, we can only know if the choices made by other types of homeless individuals have a similar complexity if we continue to respond to pleas for more and better evidence.

10   See Jencks, *The Homeless*, p. 44.

19

Whores, Slaves, and Stallions: Languages of Exploitation and Accommodation Among Prizefighters

Loïc Wacquant

Loïc Wacquant is a Researcher at the Centre de sociologie européenne du Collège de France and a Professor of Sociology and Research Fellow at the Earl Warren Legal Institute, University of California–Berkeley. He is the author of *Prisons of Poverty* (1999, translated in twelve languages), *Body & Soul: Ethnographic Notebooks of an Apprentice Boxer* (2000, translated in five languages), *Punir os pobres* (2001), *Parias Urbanos* (2001), and of the forthcoming *In the Zone: Making Do in the Dark Ghetto at Century's End*. He has recently completed an anthology of the works of Marcel Mauss, to be published by the University of Chicago Press, and is now working on a comparative historical study of racial domination as well as editing the new international journal *Ethnography*.

Boxing provides a unique prism through which to gain an understanding of structured opportunity, cultural perceptions, and individual trajectories in the lower tiers of the American metropolis. Its very nature as a radically instrumentalist bodily activity, its linkages to the informal street economy, the social and ethnoracial recruitment of its practitioners, the motivations and dispositions it requires of them make boxing the prototypal masculine ghetto institution. Indeed, the modern history of pugilism in the United States is inseparable from that of race relations and from the periodic redrawing of the urban color line in that country (Sammons, 1988). Boxing is also a particularly propitious terrain for dissecting the *lived experience and symbolic construction of exploitation* at the bottom of the class and caste structure. This article draws on 35 months of ethnographic fieldwork and apprenticeship in a boxing gym located in Chicago's black ghetto to explicate how prizefighters apperceive and express the brute fact of being live commodities of flesh and blood, and how they practically reconcile themselves to ferocious exploitation in ways that enable them to preserve a sense of personal integrity and moral purpose. It thus seeks to contribute simultaneously to the anthropology of working-class cultures as well as to the ethnosociology of body, economy, and morality.[1]

A notion commonly invoked by critics of professional boxing to explain the sport's continued existence is that fighters are naïve, overcredulous, incomprehending, or ill-informed as to the real nature of their occupation – in short, dupes (or dopes) in this "show business with blood" to which they devote a good chunk of their lives and limb(s). In reality, far from harboring any illusions, professional boxers are, if anything, hyperconscious of entering into a universe of no-holds-barred exploitation in which deception, manipulation, concealment, and mistreatment are the normal order of things, and bodily damage and personal disrepair a customary consequence of the trade. One member of the gym on the South Side of Chicago where I apprenticed for some three years describes relations between ring associates as follows: "Everybody tryinna outdo everybody an' everybody tryin' to hurt everybody an' everybody don' trust nobody." The tangible proofs of the corporeal ravages and personal misery that the profession entails are everywhere for boxers to see, notes a black middleweight from the city's West Side: "All you gotta do is go to d'gyms and look around: you got lotta guys, they *legs are shot*, y'know, they jus' hang around d'gym and well they not doin' anything. An' you look at they career when they were comin' up they were doin' pretty decent, then afterwards, *tchhh!*, (sullen) they have nuthin' to fall back on, and it's *bad*."

Fighters are unanimous in holding the view that the game is rife with "crooked managers" ("It's like a ton of them, they out to make a quick buck") and they take as axiomatic that promoters and matchmakers are "fleshpeddlers" who will not hesitate to dispatch them to "fight King Kong for a dime" so long as it is in their pecuniary interest.[2] "When you a fighter an' especially when you don't have like *high people* around you," explains an African-American lightweight who works occasionally as an electrician after a brief stint in the Marines, "it's like you in a *big bowl with a lotta sharks*, you know what I'm sayin', an' they're all like (sibilating in mock delight) 'yeah you look juicy, I'll take a bite outa your ass!'" A young Puerto-Rican light-heavyweight who moonlights as a security guard has this

telling expression: "*They're the ones walkin' around with the leather shoes, we're not*, yeah, so . . . 'cuz as a promoter, you never get a punch thrown atchyou, unless you're a real bad promoter. An' you got the money an' you don't gotta work hard for it."

Idioms of Corporeal Exploitation

The boxer's consciousness of exploitation is expressed in three kindred idioms, those of *prostitution*, *slavery*, and *animal husbandry*. The first likens the fighter–manager combo to the duet formed by the prostitute and her pimp; the second depicts the ring as a plantation and promoters and matchmakers as latter-day slave masters and drivers; the third intimates that boxers are treated in the manner of dogs, pigs, stallions, and other commercially valued livestock. All three tropes simultaneously enounce and denounce the immoral, indeed inhumane, merchandising of disquiescent live bodies.

According to the first language, pimp and manager would have this in common that, under the pretense of promoting the financial interest and protecting the physical (or emotional) integrity of their respective "partner," they use and abuse them in a ruthless quest for lucre. Much like the prostitute offers her female body's capacity for sexual performance for pay on the street, the fighter retails his male body's trained ability to dish out, as well as to withstand, physical punishment between the ropes, and managers and promoters, standing in the wings, are the ones who reap the brunt of the monies generated by this commerce of manly flesh.[3] An older ring "warhorse" who has trekked across continental Europe many times as an "opponent" for local fighters[4] put it in this cutting way:

> All boxers, are what they call, figure of speech: they're *fucked over*. You know, you see, they're *pimps*, the promoters, you know. And boxers is like the *whores*, you know, so you pimp

him. Yeah, that's the way that go, I'm pretty sure. They don't really have the bes' interes' in the fighter, you know. They jus' goin' for the gusto, *the gusto is the money*. (dejected but matter-of-fact) They jus' goin' for the money.

A younger colleague from a West Side gym who gave up a solid job as a TV cable installer in a satellite city to move to Chicago and pursue his career in the ring full-time with the financial backing of the gym's new owner seconds this view:

Oh yeah, it's a lot of managers tha' you can jus' say they're *pimps*: like they like to pimp a fighter, you know. They put' em out there an' throw'em in there with anybody, jus' for the money an' take mos' the money an' leave a fighter broke or with jus' enough to barely make it. It's a lot of managers like that who *use* fighters, jus' like a pimp will use a whore – the same way. (scornful) It's a lot of managers tha' are jus' hustlers. They jus' lookin' for any fighter to make a dime off 'em an' don' really care too much abou' the fighters health or nuthin'.

The second idiom in which the visceral sense of exploitation and subordination to external dictates is expressed borrows from the historical experience of slavery. For obvious reasons, analogies to this institution of forced labor and "natal alienation" (Patterson, 1982) is endowed with a unique resonance and high emotional charge for African-American boxers. My gym buddy and regular sparring partner Ashante, then a rising junior-welterweight with a long string of dead-end jobs on the side, recounts a particularly brutal fight which awakened him to the built-in economic inequity of boxing:

If you go in dere witha *nice tough fight, man, rewar' dis man*. I tol', I saw Highmower fight dis boy, man, *man!* (chuckle) I hated fightin', *I hated boxin' ever since*, I'm serious. Because, Louie,

(incensed) Highmower an' dat boy nearly *killed each other*. Man, d'crowd wen' crazy, Ralph [the matchmaker] – I's, I's like, "look at dis shit! Boy, *this is slavery all over again*. I mean, look at dis shit! Dese men is seriously killin' each other for (lowering his voice and whispering in joint disbelief and disgust) for a hun'red dollars ... (stressing each word to dramatize his point) Highmower-cut, that-man-cut, they-all-wen'-down, three-an'-four-time-a-piece. Botha'em wen' to d'hospital, fer what, fer two hun'red dollars, *hun'red each man?* I said, (shaking his head vigorously) "No, that ain't – tha's not right."

In the course of voicing his resolute opposition to governmental regulation of the trade, which he claims would "effectively destroy boxing," the president of one of the major so-called "federations" which sanction world titles bouts[5] (an African-American former fighter I interviewed in Atlantic City in the early 1990s), conceded that there do exist "some promoters who wanta *deviate*, who wanta get an advantage or an edge up on another guy, who don't want to have the mandatory fight [in defense of a title] because they're afraid their fighter *might lose*. Or who want to *tie up a fighter* indefinitely with five or six options – *slavery went out with Lincoln* and they want to make some of these fighters *slaves* and that's not good."

The third language of exploitation among prizefighters conjures up animal and farming metaphors that debase boxers to the rank of beasts to be reared, fed, trained, and displayed – even devoured with cannibalistic cruelty – at the will and whim of those who hold the economic levers of the game. One evening, as he was showing me the various spots near his apartment that served for the open-air sale of drugs, Luke abruptly launched into an angry tirade about the tangled disputes between his trainer, his manager, and Ralph, the white matchmaker who exercises near-monopolistic control over the city's boxing economy. He resented in particular the fact that his coach had sided with Ralph when the latter maneuvered underhandedly to prevent Luke from fighting out of town for bigger purses:

> I's like, dey want me to fight when Ralph want me to fight. Like, like, like *if I'm a horse in a barn, I get up ev'ry mornin', my trainer take me out an' run me, dey clean me, dey feed me, an' put me back in my, back in my barn room,* and den, Ralph come by and say, (in an exaggeratedly jovial voice) "Hey, how you're doin'?" He stops an' he, y'know, in d'office: (in a mellifluous voice, imitating a white inflection) *"How that black stallion doin'?"* You know, "he doin' okay." An' den, they'll pick a few of the guys who's gonta fight, keep me in my stable, I'm runnin' an' I'm trainin' *right?* Den he say: (sternly) "Never gonna let him fight."

Exploitative relations are not limited to those linking fighters to managers and promoters. They can extend, capillary-style, to trainers, gym mates and rivals, and to the collection of characters who hang in the entourage of boxers and that the lore labels "gym rats." Phonzo is a loner who never complains about anything ("I never dwell on the negative, people don' bother me, nobody bother me. Not even you: *no one*") and who has enjoyed unusual success in the squared circle: he is one of a handful of fighters from Chicago who have conquered a world title over the past two decades. Yet, when we reflect upon the economic upshot of his career, sitting together in the gym's backroom, everything about him, his demeanor, body torque, tone, and glare, reveals that he is filled to the brim with bitterness. After many long years of "sacrifice" abiding by the ascetic regimen of the prizefighter, running and training daily, following murderous diets, and curtailing his social and sexual life, he finally got to strap on a champion's

belt.[6] But what should have been the apotheosis of his professional life and motive for personal exultation turned out an empty and joyless moment.

PHONZO: You find that through *finance an' money* – money is power here in America – so, since money's power, money can make you a lotta enemies, also money can make you a whole lotta imposters frien's. (visibly pained by the remembrance) So hum, I thought I had frien's, still now . . . But when the money started gettin' decent, (his voice and gaze turning cold) those frien's turned to *scavengers.* An' when a frien' turn to a scavenger, they pick your bones *clean*: they use you, take a'vantage of yon, abuse you, jus' like you were a *pig* or anythin'. They *eat you alive.* So when I came to a position of that happenin', I didn' have the same people that when I started out, I was a very unhappy person. So when I won the championship I didn' win it with the people that *I trusted.* And the one's you trusted'll sometimes turn against you, y'know? An' uh, winnin' the championship was a satisfaction, but it wasn' d'same.

LOUIE: Not bein' with the people that you wanted to be with took the joy away?
PHONZO: Took the joy, right.

LOUIE: Is that somethin' you regret?
PHONZO: I don' regret nuthin' in life. Only God know what happen in life an' why it happen. . . . It's jus' when people look at you like bein' like *a bar of soap* an' not a human bein', they lose respect for you. An' when they lose respect for you, you lose respect for them. An' when you got two people who's doin' bus'ness that ain't got no respect for each other, you don' have a good bus'ness plan. Or you don' have a good bus'ness . . . situation. (very tense and quickly, bitterly, without taking in a breath) '*Cuz everybody tryinna outdo everybody an' everybody tryin' to hurt everybody an' everybody don' trust nobody an' when you got a situation like*

that, you got (grave and guttural) *chaos*, an' when you got chaos, well, for a game, in like boxin', you got a problem like this, you got more problems than you got to handle 'em.

So that was the reason, I don' complain: I'm glad that I got out the game, 'cuz I get out without no cauliflower ears, wi' all my teeth in my mouth, without havin' broken ribs – only thing I had broken several times was my han's, that's because I hit so hard.

These three languages of exploitation are in no way incompatible with one another and, in point of fact, boxers often deploy them together in varying combinations. In his testimony during the "Hearings on Corruption in Professional Boxing" held by the U.S. Senate in summer 1992 following the media uproar caused by a grotesquely biased decision that deprived him of a world title in a nationally televised bout, Dave "TNT" Tiberi, a white middleweight from Delaware, took the anthropophagous metaphor one step further when he declared to bemused senators that "the majority of fighters, depending upon their respective levels of talent, are viewed by their promoters as prime ribs, others pork chops, and the least talented scrapple, but rarely are they recognized as human beings." Explaining that the International Boxing Federation had allowed him to challenge for the belt of its champion James Toney only after he had first relinquished his own crown with the rival International Boxing Council and signed a three-fight option with Toney's promoter, Tiberi shifts register: "Thinking back on the circumstances, it was like being bought at a slave auction . . . I sometimes find it hard to consider boxing a sport. For many promoters, it has become their private legalized slave industry" (U.S. Senate, 1992: 10, 11). The accompanying deposition of James Pritchard, the IBF Intercontinental cruiserweight titlist, adds a vampiric touch to the haunting vision in which the lifeblood of fighters is being drained out of them to be

Table 19.1   What boxers would consider "fair pay" for a six-round fight*

<500 dollars	5	11%
500 dollars	6	13%
600–800 dollars	20	45%
>1,000 dollars	14	31%
(total)	*(45)*	*(100)*

Source: author's survey of Illinois professional fighters (1991).
* Actual purses range from 200 to 300 dollars.

consumed by parasitic profiteers. Pritchard has worked under three managers, all three of whom he characterizes as "bloodsuckers": "Like a mosquito bite, he bites you and sucks your blood. That is what they do. When they latch onto you, they just suck everything out of you they can possibly get" (U.S. Senate, 1992: 30). Blood sucked, flesh picked, bones cleaned, vitality sapped and stolen: these expressions vividly convey the boxer's carnal appreciation of being an undervalued and endangered bodily commodity.[7]

Integrity Through Accommodation

The overwhelming majority of professional fighters – 88 percent of those plying their trade in Illinois in 1991 – hold that their services are grossly underpaid and they are quite vociferous in complaining that the purses they receive amount to "chump change" and "peanuts." A full 86 percent of them consider that a "fair purse" would have to equal or exceed 100 dollars per round, *twice the going rate* in Chicago at that time (see table 19.1). When I asked him if he thought that the city's pugilists are receiving "fair pay" for their labor, an unemployed black welterweight four years in the business responded with scarcely contained anger:

No, *they're not*! No, they're bein' *cheated*, they're bein' *robbed*, uh, an' boxin' in Chicago, to me, this is my personal way of speakin', boxers in Chicago, (very loudly) has been *ABUSED an' USED an' justice has never revealed in they favor in Chicago*, okay? Because uh, the guys are *underpaid*, an' they're *overtrain'*, an' they can never make the things they need to make in boxin' because uh, no one really *cared* 'bout them.

Yet, at the same time as they express a perfervid and often pained sense of exploitation, boxers rarely rise up to denounce their economic fate as a gross injustice. Instead, in their workaday world, they practically reconcile themselves to the distinct prospect, if not actuality, of being fleshly merchandise to be bought, sold, and bartered. Three "vocabularies of motive" (Mills, 1940) enable them to achieve this compromise and to construct a sense of personal and professional integrity, understood as "taking responsibility for one's own life project, within the limits and pressures imposed by structural constraints, in accordance with consistent conceptions of the right way to live, and in partnership with others."[8]

This first vocabulary asserts plainly that *exploitation is an inescapable fact of life*, a *datum brutum* of ordinary existence for ordinary folks with which one has to make do as best as one can. The source of its persuasiveness is obvious: economic exploitation *is* a constant in the nether regions of American social space where boxers and their associates dwell; the only parameters that vary are its phenomenal forms, its intensity, and its beneficiaries.[9] Under that angle, prizefighting differs little from the other social games to which proletarian young men from inner-city neighborhoods have access, given the truncated opportunities supplied by a bankrupt public school system and the long-term marginality promised by an unskilled employment market awash with cheap labor (MacLeod, 1994; Holzer, 1996). As my gym mate

Butch, a firefighter and pug with over a decade of experience in the ring, put it succinctly:

If you have a poor class of people who have nothin, uneducated, the job market is bad and then this guy says, "well look, if you two guys fight, I'll give you a 150 dollars," *how can he say no?* They taken advantage of yer situation. If he had money in his pocket and a job, he wouldn't git him to go fight. So *yes*, the poor poverty background makes helluva fighters, 'cause they'll fight, 'cause they don't have anythin' else. And once they learn to make money, the causin' pain and injury to somebody else gits to be *easy* money and, they jus' keep doin' it till they can't do it anymore, till they become easy money for somebody else.

Much as in the informal economy of the ghetto, with which the pugilistic economy mixes and merges at many junctures, one must accept to take risks if one expects to beget some profits. The same Afro-American bantamweight who vituperates the fact that promoters "do boxers like dogs, do'em just like dogs," assimilates them in the same breath to shady operators who, like him, deploy their smarts and guile in the booty capitalism of the street. "That's not no different than doin' what I's doin': makin' money *hustlin'*."[10] Isn't life itself an immense ongoing lottery of sorts, anyway? A Mexican welterweight who insists that he is fully conscious of the abuses routinely perpetrated by promoters and yet recently signed a long-term contract with one of the four major promotion houses in the land, clarifies: "You *take your chance*: you take a chance jus' walkin' down the road, you know, of getting' run ova by a car, or somebody tryin' to rob you, while you takin' your wife to a picnic or somethin'." Under conditions of pervasive uncertainty, instead of being resentful of promoters and managers, some boxers feel thankful for the chance that the latter grant them to play this queer *lottery with one's skillful body* that is prize-fighting. This is the opinion of Surly, an intermittently employed heavyweight from one of the roughest public housing projects from the city's West Side:

> I guess a lot of 'em, if they weren't really there, you know, you woul'n' have a chance, you know. It's the chance you have to take. (huffing) It's a chance in everythin'. If you shootin' dice, you takin' a chance on winnin' or loosin'. Boxin' is jus' like gamblin' in a sense. You know, but it's jus', aspect of havin' a certain amount of skill too, so, even though *you gamblin', you have a skill abou' what you doin'*.

What is more, the odious reputation of the planet of fisticuffs is such that no one on it can credibly claim that he is genuinely being deceived: every participant knows full well that boxing is like a tank of sharks where he who does not devour others is doomed to become their meal sooner or later (Wacquant, 1998). To enter into the pugilistic economy thus presupposes *ab initio* the acceptance, tacit or explicit, of a subordinate and exploited position. Martin, a black cruiserweight, who fought "pro" for nine years while working his way up from meter reader to a desk job in the customer service division of a big utility company, muses:

> I knew in life that I wanted to fight an' whether a man comes along call himself a "promoter" an' you call him a "flesh peddler," I've already sub-scribed to that position to be a fighter an' he's the flesh peddler. So, promot-ers are only interested in you if you can fight, you know – *same as with all jobs*: all jobs only interested in us as long as we are willin' to come to work, if we don't come to work, the job is no longer interested in us. So uh, (shakes his head morosely) I understand my position, understand it clearly an'

understand that if such a person as a promoter comes along, that's his job, an' uh, yeah, but they, they are only interested in you if you can fight, if you wanna call it flesh-peddlin', yeah, that's what they are. Still I got in the game, *knowin' I would be flesh* (laughs), yeah.

A second force fostering the practical acquiescence of prizefighters to hideously exploitative arrangements is the *spirit of entrepreneurship* that pervades the craft. From the moment they step into a gym, "manly artists" are fed a steady diet of folk notions and narratives that lionize the defiant individual and portray the boxer as a lone warrior, a modern-day gladiator out to prove his mettle by seizing his own fate, as it were, with his balled fists.[11] This entrepreneurial vocabulary of motive is rooted in the occupational experience of *corporeal self-production*: in training, the boxer uses his own body as the raw materials as well as the tool to refashion that very body in accordance with the peculiar exigencies of the craft; he engages in specialized bodily work aimed at producing a specific type of corporeal capital that can be sold and valorized on the pugilistic market (Wacquant, 1995).

Through endless "roadwork" (daily morning runs of 3 to 6 miles), "floorwork" (shadow-boxing, punching an assortment of bags, rope skipping and calisthenics) and "ringwork" (rehearsing moves and sparring in the ring), the fighter "develops his slumbering powers and compels them to act in obedience to his sway" (Marx, 1856: 148). In so doing, he transforms his organism, appropriates its capacities and literally produces a new embodied being out of the old. And he is given a stage on which to affirm his moral valor and construct a heroic, transcendent self which allows him to escape the status of "non-person" (Goffman, 1959: 151–2) to which (sub)proletarians like him are typically consigned. Last but not least, the particular skills that boxers acquire in the course of their occupational activities are seated in their organism and, as such, constitute their inalienable personal property. Professional fighters are *artisans of the (violent masculine) body* who, much like their counterparts of the industrial revolution, glory in the pride of "having a trade" rather than "being in a trade" (Hobsbawm, 1984: 262).

Boxers relish being right "at the point of production," being *self-made men* in the literal sense that they produce themselves through daily bodily work in the gym and out. Many of them also initially enter the profession out of a combination of love for the game and desire to escape the "slave jobs" of downgraded manufacturing and the new service economy, in which one has to "shine somebody shoes" and put up with personal submission, cultural humiliation, and loss of masculine honor as a condition of durable employment – and all this to earn a pittance that supplies neither economic security nor chances for promotion (Bourgois, 1995). They correspondingly construe prizefighting as an escape route from the modal fate of "workin' twenty dif-f'rent jive jobs" that lead nowhere. Says Vinnie, an Italian-American pug who reluctantly turned pro after a local businessman and family friend offered to underwrite his career:

> If I hadn't found boxing, I'd probably be in the streets, either jus' workin' like an average citizen, workin' for a check, havin' to take someone's orders – yeah that *kills me* to think of it!
>
> LOUIE: Really? So boxing is a way to get away from that?
>
> VINNIE: *Definit'ly,* definit'ly. That's why I say, the kids that aren't involved in boxing or in sports and things, go to school, you don't have to do that! (gesturing animatedly) Be your own, your own entrepreneur, *be your own boss,* don't have to listen to no one, don't take no one else's shit, make your own money.

The forceful affirmation of his individual "agency" finds its counterpart in the fighter's paradoxical negation – or downplaying – of the economic responsibility of managers and promoters as it deflects attention away from the impersonal arrangements and structured relationships that effectively determine the shape, pace, and outcome of boxing careers (Wacquant, 1998).

Lastly, with the interested complicity of his peers, trainers, friends and supporters, every boxer clings to the self-serving notion that he will be the *individual exception to the collective rule*: he is the one who will buck the trend, beat the odds, and transgress the universal law of pugilistic extortion. Out of sheer dedication, unbending will, and constant vigilance, he will manage to "get his" without getting spoiled in the process. Such is the position defended by Don, a former "contender" who has lately turned into a valuable second-tier fighter on the national circuit by virtue of his solid ring skills and white skin:[12] "My own self, if I'm lookin' out for myself, I don't allow anybody to take advantage of me: (firmly) *I don't allow it.*" This determination is echoed by Roderick, a black lightweight who had a taste of "the big time" when his manager sent him to work as a sparring partner for elite fighters in the gyms of Las Vegas: "To me, yes, I agree with that all the way [that promoters exploit people]. (Yet you got into the game?) What, but the only way, *I can fight,* you know: that's the difference, that I can fight. I can back myself up. (You don't think someone will use you?) Not unless I let 'em, so if I stay aware, *stay alert,* I won't get hurt." A gym mate concurs: "*Put it that way: I know it's not goin' to happen,* you know, 'cause I'm jus' kinda person if I know it's happenin' I'll go tell you to fuck yourself." As for Martin, the black cruiserweight who admits to being "flesh" to be peddled, he invokes special protection from the heavens: "I got a *Saviour* that take care of me so I don't worry about how – I know people try to use me but uh, the good Lord not gonna let that happen to me."

In the final analysis, the responsibility for exploitation is laid squarely on the boxer who is invited to claim the paternity of his eventual misfortune in the pugilistic field alongside that of his deeds. If he wants to boast authorship of his acts in the glory of fistic success, then he must be ready to assume the agony of professional failure, economic defilement, and bodily destruction, insists a young black middleweight who boxes by day and works as a security guard by night:

> I think tha's true, *some* [that promoters exploit poor minorities], you know, not all, it's *some*. I mean, a person can on'y use you as far as you let 'em. A person can on'y hang you out to dry as far as you let 'em. You feel a person is usin' you, I thin' you shoul' stop an' talk to 'em an' fin' out wha's goin' on: you have a right you know. You shoul' have controlin' int'res' in your contrac'. Never let a promoter or a manager have controlin' int'res' in you, (blurting out) because *you the fighter, man, you the one tha's puttin' yer life on the line, not him.*

All told, boxing is nothing but a "capit'list bizness" like any other and promoters, like any good entrepreneur, are just doing their job when they earn money from the toil and sweat of others. A Puerto-Rican policeman who twice fought for the state title in the lightweight division weaves the theme of the inescapability of exploitation with that of the responsibility of the fighter as an independent operator:

> Yeah, I think pretty much, I feel the same, you know, that's their *job*, that's the way they make their livin' you know what I'm sayin'? You *can't blame them in a way* because they haveta make a livin' but you *can* blame 'em in a way because they're ruinin' somebody, they're ruinin' a kid that might

have good-good potential. Jus' 'cause that kid has no money behind 'im, he's getting used as *bait*, an' that's not right, you know what I'm sayin'? But if the kid was smart enough then he wouldn't let that happen to himself, *I know it ain't gonna happen to me,* you know what I'm sayin', 'cause I know better.

Lastly, for those who, having sunk in years of intensive bodily labor in the specific economy, possess no other qualifications and no short-term alternative – outside of the no less dangerous commerce of "hot" merchandise and narcotics – to generate the income required to cover basic living expenses, brute economic necessity takes over. This is the case of an African-American heavyweight who has been hired out repeatedly by his trainer as an "opponent" on televised shows with virtually no chance of winning and who readily admits that he is being utilized by promoters to further their own ends. Knowing that managers and promoters are exploiters does not stop him from fighting: "Yeah. (Why?) 'Cos I like it. (You don't think you might get used like that?) No. Somewhat, *to some extent yeah.* (And you're not concerned about it?) Yeah, I'm concerned, but I gotta *make a livin'*, I gotta do it."[13]

Together, the doxic belief inscribed deep in the bodily dispositions of the fighter, in the normalcy of exploitation, in the "agency" of corporeal entrepreneurship, and in the possibility of individual exceptionalism help produce the *collective misrecognition* that leads boxers to collude in their own commercialization and practically consent to "sink[ing] to the level of a commodity, and to a most miserable commodity" (Marx, 1964: 120). As for the unusual *intensity* of exploitation in that economy, it is a direct function of the social and ethnoracial distance between exploiter and exploited as well as of the gaping disparity in the volume and types of capital they possess: on the one side, fighters typically own little more than their trained organism and the moral valiancy needed to valorize it in a rough and risky trade; on the other side, managers and promoters virtually monopolize the specific competencies and assets required to run the business. The near-total absence of regulation by the bureaucratic agencies of the state, in turn, is an expression of the marginal and tainted status of the trade in the universe of professional athletics and popular entertainment, as well as of the correspondingly low class and ethnic position of its practitioners and consumers, as my gym mate Smithie perceptively notes: "See it's a profession that if you had *college grads*, if you had *diplomats*, if you had people of, of certain *cultures*, okay, that went into d'game an' was *fighters*, well then they would demand that [more regulation]. But see the callibar [caliber] of people that you have in d'game, demand that callibar [caliber] of repore [rapport], okay, that callibar [caliber] of business okay? So one can reflect upon the other."

NOTES

This article draws in part on a longer paper entitled "The Passion of the Pugilist: Desire and Domination in the Making of Prizefighters," given as the Morrison Library Inaugural Lecture, University of California, Berkeley, April 25, 1995. It benefited from the encouragement of Jack Katz and from the sharp editorial eye of Megan L. Comfort. A shorter version was presented to the Workshop on Popular Culture, Programa de Pós-Graduaçâo em Antropologia Social, Museu nacional, Rio de Janeiro, on May 3, 2000, with thanks due to José Sergio Leite Lopes, Federico Neiburg, and the workshop participants.

1 During this fieldwork, conducted in 1988–91, I learned how to box (well enough to enter the Chicago Golden Gloves and to spar on a regular basis with "pros"), attended amateur tournaments and professional "cards" throughout the Midwest and in Atlantic City, observed and engaged trainers, managers, and matchmakers in their natural setting, and generally followed my friends from the gym in their everyday lives. This article relies on the 2,200 pages of my diary, my field notebooks, the lifestories of my buddies from the Stoneland Boys Club (a pseudonym), and in-depth interviews with all fifty professional boxers active in the slate of Illinois during the summer of 1991.

2 See Wacquant (1998) for a detailed analysis of the structure and functioning of the prizefighting economy as a system of exchange and mutual conversion of bodily capital and economic capital made possible by collective misrecognition.

3 "I'm a whore who sells his blood instead of his ass. But that comes with the sport. I never made much money being good lookin', but there's always somebody who'll pay me to take a punch. And I can take a punch, darlin'. It's a natural gift. This piece of granite on my shoulders can absorb a lot of punishment. They don't pay me to be bright" (Randall "Tex" Cobb, a white journeyman heavyweight, cited in Hauser, 1986: 106). A better analog for the prizefighter across the gender line might be women performers in commercial pornography (Stoller and Levine, 1993, and Wacquant, 1997), although that activity is morally reproved even in the proximate milieu of porn actresses whereas prizefighting is held in high esteem in the lower regions of social space from which boxers issue.

4 In boxing parlance, an "opponent" is a skilled but limited (or "over-the-hill") fighter who is willing to go on the road and fight strictly for money against superior foes. He is typically brought in by a promoter to face (the lingo says: to be "fed to") an up-and-coming boxer with a view towards improving the record and advancing the career of the latter. Shapiro (1988) draws a sensitive portrait of "opponents"; Brunt (1987) depicts many of them at work.

5 These organizations, often referred to derisively by boxing people as "the alphabet bandits," are self-appointed agencies which operate in cahoots with promoters to publish rankings and collect huge "sanctioning fees" in exchange for giving the championship tag to fights sold to television networks. The three majors are the World Boxing Association (created in 1962), a

"small brotherhood of Latin Americans" which is "little more than a corrupt joke," the World Boxing Council (1963), operated as "the personal fiefdom" of José Suleiman, a Lebanese-born and US-educated industrialist from Mexico in conjunction with Don King Productions (Hauser 1986: 95, 98); and the International Boxing Federation (1983), recently placed under court receivership after its top officials were charged by federal prosecutors with multiple counts of corruption (including selling their ratings to certain managers and promoters under the table). In recent years, they have faced growing competition from a bevy of smaller self-proclaimed "world federations," such as the IBC, WBO, IBO, etc.

6   The professional ethic of "sacrifice" and training regimen of pro fighters is described at length in "Pugs at Work" (Wacquant, 1995).

7   As pointed out by Orlando Patterson (1982: 388), the image of bones being picked and cleaned is also a frequent motif in the language of slaves the world over: "You eated me when I was meat, now you must pick me when I am bones." This sentiment of being "eaten alive" is also a common form of consciousness among manual workers operating under superexploitative conditions in a physically injurious setting, e.g., most famously in the cases of the tin miners of the Bolivian highlands described by June Nash (1979) and of the Brazilian sugar factory workers dissected in José Sergio Leite Lopes's (1978) classic study, *O Vapor do Diabo*. The vampiric figure of blood sucking is recounted by Abdelmalek Sayad (1991) in his vivid depiction of Algerian migrant laborers in France.

8   To borrow the characterization of the "practice of integrity" elaborated by T. Dunbar Moodie (1994: 2) in the case of black African migrant workers toiling in the gold mines of South Africa.

9   This doxic acceptance of exploitation as a constant of life is taken to a paroxysm by this unemployed lightweight from a poor black suburb of Chicago who discerns in present inequity the unmistakable harbinger of future success with almost religious fervor: "Yeah because *I'monna make my money* an' see when it's my turn to make my money, I'monna make it. It's, *anythin' that come easy is not worth it, for havin'* so I know I gotta struggle, I gotta *struggle-struggle-struggle*, I got to go without an' stuff like that but *I chose* this field to go into so *I know* it's gonna be *rough.*"

10   At the end of his interview, in a diner near the gym one summer evening, this boxer-hustler offered to take me to his gambling den and later insisted to sell me an assortment of stolen merchandise, including a used handgun (for 150 dollars) and a submachine gun in mint condition (for 300).

11   The (auto)biographies of champions, from Papa Jack Johnson and Jack Dempsey to Joe Louis, Muhammad Ali, and Oscar de la Hoya, are nearly identical iterations of this theme of superhuman singularity and individual success in the face of formidable hardships. In these prepackaged lifestories, boxers emerge as quintessential Horatio Algers of the masculine body.

12   White fighters have become more valued economically as they have become more scarce, especially in the upper weight divisions for which gate receipts and purses are by far the highest.

13   On the motivations of "bums" and "tomato cans" to continue to fight absent the prospect of victory and in spite of their utter lack of skills, see Wacquant (1998: 12–13).

REFERENCES

Bourgois, Philippe (1995) *In Search of Respect: Selling Crack in El Barrio*, Cambridge: Cambridge University Press.

Brunt, Stephen (1987) *Mean Business: The Rise and Fall of Shawn O'Sullivan*, Harmondsworth: Penguin.

Goffman, Erving (1959) *The Presentation of Self in Everyday Life*, Harmondsworth: Penguin.

Hauser, Thomas (1986) *The Black Lights: Inside the World of Professional Boxing*, New York: McGraw-Hill.

Hobsbawm, Eric (1984) "Artisans and Labour Aristocrats?" in *Workers: Worlds of Labour*, New York: Pantheon: 252–72.

Holzer, Harry J. (1996) *What Employers Want: Job Prospects for Less-Educated Workers*, New York: Russell Sage Foundation.

Lopes, José Sérgio Leite (1978) *O Vapor do Diabo: O Trabalho dos Operários do Açúca*, Rio de Janeiro: Paz e Terra.

MacLeod, Jay (1994) *Ain't No Makin' It*. Boulder: Westview Press, 2nd edn.

Marx, Karl (1964) *Early Writings*. Translated and edited by Tom Bottomore, New York: McGraw-Hill.

Marx, Karl (1956) *Selected Writings in Sociology and Social Philosophy*. Edited by Tom Bottomore and Maximilien Rubel, New York: McGraw-Hill.

Mills, C. Wright (1940) "Situated Actions and Vocabularies of Motive." *American Sociological Review* 5 (December): 904–13.

Moodie, T. Dunbar with Vivienne Ndatsche (1994) *Going for Gold: Men, Mines and Migration*, Berkeley: University of California Press.

Nash, June (1979) *We Eat the Mines and the Mines Eat Us: Dependency and Exploitation in Bolivian Tin Mines*, New York: Columbia University Press.

Patterson, Orlando (1982) *Slavery and Social Death*, Cambridge, MA: Harvard University Press.

Sammons, Jeffrey T. (1988) *Beyond the Ring: The Role of Boxing in American Society*, Urbana and Chicago: University of Illinois Press.

Sayad, Abdelmalek (1991) *L'Immigration ou les paradoxes de l'altérité*, Brussels: Editions Universitaires-De Boeck.

Shapiro, Michael (1988) "Opponents" in Joyce Carol Oates and Daniel Halpern (ed.), *Reading the Fights*, New York: Prentice-Hall Press: 242–9.

Stoller, Robert J. and I. S. Levine (1993) *Coming Attractions: The Making of an X-Rated Video*, New Haven: Yale University Press.

U.S. Senate (1992) *Hearings on Corruption in Professional Boxing before the Permanent Committee on Governmental Affairs*, 102nd Congress, August 11–12, 1992, Washington: Government Printing Office.

Wacquant, Loïc (1995) "Pugs at Work: Bodily Capital and Bodily Labor Among Professional Boxers." *Body and Society* 1-1 (March): 65–94.

Wacquant, Loïc (1997) "Porn Exposed." *Body and Society* 3-1 (March): 119–25.

Wacquant, Loïc (1998) "A Fleshpeddler at Work: Power, Pain, and Profit in the Prizefighting Economy." *Theory and Society* 27-1 (February): 1–42.

Part V

What is to be Done? Wealth, Poverty, and Public Policy

20

In the Shadow of the Poorhouse: A Social History of Welfare in America

Michael Katz

Michael Katz is the Sheldon and Lucy Hackney Professor of History at the University of Pennsylvania; he specializes in American social history. He is co-director of the Urban Studies Graduate Certificate Program. His research and writing has focused on three areas: the history of education, the history of urban social and family structure, and the history of poverty and social welfare. His most recent books are: *In the Shadow of the Poorhouse: A Social History of Welfare in America* (10th anniversary edition) and, with Thomas J. Sugrue, eds., *W. E. B. Du Bois, Race, and the City: The Philadelphia Negro and Its Legacy*. He is writing a book on the redefinition of the American welfare state since 1980.

Throughout the century before the New Deal, the poorhouse dominated the structure of welfare – or, as it was called then, relief. Although despised, dreaded, and often attacked, the poorhouse endured as the central arch of public welfare policy. Even in the twentieth century it did not disappear. Instead, through a gradual transformation it slid into a new identity: the public old-age home. Its history shows clearly how decent and compassionate care of the poor has always remained subordinate to both low taxes and the other great purposes that have guided relief. American welfare has remained within the shadow of the poorhouse. Poorhouses, which shut the old and sick away from their friends and relatives, were supposed to deter the working class from asking for poor relief. They were, in fact, the ultimate defense against the

erosion of the work ethic in early industrial America. Miserable, poorly managed, underfunded institutions, trapped by their own contradictions, poorhouses failed to meet any of the goals so confidently predicted by their sponsors.[1]

In both England and America, local communities helped destitute people in their homes – a form of assistance known as outdoor relief – long before the first almshouse had been built. Even more, despite a century of sustained attack, outdoor relief refused to disappear. Indeed, throughout the nineteenth century, many more people – in most places three, four, or more times as many – received public outdoor relief in any year as were admitted to poorhouses. Still, the number of people affected offers only one measure with which to judge whether a practice is fundamental.

Another is its role in policy, and in both Britain and America the poorhouse was the cutting edge of poor relief policy in the late eighteenth and early nineteenth centuries, advocated by Utilitarians in England and forward-looking architects of state policy in America.

Poverty

Myths of abundance in early American history notwithstanding, poverty was a serious and growing problem. Indeed, no clear line separated ordinary working people from those in need of help, because periodic destitution was one structural result of the great social and economic transformations in American life. The reasons for this prevalence of poverty vary, although most of them may be traced in one way or another to the organization of work.

Increasingly, throughout the early nineteenth century, most people worked for someone else during their entire adult lives. "Nothing more clearly distinguishes the years in which the factory system was built from the modern age, inured to its ranks of wage and salary earners," writes Daniel Rodgers, "than that the simple fact of employment should have deeply disturbed so many Americans." This spread of wage labor can be traced in various ways: through an analysis of the proportion of workers simply called "laborers" on the New York City assessment rolls between 1750 and 1850 (the proportion rose from 6 percent to 27 percent); through manuscript censuses and city directories (which show the numerical domination of most trades by wage laborers at a ratio of ten or eleven employees for each proprietor by at least the middle of the century); or by the spread of trade unions, labor newspapers, and working-class militancy as early as the 1830s. (In Philadelphia, the General Trades Union, a loose organization of unskilled and skilled workers, staged successful collective actions in the 1830s until they were decimated by the severe depression of 1837.)[2]

The uneven character of economic development complicates attempts to generalize about the relations between the history of work and poverty. Throughout the first half of the nineteenth century, handcrafts coexisted with manufactured goods; goods were produced in homes as well as in factories. Some large workplaces were collections of hand workers; in some the work was subdivided into its component parts; a few introduced steam-driven machinery. Even within the same trades, widely different work settings and manufacturing processes coexisted. Nonetheless, everywhere, a reorganization of economic life eroded the position of independent journeymen artisans. For whatever their work setting, almost all of them became wage laborers, employees rather than independent craftsmen owning their raw materials and tools and selling their products directly. As wage workers, they lost the flexibility that had marked artisan manufacture. Most also lost their skill monopoly as the logic of production subdivided work into smaller components that required less skill and less time to learn.[3]

As young men entered trades with increased ease, apprenticeships shortened or disappeared, and a glutted labor market led to lower wages. In fact, to keep their wages as low as possible, employers often fired apprentices as soon as their term expired so that they could avoid paying them adult journeyman wages.[4] Two factors intensified the problems of apprentices and adult artisans thrown out of work. One was the absence of any cushion against unemployment. Very few workers could save enough to tide them over a prolonged period of unemployment, and, without aid from their families, their alternatives were to seek relief or to travel in search of work. Here the ecology of home and workplace – the second factor – came into play. Until very late in the nineteenth century, most working people had to live within walking distance of their jobs. Few could afford the early forms of public transportation such as the horse-drawn street railways introduced in many cities in the 1860s. Because most workplaces were relatively small, most workers found only a limited number of jobs within walking distance of their homes, and, as a consequence, losing a job often meant traveling to find new work. This is one reason historians have found extraordinary population mobility everywhere in nineteenth century America. (Recent studies rarely have discovered more than a third of households remaining in the same town or city for at least a decade around the middle of the nineteenth century.) People on the road looking for work usually had almost no money. Often hungry and desperate, they sometimes sought relief in poorhouses or from public officials. In this way, transiency helped swell the roles of public relief.[5]

Sometimes, mechanization also drove people to relief. Consider the example of threshing machines in New York, where in 1853 an observer wrote:

> It is not very long since all the grain raised in this State was threshed out with flails. It requires no intellect whatever to perform this labor; any one, not a perfect idiot, can stand and pound upon the floor of a barn. This employment was usually relied on by laborers for their winter's employment. Now there is scarcely a farmer to be found who threshes with a flail. Threshing machines are everywhere used, and have completely cut off this source of winter employment.

The replacement of hand threshing by machines underlines the existence of rural, as well as urban, poverty. Nearly every county, rural or urban, had its poorhouse. One source of rural poverty was the mechanization of agriculture, which reflected the increased influence of market forces during the first half of the nineteenth century. In the Genesee Valley, observes Hannon, after 1925, commercial wheat production "was accompanied by rapid population growth, increased average farm size, a decline in self-

sufficient household production, a shortening of the average tenant contract to one year, a decline in the tenancy rate, and increased use of seasonal labor." In 1857, the editor of a local newspaper explained that "after employment for a few weeks or months," farm laborers "were left to beg, steal, or go the poorhouse. . . . This has been the situation of farm laborers in western New York for the past ten or twenty years." As the manufacture of domestic goods – clothes, small home furnishings, and so on – began to move out of homes and into shops and factories, farm women lost an important source of supplementary income. In fact, Hannon found the decline of home manufacture, far more than either industrialization or urbanization, associated with rising rates of pauperism in antebellum New York. Another source of rural poverty was the pressure of population on land, especially in long-settled areas of the East where the productivity of land had declined and farmers had run out of land to subdivide for their children. Rural poverty arose, too, from periodic crop failures caused by bad weather or insects, as in the Kansas "Grasshopper Scourge" (1874–5) that left many families destitute, or the droughts and crop failures in the same state between 1885 and 1895.[6]

Everywhere, the seasonality of work menaced working-class security, and poorhouse populations swelled during winter months. Much unskilled labor took place outdoors: unloading ships, digging canals, building railways. In cold climates where lakes and canals froze, all this employment ended in the winter. So did most construction work, another major source of employment.[7]

For most people work remained unsteady as well as seasonal. Because the availability of work varied with demand, few manufacturers employed a consistent number of workers throughout the year, and very few people found steady work. As much as low wages, this irregular employment – in the urban South as well as in the North – often dropped families into poverty. The great periodic depressions had the same effect. During each depression, thousands of workers, their jobs lost, were left without resources, dependent on relatives, friends, or charity. At times, even the well-to-do were plunged into poverty, and many workers fled cities. Others stayed and suffered. During one depression in antebellum Philadelphia, laborers worked for fifty cents a day; the wages of handloom weavers were slashed; the demand for domestic servants and seamstresses declined; and everywhere, disease, hunger, and destitution stalked the streets.[8]

The availability of work for every able-bodied person who really wants a job is one of the enduring myths of American history. In fact, work was no more universally available in the early and mid-nineteenth century than it is today, as unskilled and semiskilled workers overstocked urban labor markets. In 1822, Josiah Quincy, addressing the Grand Jury of Suffolk County, Massachusetts, pointed to the 700 men "for whom work cannot be obtained" on the books of Boston's Employment Society. "These men long for work; they anxiously beg for it; yet it is not to be found." In 1828, Matthew Carey, attacking the proposed abolition of outdoor relief in Philadelphia, observed:

> Many citizens entertain an idea that in the present state of society in this city, every person able and willing to work may procure employment; that all those who are thus employed, may earn a decent and comfortable support; and that if not the whole, at least the chief part of the distresses of the poor, arises from idleness, dissipation, and worthlessness.

Nothing could be further from the truth, wrote Carey. Even in the "most prosperous times," he pointed out, "some trades and occupations" always were "depressed," and a "deficiency of employment" consumed the modest savings of the most "frugal and industrious."[9]

Carey highlighted another great source of poverty: the low wages paid women. Some philanthropic societies had attempted to help women – especially widows – by starting workshops where they could earn money sewing. Other women earned a little money sewing for individual masters. Carey showed that even the philanthropists did not pay women enough to survive. Even so, work was so scarce that every time contracts for making clothes for soldiers were announced, "the applications" were "too numerous to be supplied." Women in the urban South faced similar problems, as the editor of the Richmond *Daily Dispatch* pointed out in 1857. Women compelled "to make their living by their industry," he observed, were paid far less than men: fifty or sixty cents a day was considered enough to make a woman "entirely independent," and some with children to support, were "actually making up shirts and drawers for 6¼ cents each."[10]

Carey also traced the relation among the wretched wages paid male workers, their working conditions, and the growth of poverty. Thousands of laborers, he pointed out, "travel hundreds of miles in quest of employment on canals" at less than a dollar a day, paying "a dollar and a half or two dollars per week for their board, leaving families behind, depending on them for support." Often, they worked "in marshy grounds, where they" breathed "pestiferous miasmata" that destroyed "their health, often irrecoverably." They returned "to their poor families, broken hearted, and with ruined constitutions, with a sorry pittance, most laboriously earned" and took to their beds "sick and unable to work." Still, their places filled quickly with other men desperate for any work. Hundreds were "most laboriously employed on turnpikes, working from morning till night, at from half a dollar to three quarters per day, exposed to the broiling sun in summer, and all the inclemency of our severe winters." Always there was "a redundance of wood pilers in our cities, whose wages are so low, that their utmost efforts do not enable them to earn more than from thirty-five to fifty cents per day." Even the "painful situation of a watchman" was an "object of desire." There never was "a want of scavengers"; nor was there any work "whatever, how disagreeable, or loathsome, or dangerous, or deleterious soever it may be, or however reduced the wages," that did not "find some persons willing to follow it, rather than beg or steal."[11]

Usually low to begin with, wages frequently were reduced. For instance, in one Philadelphia cotton mill, handloom weavers making cotton ticking earned one dollar per cut in 1820, seventy cents in 1833, and sixty cents in 1840. When wages were reduced, Walter Channing pointed out in 1843, the effect was not only to lessen "the amount paid to each" but also to discharge "from regular employment a certain number of operatives." The net effect left large numbers of people suddenly "without the means of subsistence for themselves, and for their families. These last, after no very long time, must become dependent on foreign aid for support. They are made paupers."[12]

With figures from the Board of Canal Commissioners, Carey calculated an annual income for a laborer consisting of 10 months' work at $12 per month, 2 months' work at $5 per month, and a wife's annual income of $13. The total, which implied the availability of work throughout the year, was $143. As he stressed, this total income did not allow *"for one day's want of employment of the husband, or one day's sickness of him or his wife!"* Against the income he set a modest budget, 50 cents a week for rent, a total of $65.20 for food, $24 for clothes for the couple and $16 for their two children. With fuel and a few other expenses this bare bones budget totaled $145.74, more than they could expect to earn. Without "allowance of one day or one dollar for sickness, or want of employment," both of which were common, with no provision for unemployment, Carey's hypothetical family

still could not quite match income and expenses. Their plight would have been worse, Carey pointed out, had he increased the number of their children, which would not have been unreasonable. The same results, he said, would emerge from calculating the income and expenses of the laborers on the railroad. Nor was the plight of weavers any better.[13]

Carey was right to stress the role of sickness, because illness was a major cause of destitution. A great many almshouse inmates were sick, and in histories of families on relief, illness almost always stands out as a major theme. The reasons are not hard to find. Work was dangerous and unhealthy; diets were inadequate; sanitary conditions in cities were dreadful; medical care was poor. When men took sick and died, they usually left no life insurance and few assets, and their widows had almost no way short of prostitution to support their families. Some widows with young children combined help from family, friends, and charity with sweated work sewing or washing. But when they took sick – and not surprisingly they often did – they had no alternatives to private charity, relief, or the poorhouse. Families often survived by putting all possible members to work. Even young children were expected to help by taking care of their younger brothers and sisters, collecting bits of fuel from the streets, wharves, and woods, or by begging. Those families in which at least one person remained well enough to work survived best.[14]

Landlords and grocers often helped by giving credit that enabled poor people to weather periods of unemployment or sickness. (Indeed, the role of credit as a form of relief never has received the attention it deserves from students of poverty.) Yet, often no one could earn any money. Fathers were dead or sick; mothers were consumed with the care of very young children or ill; children were too young to work, sick themselves, or had left home. To be sure, kin were expected to help each other, and charity workers almost always tried to find relatives who could assist a family before they gave it very much relief. But most poor families only had very poor relatives with no surplus to share. In other cases, kin lived too far away from each other to be of any help.[15]

Problems intensified in old age. Men did not retire. They worked until they were fired or could continue no longer. Women, who usually outlived their husbands, inherited almost nothing. A few men had small life insurance policies, and a fortunate minority of working-class people had bought and paid for a home. Otherwise, elderly people usually lived with their children. With no savings, no pension, no social security, or if they lacked children willing or able to care for them, old people often found themselves completely destitute.[16]

Immigration also intensified the problem of poverty. Between 1820 and 1860 more than five million immigrants entered the United States. Although it seems unlikely that foreign countries, as protesters claimed at the time, were dumping their paupers on American shores, the massive antebellum immigration – especially because of the Irish famine in the 1840s and early 1850s – did exacerbate the problem of poverty and poor relief. Many immigrants had used up all their money simply to get to America; some arrived sick from the trip; others could not find work; many, contemporaries said, "had been accustomed to receiving relief in their old homes, and so were not abashed to ask for it when they came to the New World." And, of course, immigrants helped overstock the labor market for unskilled work. (However, it is crucial to remember that without massive immigration America would have lacked an adequate labor supply to build its infrastructure of canals, railroads, and turnpikes. American homes would have lacked domestic servants, and American factories would have lacked enough hands.)[17]

Even this cursory overview shows why poverty was a major problem in early and mid-nineteenth century America. The great transformation of social and economic structure disrupted social relations and created a class of highly mobile wage laborers subject to irregular, seasonal, dangerous, unhealthy, often badly paid work. Even in the urban South, "the incidence of poverty increased throughout the antebellum period." Public policy made no provision for the periodic unemployment endemic to the emerging system, no provision for the women left widows, or for the elderly without families. Those in need of relief were young men thrown out of apprenticeships or looking for work, unemployed household heads with families, widows without working children, and those sick and elderly people without kin who could care for them. Crises were woven into the very fabric of working-class experience, and periods of dependence were normal. They were integral to the structure of social and economic life. With luck, some people pulled themselves out. They got well or found work. Others were not so fortunate. Working-class experience was a continuum; no clear line separated the respectable poor from paupers. This is why all attempts to divide the poor into classes and all policies based on those divisions ultimately failed. In no instance was the failure more spectacular than in the history of the poorhouse.[18]

Poorhouses and Other Social Institutions

Poorhouses were one among a set of social institutions invented or redesigned early in the nineteenth century, all of which embodied similar assumptions and strategies. Together, they were a collective response to the great transformation of social experience that both frightened and exhilarated women and men confronted with the task of raising families, earning a living, and shaping public life at a time when old expectations crumbled, past practice offered few reliable guides, and the future remained unpredictable, even, to a very real extent, unimaginable.

Few formal, specialized institutions existed in colonial America. Criminals, for instance, were not punished by long jail sentences. Rather, they were held in jail only until trial; if found guilty, they were punished by fines, whipping, or execution. The mentally ill were cared for by their families or dumped in the few large almshouses built in the eighteenth century. The poor were cared for largely through some form of outdoor relief or auctioned off to local farmers. Poor strangers were told to leave town. Children of the poor learned to read in a variety of ways: at home, in small dame schools, or in town schools that they attended irregularly.

By 1850, all of this had changed. Specialized institutions had been founded to care for the mentally ill, to rehabilitate juvenile delinquents, to educate the blind, deaf, and dumb, and to eradicate ignorance. New penitentiaries had been built on novel principles, and even almshouses became instruments of social policy.[19]

The new institutions all rested on optimistic assumptions about the possibilities of reform, rehabilitation, and education. Their sponsors believed that institutions could improve society through their impact on individual personalities. Because of their environmental sources, crime, pauperism, ignorance, and mental illness – which observers at the time usually confounded as different manifestations of an underlying and pathological condition of dependence – could be eradicated. Even intemperance could be treated in institutions because it originated in causes extrinsic to individual character, most often a faulty family life in childhood and an absence of religious and secular education. Institutions would seal off individuals from the corrupting, tempting, and distracting influences of the world long enough for a kind but firm regimen to transform their behavior and reorder their personalities. Even poorhouses shared in this rehabilitative vision; they would sup-

press intemperance, the primary cause of pauperism, and inculcate the habit of steady work.

The institutional explosion burst forth from both voluntary and state sponsorship; dotted the landscape with both residential asylums and nonresidential schools; and eventually encompassed almost everyone. (Many institutions were founded by philanthropists or voluntary groups and then taken over by the state; in some cases, philanthropists gave money to states to start new institutions; states, on the other hand, often gave money to voluntary associations to perform public functions, for instance, to run the educational system for New York City. This all points not only to the intermingling of voluntary and state activity but also to the very different, protean definition of *public* in early American history.) Early nineteenth century institutional development was defined by the creation of formal organizations to build or reform the character of distinct categories of clients: the mentally ill, criminals, juvenile delinquents, paupers, and children. This use of secular institutions as deliberate agencies of social policy, their specialization, and their emphasis on the formation or reformation of character represented a new and momentous development in modern history.[20]

What accounts for this institutional explosion? How are we to interpret the sudden emergence of the institutional state in early nineteenth century America? Answers are both general and specific. Each institution responded to a specific set of concerns. However, all of them confronted problems inherent in the great transformation of social experience that accompanied the emergence of capitalism in America.

The new institutions were heavy artillery in an assault on popular culture that accompanied the diffusion of wage labor as the template for human relations. Consider two great issues: the problem of time and work discipline and the question of universal standards. Wage labor breaks the noneconomic ties between employers and employees. It frees workers by setting them adrift. An exchange of labor for money, nothing more, governs their relation to their employers. Wages depend on the price of finished products, local labor markets, and the demand for goods. Within wage labor, time is essential. Except for piece work, time is the unit through which labor is measured and paid. Wasted time costs employers extra money, raises the cost of finished goods, and lowers their competitive position in the market. For these reasons, it is imperative that workers labor steadily and efficiently.

All this may seem commonplace. But remember that wage work was novel in the early nineteenth century and that, even more than wages, time and work discipline were at the heart of conflicts between masters and workers. Flexible work schedules had defined the artisan life. In weaving, to take one example, each month masters gave out material to be woven. During the month weavers could organize their work as they wished, and many worked hardest at the end of the month when their work was due. Cordwainers traditionally took "blue Monday," a holiday that extended the weekend but interfered with masters' increasing demands for reliable, steady output; cabinetmakers, too, largely set their own work schedules.[21]

The transformation of casual, episodic, and flexible work patterns into steady, punctual, and predictable labor underlay many of the key struggles surrounding the creation of a working class in both England and North America, and through their emphasis on time and work discipline all of the new social institutions took a leading role in these conflicts.[22] As an example, consider public schools. In their early reports, even public school boards in small towns and villages discussed no question as often as punctual and regular attendance. Sometimes they even advocated locking the school door at the start of the day, turning away latecomers who had trudged miles through the snow. Within every other in-

stitution, order, predictability, and work also were central. Penitentiaries stressed a rigid, mechanical, "machine-like" schedule. Reform schools, "large congregate institutions with workshop routines," had unbending programs. The "orderly, predictable, and regular" routine in early mental hospitals was itself part of the therapy. And the work ethic – as will become clear – is what poorhouses were all about.[23]

An emphasis on universal standards also joined the culture of wage labor to the emergence of social institutions. Reformers assaulted the personalistic, ascriptive basis of much public life and advocated its replacement with universal standards that stressed achievement. Merit, or worthiness, should be defined by productive capacity, the ability to do a job better than someone else, or by meeting a bureaucratic standard, such as passing an examination. Above all, rewards should be earned, not distributed on the basis of kinship, friendship, patronage, or some other particularistic relation. Everywhere, reformers wanted to classify: to divide children into grades with clear criteria for promotion; to sort the poor into moral categories: to classify the insane; to grade prisoners and delinquents and demarcate clear standards for passage from one category to another. Rewards should be distributed by clear criteria applied without favor to everyone who fell into one of the narrow and proliferating categories through which nineteenth century policy entrepreneurs viewed their world. All of this reflected what Christopher Lasch has called the emergence of a "single standard of honor." The corollary, as Harry Braverman pointed out, was disposing of the rest as cheaply and conveniently as possible through the creation of institutions that cleared the marketplace of all but the economically active and productive.[24]

Despite their key role in a general cultural offensive, each new social institution had goals of its own. Each responded to a social problem exacerbated or redefined by the great social and economic transformation of the age. In the case of poorhouses, the problem was the forces that made poverty a major problem in late eighteenth and early nineteenth century America and the dramatic increase in the number of poor people asking for relief.

Pauperism and Relief Before the Poorhouse

Throughout the colonial period and the early nineteenth century, poor relief policy in England profoundly influenced American practice. On both sides of the Atlantic, rising expenses for relief and anxieties about both labor supplies and social order stimulated searching reexaminations of poor laws. Reformers predicted that the replacement of outdoor relief with poorhouses would curb the demand for relief, check the threatened demoralization of the poor, avoid interference with labor supplies, and inculcate a work ethic. However, reformers never managed to eliminate outdoor relief completely, and their great innovation – poorhouses – proved an abject failure.

Early American poor relief, it is important to stress, drew heavily on English precedents. In fact, four principles inherited from England underlay the local practice. First, poor relief was a public responsibility, usually assigned to officials called overseers of the poor. Second, it was profoundly local. Each parish in England organized its own system of relief and retained responsibility for its own people, even when they had temporarily moved away. This made the question of legal residence, or settlement, the most contentious practical problem in aid to the poor. Kin responsibility, the third principle, denied public aid to individuals with parents, grandparents, adult children, or grandchildren who could take them into their homes. Finally, concerns about children and about work were combined in legislation that authorized overseers to apprentice the children of paupers to farmers and artisans who agreed to train and care for them in their homes.[25]

At first, the colonies more or less copied the major features of English legislation. In fact, Rhode Island merely stated that the basis of its poor law would be 43 Elizabeth (the basis of the Elizabethan poor law). In America, as in England, poor relief was a local (at first township, later usually county) responsibility assigned to overseers of the poor. (In the South, until after the Revolution, the parish remained the unit for relief, which was administered by the Anglican clergy.) Relief policy, also as in England, authorized overseers only to aid those poor with a settlement and to bind out children of paupers as apprentices.[26]

Poorhouses were only one of the four methods of poor relief practiced in most states. As late as 1851, in a report to the Rhode Island legislature, Thomas Hazard found all four within that small state.

> 1st. By venduing [auctioning or selling] them to the lowest bidder. 2nd. By contracting for their maintenance, with an individual, or individuals, through the agency of a committee or otherwise. 3d. By placing all the poor in one Asylum, owned by the town. 4th. By placing all such in an asylum as are bereft of home and friends, and administering out-door relief to such as have.

Although detailed practices varied greatly, the mixture of auction, contract, outdoor relief, and poorhouses, described by Thomas Hazard in Rhode Island in 1851, existed in most colonies a century earlier, although auctioning was less common in the South. It was mainly larger towns and cities that had built poorhouses (Boston, 1664; Salem, 1719; Portsmouth, New Hampshire, 1716; Newport, Rhode Island, 1723; Philadelphia, 1732; New York City, 1736; Charlestown, 1736; Providence, 1753; Baltimore, 1773). Smaller towns and villages usually followed the other practices.[27] The worst of these practices – and all other writers on poor relief seem to agree – was the first. "When stripped of all disguises, selling the poor to the lowest bidder is simply offering a reward for the most cruel and avaricious man that can be found to abuse them." The poor were auctioned most often in country towns, because it was a cheap way to care for them and because there were too few poor to make an almshouse practical.[28]

In time, most places chose poorhouses. However, despite their alleged economy – one of their principal selling points – in Britain and America it invariably cost more to keep paupers in almshouses than to support them in their homes. As with criminals or the mentally ill today, institutions have been an expensive response to a social problem. Given their cost and the availability of cheaper alternatives, the reasons state and local governments clung so long to poorhouses as the cornerstone of public relief are not transparent.[29]

Of course, not every town or county chose among alternatives in quite the same way. Everywhere, practices differed within the same state: towns and counties spent different amounts to help the destitute, varied the balance between indoor and outdoor relief, and ran their poorhouses differently. Despite variations, the contours of poor relief paralleled each other in critical ways from Maine to North Carolina, from Rhode Island, New York, and Pennsylvania to Kansas, Indiana, and Michigan. Poor relief history, therefore, exemplifies one of the great themes of American social experience: the continuities in institutional patterns across a sprawling, decentralized, and diverse nation. Looked at this way, the issue is not diversity. Rather, it is this: all over the country those nineteenth century Americans who controlled social policy made similar choices about poor relief. We should try to understand why.[30]

By the end of the eighteenth century, the two general patterns of relief were the township system of New England and the county system of Pennsylvania. The latter, which made the county rather than the town responsible for the poor, eliminated many settlement disputes, which had arisen between towns within the same county. In fact, Pennsylvania's poor laws became the most influential in the new nation because they were copied in the Northwest Territories and, subsequently, in the states created out of them. The Pennsylvania legislation was enabling, not mandatory. Counties asked for and were granted permission to build poorhouses. Except for New York, which passed a mandatory law, this was the pattern in most of the country. Nonetheless, even without coercion, the poorhouse became a familiar institution during the first decades of the nineteenth century. By the Civil War poorhouses had spread from cities and the more densely populated seaboard to rural towns and counties throughout most of the settled regions of the country, North and South. In the South, rural counties often abandoned their poorhouses in the first decades of the nineteenth century. With most of the dependent members of the population the responsibility of the slaveholders who owned them, official relief rates in the South remained, of course, much lower than in the North.[31]

When state reports in Massachusetts, New York, Pennsylvania, and New Hampshire in the 1820s all advocated almshouses as the major public policy for poor relief, they drew not only on English theory and practice, about which they were very well informed, but on American experience with almshouses in the preceding two decades. So uniformly positive were the towns with almshouses, that officials everywhere felt confident about recommending a shift away from existing, noninstitutional relief. The American pattern that emerged did not simply imitate English practice. The English attempted to ban all outdoor relief to ablebodied paupers. In America, only Delaware seriously tried to prohibit outdoor relief for any group. Moreover, not only did America lack a national system, but practices within states remained varied and permissive, and, as a consequence, arrangements differed among towns and counties within the same states.[32]

What, exactly, did poorhouse advocates hope to accomplish and why did poor law reform appear so urgent? First, in the early decades of the nineteenth century, state and local officials everywhere claimed pauperism was rising at an alarming rate. In 1821, a Massachusetts Committee, chaired by Josiah Quincy (hereafter Quincy Report), reported that "the increase of the pauper burden [in Massachusetts] has exceeded, in a given number of years, the proportion of the increase of the pauper burden of Great Britain." About 6 years later the secretary of New Hampshire wrote of the "rapid increase in the number of paupers supported by the public, and in the expense of supporting them."[33]

Relief roles grew most in cities. Yates, secretary of state of New York, pointed to the "dense population" of New York City "and of the large villages and towns, which, from their convenient situation for navigation and commerce, allure to their haunts and recesses, the idle and dissolute of every description." In the same year, the mayor of Schenectady pointed out "that cities are the great resorts for the straggling and vagrant poor, who although having no permanent settlement amongst us, still at times call loudly for relief and assistance." Unlike some social fears, the increase in the number and expense of paupers was tangible. In contrast to moral decay, lax family discipline, a decline in civility, or, even, to some extent the safety of the streets, it was not nebulous or largely a product of perception. Rather, it was concrete, measurable, translated into tax dollars. Because poor rates (taxes for poor relief) often were billed separately from other taxes, taxpayers immediately felt every increase in municipal expenses.[34]

As they reluctantly paid the mounting poor rates, early nineteenth century taxpayers tried to account for the increase in pauperism, and they developed a clear explanation. They placed some of the blame on the growth of cities and immigration. Even more, they stressed the role of intemperance.

But the real villains were existing public poor relief practice and the indiscriminate generosity of private charity. In Massachusetts, the Quincy Report (1821) concluded, "That of all the causes of pauperism, intemperance, in the use of spiritous liquors, is the most powerful and universal." Three years later the articulate overseer of the poor in Albany claimed, "that if any measure could be devised, to diminish the use of spiritous liquors, the condition of the poor would at once be improved; for it is doubtless the principal cause of the suffering of a large proportion of the poor." European countries, many observers believed, increased America's problem by dumping their paupers on its shore. In 1850, for instance, the mayor of Bangor, Maine, argued that only the federal government could prevent European countries from assessing "a tax upon the property of this country sufficient for the maintenance of all the paupers on the face of the earth." In 1827, the Philadelphia Board of Guardians of the Poor wrote, "One of the greatest burthens that falls upon this corporation, is the maintenance of the host of worthless foreigners, disgorged upon our shores," and in the 1850s, to take a final example, a well-informed observer noted that one cause "for the increase of pauperism amongst us . . . is the increase of our foreign population."[35]

Despite immigration, the growth of cities, and drink, to many observers the great source of pauperism lay within poor relief practice itself. For private charity and outdoor relief encouraged idleness by undermining the relation between work and survival. To nineteenth century observers, the poor laws interfered with the supply of energy available for productive labor by draining the working class of its incentive. Paupers were living proof that a modestly comfortable life could be had without hard labor. Their dissipation was a cancer demoralizing the poor and eroding the independence of the working class.

Overseers of the poor in Beverly, Massachusetts, claimed that poor relief encouraged "idleness" and "improvidence." "The idle will beg in preference to working; relief is extended to them without suitable discrimination. They are not left to feel the just consequences of their idleness." Meanwhile, the "industrious poor" were "discouraged by observing that bounty bestowed upon the idle, which they can only obtain by the sweat of their brow." Massachusetts's climate made saving for winter necessary. If the poor spent all their money in the summer, in winter they would "be in want. This improvidence may be and often is encouraged by the facility with which relief is obtained." The Yates Report in New York put forth as "propositions very generally admitted" that "our poor laws are manifestly defective in principle, and mischievous in practice, and that under the imposing and charitable aspect of affording relief exclusively to the poor and infirm, they frequently invite the ablebodied vagrant to partake of the same bounty." Poor relief practices operated "as so many invitations to become beggars."[36]

Indiscriminate charity and outdoor relief eroded more than the will to work. They also destroyed character. When the poor started to think of relief "as a right," they began to count on it "as an income." All "stimulus to industry and economy" was "annihilated, or weakened" while "temptations to extravagance and dissipation . . . increased." As a consequence, "The just pride of independence, so honorable to a man, in every condition" was "corrupted by the certainty of public provision."[37]

Even more, Charles Burroughs warned, the generous public aid that had begun to teach the poor that relief was a right promoted militancy and eroded the deference that should govern class relations. "The poor tax," he asserted, made relief impersonal. It was paid "without any comparative rememberance of the poor." At the same time, as poor people began to claim relief "as an obligation" owed to their "wretched condition," they became "jealous about the proper administration of the poor

laws, and the encroachments [on their] . . . prerogatives." They started to "utter the language of discontent, complaint, and even vengeance." The indifference of the taxpayers and the militance of the poor widened "the breach between [them] . . . and the affluent. . . . The poor look to the rich, as hard hearted oppressors . . . and the rich look to the poor, as so many poachers in their domains."[38]

None of the critics of poor relief, it must be stressed, proposed to eliminate poverty. To most people of the time, the idea would have been preposterous. Even in America, the vast majority would have to scrabble hard for a living. Nor was the issue redistributing wealth; rather, it was this: how to keep the genuinely needy from starving without breeding a class of paupers who chose to live off public and private bounty rather than to work. These were the goals most commentators felt current poor relief practice defeated.

As the Quincy Report made clear, policy assumed the existence of two classes of paupers.

> 1. The impotent poor; in which denomination are included all, who are wholly incapable of work, through old age, infancy, sickness or corporeal debility. 2. The able poor; in which denomination are included all, who are capable of work, of some nature, or other; but differing in the degree of their capacity, and in the kind of work, of which they are capable.

No one should hesitate to help the first class of poor. Christian charity and ordinary human compassion made their care a clear duty, although it was not so clear where and by whom they should be aided. The real issue concerned the ablebodied poor. According to the Quincy Report, all the "evils" attributable to the current system of poor relief could be traced to the same root: "the difficulty of discriminating between the able poor and the impotent poor and of apportioning the degree of public provision to the degree of actual impotency." The able poor, so it was assumed, should fend for themselves. Indeed, it is only a slight exaggeration to say that the core of most welfare reform in America since the early nineteenth century has been a war on the able-bodied poor: an attempt to define, locate, and purge them from the roles of relief.[39]

Perhaps the difficulty of drawing the line between the ablebodied and impotent poor led Yates, in New York, to use a different definition: the distinction between the permanent poor, "or those who are regularly supported, during the whole year, at the public expense," and the occasional or "temporary poor . . . who receive occasional relief, during a part of the year chiefly in the autumn or winter." However the poor were divided, the problem that eluded all commentators was finding a satisfactory way to limit relief to a portion of those who asked for help. As the seemingly straightforward behavioral categories proposed by Quincy and Yates proved difficult to put into practice, observers turned increasingly toward moral distinctions. Charles Burroughs pointed the way to the newer distinction in 1834 when he attempted to distinguish poverty from pauperism. Poverty was an "unavoidable evil, to which many are brought from necessity, and in the wise and gracious Providence of God." Poverty resulted not from "our faults" but from "our misfortunes," and the poor should "claim our tenderest commiseration, our most liberal relief." But pauperism was a different story. "Pauperism is the consequence of wilful error, of shameful indolence, of vicious habits. It is a misery of human creation, the pernicious work of man, the lamentable consequence of bad principles and morals." Relief to the poor was charity; relief to paupers increased "the evil in a tenfold degree." (Later in the century, Burroughs's moral categories were formalized into the distinction between the "worthy" and "unworthy" poor.)[40]

In the South, explanations of poverty among whites sometimes blurred the familiar distinction between worthy and unworthy poor. For distinctions of race ultimately proved more important than those of class. Whatever else it accomplished, poor relief was supposed to shore up white supremacy by assuring even needy whites a standard of living and work superior to blacks. "The *leitmotif* of the Southern public relief system," writes Bellows, "was to give definition to the role of the white laborer in the urban economy. Even in indigency and unemployment, a distinction had to exist between the white hireling and the black slave if the grand illusion of white supremacy was not to be eroded at its base." As a consequence, white Southerners often transmuted the distinction between worthy and unworthy poor into a division between neighbors and strangers. "Fear of strangers, vagrants and vagabonds better describes the antipathy aimed at some indigents of the city, rather than horror at their personal conduct."[41]

Critics also attacked two other major features of poor relief: the practice of auctioning off the poor and settlement laws. The case against auctions had two sides. One was its brutality. In New York, the Yates Report concluded, "The poor, when farmed out, or sold, are frequently treated with barbarity and neglect by their keepers," and "in more than one instance" the "cruelty and torture" inflicted by keepers had killed the paupers with whose care they were charged. Even more graphically, Abijah Hammond, in an address to the agricultural society of Westchester County in October, 1820, thundered:

> Most of the poor are *sold*, as the term is, that is, *bid off*, to those who agree to support them on the lowest terms, to purchasers nearly as poor as themselves, who treat them in many instances more like brutes than like human beings; and who, instead of applying the amount received from the poor-master, for the comfort of the pauper, spend it to support their own

families, or, which is too often the case, in purchasing ardent spirits; under the maddening influence of which, they treat these wretched pensioners, and not unfrequently their own wives and children, with violence and outrage.[42]

Nonetheless – and this was the other criticism – the poor sometimes turned the system of auction or sale to their own advantage. Families sometimes put in the low bid for their own relatives because they were willing or able to care for them with very little extra money. When this happened, public funds subsidized a modestly comfortable life for dependent people with their kin. To poor law critics, these subsidies were an outrageous abuse of the taxpayers. The supervisor of Hunter, New York, wrote:

> Every pauper has more or less relations in the town, who seem to feel that it is a fine thing to get some money from the town, and yet keep the poor themselves. They dread the idea of their being sent to a house of industry, because they lose the money they draw from the town. Hence they raise a clamor against such a project, and enlist with them all the connexions of the pauper, his neighbors, etc. and the plan is defeated.[43]

Here is a hint that the attempt to replace older methods of relief with poorhouses met popular resistance in America as well as in Britain, where local opposition, especially in northern England, frequently was fierce. Although American historians have not studied this topic, there is no reason to believe that American working people understood the meaning of reformed poor laws less well than their British counterparts. Poorhouses, they heard, were designed to enforce discipline and help regulate labor markets and wages. Their advocates wanted to remove people too poor, sick, or old to care for themselves from their friends and families and put them

into a harsh, degrading institution. In these circumstances, resistance became neither venal nor unreasonable. Poor people found allies in their resistance to poorhouses among the professionals and merchants who profited from their business and among the justices of the peace and overseers of the poor who earned at least some of their living from the unreformed system. As the Yates Report pointed out:

> The interests of the physician and the shopkeeper or merchant, in those towns in which the alms-house might not be located, would perhaps be affected by the proposed system [of county almshouses], and some hostilities might arise from that source. . . . in some towns the local feelings and interests of justices, overseers and constables may also be arrayed in some degree against this plan; nor is it the least item in the objections that will probably be made, that the paupers themselves and their connexions, and those who derive a profit from supporting the paupers, or expect to derive it, will also indulge in feelings hostile to the system.[44]

Except for the South, settlement remained the other great problem with the poor laws. Towns often spent more money ridding themselves of paupers than they would have spent supporting them. Aside from the trouble and expense of endless litigation, the system often was cruel, for old and sick paupers frequently were shipped from town to town, even in the middle of winter. The Yates Report estimated that one-ninth of all the taxes raised for poor relief were spent "in the payment of fees of justices, overseers, lawyers and constables" who decided and administered settlement questions. Part of the problem lay in the laws themselves, which were "so technical, numerous, and complicated, if not obscure, that even eminent counsel" often could not "determine questions arising" from them. What then could be expected from the decisions of local officials "unlearned in our laws"? The Albany overseer of the poor explained that the local constable charged with sending the poor on their way had to advance his own money to support and transport them. Often, he was not reimbursed for several months, sometimes not for a year, and, even then, his accounts were often examined in "a most rigid and . . . unjustifiable" way. For this reason, the constable tried to "rid himself of [paupers] at the least possible expense," and, as a result, the individual pauper was "bandied about from constable to constable, not unfrequently from one extremity of the state to another, generally in feeble health, and during the inclemency of the winter season."[45]

Although unsatisfactory for everyone, the mix of outdoor relief, the auction of paupers, and their transport from town to town was especially harsh on children. According to the Yates Report, "The education and morals of the children of paupers, (except in alms houses) are almost wholly neglected. They grow up in filth, idleness, ignorance and disease, and many become early candidates for the prison or the grave. The evidence on this head is too voluminous even for reference." Although many adult poor had passed beyond redemption, their children were quite another matter. By failing to intervene between parents and their children, reformers argued, the state had abandoned – temporarily, as it turned out – the opportunity to break the mechanism through which pauperism and its allies, crime and ignorance, perpetuated each other. This inability to break the cycle of pauperism added urgency to appeals for reform.[46]

The Case for the Poorhouse

Both the Quincy and Yates reports rejected the views of those English political economists who advocated the total abolition of all poor relief. They found such a draconian solution offensive and contrary to American

sentiment. Rather, they recommended replacing most forms of outdoor relief, the auction, and the contract system with a network of almshouses (or poorhouses). Within the almshouses, work – especially farm labor – would be mandatory for all inmates neither too sick nor too feeble, and both idleness and alcohol would be prohibited. Ablebodied men would be pruned rigorously from the relief roles; begging would be barred and punished; children would be schooled; and settlement laws would be greatly simplified.[47]

Especially in England, the replacement of outdoor relief with poorhouses has echoed through time as a cruel solution to the problem of pauperism. And so it was. But in America, the goals of poorhouse sponsors were not entirely repressive. For they reflected an attempt to mitigate the harshness of contemporary poor relief practice by ending the auctioning of the poor to the lowest bidder and stopping the shunting of the poor from town to town regardless of their health or the weather. To their sponsors, poorhouses appeared an ideal way to accomplish a broad array of economic, disciplinary, rehabilitative, and humanitarian objectives.

Poorhouses had very clear goals: they were supposed to check the expense of pauperism through cheaper care and by deterring people from applying for relief. According to the Quincy Report, all the towns that had already built a poorhouse "without exception claimed a reduction in their expenses." In New York, the Yates Report estimated the annual cost of a pauper in an almshouse at twenty to thirty-five dollars and on outdoor relief not less than thirty-three to sixty-five dollars; if the pauper was old or sick, outdoor relief would cost at least eighty or one hundred dollars each year. County poorhouses, it was also argued, would spread the financial burden of relief more evenly among rural and urban areas, in contrast to the current system under which urban areas often paid three times as much as rural ones. Another projected benefit of a county poorhouse system was its contribution to the reduction of settlement problems. "The expenses of removals from extreme parts, and the consequent grievous litigation, as well as the payment of the innumberable host of officers, would be avoided."[48]

As for cutting the cost of poor relief through deterrence, consider the experience of New Bedford, Massachusetts, with its poorhouse. Since its construction the town had "experienced a diminution of that class of vagrants who have for years annoyed us." Before the poorhouse, the town's poor had been helped with outdoor relief, and very often people applied "for assistance for supporting their aged and infirm relations." With the opening of the poorhouse, "their applications" had "almost entirely ceased." Once people knew "that every Pauper must be removed to the Poor House, many causes combined to prevent their application for assistance." Franklin, New York, expected that a poorhouse would "in a great measure, deter many persons from applying for relief, except in cases of absolute necessity." "The prohibition against alcohol and mandatory work," predicted Charles Burroughs, "will deter many intemperate wretches, and lazy vagrants from seeking admission to these walls" and act "as a stimulant on their industry and moral feelings."[49]

Poorhouses were expected to do more than cut the expense of poor relief and deter potential paupers from asking for help. In the North – but much less so in the South – they also were supposed to transform the behavior and character of their inmates. Every town, an official from Pepperell, Massachusetts, pointed out, harbored "a class of people naturally disposed to be lazy and indolent." When boarded with private families, they indulged their habits, caring only for "what is sufficient to nourish the body," passing "their time in sloth and inactivity." But put "these characters" in a poorhouse, and "you find they are uneasy and discontented. A degree of pride begins to operate in their bosom; this proves an incen-

tive to exertion; they quit their station and shift for themselves." Under the influence of a poorhouse superintendent who made them work and watched their behavior, paupers would "possibly in time become renovated." At the same time, poorhouses would strike a blow at intemperance, the great immediate cause of pauperism, first by prohibiting alcohol, second by deterrence. For magistrates should be given authority "to send any person, on view, found intoxicated, or in the habit of intoxication, for a certain period, to labor in a house of industry."[50]

Almshouses, their advocates predicted confidently, also would improve the lives of pauper children. Pauper children outside of almshouses, observed the Yates Report, were "not only brought up in ignorance and idleness"; their "health" was "precarious," and, often, they died "prematurely." Just the reverse happened in almshouses. Children's "health and morals" were "alike improved and secured," and they received "an education to fit them for future usefulness." For all these reasons, to its sponsors the poorhouse seemed a just, humane alternative to the practice of boarding out the poor. As one official from a New York town claimed, "The *infirm* could be more readily healed – the *idiot* more humanely provided for – the *lunatic* more securely kept, and the *youth* better prepared for society."[51]

Poorhouse advocates believed they had good grounds for optimism. Although poorhouses were novel, enough of them existed to compile a swelling body of evidence about their virtues. The verdict appeared unanimous. Every town or city that had established a poorhouse before the early 1820s reported a reduction in the cost of poor relief and an improved moral climate. Yates's survey of pauperism throughout the country concluded, "where the poor-house system has prevailed for the greatest length of time, and to the greatest extent, the ratio of pauperism, and of the amount of expense is less than it is in any other state in which that system has been more recently or partially introduced." This is why Pennsylvania, Delaware, Rhode Island, and Virginia had the lowest ratios of paupers in the country. At a local level, to take only one example, the supervisor of Brookhaven, New York, estimated that the establishment of a poorhouse in 1817 had reduced expenses for pauperism by one-third.[52]

Poorhouse advocates even exuded optimism about paupers' ability to produce their own food and do other useful work. Salem, Massachusetts, for instance, appears to have been especially successful at employing its poorhouse inmates. The town had opened a new almshouse in 1816. In the next year, about 18 acres of land were broken up and planted, producing 4,391 pounds of pork (of which 2,000 pounds were sold for $280), 1,000 bushels of turnips, and 2,700 bushels of potatoes. Besides farming, inmates worked at "spinning, weaving, coopering, the manufacture of small articles of cabinet furniture, making the wood work of all the tools used on the farm, corn brooms, etc. etc." All the shoes worn by the inmates had been made in the almshouse as had most of the clothes. Picking oakum, probably the major employment of paupers in most almshouses, was "restricted to those who are confined to their rooms by age and infirmity, or are otherwise incapable of hard labor." Even New York City reported a large and varied product from its almshouse inmates, and as late as 1843, Walter Channing could write glowingly about the industry in Boston's Almshouse.[53]

The optimism of early almshouse sponsors and administrators contradicts most reports made only a few years later. Clearly, in their early years, it was at least plausible to think of almshouses positively, as humane, reformatory institutions, reducing expenditures for poor relief and checking the growth of a demoralized pauper class. But it is difficult to believe that even in these early years the picture was quite as cheery as poor law reformers would have had their contemporaries believe. For one example,

recall the hints of opposition, the local resistance to poorhouses. From the start, poorhouses were not popular institutions. Nor were they supposed to be. Here is the heart of the issue. Irreconcilable contradictions had been stamped into the foundations of almshouses. The almshouse was to be at once a refuge for the helpless and a deterrent to the ablebodied; it was supposed to care for the poor humanely and to discourage them from applying for relief. In the end, one of these poles would have to prevail. The almshouse was to be both a voluntary institution, entered with no more coercion than the threat of starvation, and, in some cases, a penal institution for vagrants and beggars. Asserting that poverty was not a crime, almshouse sponsors protested against the inhumanity of existing poor relief practices such as auctioning the poor or shunting them around from town to town. At the same time, their own comments confounded crime and poverty. Not least, they expected institutions designed to house only the most helpless and infirm paupers to be hives of industry and productivity. If the almshouses worked, the aged and infirm would be held hostage to the war on ablebodied paupers. In essence, social policy advocated shutting up the old and sick away from their friends and relatives to deter the working class from seeking poor relief. In this way, fear of the poorhouse became the key to sustaining the work ethic in nineteenth century America.

The Failure of the Poorhouse

By the 1850s, almost every major institution founded in the early nineteenth century had lost its original promise. For a short time it had appeared that most of them would work in the way their promoters had predicted. Early mental hospitals reported astonishing rates of cure; reform schools allegedly transformed young delinquents; and poorhouses purportedly slowed the growth of pauperism and sheltered the helpless. But within several years this early optimism faded. Mental hospitals did not cure; prisons and reform schools did not rehabilitate; public schools did not educate very well; and poorhouses did not check the growth of outdoor relief or promote industry and temperance. A preoccupation with order, routine, and cost replaced the founders' concern with the transformation of character and social reform. Everywhere, reform gave way to custody as the basis of institutional life.[54]

Poorhouses had degenerated especially badly. A select committee of the New York State Senate visited the state's poorhouses in 1856 and issued a scathing indictment. "The poor houses throughout the State," wrote the committee, "may be generally described as badly constructed, ill-arranged, ill-warmed, and ill-ventilated. The rooms are crowded with inmates; and the air, particularly in the sleeping apartments, is very noxious, and to casual visitors, almost insufferable." Sometimes forty-five inmates slept in one dormitory "with low ceilings, and sleeping boxes arranged in three tiers one above another." Within poorhouses good health was an "impossibility." Almost none of them had adequate hospital facilities, and the sick were "even worse cared for than the healthy." Medical attendance was "inadequate" and physicians "poorly paid." Sometimes inmates died with no medical attention at all. One county poorhouse that averaged 137 inmates reported 36 deaths in the previous year, "yet none of them from epidemic or contagious disease," a death rate that indicated "most inexcusable negligence." With almost no classification of their inmates, men and women mingled freely during the day and, even, at night. As a result, many of the births in poorhouses were "the offspring of illicit connections." Petty graft exacerbated the problem of poorhouse administration. In two counties the contractor who supplied the poorhouse was "allowed to profit by all the labor which he could extort from the paupers." In both these cases, the contractor was also one of the superintendents of the poor and in one

case, even, the superintendent of the poorhouse himself. In 1857, in Charleston, South Carolina, shocked commissioners of the poor reported:

> The Yard was uncleansed – the surface drains filled with offensive matter – the Privies in a most filthy state – the floors most unwashed, many of the windows obscured by apparently many months accumulation of dust and cobwebs – nearly all the beds and bedding in a disgustingly neglected state, and in some localities, swarming with vermin.[55]

Managerial problems in poor relief began with the office of overseer of the poor. So unpopular was the job that it sometimes took fines to force men to serve. In Philadelphia, for example, until the late 1820s men usually did not serve as Guardians of the Poor for more than a year. Only when paid, full-time officials assumed more of the day-to-day burden of handling applications for relief and investigating the merit of individual cases, did guardians begin to accept longer terms. Philadelphia's guardians disliked most dealing with the outdoor poor. However, some of them managed to win a potentially lucrative place among the managers of the almshouse, who often sold the institution supplies.[56]

Indeed, because superintendents or overseers of the poor often used their offices as sources of graft, petty corruption infected the administration of poor relief. In New York State, said one experienced observer, one of the superintendents of the poor usually was a "country merchant" and two were farmers. They divided the "purchasing of supplies" among themselves. The merchant sold the poorhouse its meat and other articles from his own store at the "highest retail prices," charging even "for the very wrapper and twine" used to package the goods. He had little incentive to "restrain waste and extravagance" because the more he sold, the larger his profits. Farmers also had their own intricate fiddles that brought them a "nice profit." The whole process of supplying poorhouses, in fact, was "reduced to a regular system in most counties in the State." Petty corruption proved hard to eradicate. Almost forty years later in the 1890s, Amos Warner included in his complaints about poor relief administration "dishonest or wasteful mismanagement of funds."[57]

Warner also pointed to the limited ability of most poorhouse keepers and described how job pressures drove even well-meaning men to brutality. With "dreary work, small pay, and practically no general recognition" for their services, whatever their quality, "a sensitive, high-minded, ambitious man" was not likely to accept the job, and, "almost of necessity," the typical keeper was "a tolerably stolid, unsympathetic person, and one who had not been very successful in other lines." Unfortunately, the job usually exceeded his abilities. He was sent "a miscellaneous assortment of the diseased, defective, and incapable" and told to care for them without "the proper facilities." Although the county "cut his appropriations to the lowest possible point," he did not complain for fear of losing his job. Most of the inmates, moreover, were "bad-tempered, unreasonable, and inveterately querulous. They would complain no matter what might be done for them." In these circumstances, he gradually came to feel that "it does not matter what is done for them – that anything is good enough for them." The result was brutality. "He becomes brutal unconsciously, and almost in self-defense. After a few years he does, without question, things that would have seemed absolutely awful to him when he first entered his duties."[58]

In North Carolina, even in the early twentieth century, it was not "unusual to find a superintendent" who belonged "to a class only slightly superior to most of his inmates." Rarely could he be compared with "the other officials of the county." He was "not the type of man who could be elected register of deeds or clerk of the court." His wife, of course, usually belonged "to the

same class as he." In 1922, a survey of poorhouse superintendents in eighty counties found that seventy-four had less than a high school education. "The only superintendent who had any college training" had been "removed because he did not belong to the same political faction as the county commissioners." Many superintendents were "practically illiterate," and a few could not read and write. Most – sixty-nine of eighty – had been farmers, and thirty had been tenant farmers. The eleven nonfarmers "came from various occupations – merchant, salesman, carpenter, mason, jailer, policeman, 'moonshiner.'"[59]

Like other new service professions that developed during the nineteenth century, poorhouse administration had to forge an occupational identity. The first school systems, penitentiaries, reform schools, mental hospitals, and poorhouses could not draw on a pool of trained administrators or a body of technical and managerial knowledge. In each case, however, as officials created a new role and accumulated practical experience, they developed their own organizations, journals, and training procedures. As a result, by the early twentieth century, each new service activity had generated a new profession: school superintendent, penologist, psychiatrist, social worker, public welfare official. Each of these professions originated in practice, that is, from the attempt to build and run novel institutions.[60]

In New York State, the Annual Convention of the County Superintendents of the Poor, which met first in 1870, was a loosely knit organization that held annual conventions, published its proceedings, and sometimes lobbied the state legislature. Over the years, its proceedings show the gradual development of an occupational identity, fostered, especially late in the century, by attacks on county poorhouses and attempts to remove the insane to state institutions. A few superintendents, who held their jobs for many years (such as the one from Rochester), obviously were well read in contemporary literature about pauperism and poor relief, and they tried to run their own institutions professionally and to stimulate their colleagues throughout the state to higher standards. Indeed, by 1913 the County Convention felt sufficiently professional to change its name to the New York Association of Public Welfare Officials.

Nonetheless, probably no more than a few poorhouses were very well administered. Small county poorhouses had few staff besides the keeper or superintendent and his wife. Cities such as Philadelphia or New York developed elaborate hierarchies for administering their large poorhouses, but these, too, were understaffed. Medical care, always insufficient, sometimes was left to local doctors for whom the poorhouse offered a lucrative and steady source of income – and a source of contention among local physicians who sometimes underbid one another for the contract. Occasionally, as in Philadelphia, medical students provided much of the medical care. Professional nurses were almost nonexistent, and most of the nursing was done by other inmates.[61]

Inmates, in fact, did a great deal of the routine work around poorhouses. They not only nursed other inmates and gardened but also often cooked, cleaned, sewed, and did other small jobs. Inmates virtually ran the larger poorhouses, as in Philadelphia, where they greatly outnumbered the paid staff. With inmates serving as attendants, officials had little control over life on the wards, and large poorhouses turned into rowdy, noisy places in which discipline was almost impossible. According to Clement, in Philadelphia some of the inmates formed their own organizations; others fought with each other; and the city's ethnic tensions erupted into conflicts within the almshouse. Other inmates peddled small goods – "pins, needles, thread, and other small personal articles" – to one another while the "gate-keepers peddled drugs, fruits, and candy." (Inmates were supposed to turn all their money over to the agent who admitted them; so the medium of exchange remains unclear.) Even liquor was easily available. Doctors failed to hide the keys to the liquor cabinet; the inmates stole liquor from the managers' private stock; employees smuggled in liquor which they sold; and doctors prescribed a great deal of liquor as medicine. In 1825–6, for example, they authorized the purchase of 1,624 gallons for the hospital, or an average of one-half gallon for every person admitted during the year. This easy availability of liquor, of course, defeated attempts to curb the intemperance thought to be the major immediate cause of pauperism.[62]

The ease with which inmates could enter or leave almshouses made discipline problems worse. Despite a rule that required inmates to work off the cost of their care, in Philadelphia inmates left the almshouse easily: they went to an official who checked their records and, usually, finding nothing amiss, handed them their clothes and allowed them to leave. (Inside the almshouse all the inmates had to wear the same uniform.) Warner complained of the "laxness" of admission and discharge policies. Because everyone was "entitled to be saved from starvation and death and exposure," anyone could enter an almshouse. But the almshouse, after all, was not a penal institution and it "was in the interest of no one to have persons there who" could "support themselves outside." This meant that inmates virtually could discharge themselves at will; "the door swings . . . outward or inward with the greatest ease." As a result, the almshouse became a temporary refuge for the degenerate poor, "a winter resort for tramps . . . a place where the drunkard and the prostitute" recuperated "between debauches." The open-door policy, as characteristic of Charleston as of Philadelphia, had spawned a class of almshouse recidivists. Citing a study in Hartford, Warner reported the case of one woman who "came and went thirteen times in twenty-two and one-half months."[63]

A failure to classify inmates underlay the administrative problems of poorhouses. Critics throughout the century complained that many poorhouses did not separate paupers by age, condition, sex, and color; allowed the worthy poor to mingle with the degraded; and failed to send the insane or other handicapped inmates to special institutions. In 1855, a New York critic complained that the "poor of all classes and colors, all ages and habits, partake of a common fare, a common table, and a common dormitory." Respectable widows who found themselves in poorhouses as a result of financial "misfortunes" had to sit at the same table as "a negro wench . . . and a filthy prostitute." Nearly forty years later, Warner charged, "Probably a majority of the grave evils which could be charged at the present time to the American almshouse have their origin in a lack of proper classification," by which he meant both the reluctance to remove some categories of people – children and the insane particularly – to special institutions as well as the failure to sort out the inmates who remained. He recommended classification by color, "separation of the sexes," "isolation of defectives," "special provision for the sick," and "classification by age . . . and . . . character." Classification remained a defect in poorhouses well into the twentieth century. Writing in the mid-1920s, Harry C. Evans claimed, "The poor-farm is our human dumping ground into which go our derelicts of every description. Living in this mass of insanity and depravity, this prison place for criminals and the insane, are several thousand children and respectable old folk, whose only offense is that they are poor."[64]

One other problem made classification impossible and prevented the poorhouse from reaching any of its goals other than deterrence. That, of course, was the cheapness that governed poor relief, what Warner called the "culpable stinginess . . . of the appropriating power, resulting in inadequate or unhealthful food, lack of proper building, heating apparatus, clothing and so

forth." Everywhere, the real concern of public officials was to keep poor relief as inexpensive as possible. In the end, all the various goals of poor law reform throughout the century could be sacrificed, as long as taxes for poor relief went down.[65]

Within poorhouses, the insane suffered especially badly. Often treated abusively, the insane poor were "confined" to "cells and sheds," that were "wretched abodes, often wholly unprovided with bedding." For the most part, male attendants looked after female inmates; sometimes they whipped inmates; in other cases they chained them in their "loathsome cells." "In some poor houses, the committee found lunatics, both male and female, in cells, in a state of nudity. The cells were intolerably offensive, littered with the long accumulated filth of the occupants, and with straw reduced to chaff by long use as bedding, portions of which, mingled with the filth, adhered to the persons of the inmates and formed the only covering they had." Children, however, worried the New York Senate committee most. Outside of New York City and Kings County (Brooklyn), at least thirteen hundred children lived in the state's poorhouses, "enough, in these nurseries, if not properly cared for, to fill some day all the houses of refuge and prisons of the State."[66]

Nor did most poorhouse superintendents manage to find useful work for their inmates. In fact, "idleness" remained "a great evil," most notable during the winter "when the houses are crowded, where there is little out door work to be done, and when the inmates are in the most vigorous state to do full work." In most poorhouses, the best source of work, farming or gardening, was "unavailable in the winter, just at the time when a rigid work-test is most essential." Work remained a problem that plagued poorhouse administrators throughout the century. Writing in 1894, Amos Warner pointed out how much more it usually cost to "set the inmates of an almshouse to work than their work is worth." They could be supported "more cheaply in idleness," he said. Finding work for women inmates, however, was easier. There were "relatively so few" of them that they usually could be put to work usefully "taking care of the house and in doing the laundry-work and sewing."[67]

In the Philadelphia almshouse, managers repeatedly tried to organize profitable factories run by inmates. They never succeeded. Only a minority of inmates were healthy enough or strong enough to work; often goods were produced more cheaply outside the almshouse; and inmates had few skills. Nonetheless, managers clung to the importance of work for its moral as well as its economic returns. In the 1820s, they sold the poorhouse horses and instead constructed tread wheels with which to punish inmates. When there were too few men and women who needed punishment because they were lazy or had venereal disease, the managers used mentally ill inmates to work the tread wheels. Despite their inefficiency and a committee's recommendation to replace them with steam-driven machinery, most officials wanted to keep the tread wheels to deter the poor from seeking public relief.[68]

Disturbed by the idleness of most poorhouse inmates, the New York Commissioners of Public Charities observed "that pauper labor still remains very far behind what it should be in productiveness." Even discounting the sick and old, inmates did not earn a third of the cost of their support. Given this situation, the commissioners urged sentencing the ablebodied and others convicted of minor offenses to special workhouses for as long as possible (at least 3 months), where they would be made to "labor systematically" and be taught a trade. In Kansas, the discipline on poor farms was penal. A visitor found inmates forbidden to speak to each other, "except concerning their work," and if they "became unruly, a jail room was used. . . . They were also sometimes deprived of their meals as a punishment." These examples show how social

policy confounded crime and poverty. Extreme poverty among ablebodied men itself was a crime that justified their detention; criminals differed so little from ablebodied paupers that they could be sentenced to the same institution. Work was important, first, because wherever possible paupers should earn their support. Second, it could help make paupers independent by teaching them a trade. But most of all, it deterred shirkers from applying for public relief.[69]

In his letters on pauperism, "Franklin," a well-informed New York newspaper correspondent, unintentionally highlighted the ambiguities in the stress on work within poorhouses. Whether work returned a profit ultimately was irrelevant; any work was better than none because its greatest value was deterring others from seeking public relief. Everywhere, noted Franklin, paupers earned only a tiny amount. The average for New York State was $3.15 per year; in Boston, it was $4.73; in Philadelphia, $4.71; in Essex County, Massachusetts, $4.53. Only Providence, Rhode Island, where paupers annually averaged $16.37, stood out as an exception. Not only did paupers in Providence earn more, but the city supported more paupers who, for one reason or another, were incapable of working. The Providence Poorhouse rigidly enforced "the rule . . . that every one able to work must work." If no profitable work was available, "they set them at something which is not profitable, at all events they must be kept employed." During his last visit, Franklin had seen "a party of men carrying wood from one corner of the yard to another and piling it there; when it was all removed it was brought back again and piled in the old place." This sort of practice rid "Providence of all lazy drones, such as infest our poor houses to a great degree." "Franklin" had begun his argument by stressing the need to increase the profitability of pauper labor, but he slipped without transition into the virtues of labor, any hard labor, for its own sake. In the end, it was deterrence, not profitability, that mattered.[70]

Satisfactory work arrangements rarely existed. Work's deterrent, educational, and moneymaking purposes contradicted each other, and the large share of old, sick, and disabled inmates left only a minority able to labor. The most successful work was farming, and poorhouses often were built in the country with farms attached to them. Indeed, in many states they were called poor-farms rather than poorhouses. In some instances, superintendents who were both good managers and good farmers ran productive farms that grew a large share of the inmates' food. Even in Philadelphia, the farm attached to the poorhouse was relatively successful. However, in many instances, farms, like manufacturing operations, were failures. In 1872, for example, Dr. C. T. Murphey criticized the failure of the farms attached to North Carolina's poorhouses. "If it be possible to contemplate any one feature more than another of the faulty management of our houses," he wrote, "it is the neglect and want of proper cultivation of vegetable gardens." At least half of the inmates' food could be grown on one well-cultivated acre, but the year's crops were "barely sufficient" for "the overseer and his family, and apples and fruit during their season (so abundant in North Carolina)" were "regarded as a great luxury by the inmate poor, and . . . seldom found among them either as a relish or food." Poorhouse farms often failed because in the summer when they needed ablebodied labor, healthy younger men left to work elsewhere. Indeed, poorhouses remained most crowded in the winter when they could offer their inmates little outdoor work. This is why even most country poorhouses failed to employ their inmates usefully.[71]

Poorhouses not only failed to find work for their inmates; they did not even manage to reduce the expense of poor relief. Despite the confident predictions of their founders in the 1820s, it proved more expensive to support someone in a poorhouse than on outdoor relief. The New York Senate Committee pointed out that "half the sum requisite" to support a person in a poorhouse "would often save them from destitution, and enable them to work in their households and their vicinity, sufficiently to earn the remainder of their support during the inclement season when indigence suffers the most." Dirty, dangerous, brutal, demoralizing, and expensive, poorhouses had become "unsuitable refuges for the virtuous poor, and mainly places of confinement for the degraded." Poor inmates received worse treatment than criminals, worse even than animals. "Common domestic animals are usually more humanely provided for than the paupers in some of these institutions; where the misfortune of poverty is visited with greater deprivations of comfortable food, lodging, clothing, and warmth and ventilation than constitute the usual penalty of crime."[72]

The New York Senate Committee did not evaluate how well poorhouses played their other role. For they had been founded not only to care for the indigent and helpless but to deter the poor from asking for relief. No one was supposed to want to go to a poorhouse. By their very existence, poorhouses were supposed to spur the working class to independence. Most commentators implied that poorhouses succeeded as deterrents, but the actual situation was more complex. In the 1850s, one poor relief critic argued that poorhouses had made the poor "less independent than they had been twenty years" earlier. In the 1830s, he said, "there was a strong repugnance on the part of the poor to go to the County house, or to accept public relief in any form," and they would suffer an "astonishing" amount "rather than become a public charge." Equally "astonishing" was "the extent to which they carried the science of frugality." Now, the poor had become "more wasteful," with "less sense of shame in living on the public." Public policy bore much of the blame for this demoralization of the poor, for it was common to hear the inmates in county poorhouses "discussing the merits of Poor Houses in different parts of the State, just as fashionable travelers discuss the merits of the Ocean House at Newport, or the United States at Saratoga." Paupers had begun to think of "County Houses as places of rest and repose, intended to shield them from effort and labor" and could see no reason not to "avail themselves of their comforts without scruple, as often and as long as it suits their convenience."[73]

One lesson observers learned was the incompatibility of deterrence and compassion: the spread of fear and the kindly treatment of decent poverty could not coexist. One or the other always prevailed. This was the reason poorhouse critics increasingly argued for the separation of the ablebodied into special workhouses. By dividing the inmates into the ablebodied and deserving two separate policies could exist: one harsh, punitive, and centered on work, the other more compassionate and generous. However, very few places managed to create both a workhouse and an almshouse, and, in any event, in practice, the division of individual cases rarely was as easy as commentators implied. Some people were helpless because they were sick, insane, or old. But for others, the line was not nearly so clear. Maintaining two institutions, moreover, would have strained the administrative capacity and financial resources of towns and counties already reluctant to provide more than the most minimal support, even for the impotent poor. Even more, occasional bursts of sentiment aside, poorhouses were not supposed to do more than keep old and helpless inmates from starvation. They existed to deter the impotent as well as the ablebodied poor from seeking their shelter. Whether some poorhouses chose compassion over deterrence in the mid-nineteenth century and so encouraged homeless men to seek them out is not the main point. Most poorhouses offered few comforts or attractions. By the close of the century, at the latest, dread of the poorhouse was virtually universal. In the end, deterrence won.

By ignoring the contradiction in poorhouse goals, the New York Senate Committee could retain some optimism, a faith that honest, capable management could turn poorhouses around. But poorhouse managers needed support, and the committee, worried about public neglect, complained that citizens generally showed "little interest in the condition even of those" poorhouses "in their immediate neighborhood." Even people who took a "great interest in human suffering" never visited poorhouses and were "entirely uninformed" of the horrors that lurked in a "county house almost at their own doors." A correspondent to the Savannah *Republican* made a similar criticism of public involvement with poorhouses in the urban South. In the last analysis, the New York Senate Committee concluded, this "apparent indifference on the part of the citizens" accounted for the "miserable state to which these houses have fallen." Twelve years later, in 1869, the newly appointed Commissioners of Public Charity reviewed the state's poorhouses and found them in much the same condition as had the earlier Senate committee. Quoting at length from the committee's report, the commissioners observed, "the condition of things twelve years ago corresponds with our representations today." They pointed out that the Senate committee had criticized the "little interest taken by citizens in the counties in the condition of the poorhouses" and attributed much of their miserable state to "this apparent indifference." Though the committee had made "a strong and urgent appeal to the benevolent to look into the condition of the poor," there had been "little, if any, response."[74]

The commissioners' complaints about public indifference reflected a growing fear that the well-to-do had abandoned their public responsibilities. Not only the corruption of politics but the decay of public institutions and the emergence of a militant, undeferential working class, so it was argued, resulted from the withdrawal of educated, well-off citizens from an active role in local government, the oversight of public institutions, and their former close and personal contact with the poor. The commissioners hammered at public indifference by pointing out that paying taxes did "not include the whole sphere of duty of the citizen to the community of which he is a member. He should take part at least in a general oversight of its municipal management, and constitute himself a moral policeman in home affairs."[75]

The reassertion of the citizen as "moral policeman" – a major theme of late nineteenth-century history, reflected in scientific charity, the temperance movement, and the wars against sexuality – helped shape the history of poorhouses. "Moved by considerations of a purely benevolent character," reported the commissioners in 1872, "some public spirited citizens of Westchester county, acting under the suggestions of Miss Louisa L. Schuyler, have taken initiatory steps looking toward a local supervision of its poor house, by the organization of a local visiting committee." The criticism of indifference had worked; the women of Westchester County became the nucleus of a new organization, the New York State Charities' Aid Association, a coalition of county associations of well-to-do citizens, mainly women, whose members attempted to stimulate improvements in local poorhouses through systematic visiting. As might be expected, poorhouse keepers did not always welcome their new observers. In fact, the Westchester visitors at first were denied entrance to the poorhouse. Using its influence, however, the association turned to the state legislature and, within a year, had sponsored a bill granting them access to poorhouses. Their success revealed the power and influence of their members, the close, complex relations between the state and voluntarism, and the indistinct boundaries between public and private that have always been a feature of American life.[76]

The watchfulness of the State Charities' Aid Association failed to transform poorhouses into decent, compassionate refuges for the destitute. Not only in New York but throughout the country, trapped by their contradictory purposes, undercut by poor management and inadequate funds, poorhouses never could find useful work for their inmates or offer the old, sick, and helpless, not to mention the ablebodied unemployed, much more than a roof and escape from death by starvation. Nor did they reduce pauperism or cut the cost of poor relief. In fact, despite the diffusion of poorhouses, the volume of outdoor relief continued to grow.

NOTES

1   Although outdoor relief – or, our modern euphemism, public welfare – is as old as the colonies, as American as Thanksgiving, there is, in contrast to England, almost no modern American historical writing about poor laws, and outdoor relief remains one of the dirty little secrets of American history. Even the one brief American flurry of interest in poor law history virtually ignored outdoor relief. Primarily in the 1920s and 1930s, a series of books sponsored by two pioneers in social welfare, Edith Abbott and Sophonisba Breckenridge, traced the history of poor laws in various states. All of them emphasized the origins and history of poorhouses and told a dreary tale of meanness and misery gradually supplanted by professional administration and specialized institutions that took children, the insane, and the sick out of poorhouses. These accounts reflected their authors' primary purpose, which was not to write social history. Rather, they wanted to stimulate the nascent growth of state power in social welfare, the development of specialized institutions, and the professionalization of social work and public administration. See, for example, Grace Abbott, *Public Assistance* (Chicago: University of Chicago Press, 1940) and Sophonisba Breckenridge, *Public Welfare Administration* (Chicago: University of Chicago Press, 1927; rev. ed., 1938). For a recent biography, see Lela B. Costin, *Two Sisters for Social Justice: A Biography of Grace*

and Edith Abbott (Urbana and Chicago: University of Illinois Press, 1983). For overviews of the history of social welfare in America, see James Leiby, *A History of Social Welfare and Social Work in the United States* (New York: Columbia University Press, 1978); Walter I. Trattner, *From Poor Law to Welfare State*, 3d ed. (New York: Free Press, 1984); David M. Schneider, *The History of Public Welfare in New York State, 1876–1940* (Chicago: University of Chicago Press, 1938); David M. Schneider and Albert Deutsch, *The History of Public Welfare in New York State, 1867–1940* (Chicago: University of Chicago Press, 1941); Blanche Coll, *Perspectives in Public Welfare* (Washington, D.C.: U.S. Government Printing Office, 1969) and "Public Assistance in the United States: From Colonial Times to 1860," in *Comparative Development in Social Welfare*, ed. E. W. Martin (London: Allen and Unwin, 1972) pp. 128–58; June Axinn and Herman Levin, *Social Welfare: A History of the American Response to Need* (New York: Dodd, Mead, 1970).

2   David M. Gordon, Richard Edwards, Michael Reich, *Segmented Work, Divided Workers: The Historical Transformation of Labor in the United States* (New York: Cambridge University Press, 1982), pp. 48–99; Maurice Dobb, *Studies in the Development of Capitalism*, rev. ed. (New York: International Publishers, 1967), chs. 1–2; Charles Tilly, *As Sociology Meets History* (New York: Academic Press, 1981), ch. 7; Daniel Rodgers, *The Work Ethic in Industrial America, 1850–1920* (Chicago: University of Chicago Press, 1978), p. 30; Kaestle, *Evolution of an Urban School System, New York City, 1750–1850* (Cambridge: Harvard University Press, 1973) p. 102; Katz, Doucet, and Stern, *Social Organization of Early Industrial Capitalism* (Cambridge: Harvard University Press, 1982), ch. 1; David Montgomery, "The Shuttle and the Cross: Weavers and Artisans in the Kensington Riots of 1844," *Journal of Social History* (Summer, 1972), pp. 411–46.

3   Richard A. McLeod, "The Philadelphia Artisans 1828–1850," Ph.D. diss. Univ. of Missouri, 1971, pp. 35 and 54–74, is good on these points. See, also, Bruce Laurie and

Mark Schmitz, "Manufacture and Productivity: The Making of an Industrial Base: Philadelphia, 1850–1880," in Theodore Hershberg, ed., *Philadelphia: Work, Space, Family, and Group Experience in the Nineteenth Century* (New York: Oxford University Press, 1981), ch. 2.

4   McLeod, "Philadelphia Artisan," p. 61.

5   There are many studies of population mobility in nineteenth century America. The first book to call attention to the phenomenon was Stephan Thernstrom, *Poverty and Progress: Social Mobility in a Nineteenth-Century City* (Cambridge: Harvard University Press, 1964). For a review of the field and the presentation of somewhat less problematic data than most other studies, see Katz, Doucet, and Stern, *Social Organization*, ch. 3.

6   "Letters to the Secretary of State on the Subject of Pauperism," first published in the *Columbia Republican*, in the fall of 1853, in New York Secretary of State Annual Report on Statistics of the Poor, 1855, New York Senate Documents, No. 72, 1855, p. 79; Nancy Cott, *The Bonds of Womanhood: "Women's Sphere" in New England, 1780–1835* (New Haven: Yale University Press, 1977), pp. 23–46; Joan Underhill Hannon, "Poverty in the Antebellum Northeast: The View from New York State's Poor Relief Rolls," *Journal of Economic History*, XIV, No. 4 (December, 1984), pp. 1028–31 (quote p. 1030; newspaper quote, pp. 1030–1); Grace A. Browning, *The Development of Poor Relief Legislation in Kansas* (Chicago: University of Chicago Press, 1935), pp. 76–84.

7   Benjamin Joseph Klebaner, "Public Poor Relief, America 1790–1860," Ph.D. diss., Columbia University, 1952, pp. 74–5.

8   Priscilla F. Clement, "The Response to Need: Welfare and Poverty in Philadelphia, 1800–1850," Ph.D. diss., University of Pennsylvania, 1977, pp. 267–70; Barbara Lawrence Bellows, "Tempering the Wind: The Southern Response to Urban Poverty, 1850–1865," Ph.D. diss., University of South Carolina, 1983, pp. 199–201.

9   Matthew Carey, "Essays on the Public Charities of Philadelphia," (1828), p. 171, reprinted in David J. Rothman, ed., *The*

Jacksonians on the Poor: Collected Pamphlets (New York: Arno Press and New York Times, 1971).

10 Carey, "Essays," pp. 167, 172; Bellows, "Tempering the Wind", p. 204.

11 Carey, "Essays," p. 173.

12 McLeod, "Philadelphia Artisan," p. 151; Walter Channing, "An Address on the Prevention of Pauperism," p. 35, in Rothman, ed., *Jacksonians*.

13 Carey, "Essays," p. 11.

14 As an example of the problem of widows, see the case history in Michael B. Katz, *Poverty and Policy in American History* (New York: Academic Press, 1983), pp. 18–54.

15 The best way to get a sense of how families survived and of the awesome pressures under which they lived is to read the case histories compiled by agents and visitors for various voluntary societies, such as charity organization societies.

16 On life insurance, see Viviana A. Zelizer, *Morals and Markets: The Development of Life Insurance in the United States* (New York: Columbia University Press, 1979). In most medium-sized cities around the middle of the nineteenth century, about one-quarter to one-third of families owned their own homes. In big cities the proportion was smaller, about 11 percent in Philadelphia and probably less than half that in New York. For a discussion of property ownership in the nineteenth century, see Katz, Doucet, and Stern, *Social Organization*, ch. 4. For an estimation of the proportion of elderly who lived with their children see, Steven Ruggles, "Prolonged Connections: Demographic Change and the Rise of the Extended Family in Nineteenth Century England and America," Ph.D. diss., University of Pennsylvania, 1984.

17 Klebaner, "Public Poor Relief," pp. 612–13.

18 Bellows, "Tempering the Wind," p. 199.

19 Gerald N. Grob, *Mental Institutions in America: Social Policy to 1875* (New York: Free Press, 1973), p. 81. On the development of social institutions in this period see also, David J. Rothman, *The Discovery of the Asylum: Social Order and Disorder in the New Republic* (Boston: Little Brown, 1971) and Katz, Doucet, and Stern, *Social Organization*, pp. 349–91.

20 In addition to the sources already cited on institutional development see, Barbara Brenzel, *Daughters of the State: A Social Portrait of the First Reform School for Girls in North America, 1846–1905* (Cambridge: MIT Press, 1983); F. Kaestle, *The Evolution of an Urban School System*; Michael B. Katz, *The Irony of Early School Reform: Educational Innovation in Mid-Nineteenth Century Massachusetts* (Cambridge: Harvard University Press, 1968); Klebaner, "Public Poor Relief in America"; W. D. Lewis, *From Newgate to Dannemora: The Rise of the Penitentiary in New York, 1796–1848* (Ithaca: Cornell University Press, 1965); Robert M. Mennel, *Thorns and Thistles: Juvenile Delinquents in the United States, 1825–1840* (Hanover, N.H.: University Press of New England, 1973).

21 McLeod, "Philadelphia Artisan," pp. 26–7.

22 The classic statement of the problem of time and work discipline in this period is, E. P. Thompson, "Time, Work Discipline, and Industrial Capitalism," *Past and Present* 38 (December 1967), pp. 56–97. See also, Herbert Gutman, *Work, Culture, and Society in Industrializing America* (New York: Knopf, 1976), ch. 1.

23 Katz, *Irony*, pp. 207–9; Lewis, *From Newgate to Dannemora*, p. 90; Mennel, *Thorns and Thistles*, pp. 51–2; Grob, *Mental Institutions*, p. 176.

24 Christopher Lasch, "Origins of the Asylum," in C. Lasch, ed., *The World of Nations: Reflections on American History, Politics, and Culture* (New York: Basic Books, 1973); Harry Braverman, *Labor and Monopoly Capital: The Degradation of Work in the Twentieth Century* (New York: Monthly Review Press, 1974), pp. 279–80.

25 Geoffrey W. Oxley, *Poor Relief in England and Wales, 1601–1834* (London, Vermont, and Vancouver, B.C.: David and Charles, 1974); Ursula R. Henriques, *Before the Welfare State: Social Administration in Early Industrial Britain* (London and New York: Longmans, 1979); M. A. Crowther, *The Workhouse System, 1834–1929* (Athens, Ga.: University of Georgia Press, 1981); Leiby, *History of Social Welfare*, p. 9; Klebaner, "Public Poor Relief,"; S. E. Wiberly, "Four Cities: Public Poor Relief in Urban America," Ph.D. diss., Yale University, 1975.

26 Klebaner, "Public Poor Relief," p. 682; James Leiby, *History of Social Welfare*, pp. 39–40; Elizabeth Wisner, *Social Welfare in the South: From Colonial Times to World War I* (Baton Rouge, LA: Louisiana State University Press, 1979), pp. 11, 23.

27 Klebaner, "Public Poor Relief," pp. 71–2; Wisner, *Social Welfare*, p. 40.

28 Thomas R. Hazard, *Report on the Poor and Insane in Rhode Island* (Providence, R.I.: J. Knowles, 1851; New York: Arno Press, 1973), pp. 85–7. The practice of auction or vendue resembled the older British custom of "roundsmen," where the poor were sent round from farm to farm, often to work for farmers who had made a low bid for their care. "Roundsmen" kept agricultural wages low because laborers had to compete for jobs with paupers. No one yet has tried to learn whether the vendue system played a similar role in America.

29 Consider just one example. In 1870, 15,343 people were helped for some period of time in New York state's poorhouses at a cost of $1,681,470. In the same year, 101,796 people received public outdoor relief at a cost of $911,855. The cost per person in the poorhouse was $109.59; for outdoor relief it was $8.96. New York Board of State Charities, 13th annual report, p. 113; Joan Underhill Hannon, "The Generosity of Antebellum Poor Relief," *Journal of Economic History* XLIV:3 (September 1984), p. 814 and "Poverty in the Antebellum Northeast," pp. 1019–31.

30 In 1880, a committee of the New York State Assembly prefaced their recommendation for drafting a new poor law by observing that "The laws of the government of poorhouses and for the relief of the poor in the several towns, counties, and cities of this State are administered according to no uniformity of interpretation, fixed by an appellate authority, having jurisdiction therein, but according to the caprice or interest of the various officers exercising authority therein." [New York] Assembly Document No. 57, February 13, 1880, "Report of Committee on General Laws of 1879, in Relation to Poor houses and Relief of the Poor." Roy M. Brown, *Public Poor Relief in North Carolina* (Chapel Hill: University of North Carolina Press, 1928), pp. 73–4;

Amos G. Warner, *American Charities: A Study in Philanthropy and Economics* (Boston: Crowell, 1894), pp. 141–3. Warner was professor of economics and social science at Stanford and formerly superintendent of charities for the District of Columbia and general agent of the Charity Organization Society of Baltimore. His book was widely used and often reprinted.

31 William C. Heffner, *History of Poor Relief Legislation in Pennsylvania* (Cleona, Pa.: published by the author, 1913), pp. 39–145; Klebaner, "Public Poor Relief," p. 69.

32 Klebaner, "Public Poor Relief," pp. 682–3.

33 "Report of the Committee on the Pauper Laws of this Commonwealth [1821]," hereafter referred to as Quincy Report, p. 32 and "Report of the Secretary of State [of New York] in 1824 on the Relief and Settlement of the Poor," hereafter referred to as Yates Report, pp. 1069, 1081, 966, 942, both reprinted in David J. Rothman, ed., *The Almshouse Experience: Collected Reports* (New York: Arno Press and New York Times, 1971).

34 Yates Report, pp. 942 and 1041.

35 Yates Report, p. 966; Samuel Chipman, *Report of an Examination of Poorhouses, Jails, etc. in the State of New York and in the Counties of Berkshire, Massachusetts; Litchfield, Connecticut; and Bennington, Vermont, etc.* (Albany, New York: Executive Committee of the New-York State Temperance Society, 1834), passim.; Klebaner, "Public Poor Relief," pp. 602–3; "Report of the Committee Appointed by the Board of Guardians of the Poor of the City and Districts of Philadelphia, to Visit the Cities of Baltimore, New-York, Providence, Boston, and Salem [1827]," hereafter referred to as Philadelphia Report, p. 28, reprinted in Rothman, *Almshouse Experience*; "Franklin," "Letters to the Secretary of State on the Subject of Pauperism," p. 80.

36 Quincy Report, pp. 17 and 31; Yates Report, pp. 952 and 966. Charles Burroughs, "A Discourse Delivered in the Chapel of the New Almshouse, in Portsmouth, N.H. Dec. 15, 1834 on the Occasion of its First Being Opened for Religious Service," pp. 49–50 and R. C. Waterston, "An Address on Pauperism, Its Extent, Causes, and the Best Means of Prevention; Delivered at the

Church in Bowdoin Square, February 4, 1844, pp. 19–20, both reprinted in David J. Rothman, ed., *The Jacksonians.*

37 Quincy Report, p. 51.

38 Burroughs, "Discourse," p. 56.

39 Quincy Report, p. 4.

40 Yates Report, p. 941; Burroughs, "Discourse," pp. 3–10.

41 Bellows, "Tempering the Wind," pp. 181, 250.

42 Yates Report, pp. 952, 1056.

43 Yates Report, p. 993.

44 Yates Report, p. 1061.

45 Yates Report, pp. 967 and 952; Wisner, *Social Welfare*, pp. 32–3.

46 Yates Report, p. 952.

47 Yates Report, pp. 956–7; Quincy Report, pp. 5–10.

48 Quincy Report, p. 8; Yates Report, p. 995.

49 Quincy Report, p. 25; Yates Report, p. 984; Burroughs, "Discourse," p. 91.

50 Quincy Report, pp. 34–5; Yates Report, pp. 1007–8; Bellows, "Tempering the Wind," p. 213.

51 Yates Report, pp. 1060, 995.

52 Yates Report, pp. 943, 1041, 1047; Quincy Report, p. 19.

53 Quincy Report, pp. 28–30; Yates Report, pp. 1009–11; Walter Channing, "An Address on the Prevention of Pauperism," 1843, pp. 62–3, reprinted in Rothman, *Jacksonians on the Poor.*

54 All the books on institutions previously cited tell a similar story of decline. Grob's account in *Mental Illness* (pp. 174–5) is especially graphic and his explanation detailed and convincing.

55 New York State Senate, "Report of Select Committee to visit Charitable Institutions supported by the State, and all city and county poor and work houses and jails. In Senate, January 9, 1857. No. 8, p. 3; Charleston commissioners quoted in Bellows, "Tempering the Wind," p. 224.

56 Clement, "Response to Need," pp. 43–64; 156–64.

57 "Franklin," "Letters," pp. 97–8; Warner, *American Charities*, p. 150.

58 Warner, *American Charities*, p. 152.

59 Brown, *Public Poor Relief*, pp. 114–19.

60 On the professionalization of psychiatry see, Grob, *Mental Illness*; on social work, Roy Lubove, *The Professional Altruist: The Emergence of Social Work as a Career: 1880–1935* (Cambridge: Harvard University Press, 1965); on school superintendents, David Tyack and Elisabeth Hansot, *Managers of Virtue: Public School Leadership in America, 1820–1980* (New York: Basic Books, 1982).

61 Clement, "Response to Need," p. 400; Klebaner, "Public Poor Relief," pp. 180–3.

62 Clement, "Response to Need," pp. 337–8, 170, 400.

63 Clement, "Response to Need," p. 335; Warner, *American Charities*, pp. 155–9; Bellows, "Tempering the Wind," p. 235.

64 "Franklin," "Letters", p. 108; Warner, *American Charities*, pp. 152–4; Brown, *Public Poor Relief*, p. 160.

65 Warner, *American Charities*, p. 150.

66 New York Senate Report, p. 4.

67 Warner, *American Charities*, p. 160; New York Senate Report, pp. 4–5.

68 Priscilla F. Clement, "The Response to Need," pp. 172–3, 307–9.

69 *Fifth Annual Report of the Board of State Commissioners of Public Charities.* State of New York. In Senate, April 4, 1872. No. 97, pp. 37–42; Grace A. Browning, *The Development of Poor Relief Legislation in Kansas* (Chicago: University of Chicago Press, 1935), p. 51,

70 "Franklin," "Letters," pp. 103–4.

71 Brown, *Public Poor Relief in North Carolina*, p. 80; Klebaner, "Public Poor Relief," p. 200; Bellows, "Tempering the Wind," pp. 243–9, is good on the problems of providing work in poorhouses.

72 New York Senate Committee, p. 6.

73 "Franklin," "Letters", p. 92.

74 New York Senate Committee Report, pp. 3–9; *Second Annual Report of the Board of Commissioners of Public Charities.* State of New York. In Senate, March 22, 1869. No. 61, pp. lxxi–lxxiii; Bellows, "Tempering the Wind," p. 226.

75 *Fifth Annual Report of the Board*, p. 64.

76 *Fifth Annual Report of the Board*, p. 64.

21

The Hidden Agenda

William Julius Wilson

William Julius Wilson is the Malcolm Wiener Professor of Social Policy at Harvard University's John F. Kennedy School of Government. Professor Wilson's books include *The Declining Significance of Race: Blacks and Changing American Institutions* (University of Chicago Press, 1978), *The Truly Disadvantaged: The Inner City, the Underclass and Public Policy* (University of Chicago Press, 1987), and more recently *The Disappearance of Work: The World of the New Urban Poor* (Knopf, 1996). His current research focuses on the increasing concentration of poverty in many large central cities. Recent studies examine this "new urban poverty" from a broad perspective and consider the causative role of macroeconomic conditions, culture, social welfare policy, and historical circumstances. In addition, Professor Wilson's research addresses the impact of inequality and poverty concentration on racial and ethnic relations, family structure, and joblessness, as well as the role of public policies in both alleviating and exacerbating these problems. Professor Wilson is Past President of the Consortium of Social Science Associations, Past President of the American Sociological Association, and is a MacArthur Prize Fellow. He was elected to the American Academy of Arts and Sciences in 1988, the American Philosophical Society in 1990, and the National Academy of Sciences in 1991. He is also a member of the President's Commission on White House Fellowships.

The Hidden Agenda: From Group-specific to Universal Programs of Reform

It is not enough simply to recognize the need to relate many of the woes of truly disadvantaged blacks to the problems of societal organization; it is also important to describe the problems of the ghetto underclass candidly and openly so that they can be fully explained and appropriate policy programs can be devised. It has been problematic, therefore, that liberal journalists, social scientists, policymakers, and civil rights leaders were reluctant throughout the decade of the 1970s to discuss inner-city social pathologies. Often, analysts of such issues as violent crime or teenage pregnancy deliberately make no references to race at all, unless perhaps to emphasize the deleterious consequences of racial discrimination or the institutionalized inequality of American society. Some scholars, in an effort to avoid the appearance of "blaming the victim" or to protect their work from charges of racism, simply ignore patterns of behavior that might be construed as stigmatizing to particular racial minorities.

Such neglect is relatively recent. During the mid-1960s, social scientists such as Kenneth B. Clark, Daniel Patrick Moynihan, and Lee Rainwater forthrightly examined the cumulative effects of racial isolation and class subordination on inner-city blacks. They vividly described aspects of ghetto life that, as Rainwater observed, are usually not discussed in polite conversations. All of these studies attempted to show the connection between the economic and social environment into which many blacks are born and the creation of patterns of behavior that, in Clark's words, frequently amounted to "self-perpetuating pathology."

Why have scholars tended to shy away from this line of research? One reason has to do with the vitriolic attack by many blacks and liberals against Moynihan upon publication of his report in 1965 – denunciations that generally focused on the author's unflattering depiction of the black family in the urban ghetto rather than on the proposed remedies or his historical analysis of the black family's social plight. The harsh reception accorded *The Negro Family* undoubtedly dissuaded many social scientists from following in Moynihan's footsteps.

The "black solidarity" movement was also emerging during the latter half of the 1960s. A new emphasis by young black scholars and intellectuals on the positive aspects of the black experience tended to crowd out older concerns. Indeed, certain forms of ghetto behavior labeled pathological in the studies of Clark and colleagues were redefined by some during the early 1970s as "functional" because, it was argued, blacks were displaying the ability to survive and in some cases flourish in an economically depressed environment. The ghetto family was described as resilient and capable of adapting creatively to an oppressive, racist society. And the candid, but liberal writings on the inner city in the 1960s were generally denounced. In the end, the promising efforts of the early 1960s – to distinguish the socioeconomic characteristics of different groups within the black community, and to identify the structural problems of the United States economy that affected minorities – were cut short by calls for "reparations" or for "black control of institutions serving the black community."

If this ideologically tinged criticism discouraged research by liberal scholars on the poor black family and the ghetto community, conservative thinkers were not so inhibited. From the early 1970s through the first half of the 1980s, their writings on the culture of poverty and the deleterious effects of Great Society liberal welfare policies on ghetto underclass behavior dominated the public policy debate on alleviating inner-city social dislocations.

The Great Society programs represented the country's most ambitious attempt to implement the principle of equality of life chances. However, the extent to which these programs helped the truly disadvantaged is difficult to assess when one considers the simultaneous impact of the economic downturn from 1968 to the early 1980s. Indeed, it has been argued that many people slipped into poverty because of the economic downturn and were lifted out by the broadening of welfare benefits. Moreover, the increase in unemployment that accompanied the economic downturn and the lack of growth of real wages in the 1970s, although they had risen steadily from 1950 to about 1970, have had a pronounced effect on low-income groups (especially black males).

The above analysis has certain distinct public policy implications for attacking the problems of inner-city joblessness and the related problems of poor female-headed families, welfare dependency, crime, and so forth. Comprehensive economic policies aimed at the general population but that would also enhance employment opportunities among the truly disadvantaged – both men and women – are needed. The research presented in this study suggests that improving the job prospects of men will strengthen low-income black families. Moreover, underclass absent fathers with more stable employment are in a better position to contribute financial support for their families. Furthermore, since the majority of female householders are in the labor force, improved job prospects would very likely draw in others.[1]

I have in mind the creation of a macroeconomic policy designed to promote both economic growth and a tight labor market.[2] The latter affects the supply-and-demand ratio and wages tend to rise. It would be necessary, however, to combine this policy with fiscal and monetary policies to stimulate noninflationary growth and thereby move away from the policy of controlling inflation by allowing unemployment to rise. Furthermore, it would be important to develop policy to increase the competitiveness of American goods on the international market by, among other things, reducing the budget deficit to adjust the value of the American dollar.

In addition, measures such as on-the-job training and apprenticeships to elevate the skill levels of the truly disadvantaged are needed. I will soon discuss in another context why such problems have to be part of a more universal package of reform. For now, let me simply say that improved manpower policies are needed in the short run to help lift the truly disadvantaged from the lowest rungs of the job market. In other words, it would be necessary to devise a national labor-market strategy to increase "the adaptability of the labor force to changing employment opportunities." In this connection, instead of focusing on remedial programs in the public sector for the poor

and the unemployed, emphasis would be placed on relating these programs more closely to opportunities in the private sector to facilitate the movement of recipients (including relocation assistance) into more secure jobs. Of course there would be a need to create public transitional programs for those who have difficulty finding immediate employment in the private sector, but such programs would aim toward eventually getting individuals into the private sector economy. Although public employment programs continue to draw popular support, as Weir, Orloff, and Skocpol point out, "they must be designed and administered in close conjunction with a nationally oriented labor market strategy" to avoid both becoming "enmeshed in congressionally reinforced local political patronage" and being attacked as costly, inefficient, or "corrupt."[3]

Since national opinion polls consistently reveal strong public support for efforts to enhance work in America, political support for a program of economic reform (macroeconomic employment policies and labor-market strategies including training efforts) could be considerably stronger than many people presently assume.[4] However, in order to draw sustained public support for such a program, it is necessary that training or retraining, transitional employment benefits, and relocation assistance be available to all members of society who choose to use them, not just to poor minorities.

It would be ideal if problems of the ghetto underclass could be adequately addressed by the combination of macroeconomic policy, labor-market strategies, and manpower training programs. However, in the foreseeable future employment alone will not necessarily lift a family out of poverty.[5] Many families would still require income support and/or social services such as child care. A program of welfare reform is needed, therefore, to address the current problems of public assistance, including lack of provisions for poor two-parent families, inadequate levels of support, inequities between different states, and work disincentives. A national AFDC benefit standard adjusted yearly for inflation is the most minimal required change. We might also give serious consideration to programs such as the Child Support Assurance Program developed by Irwin Garfinkel and colleagues at the Institute for Research on Poverty at the University of Wisconsin, Madison.[6] This program, currently in operation as a demonstration project in the state of Wisconsin, provides a guaranteed minimum benefit per child to single-parent families regardless of the income of the custodial parent. The state collects from the absent parent through wage withholding a sum of money at a fixed rate and then makes regular payments to the custodial parent. If the absent parent is jobless or if his or her payment from withholdings is less than the minimum, the state makes up the difference. Since all absent parents regardless of income are required to participate in this program, it is far less stigmatizing than, say, public assistance. Moreover, preliminary evidence from Wisconsin suggests that this program carries little or no additional cost to the state.

Many western European countries have programs of family or child allowances to support families. These programs provide families with an annual benefit per child regardless of the family's income, and regardless of whether the parents are living together or whether either or both are employed. Unlike public assistance, therefore, a family allowance program carries no social stigma and has no built-in work disincentives. In this connection, Daniel Patrick Moynihan has recently observed that a form of family allowance is already available to American families with the standard deduction and the Earned Income Tax Credit, although the latter can only be obtained by low-income families. Even though both have been significantly eroded by inflation, they could represent the basis for a more comprehensive family allowance program that approximates the European model.

Neither the Child Support Assurance Program under demonstration in Wisconsin nor the European family allowances program is means tested; that is, they are not targeted at a particular income group and therefore do not suffer the degree of stigmatization that plagues public assistance programs such as AFDC. More important, such universal programs would tend to draw more political support from the general public because the programs would be available not only to the poor but to the working- and middle-class segments as well. And such programs would not be readily associated with specific minority groups. Nonetheless, truly disadvantaged groups would reap disproportionate benefits from such programs because of the groups' limited alternative economic resources. For example, low-income single mothers could combine work with adequate guaranteed child support and/or child allowance benefits and therefore escape poverty and avoid public assistance.

Finally, the question of child care has to be addressed in any program designed to improve the employment prospects of women and men. Because of the growing participation of women in the labor market, adequate child care has been a topic receiving increasing attention in public policy discussions. For the overwhelmingly female-headed ghetto underclass families, access to quality child care becomes a critical issue if steps are taken to move single mothers into education and training programs and/or full- or part-time employment. However, I am not recommending government-operated child care centers. Rather it would be better to avoid additional federal bureaucracy by seeking alternative and decentralized forms of child care such as expanding the child care tax credit, including three- and four-year-olds in preschool enrollment, and providing child care subsidies to the working-poor parents.

If the truly disadvantaged reaped disproportionate benefits from a child support enforcement program, child allowance program, and child care strategy, they would also benefit disproportionately from a program of balanced economic growth and tight-labor-market policies because of their greater vulnerability to swings in the business cycle and changes in economic organization, including the relocation of plants and the use of labor-saving technology. It would be shortsighted to conclude, therefore, that universal programs (i.e., programs not targeted at any particular group) are not designed to help address in a fundamental way some of the problems of the truly disadvantaged, such as the ghetto underclass.

By emphasizing universal programs as an effective way to address problems in the inner city created by historic racial subjugation, I am recommending a fundamental shift from the traditional race-specific approach of addressing such problems. It is true that problems of joblessness and related woes such as poverty, teenage pregnancies, out-of-wedlock births, female-headed families, and welfare dependency are, for reasons of historic racial oppression, disproportionately concentrated in the black community. And it is important to recognize the racial differences in rates of social dislocation so as not to obscure problems currently gripping the ghetto underclass. However, as discussed above, race-specific policies are often not designed to address fundamental problems of the truly disadvantaged. Moreover, as also discussed above, both race-specific and targeted programs based on the principle of equality of life chances (often identified with a minority constituency) have difficulty sustaining widespread public support.

Does this mean that targeted programs of any kind would necessarily be excluded from a package highlighting universal programs of reform? On the contrary, as long as a racial division of labor exists and racial minorities are disproportionately concentrated in low-paying positions, antidiscrimination and affirmative action programs will be needed even though they tend to benefit the more advantaged minority members.

Moreover, as long as certain groups lack the training, skills, and education to compete effectively on the job market or move into newly created jobs, manpower training and education programs targeted at these groups will also be needed, even under a tight-labor-market situation. For example, a program of adult education and training may be necessary for some ghetto underclass males before they can either become oriented to or move into an expanded labor market. Finally, as long as some poor families are unable to work because of physical or other disabilities, public assistance would be needed even if the government adopted a program of welfare reform that included child support enforcement and family allowance provisions.

For all these reasons, a comprehensive program of economic and social reform (highlighting macroeconomic policies to promote balanced economic growth and create a tight-labor-market situation, a nationally oriented labor-market strategy, a child support assurance program, a child care strategy, and a family allowances program) would have to include targeted programs, both means tested and race-specific. However, the latter would be considered an offshoot of and indeed secondary to the universal programs. The important goal is to construct an economic-social reform program in such a way that the universal programs are seen as the dominant and most visible aspects by the general public. As the universal programs draw support from a wider population, the targeted programs included in the comprehensive reform package would be indirectly supported and protected. Accordingly, *the hidden agenda for liberal policymakers is to improve the life chances of truly disadvantaged groups such as the ghetto underclass by emphasizing programs to which the more advantaged groups of all races and class backgrounds can positively relate.*

I am reminded of Bayard Rustin's plea during the early 1960s that blacks ought to recognize the importance of fundamental economic reform (including a system of national economic planning along with new education, manpower, and public works programs to help reach full employment) and the need for a broad-based political coalition to achieve it. And since an effective coalition will in part depend upon how the issues are defined, it is imperative that the political message underline the need for economic and social reforms that benefit all groups in the United States, not just poor minorities. Politicians and civil rights organizations, as two important examples, ought to shift or expand their definition of America's racial problems and broaden the scope of suggested policy programs to address them. They should, of course, continue to fight for an end to racial discrimination. But they must also recognize that poor minorities are profoundly affected by problems in America that go beyond racial considerations. Furthermore, civil rights groups should also recognize that the problems of societal organization in America often create situations that enhance racial antagonisms between the different racial groups in central cities that are struggling to maintain their quality of life, and that these groups, although they appear to be fundamental adversaries, are potential allies in a reform coalition because of their problematic economic situations.

The difficulties that a progressive reform coalition would confront should not be underestimated. It is much easier to produce major economic and social reform in countries such as Sweden, Norway, Austria, the Netherlands, and West Germany than in the United States. What characterizes this group of countries, as demonstrated in the important research of Harold Wilensky,[7] is the interaction of solidly organized, generally centralized, interest groups – particularly professional, labor, and employer associations with a centralized or quasi-centralized government either compelled by law or obliged by informal agreement to take the recommendations of the interest groups into account or to rely on their counsel. This

arrangement produces a consensus-making organization working generally within a public framework to bargain and produce policies on present-day political economy issues such as full employment, economic growth, unemployment, wages, prices, taxes, balance of payments, and social policy (including various forms of welfare, education, health, and housing policies).

In all of these countries, called "corporatist democracies" by Wilensky, social policy is integrated with economic policy. This produces a situation whereby, in periods of rising aspirations and slow economic growth, labor – concerned with wages, working conditions, and social security – is compelled to be attentive to the rate of productivity, the level of inflation, and the requirements of investments, and employers – concerned with profits, productivity, and investments – are compelled to be attentive to issues of social policy.[8]

The corporatist democracies, which are in a position to develop new consensus on social and economic policies in the face of declining economies because channels for bargaining and influence are firmly in place, stand in sharp contrast to the decentralized and fragmented political economies of the United States, Canada, and the United Kingdom. In these latter countries – none of which is a highly progressive welfare state – the proliferation of interest groups is not restrained by the requisites of national trade-offs and bargaining, which therefore allows parochial single issues to move to the forefront and thereby exacerbates the advanced condition of political immobilism. Reflecting the rise of single-issue groups has been the steady deterioration of political organizations and the decline of traditional allegiance to parties among voters. Moreover, there has been a sharp increase in the influence of the mass media, particularly the electronic media, in politics and culture. These trends, typical of all Western democracies, are much more salient in countries such as the United States, Canada, and the United Kingdom because their decentralized and fragmented political economies magnify the void created by the decline of political parties – a void that media and strident, single-issue groups rush headlong to fill.[9]

I raise these issues to underline some of the problems that a political coalition dedicated to developing and implementing a progressive policy agenda will have to confront. It seems imperative that, in addition to outlining a universal program of reform including policies that could effectively address inner-city social dislocations, attention be given to the matter of erecting a national bargaining structure to achieve sufficient consensus on the program of reform.

It is also important to recognize that just as we can learn from knowledge about the efficacy of alternative bargaining structures, we can also benefit from knowledge of alternative approaches to welfare and employment policies. Here we fortunately have the research of Alfred J. Kahn and Sheila Kamerman, which has convincingly demonstrated that countries that rely the least on public assistance, such as Sweden, West Germany, and France, provide alternative income transfers (family allowances, housing allowances, child support, unemployment assistance), stress the use of transfers to augment both earnings and transfer income, provide both child care services and day-care programs, and emphasize labor-market policies to enhance high employment. These countries, therefore, "provide incentives to work, supplement the use of social assistance generally because, even when used, it is increasingly only one component, at most, of a more elaborate benefit package." By contrast, the United States relies more heavily than all the other countries (Sweden, West Germany, France, Canada, Austria, the United Kingdom, and Israel) on public assistance to aid poorer families. "The result is that these families are much worse off than they are in any of the countries."[10]

In other words, problems such as poverty, joblessness, and long-term welfare dependency in the United States have not been addressed with the kinds of innovative approaches found in many western European democracies. "The European experience," argue Kamerman and Kahn, "suggests the need for a strategy that includes income transfers, child care services, and employment policies as central elements." The cornerstone of social policy in these countries is employment and labor-market policies. "Unless it is possible for adults to manage their work and family lives without undue strain on themselves and their children," argue Kamerman and Kahn, "society will suffer a significant loss in productivity, and an even more significant loss in the quantity and quality of future generations."[11]

The social policy that I have recommended above also would have employment and labor-market policies as its fundamental foundation. For in the final analysis neither family allowance and child support assurance programs, nor means-tested public assistance and manpower training and education programs can be sustained at adequate levels if the country is plagued with prolonged periods of economic stagnation and joblessness.

A Universal Reform Package and the Social Isolation of the Inner City

The program of economic and social reform outlined above will help address the problems of social dislocation plaguing the ghetto underclass. I make no claims that such programs will lead to a revitalization of neighborhoods in the inner city, reduce the social isolation, and thereby recapture the degree of social organization that characterized these neighborhoods in earlier years. However, in the long run these programs will lift the ghetto underclass from the throes of long-term poverty and welfare dependency and provide them with the economic and educational resources that would expand the limited choices they now have with respect to living arrangements. At the present time many residents of isolated inner-city neighborhoods have no other option but to remain in those neighborhoods. As their economic and educational resources improve they will very likely follow the path worn by many other former ghetto residents and move to safer or more desirable neighborhoods.

It seems to me that the most realistic approach to the problems of concentrated inner-city poverty is to provide ghetto underclass families and individuals with the resources that promote social mobility. Social mobility leads to geographic mobility. Geographic mobility would of course be enhanced if efforts to improve the economic and educational resources of inner-city residents were accompanied by legal steps to eliminate (1) the "practice at all levels of government" to "routinely locate housing for low-income people in the poorest neighborhoods of a community where their neighbors will be other low-income people usually of the same race"; and (2) the manipulation of zoning laws and discriminatory land use controls or site selection practices that either prevent the "construction of housing affordable to low-income families" or prevent low-income families "from securing residence in communities that provide the services they desire."[12]

This discussion raises a question about the ultimate effectiveness of the so-called self-help programs to revitalize the inner city, programs pushed by conservative and even some liberal black spokespersons. In many inner-city neighborhoods, problems such as joblessness are so overwhelming and require such a massive effort to restabilize institutions and create a social and economic milieu necessary to sustain such institutions (e.g., the reintegration of the neighborhood with working- and middle-class blacks and black professionals) that it is surprising that advocates of black self-help have received so much serious attention from the media and policy makers.[13]

Of course some advocates of self-help subscribe to the thesis that problems in the inner city are ultimately the product of ghetto-specific culture and that it is the cultural values and norms in the inner city that must be addressed as part of a comprehensive self-help program.[14] However, cultural values emerge from specific circumstances and life chances and reflect an individual's position in the class structure. They therefore do not ultimately determine behavior. If ghetto underclass minorities have limited aspirations, a hedonistic orientation toward life, or lack of plans for the future, such outlooks ultimately are the result of restricted opportunities and feelings of resignation originating from bitter personal experiences and a bleak future. Thus the inner-city social dislocations emphasized in this study (joblessness, crime, teenage pregnancies, out-of-wedlock births, female-headed families, and welfare dependency) should be analyzed not as cultural aberrations but as symptoms of racial-class inequality.[15] It follows, therefore, that changes in the economic and social situations of the ghetto underclass will lead to changes in cultural norms and behavior patterns. The social policy program outlined above is based on this idea.

Before I take a final look, by way of summary and conclusion, at the important features of this program, I ought briefly to discuss an alternative public agenda that could, if not challenged, dominate the public policy discussion of underclass poverty in the next several years.

A Critical Look at an Alternative Agenda: New-Style Workfare

In a recent book on the social obligations of citizenship, Lawrence Mead contends that "the challenge to welfare statesmanship is not so much to change the extent of benefits as to couple them with serious work and other obligations that would encourage functioning and thus promote the integration of recipients." He argues that the programs of the Great Society failed to overcome poverty and, in effect, increased dependency because the "behavioral problems of the poor" were ignored. Welfare clients received new services and benefits but were not told "with any authority that they ought to behave differently." Mead attributes a good deal of the welfare dependency to a sociological logic ascribing the responsibilities for the difficulties experienced by the disadvantaged entirely to the social environment, a logic that still "blocks government from expecting or obligating the poor to behave differently than they do."[16]

Mead believes that there is a disinclination among the underclass to either accept or retain many available low-wage jobs. The problem of nonwhite unemployment, he contends, is not a lack of jobs, but a high turnover rate. Mead contends that because this kind of joblessness is not affected by changes in the overall economy, it would be difficult to blame the environment. While not dismissing the role discrimination may play in the low-wage sector, Mead argues that it is more likely that the poor are impatient with the working conditions and pay of menial jobs and repeatedly quit in hopes of finding better employment. At the present time, "for most jobseekers in most areas, jobs of at least a rudimentary kind are generally available." For Mead it is not that the poor do not want to work, but rather that they will work only under the condition that others remove the barriers that make the world of work difficult. "Since much of the burden consists precisely in acquiring skills, finding jobs, arranging child care, and so forth," states Mead, "the effect is to drain work obligation of much of its meaning."[17]

In sum, Mead believes that the programs of the Great Society have exacerbated the situation of the underclass by not obligating the recipients of social welfare programs to behave according to mainstream norms – completing school, working, obeying the law, and so forth. Since virtually nothing was demanded in return for benefits, the underclass remained socially isolated and could not be accepted as equals.

If any of the social policies recommended by conservative analysts are to become serious candidates for adoption as national public policy, they will more likely be based on the kind of argument advanced by Mead in favor of mandatory workfare. The laissez-faire social philosophy represented by Charles Murray is not only too extreme to be seriously considered by most policymakers, but the premise upon which it is based is vulnerable to criticism that the greatest rise in black joblessness and female-headed families occurred during the very period (1972–80) when the real value of AFDC plus food stamps plummeted because states did not peg benefit levels to inflation.

Mead's arguments, on the other hand, are much more subtle. If his and similar arguments in support of mandatory workfare are not adopted wholesale as national policy, aspects of his theoretical rationale on the social obligations of citizenship could, as we shall see, help shape a policy agenda involving obligational state programs.

Nonetheless, whereas Mead speculates that jobs are generally available in most areas and therefore one must turn to behavioral explanations for the high jobless rate among the underclass, data reveal (1) that substantial job losses have occurred in the very industries in which urban minorities are heavily concentrated and substantial employment gains have occurred in the higher-education-requisite industries that have relatively few minority workers; (2) that this mismatch is most severe in the Northeast and Midwest (regions that also have had the sharpest increases in black joblessness and female-headed families); and (3) that the current growth in entry-level jobs, particularly in the service establishments, is occurring almost exclusively outside the central cities where poor minorities are concentrated. It is obvious that these findings and the general observations about the adverse effects of the recent recessions on poor urban minorities raise serious questions not only about Mead's assumptions regarding poor minorities, work experience, and jobs, but also about the appropriateness of his policy recommendations.

In raising questions about Mead's emphasis on social values as an explanation of poor minority joblessness, I am not suggesting that negative attitudes toward menial work should be totally dismissed as a contributing factor. The growing social isolation, and the concentration of poverty in the inner city, that have made ghetto communities increasingly vulnerable to fluctuations in the economy, undoubtedly influence attitudes, values, and aspirations. The issue is whether attitudes toward menial employment account in large measure for the sharp rise in inner-city joblessness and related forms of social dislocation since the formation of the Great Society programs. Despite Mead's eloquent arguments the empirical support for his thesis is incredibly weak.[18] It is therefore difficult for me to embrace a theory that sidesteps the complex issues and consequences of changes in American economic organization with the argument that one can address the problems of the ghetto underclass by simply emphasizing the social obligation of citizenship. Nonetheless, there are clear signs that a number of policymakers are now moving in this direction, even liberal policymakers who, while considering the problems of poor minorities from the narrow visions of race relations and the War on Poverty, have become disillusioned with Great Society-type programs. The emphasis is not necessarily on mandatory workfare, however. Rather the emphasis is on what Richard Nathan has called "new-style workfare," which represents a synthesis of liberal and conservative approaches to obligational state programs.[19] Let me briefly elaborate.

In the 1970s the term *workfare* was narrowly used to capture the idea that welfare recipients should be required to work, even to do make-work if necessary, in exchange for receiving benefits. This idea was generally rejected by liberals and those in the welfare establishment. And no workfare program, even Gov. Ronald Reagan's 1971 program, really got off the ground. However, by 1981 Pres. Ronald Reagan was able to get congressional approval to include a provision in the 1981 budget allowing states to experiment with new employment approaches to welfare reform. These approaches represent the "new-style workfare." More specifically, whereas workfare in the 1970s was narrowly construed as "working off" one's welfare grant, the new-style workfare "takes the form of obligational state programs that involve an array of employment and training services and activities – job search, job training, education programs, and also community work experience."[20]

According to Nathan, "we make our greatest progress on social reform in the United States when liberals and conservatives find common ground. New-style workfare embodies both the caring commitment of liberals and the themes identified with conservative writers like Charles Murray, George Gilder, and Lawrence Mead." On the one hand, liberals can relate to new-style workfare because it creates short-term entry-level positions very similar to the "CETA public service jobs we thought we had abolished in 1981"; it provides a convenient "political rationale and support for increased funding for education and training programs"; and it targets these programs at the most disadvantaged, thereby correcting the problem of "creaming" that is associated with other employment and training programs. On the other hand, conservatives can relate to new-style workfare because "it involves a strong commitment to reducing welfare dependency on the premise that dependency is bad for people, that it undermines their motivation to self-support and isolates and stigmatizes welfare recipients in a way that over a long period feeds into and accentuates the underclass mind set and condition."[21]

The combining of liberal and conservative approaches does not, of course, change the fact that the new-style workfare programs hardly represent a fundamental shift from the traditional approaches to poverty in America. Once again the focus is exclusively on individual characteristics – whether they are construed in terms of lack of training, skills, or education, or whether they are seen in terms of lack of motivation or other subjective traits. And once again the consequences of certain economic arrangements on disadvantaged populations in the United States are not considered in the formulation and implementation of social policy. Although new-style workfare is better than having no strategy at all to enhance employment experiences, it should be emphasized that the effectiveness of such programs ultimately depends upon the availability of jobs in a given area. Perhaps Robert D. Reischauer put it best when he stated that: "As long as the unemployment rate remains high in many regions of the country, members of the underclass are going to have a very difficult time competing successfully for the jobs that are available. No amount of remedial education, training, wage subsidy, or other embellishment will make them more attractive to prospective employers than experienced unemployed workers."[22] As Reischauer also appropriately emphasizes, with a weak economy "even if the workfare program seems to be placing its clients successfully, these participants may simply be taking jobs away from others who are nearly as disadvantaged. A game of musical underclass will ensue as one group is temporarily helped, while another is pushed down into the underclass."[23]

If new-style workfare will indeed represent a major policy thrust in the immediate future, I see little prospect for substantially alleviating inequality among poor minorities if such a workfare program is not part of a more comprehensive program of economic and social reform that recognizes the dynamic interplay between societal organization and the behavior and life chances of individuals and groups – a program, in other words, that is designed to both enhance human capital traits of poor minorities and open up the opportunity structure in the broader society and economy to facilitate social mobility. The combination of economic and social welfare policies discussed in the previous section represents, from my point of view, such a program.

Conclusion

In this chapter I have argued that the problems of the ghetto underclass can be most meaningfully addressed by a comprehensive program that combines employment policies with social welfare policies and that features universal as opposed to race- or group-specific strategies. On the one hand, this program highlights macroeconomic policy to generate a tight labor market and economic growth; fiscal and monetary policy not only to stimulate noninflationary growth, but also to increase the competitiveness of American goods on both the domestic and international markets; and a national labor-market strategy to make the labor force more adaptable to changing economic opportunities. On the other hand, this program highlights a child support assurance program, a family allowance program, and a child care strategy.

I emphasized that although this program also would include targeted strategies – both means tested and race-specific – they would be considered secondary to the universal program so that the latter are seen as the most visible and dominant aspects in the eyes of the general public. To the extent that the universal programs draw support from a wider population, the less visible targeted programs would be indirectly supported and protected. To repeat, the hidden agenda for liberal policymakers is to enhance the chances in life for the ghetto underclass by emphasizing programs to which the more advantaged groups of all class and racial backgrounds can positively relate.

Before such programs can be seriously considered, however, cost has to be addressed. The cost of programs to expand social and economic opportunity will be great, but it must be weighed against the economic and social costs of a do-nothing policy. As Levitan and Johnson have pointed out, "the most recent recession cost the nation an estimated $300 billion in lost income and production, and direct outlays for unemployment compensation totaled $30 billion in a single year. A policy that ignores the losses associated with slack labor markets and forced idleness inevitably will underinvest in the nation's labor force and future economic growth." Furthermore, the problem of annual budget deficits of around $200 billion dollars (driven mainly by the peacetime military buildup and the Reagan administration's tax cuts), and the need for restoring the federal tax base and adopting a more balanced set of budget priorities have to be tackled if we are to achieve significant progress on expanding opportunities.[24]

In the final analysis, the pursuit of economic and social reform ultimately involves the question of political strategy. As the history of social provision so clearly demonstrates, universalistic political alliances, cemented by policies that provide benefits directly to wide segments of the population, are needed to work successfully for major reform.[25] The recognition among minority leaders and liberal policymakers of the need to expand the War on Poverty and race relations visions to confront the growing problems of inner-city social dislocations will provide, I believe, an important first step toward creating such an alliance.

NOTES

1   Kathryn M. Neckerman, Robert Aponte, and William Julius Wilson, "Family Structure, Black Unemployment, and American Social Policy," in *The Politics of Social Policy in the United States*, ed. Margaret Weir, Ann Shola Orloff, and Theda Skocpol (Princeton, N.J.: Princeton University Press, 1988).

2   The essential features of such a policy are discussed in chap. 5 [of original publication], "The Case for a Universal Program."

3   Margaret Weir, Ann Shola Orloff, and Theda Skocpol, "The Future of Social Policy in the United States: Political Constraints and Possibilities," in Weir, Orloff, and Skocpol, *Politics of Social Policy in the United States*.

4   Theda Skocpol, "Brother Can You Spare a Job?: Work and Welfare in the United States," paper presented at the Annual Meeting of the American Sociological Association, Washington, D.C., August 27, 1985.

5   Part of the discussion on welfare reform in the next several pages is based on Neckerman, Aponte, and Wilson, "Family Structure, Black Unemployment, and American Social Policy."

6   Irwin Garfinkel and Sara S. McLanahan, *Single Mothers and Their Children: A New American Dilemma* (Washington, D.C.: Urban Institute Press, 1986).

7   Harold L. Wilensky, "Evaluating Research and Politics: Political Legitimacy and Consensus as Missing Variables in the Assessment of Social Policy," in *Evaluating the Welfare State: Social and Political Perspectives*, ed. E. Spiro and E. Yuchtman-Yarr (New York: Academic Press, 1983). I am indebted to Wilensky for the following discussion on corporatist democracies.

8   Ibid.

9   Ibid.

10 Sheila S. Kamerman and Alfred J. Kahn, "Income Transfers, Work and the Economic Well-being of Families with Children," *International Social Security Review* 3 (1982): 376.

11 Sheila S. Kamerman and Alfred Kahn, "Europe's Innovative Family Policies," *Transatlantic Perspectives*, March 1980, p. 12.

12 William L. Taylor, "*Brown*, Equal Protection, and the Isolation of the Poor," *Yale Law Journal* 95 (July 1986): 1729–30.

13 I have in mind the numerous editorials and op-ed columns on self-help in widely read newspapers such as the *Washington Post, New York Times, Wall Street Journal*, and *Chicago Tribune*; articles in national magazines such as *The New Republic* and *Atlantic Monthly*; and the testimony that self-help

advocates, particularly black conservative supporters of self-help, have given before the U.S. Congress.

14   The most sophisticated and articulate black spokesperson of this thesis is Harvard University professor Glenn Loury. See, e.g., Glenn Loury, "The Need for Moral Leadership in the Black Community," *New Perspectives* 16 (Summer 1984): 14–19.

15   Stephen Steinberg makes a compelling case for this argument in his stimulating book *The Ethnic Myth: Race, Ethnicity and Class in America* (New York: Atheneum, 1981).

16   Lawrence M. Mead, *Beyond Entitlement: The Social Obligations of Citizenship* (New York: Free Press, 1986), pp. 4, 61.

17   Ibid., pp. 73, 80.

18   See, for example, Michael Sosin's excellent review of *Beyond Entitlement* in *Social Service Review* 61 (March 1987): 156-9.

19   R. Nathan, "The Underclass – Will It Always Be with Us?" Paper presented at a symposium on the Underclass, New School for Social Research, New York, N.Y., November 14, 1986.

20   Ibid., p. 18.

21   Ibid., pp. 19–21. Although Lawrence Mead is highly critical of new-style workfare (because it reinforces the sociological view of the disadvantaged by assuming that before the recipients can work, the program has to find the client a job, arrange for child care, solve the client's help problems, and so on), his elaborate theory of the social obligation of citizenship is being adopted by policymakers to buttress the more conservative side of the new workfare programs.

22   Robert D. Reischauer, "America's Underclass: Four Unanswered Questions," paper presented at The City Club, Portland, Oreg., January 30, 1986.

23   Robert D. Reischauer, "Policy Responses to the Underclass Problem," paper presented at a symposium at the New School for Social Research, November 14, 1986.

24   S. A. Levitan and C. M. Johnson, *Beyond the Safety Net: Reviving the Promising of Opportunity in America* (Cambridge, Mass.: Ballinger Publishing Co., 1984), pp. 169–70.

25   Skocpol, "Brother Can You Spare a Job?"

22

The Stakeholder Society

Bruce Ackerman and Anne Alstott

Bruce Ackerman is the Sterling Professor of Law and Political Science at Yale University. He is author of *Against Lameduck Impeachment* (1999); *The Uncertain Search for Environmental Quality* (with Rose-Ackerman, Sawyer, and Henderson, 1974); *Economic Foundations of Property Law* (ed., 1975); *Private Property and the Constitution* (1977); *Social Justice in the Liberal State* (1980); *Clean Coal/Dirty Air* (with Hassler, 1981); *Reconstructing American Law* (1984); *We the People: Foundations* (1991); *The Future of Liberal Revolution* (1992); *Is NAFTA Constitutional?* (with Golove, 1995); *Perspectives on Property Law* (with C. Rose and R. Ellickson, 1995); *We the People: Transformations* (1998).

Anne Alstott is a professor in the Yale Law School. Her research interests are in the fields of tax policy and social welfare policy. Recent publications include *The Stakeholder Society* (with Bruce Ackerman), "Work vs. Freedom: A Liberal Challenge to Employment Subsidies" *Yale Law Journal* (1999), vol. 108, pp. 967; "Tax Policy and Feminism: Competing Goals and Institutional Choices" *Columbia Law Review* (1996), vol. 96, pp. 2001; and "The Earned Income Tax Credit and the Limitations of Tax-Based Welfare Reform" *Harvard Law Review* (1995), vol. 108, p. 533. From 1992 to 1997, Professor Alstott was associate professor of law at Columbia University School of Law.

Americans have always had an uncertain love affair with equal opportunity. We believe in it, we know it really doesn't exist in today's world, and yet we have learned to live comfortably in the gap between ideal and reality. After all, aren't all ideals elusive?

Perhaps unequal opportunity was easier to accept when a booming economy guaranteed that children from every class did better than their parents. Even if lower-class kids still ended up near the bottom, they had a sense of participating in the general upward movement. But those halcyon days are over.[1] Although the economy as a whole continues to prosper, the last generation's vast increase in wealth has utterly failed to "trickle down" to the overwhelming majority of Americans. The indisputable fact is that almost all our newfound abundance has gone to the top 20 percent.[2]

The statistics on income and wages are no less grim. Since the early 1970s, the average family's income has grown little, and the typical male worker has seen his real wages decline. Only the entry of vast numbers of women into the labor force has produced meager gains in median family income.[3] In contrast, real wages for college graduates have continued to go up.[4] By the mid-1990s, the top 5 percent of American families received 20 percent of total income – a larger share than at any time since 1947.[5]

These economic disparities are profoundly shaping the future of the next generation. Rich kids get a big head start in life – they go to the best schools, the best colleges, get generous financial help from Mom and Dad, and eventually receive a tidy inheritance. But things look different at the bottom, where an increasing proportion of children live out their early years. In 1996, children represented 40 percent of all Americans living below the poverty line – but only one-quarter of the total population.[6] We are reaching the point of no return: it is one thing to tolerate a gap between ideals and reality, quite another to allow the ideal to disappear from our moral horizon. Do Americans believe in equal opportunity anymore?

There is only one way to find out, and that is by offering a range of serious proposals that might revitalize our collective commitment. In this neoconservative age, it is all too easy to assert that nothing practical can be done. Isn't increasing inequality the price we pay for progress?

Our answer is no. If America drifts away from the promise of equal opportunity, it is not because practical steps are unavailable, but because we have lost our way.

In developing our vision of the stakeholder society, we also challenge some familiar platitudes of the Left. Instead of focusing on the widening economic gap, American liberals have been increasingly preoccupied with the politics of identity. Insofar as economics has been important, the focus has been on assuring equal opportunity in the workplace. This is a fine goal, but it is not enough. Nor is it enough to redeem the faded promise of *Brown v. Board of Education* and seek new ways of providing a more equal education to all. We must also recognize that increasing inequality of wealth is endangering our sense of community.

We offer a practical plan for reaffirming the reality of a common citizenship. As each American reaches maturity, he or she will be guaranteed a stake of eighty thousand dollars. Our plan seeks justice by rooting it in capitalism's preeminent value: the importance of private property. It points the way to a society that is more democratic, more productive, and more free. Bear with us, and you will see how a single innovation once proposed by Tom Paine can achieve what a thousand lesser policies have failed to accomplish. Through stakeholding, Americans can win a renewed sense that they do indeed live in a land of equal opportunity, where all have a fair chance.

Our vision of economic citizenship is rooted in the classical liberal tradition. It is up to each citizen – not the government – to decide how she will use her fair share of the nation's patrimony. By putting this ideal of free and equal citizenship at the center of our political economy, we challenge two master themes that have dominated discussion throughout the twentieth century.

The first theme is the maximization of social welfare. This goal provides a ready argument for progressive taxation. Because a marginal dollar is worth more to the poor than to the rich, government should tax the rich at higher rates. The same logic implies a safety net for those whose incomes fall below a minimally decent floor. But these progressive tendencies are held in check by a final factor. Excessive redistribution reduces incentives for production and growth. The big tradeoff, then, is between more equality and more wealth to share.[7]

This familiar conclusion is challenged by a second, and recently resurgent, theme. It proceeds from a libertarian model of society:

the government does not "own" society's wealth and therefore has no right to redistribute it. Taxes should be low and welfare spending minimal. People have an equal right to exploit the opportunities that come their way. Freedom comes first, and whenever taxes go up, individual freedom goes down.

We mean to define a third way. Like libertarians, we emphasize each person's right to make the most of his or her opportunities. But we deny that the "invisible hand" distributes these opportunities in a morally defensible way. Like welfarists, we believe in social responsibility. But for us, the central task of government is to guarantee *genuine* equality of opportunity. Americans who begin life with greater opportunities cannot complain when their tax dollars go toward expanding the life-options of the less privileged. Such a program redistributes opportunities more fairly, permitting all citizens to begin life on a level playing field.

Our proposal for a stakeholder society takes one large step toward this ideal. The program we describe is very different from the status quo, yet it is both realistic and politically attractive. Our reforms are unfamiliar because our goal challenges the existing mix of libertarian and welfarist policies of American government. We hope to displace the tired debate between supporters and critics of the welfare state with a new question: How do we achieve genuinely equal opportunity for all?

We reject the idea that there is an inexorable tradeoff between liberty and equality. The stakeholder society promises more of both.

The Basic Proposal: Stakeholding and Its Responsibilities

As a citizen of the United States, each American is entitled to a stake in his country: a one-time grant of eighty thousand dollars as he reaches early adulthood. This stake will be financed by an annual 2 percent tax levied on all the nation's wealth. The tie between wealthholding and stakeholding expresses a fundamental social responsibility. Every American has an obligation to contribute to a fair starting point for all.

Stakeholders are free. They may use their money for any purpose they choose: to start a business or pay for more education, to buy a house or raise a family or save for the future. But they must take responsibility for their choices. Their triumphs and blunders are their own.

At the end of their lives, stakeholders have a special responsibility. Because the eighty thousand dollars was central in starting them off in life, it is only fair that they repay it at death if this is financially possible. The stakeholding fund, in short, is enriched each year by the ongoing contributions of all wealth-holders and by a final payback at death.

There are many possible variations on the stakeholding theme. But we have said enough to suggest the broad political appeal of equal opportunity. How many young adults start off life with eighty thousand dollars? How many parents can afford to give their children the head start that this implies?

Stakeholding liberates college graduates from the burdens of debt, often with something to spare. It offers unprecedented opportunities for the tens of millions who don't go to college and have often been shortchanged by their high school educations. For the first time, they will confront the labor market with a certain sense of security. The stake will give them the independence to choose where to live, whether to marry, and how to train for economic opportunity. Some will fail. But fewer than today.

A Common Bond

Turn back the clock half a century and consider a very different America. For most citizens, World War II had marked a great collective achievement for the nation. Both on the battlefront and on the home front, men and women experienced a sense of genuine contribution to a common enterprise of high moral importance. The military draft created a strongly democratic ethos which endured in American life long after the war was over. This sense of common enterprise was sustained during the next era of economic growth – through the 1960s, most Americans really did share in the growing abundance.[8]

But these bonds have unraveled over the past quarter-century. Citizenship is now a largely formal exercise. Voting rights are important, but confer no sense of individual efficacy. Guarantees against discrimination in employment and the like are too thin to generate an everyday sense of common commitment. With the top 20 percent appropriating the lion's share of the nation's economic growth, most Americans no longer share fully in the free enterprise system. If a deep sense of national community is to endure, the next generation will require new institutions that express America's enduring aspirations.

Consider the fate of the GI Bill of Rights, the last great initiative that targeted young adults. First formulated after World War II, it was designed to provide citizen-soldiers with the funds needed to go to college, start a small business, or buy a home. While its direct benefits went mostly to men, it shared the universalistic aspirations of stakeholding, seeking to redeem America's promise of freedom in concrete terms. But after half a century, the meaning of the GI Bill has changed in the context of a professional military. It has become an employee benefit, not an expression of common citizenship.

Conventional forms of worker protection cannot be expected to fill this gap. Our current social security system reflects the traditional ideal of lifelong employment at a decent wage, with a safety net for occasional unemployment, catastrophic disability, and eventual retirement. That is a pretty picture. But it is no longer a reality for most American workers. The college-educated workforce is doing better than ever, but the least-skilled workers face a labor market that promises high unemployment and poverty-level wages.[9] For this group, traditional social insurance provides very little economic security. And the future promises more of the same: free trade, global capital markets, and technological change are likely to hold down blue-collar wages in the United States.[10] While it may be politically popular for pundits on the Right to deny this fact, it is far more constructive to confront it. How can we reconcile free trade and open markets with real equality of opportunity?

Through stakeholding. Our initiative does not seek to reverse world economic forces. It fully endorses the open economy and the great wealth made possible by the worldwide division of labor. But it insists that the American political community is strong enough to shape this wealth for its own purposes. Is America more than a libertarian marketplace? Can we preserve a sense of ourselves as a nation of free and equal citizens?

As young adults receive their stakes, they will have little doubt about America's answer to this question. As they come forward to claim their eighty thousand dollars, each of America's children will do more than gain the ability to shape their individual destinies. They will locate themselves in a much larger national project devoted to the proposition that all men *are* created equal. By invoking this American ideal in their own case, they link themselves not only to all others in the past who have taken steps to realize this fundamental principle but also to all those who will do so in the future.

To be sure, there are risks as well as rewards. Are twenty-somethings really up to the task of responsible stakeholding? Can they be trusted to invest the money wisely in themselves, their families, their businesses, and their communities? Won't they fritter away the nation's patrimony on drugs and decadence?

We will be discussing ways to structure stakeholding to enhance the prospect of responsible decision-making. For example, no citizen should be allowed free use of his eighty thousand dollars without gaining a high school diploma. Nor should he get all the money at once; the stakeholding fund should provide payments of twenty thousand dollars every year or two as citizens move through their early twenties. And so forth.

But it is better to defer questions of program design for now and consider more basic issues of principle.

Beyond the Welfare State

We are trying to break the hold of a familiar vision of the welfare state in America. In this view, modern government has succeeded to the traditional tasks of the church – tending to the old, the sick, the disabled. Like the church, the welfare state is concerned with providing the weak with a decent minimum.

Given this statement of the problem, debate centers on how minimal the minimum should be. Even libertarians grudgingly concede that some vulnerable Americans must be provided with some care some of the time; welfarists push the minimum higher.

We reject the organizing premise of this unending argument. Our primary focus is on the young and energetic, not the old and vulnerable. Our primary values are freedom and equal opportunity, not decency and minimum provision. We do not deny that old-fashioned decency has a role to play, and we will try to define its place later on.[11] For now, it is enough to see that stakeholding is intended not as "welfare reform" but as an entirely new enterprise. Our first concern is not with safety nets but with starting points; not with misfortune, but with opportunity; not with welfare, but with economic citizenship.

From this vantage, it is hardly news that America only promises its children the pursuit of happiness and does not guarantee them success. But it is one thing to make a mess out of your life, quite another never to have had a fair chance. The key question, then, is not whether some stakeholders will fail to make good use of their stake. Some will fail, and in ways that they will come to regret bitterly. The question is whether these predictable failures should serve as a reason to deprive tens of millions of others of *their* fair chance to pursue happiness.

We say no. Each individual citizen has a right to a fair share of the patrimony left by preceding generations. This right should not be contingent on how others use or misuse their stakes. In a free society, it is inevitable that different stakeholders will put their resources to different uses, with different results. Our goal is to transcend the welfare state mentality, which sets conditions on the receipt of "aid." In a stakeholding society, stakes are a matter of right, not a handout. The diversity of individuals' life choices (and the predictable failure of some) is no excuse for depriving each American of the wherewithal to attempt her own pursuit of happiness.

Nor is it a reason to transform stakeholding into yet another exercise in paternalistic social engineering. In our many conversations on the subject, somebody invariably suggests the wisdom of restricting the stake to a limited set of praiseworthy purposes – requiring each citizen to gain bureaucratic approval before spending down his eighty thousand dollars. Won't this allow us to redistribute wealth and make sure the money is well spent?

This question bears the mark of the welfarist mindset. The point of stakeholding is to liberate each citizen from government, not to create an excuse for a vast new bureaucracy intervening in our lives. If stakeholders want advice, they can buy it on the market. If people in their twenties can't be treated as adults, when will they be old enough?

Admittedly, there will always be some Americans who are profoundly unequal to the challenges of freedom. It would be silly to suppose that victims of profound mental disability were capable of managing their eighty thousand dollars on their own. More controversially, we would also deny full control over their stakes to Americans who cannot demonstrate the self-discipline needed to graduate from high school. We agree, alas, that more traditional forms of bureaucratic control may be needed to deal sensibly with these tough cases. But we refuse to allow trendy talk of "underclass" pathologies to divert our attention from another and equally pressing problem. Quite simply, there are tens of millions of ordinary Americans who are perfectly capable of responsible decision-making in a stakeholding society but are now becoming the forgotten citizens of our globalizing economy.

We are speaking of the ordinary Joe or Jane who graduates from high school or maybe a two-year college and who then confronts an increasingly harsh labor market. For this enormous group, stakeholding will provide a priceless buffer against the predictable shocks of the marketplace. A temporary economic setback will no longer quickly spiral into a devastating loss of self-confidence or a grim period of deprivation. The stake will provide a cushion in hard times and a source of entrepreneurial energy in better ones.

In emphasizing these ordinary Americans, we do not wish to belittle the importance of stakeholding for those at the top and the bottom of our economic hierarchy. For the top quarter of the population, those graduating from four-year colleges, stakeholding will not only eliminate the crushing burden of student loans. It will also inject much-needed competition among universities for the stakeholding dollar, generating a more responsive and effective system of higher education. For those growing up in the ghettos of America, stakeholding will provide a beacon of hope: stay in school and graduate, and you will not be forgotten. You will get a solid chance

to live out the American dream of economic independence.

But stakeholding's message will have a special salience to the broad middle group of Americans, who constitute about two-thirds of the entire population. After all, existing governmental programs already heap large educational subsidies on those who can successfully negotiate the challenges of four-year college; even in today's conservative climate, we have not entirely given up on special programs that address the needs of ghetto youth. But at present, ordinary Americans really are forgotten Americans. After they leave school, they confront the market without much to fall back on. While stakeholding offers economic independence for all, its promise will have special meaning to middle America – which should rally to its support once it has been persuaded that government *can* be made to work again for ordinary people.

This leads us to our larger political objectives. We propose to revitalize a very old republican tradition that links property and citizenship into an indissoluble whole. In earlier times, this linkage was often used for exclusionary purposes.[12] In colonial America, for example, suffrage and office-holding were often restricted to those with substantial property. But during the nineteenth century, a serious effort was made to reverse the linkage. Most famously, the Homestead Act refused to offer up America's vast resources to the highest bidders, but encouraged citizens to stake their claims for a fair share of the common wealth. During Reconstruction, Radical Republicans led a spirited campaign to couple the Fourteenth Amendment's grant of citizenship to black Americans with a stake carved out of rebel property.

This campaign failed, and the closing of the frontier heralded an increasing split between property and citizenship in American thought and practice. Even those genuinely concerned with economic dignity looked elsewhere: socialists would settle for nothing less than the abolition of private property itself; more moderate re-formers aimed to build a strong state apparatus capable of regulating the capitalist system. Now that we have had experience with the limitations of both these experiments, isn't it time to consider another path?

We do not join those who would cheerfully sweep away the legislative achievements of the Progressives, the New Deal, and the Great Society. Many of these reforms have withstood the test of time, and others merely require adaptations and refinements. But if we are to confront the emerging problems of our own age, we must once again attempt a fundamental redefinition of the progressive vision. Rather than abolishing private property or regulating it more intensely, we should be redistributing it.

This is the time to make economic citizenship a central part of the American agenda. The task is to enable *all* Americans to enjoy the promise of economic freedom that our existing property system now offers to an increasingly concentrated elite.

Experiments in Stakeholding

Stakeholding is a simple idea, and one whose time has come. This seems to be the assessment of some astute politicians who have gained great followings through initiatives that bear a family resemblance to our proposal. Margaret Thatcher is a case in point. When she became prime minister of Great Britain in 1979, 32 percent of all housing was publicly owned. Although bent on sweeping privatization, Thatcher refused to sell off these vast properties to big companies. She invited residents to buy their own homes at bargain rates. With a single stroke, she created a new property-owning citizenry, and she won vast popularity in the process.[13]

A more sweeping initiative took place in the Czech Republic in the aftermath of the Communist overthrow of 1989. The prime minister elected in 1992, Václav Klaus, confronted a much larger task than Thatcher's: the state sector contained seven thousand

medium and large-scale enterprises, twenty-five to thirty-five thousand smaller ones. How to distribute this legacy of Communism? Klaus saw his problem as an opportunity to create a vast new property-owning class of Czech citizens.

The mechanism was the ingenious technique of "voucher privatization." Each Czech citizen could subscribe to a book of vouchers that he could use to bid for shares in state companies as they were put on the auction block. An overwhelming majority – 8.5 out of 10.5 million – took up Klaus's offer and claimed their fair share of the nation's wealth as they moved into the new free-market system. Klaus's creative program helped cement his position as the leading politician of the Republic. More importantly, the broad involvement of citizen-stakeholders played a central role in legitimating the country's transition to liberal democracy.[14]

Thatcher and Klaus conceived of their initiatives as one-shot affairs. But the citizens of Alaska have made stakeholding a regular part of their political economy. Once again, the occasion was the distribution of a major public asset, in this case the revenues from North Slope oil. Rather than using it all for public expenditures, the Republican leadership designed a stakeholding scheme that is now distributing about one thousand dollars a year to every Alaskan citizen. Once again, the system has become broadly popular, with politicians of both parties regularly pledging that they will not raid the symbolically named Permanent Fund.[15]

Taxing Wealth

The biggest difference between these initiatives and our proposal should be obvious. Brits, Czechs, and Alaskans funded stakeholding out of public property. We look to two other sources. Over the short term – the first forty or fifty years – we rely principally upon an annual 2 percent tax on wealth. Over the longer run, stakeholding will be financed increasingly by recipients' payments at death.

These particular choices deserve their own chapters – and then some. Perhaps you will find yourself unconvinced by our case for the wealth tax and will conclude that some other short-run source of revenue is more appropriate. If so, we would be happy to marry stakeholding with your alternative taxing scheme. But beyond these (important) questions of program design lies a deeper point. In our view, there is no good reason to limit stakeholding to cases involving physical assets like housing or factories or oil. Americans have created other assets that are less material but have even greater value. Most notably, the free enterprise system did not drop from thin air. It has emerged only as the result of a complex and ongoing scheme of social cooperation. The free market requires heavy public expenditures on the police and the courts and much else besides. Without billions of voluntary decisions by Americans to respect the rights of property in their daily lives, the system would collapse overnight.[16] All Americans benefit from this cooperative activity – but some much more than others. Those who benefit the most have a duty to share some of their wealth with fellow citizens whose cooperation they require to sustain the market system. This obligation is all the more exigent when the operation of the global market threatens to split the country more sharply into haves and have-nots.

This view gives our proposal a different ideological spin from those pioneered by Margaret Thatcher and Václav Klaus. Surely there will be some on the Right who will blanch at the implications of our proposal. But we do hope that many others will come to see its justice. We expect a similar split on the Left. Some will be deeply suspicious of our proposal to liberate stakeholding assets from the grip of the regulatory state, leaving it to each citizen to spend his eighty thousand in the way that makes sense to him. Others will be more impressed by the justice of empowering all Americans to share in the pursuit of happiness.

We expect less resistance to the long-run aspect of our funding proposal, which relies on stakeholders making substantial paybacks at death. This will require us, however, to put some old questions about inheritance in a new light.

Expanding the Stake

Our first task will be to explore the many moral and practical questions presented by the basic stakeholding proposal. But we have a larger aim as well. We believe that our initiative provides a framework for a more general reconstruction of the existing welfare state.

In building support for his New Deal proposals, Franklin Roosevelt had one overriding aim. He wanted to entrench social security so deeply in our institutional life that it would be politically impossible for his opponents to repeal it. Somehow or other, his program must express the idea that social security was not charity but a fundamental right. What image would convey the requisite notion of entitlement?

Drawing on European traditions, Roosevelt embraced a system that emphasized the workplace. Social security was not charity because workers would earn it by contributing to an insurance fund through payroll taxes. Here as elsewhere, Roosevelt proved himself the master politician of the age: to the libertarians' despair, social security remains a bulwark of economic citizenship. Thanks in large part to social security, the poverty rate among the elderly has plummeted in the past decades, and many more workers can look forward to retirement with a modicum of dignity.[17]

But Roosevelt's enduring political triumph has come at a heavy price. Because "premiums" are paid only at the workplace, nonworkers get nothing in their own right. Of course, many of these people live productive lives. Millions of women spend years out of the paid work force, or in low-paid part-time work, while they rear young children. As a consequence, the insurance metaphor provides them with little or no independent social security. The system ties their economic fate to their husbands' – if they have them. As we shall see, this is only the beginning of many other questionable discriminations and taxation decisions encouraged by the Rooseveltian link between retirement income and the workplace.

Don't get us wrong. Social security is one of the great achievements of American social policy. But as we look forward to the twenty-first century, it is time to move on to a more progressive and more inclusive system. What is required is a new master metaphor to displace the insurance analogy – and to symbolize the transition from worker citizenship to universal economic citizenship.

Stakeholding provides this metaphor. It creates a new way of expressing Roosevelt's idea that a decent retirement is a matter of right, not a question of charity. And it allows us to restructure this right in a much fairer way. Under our expanded proposal, each American citizen not only gets to stake her claim to eighty thousand dollars. She also gets an entitlement to a basic retirement pension. In contrast to the existing system, this citizen's pension would not depend on the vagaries of her work history, her wage rate, or her marital status. Instead, it would be a fundamental aspect of economic citizenship. Each American would receive a monthly retirement check that represented the minimum amount needed to live a decent life. Of course, this check would represent a floor, not a ceiling. People who wanted more money in retirement would remain perfectly free to invest in private pension plans. But it would be up to each of us to make this decision.

The stakeholding system will also open up a long overdue reconsideration of the methods through which we now pay for a secure retirement. Once we remove pensions from the workplace, it will no longer seem natural to fund them through payroll taxes. Instead, Americans will begin to see the payroll tax for what it is – a *tax*, and one that hits the working poor hardest. We urge its replacement by a new system that is more in keeping with the principles of equal opportunity at the core of the stakeholder society.

Stakeholding as a Catalytic Reform

Most reforms, when they are adopted, don't lead anywhere. They may fix a problem, and that is a good thing, but they don't precipitate a larger wave of reconstructive activity.

Stakeholding, by contrast, is a catalytic reform. It can generate further waves of activity that might, over time, lead to the construction of a more just retirement system for older Americans – and much else besides.

Or it may not. Indeed, we are a bit concerned that the greater complexity of expanded stakeholding might distract attention from one of the greatest virtues of our basic proposal.

And that is its direct appeal to ordinary Americans. Everybody understands eighty thousand dollars and what it might mean in the lives of young adults. Everybody understands a flat tax of 2 percent on net wealth. Because our proposal exempts the first eighty thousand dollars of each citizen's wealth from the new tax, the overwhelming share will be paid by America's upper classes – the very group that has seen its wealth increase over the past twenty-five years. Our basic proposal, then, makes it plain to the general public that something effective *can* be done about America's increasing maldistribution of wealth – and that stakeholding is well within our political reach.

This is, is it not, a democracy where each citizen casts an equal vote, and the majority rules? If we work together, there is nothing that can stop us from building a new foundation for economic citizenship. The effort will require political effort by many, inspired leadership by some, and a certain sophistication by all in dealing with the advertising campaigns launched by those who have so much to lose.

But Americans have managed to overcome larger obstacles in the past. It is past time to begin a new era of reform.

NOTES

1 See McMurrer, Condon, and Sawhill (1997), pp. 8–9 (in past years, children were more likely to do better than their parents because of economic growth or changes in the occupational structure); for more detail, see Chaps. 2 and 9.
2 See Wolff (1998), pp. 136–7 (from 1983 to 1995, only the top 5 percent experienced an increase in net worth; in every other group, wealth declined, with the bottom 40 percent experiencing the sharpest decline); for more detail, see Chap. 6 [of original publication].
3 See Gottschalk (1997), pp. 21–40; Blank (1997), pp. 60–4.
4 Gottschalk (1997), p. 30 (between 1979 and 1994, real wages for college graduates increased by 5 percent, while real wages for high school graduates fell by 20 percent).
5 See U.S. Bureau of the Census (1997b), p. 470, table 725 (showing that in 1993, 1994, and 1995, the top 5 percent received 20.0 to 20.3 percent of total income); and Danziger and Gottschalk (1995), p. 42, table 3.1 (in 1947, the richest 5 percent of U.S. families received 17.5 percent of aggregate income; in 1989, 17.9 percent; in 1991, 17.1 percent).
6 U.S. Bureau of the Census (1997a), p. vi.
7 See, e.g., Okun (1975).
8 See Levy (1987), p. 17.
9 See Blank (1997), pp. 57–72.
10 See Wilson (1996), pp. 150–3; Blank (1997), pp. 66–7.
11 See Chap. 8 of full text of *The Stakeholder Society*.
12 See Smith (1997).
13 See Silver (1990), pp. 163–95. In contrast to stakeholding, Thatcher's program lacked evenhandedness and was justly criticized for it. Not only were poor people living in private housing excluded, but the value of the "Right to Buy" depended on the quality of each tenant's house. Moreover, despite the substantial discounts, many tenants found it difficult to come up with the money needed to exercise their option. As a consequence, Thatcher's program tended to leave the least advantaged as tenants in worsening accommodations. See Flynn (1990).
14 See Rapaczynski and Frydman (1994); Shafik (1995). Unfortunately, Klaus did not combine his support of voucher privatization with a regulatory regime – like the American Securities and Exchange Commission – that would have protected the interests of citizen-stakeholders from predictable abuse by insiders. This failure has led to increasing public dissatisfaction with Klaus, but it would be a mistake to allow it to cast a shadow upon his earlier successes as a policy innovator.
15 See Brown and Thomas (1994), p. 43. The popularity of the program is so great that some believe that it prevents the use of the funds for more important purposes. Compare Brown and Thomas (1994) with O'Brien and Olson (1990). While this may be correct in the Alaska case, we will argue that the value of stakeholding is sufficiently great to justify a priority over most other competing programs.
16 See Holmes and Sunstein (1998).
17 See Moon (1997), pp. 67–8; Kingson and Schulz (1997), pp. 51–2.

REFERENCES

Blank, Rebecca. *It Takes a Nation* (New York: Russell Sage Foundation; Princeton, N.J.: Princeton University Press, 1997).

Brown, William S., and Clive S. Thomas. "The Alaska Permanent Fund: Good Sense or Political Expediency?" 37 *Challenge* 38 (1994).

Danziger, Sheldon, and Peter Gottschalk. *America Unequal* (New York: Russell Sage Foundation; Cambridge: Harvard University Press, 1995).

Flynn, Rob. "Political Acquiescence, Privatisation, and Residualisation in British Housing Policy." In *Privatization and Its Alternatives*

(William T. Gormley, Jr., ed.) (Madison: University of Wisconsin Press, 1990).

Gottschalk, Peter. "Inequality, Income Growth, and Mobility: The Basic Facts," 11 J. Econ. Persp. 21 (Spring 1997).

Holmes, Stephen, and Cass Sunstein. The Costs of Rights (New York: W. W. Norton, 1998).

Kingson, Eric R., and James H. Schulz. "Should Social Security Be Means-Tested?" In Social Security in the Twenty-First Century (Kingson and Schulz, eds.) (New York: Oxford University Press, 1997).

Levy, Frank. Dollars and Dreams: The Changing American Income Distribution (New York: Russell Sage Foundation, 1987).

McMurrer, Daniel P., Mark Condon, and Isabel V. Sawhill. Intergenerational Mobility in the United States, The Urban Institute (May 1997).

Moon, Marilyn. "Are Social Security Benefits Too High or Too Low?" In Social Security in the Twenty-First Century (Eric R. Kingson and James H. Schulz, eds.) (New York: Oxford University Press, 1997).

O'Brien, J. Patrick, and Dennis Olson. "The Alaska Permanent Fund and Dividend Distribution Program," 18 Pub. Fin. Q. 139 (1990).

Okun, Arthur. Equality and Efficiency: The Big Tradeoff (Washington, D.C.: Brookings Institution, 1975).

Rapaczynski, Andrzej, and Roman Frydman. Privatization in Eastern Europe: Is the State Withering Away? (Budapest and New York: Central European University Press, 1994).

Shafik, Nemat. "Making a Market: Mass Privatization in the Czech and Slovak Republics," 23 World Dev. 1143 (1995).

Silver, Harry. "The Privatization of Public Housing in Great Britain." In Privatization and Its Alternatives (William T. Gormley, Jr., ed.) (Madison: University of Wisconsin Press, 1990).

Smith, Rogers. Civic Ideals (New Haven: Yale University Press, 1997).

U.S. Bureau of the Census. Poverty in the U.S.: 1996 (Current Population Reports, P60–198) (1997a).

———. Statistical Abstract of the United States, 117th ed. (1997b).

Wilson, William J. When Work Disappears (New York: Alfred A. Knopf, 1996).

Wolff, Edward N. "Recent Trends in the Size Distribution of Household Wealth," 12 J. Econ. Persp. 131 (Summer 1998).

23

Black Economic Progress in the Era of Mass Imprisonment

Bruce Western, Becky Pettit, and Josh Guetzkow

Bruce Western is Professor of Sociology and Faculty Associate of the Office of Population Research at Princeton University. His research focuses on the influence of public policy and labor relations on patterns of earnings and employment.

Becky Pettit is an assistant professor of Sociology and faculty affiliate of the Center for Studies in Demography and Ecology, University of Washington. Her research focuses on the relationship between demographic processes and inequality.

Josh Guetzkow is a graduate student in the Department of Sociology at Princeton University. His research focuses on the political and cultural sociology of the criminal justice system.

The 1990s was a decade of extraordinary prosperity. After nearly 20 years of slow growth and periodically high unemployment, the US economy expanded rapidly, gathering speed as the decade unfolded. By most accounts, the labor market performed impressively, sharing the spotlight only with the stock market in the extraordinary story of the 1990s economic expansion. As unemployment fell across the labor force as a whole, black workers registered strong employment gains. By the end of the decade it appeared that wages for young black men were growing faster than for any other group. More than any jobs program or hiring policy, it seemed that sustained economic growth had brought prosperity to the most disadvantaged workers.

While the renewal of the American economy is relatively recent, the expansion of the penal system dates from the early 1970s. After 50 years of relative stability in the proportion of people incarcerated, the prison population doubled in size between 1970 and 1982. Between 1982 and 1999, the prison population increased threefold. These broad trends conceal substantial inequality. Prison incarceration rates are about eight times higher for blacks than whites, and high school dropouts are more than twice as likely to be in prison than high school graduates. Consequently, much of the growth in imprisonment in the three decades after 1970 was concentrated among young minority men with little education. By the late 1990s, about two-thirds of all state prison inmates were black or

Hispanic, and about half of all minority inmates had less than twelve years of schooling.

The growth of the penal system has profoundly affected the economic situation of the young low-skill African American men whose incarceration rates are highest. The economic effects of incarceration operate on two levels. First, the predominantly low-skill and minority men locked up in prisons and jails are not included in the standard labor force surveys used to measure employment or wages. Imprisonment conceals economic inequality by excluding large numbers of poor men from official accounts of the labor market. As we will see, the economic progress of young black men has been substantially overstated. Second, the penal system fuels inequality by weakening the economic opportunities of prison and jail inmates after they are released. In this case, incarceration has widened the earnings and employment gap between young black and white men.

The growth of the penal system puts the economic boom of the 1990s in a different light. Although most sections of the labor force were not dramatically affected by mass incarceration, young black men – particularly those with little schooling – routinely faced the risk of imprisonment. They thus obtained few of the benefits of economic growth and low unemployment that buoyed the labor market as a whole. We begin this story by documenting the concentration of incarceration among young low-skill men. We then detail the effects of incarceration on conventional employment and earnings statistics. Finally, we examine how the experience of time in prison or jail affects the life chances of ex-convicts after release.

Inequality in Incarceration

The economic disadvantage of prison and jail inmates is the basic precondition for the effects of mass incarceration on racial inequality in the labor market. The level of imprisonment in a population is usually described by the incarceration rate. The incarceration rate quantifies the proportion of a population in prison or jail on an average day in a given year. For example, if 1 out of 100 white high school dropouts are locked up on average in 1990, the incarceration rate for that group is 1 percent. The Bureau of Justice Statistics reports incarceration rates for demographic groups such as men or non-Hispanic whites. For our purposes, it is useful to focus on the incarceration rates of young men at different levels of schooling.

Combining data from correctional and labor force surveys, we estimated prison and jail incarceration rates for non-Hispanic black and white men in different age and education groups.[1] (Unless otherwise noted, we report incarceration rates for jail and prison inmates throughout the paper.) Figure 23.1 plots incarceration rates for working-age men, between 18 and 65, and young men, aged 22–30. Among the young men, incarceration rates for those with less than 12 years of schooling are also reported. Figure 23.1 shows that incarceration rates broadly increased for all groups of black and white men in the two decades after 1980. Among whites, incarceration rates are about 50 percent higher for young men in their twenties than for the working-age male population as a whole. Among young high school dropouts, incarceration rates are higher still. By the end of the 1990s, 1 out of 10 young white men with little schooling was in prison or jail.

The lower panel of figure 23.1 shows a similar pattern for African Americans. The absolute level of incarceration rates for black men (indicated by the scale on the vertical axis) is much higher than for whites. Among all working-age black men, 7.5 percent were incarcerated on an average day in 1999, compared to 11.7 percent of black men in their twenties. The incarceration rates for young black unskilled men are dramatically higher. In the early stages of the prison boom, in 1980, 14 percent of young black male dropouts were behind bars. By

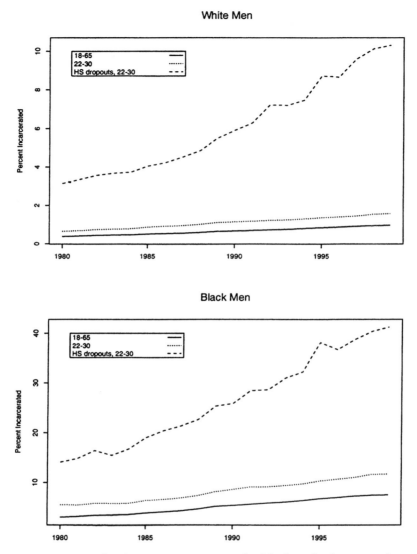

Figure 23.1 Prison and jail incarceration rates for black and white men by age and education

1999, the incarceration rate had climbed to 41.2 percent.

The growth in incarceration rates and racial disparity in incarceration are reported in table 23.1. The table shows that the rate of growth in incarceration was slightly faster for whites than blacks. Thus racial dis-

parity in imprisonment, measured by the black–white ratio in incarceration rates, declined slightly from 1980 to 1999. Even so, black men between the ages of 18 and 65 were nearly 8 times as likely as whites to be in prison or jail in 1999. Despite small declines in racial disparity, the largest

Table 23.1 Prison and jail incarceration rates for black and white men by age and education, 1980, 1999

	Ages 18–65	*Ages 22–30*	*H.S. Dropouts Ages 22–30*
White Men			
1980	.4	.7	3.1
1999	1.0	1.6	10.3
Increase 1980–1999	.6	1.0	7.2
Black Men			
1980	3.1	5.5	14.0
1999	7.5	11.7	41.2
Increase 1980–1999	4.4	6.2	27.2
Black–White ratio 1980	7.8	7.9	4.5
Black–White ratio 1999	7.5	7.3	4.0

absolute gains in incarceration were recorded by black men. Racial disparity in incarceration is partly explained by the relatively low level of schooling of young black men compared to young whites. If we look just at high school dropouts, the black–white ratio in incarceration rates is just half as large as for the population as a whole. Even among dropouts, however, blacks remain four times more likely to be in prison or jail than whites.

Although black–white disparity in incarceration rates declined between 1980 and 1999, much of this can be explained by the increasing incarceration of other minorities (including Hispanics). Hispanics accounted for only a few percentage points of the prison and jail population in 1980 but around 15 percent of all inmates by the end of the 1990s. The disparity in incarceration between whites and non-whites has increased as a result. For example, in 1980, the combined prison incarceration rate of blacks and Hispanics outnumbered that of whites by 5.9 to 1; by 1996, that ratio was 6.2 to 1.[2]

Incarceration rates indicate high levels of imprisonment, but because the rates record imprisonment at a single point in time they understate the frequency of prison admis-sion over the life course. An alternative measure of incarceration records the frac-tion of the population that have ever served time in prison. We estimated the proportion of men who had ever served time in prison by age 30–34 in 1989 and 1999 (table 23.2). In 1989, 2.1 percent of white men compared to 13.1 percent of black men in their thirties had prison records. By 1999, more than 1 in 5 black men aged 30–34 had been to prison. The high concentration of incarceration among poorly-educated men is also reflected in these figures. At the end of the 1990s, more than half of all black male dropouts in their early thirties had served time in prison. Cumulative risks of incarceration are even extremely high among men with high school diplomas. By 1999, nearly one quarter of black men with 12 years of schooling had been to prison. Unlike incarceration rates, racial disparity in the cumulative risk of incarceration over the life course clearly increased through the 1990s. By the end of the decade, African American men were about 7 times more likely to have a prison record than white men. In short, serving time in prison is now extremely common for young black men, and has become a modal experience among young African American men with little schooling.[3]

Table 23.2   Percentage of men born 1955–1959 and 1965–1969 with prison records by 1989 and 1999, by race and education

	All	*Education*		
		High School Dropouts	*H.S./GED*	*Some College*
White Men				
1989	2.1	8.4	2.5	.7
1999	3.2	12.6	4.3	1.1
Black Men				
1989	13.1	33.3	12.0	5.2
1999	22.3	52.1	23.5	8.6
Black–white ratio, 1989	6.2	4.0	4.8	7.4
Black–white ratio, 1999	7.0	4.1	5.5	7.8

These disaggregated incarceration statistics suggest that the experience of prison or jail is common for young black men, and virtually pervasive for young unskilled black men in recent birth cohorts. Because incarceration is so highly concentrated among the most disadvantaged on the labor market the effects of the penal system on this group are large.

Incarceration and Invisible Inequality

Incarceration conceals inequality by locking up large numbers of poor and minority men. In the early 1970s, before the growth of the penal system, the inequality-concealing effect of incarceration was negligible. By the 1990s, however, the invisible inequality generated by the penal system accounted for large portions of the black–white difference in employment and earnings among young men.

Usually, the utilization of labor is measured by either an unemployment rate or employment-to-population ratio. The unemployment rate is often too restrictive for assessing the economic status of socially marginal groups because it does not count the long-term jobless who are discouraged from actively seeking work. The unemployment rate also excludes consideration of the institutionalized population. Although the employment–population ratio provides a more accurate indication of the prevalence of employment, official tabulations count only the noninstitutional population. This means that prison and jail inmates are ignored in conventional measures of employment and joblessness. By excluding prison and jail inmates from the population count, standard labor force figures overstate the rate of employment.

It might be objected that many in the penal system are working in some kind of prison industry and are thus employed in some sense. By counting prison and jail inmates among the jobless we follow the definition of employment used by the Bureau of the Census. The Census expressly excludes from the employment count those in correctional facilities. The Census employment concept recognizes that a paying job on the open labor market confers a degree of economic independence, rights to a minimum wage and union membership. Employment in prison work programs carries few of these benefits.

Table 23.3 contrasts the usual employment–population ratio defined on the noninstitutional population with an adjusted employment statistic that includes prison and jail inmates among the jobless. For white men, adjusting for the size of the

Table 23.3 Percentage of the population employed, black and white men by age and education, 1980, 1999

	1980		1999	
	Unadjusted	Adjusted	Unadjusted	Adjusted
White Men				
Ages 18–65	84.2	83.9	84.8	83.9
Ages 22–30	86.5	85.9	88.6	87.2
H.S. dropouts, 22–30	77.1	74.7	81.3	72.9
Black Men				
Ages 18–65	70.1	68.0	72.1	66.7
Ages 22–30	73.9	69.8	76.4	67.4
H.S. dropouts, 22–30	64.5	55.5	50.9	29.9

Note: Unadjusted employment rates are calculated as a percentage of the noninstitutional population; adjusted employment rates are calculated as a fraction of the noninstitutional and incarcerated population.

penal population makes little difference to the employment rates of those aged 18 to 65, or 22 to 30. Among young white male dropouts, however, counting the incarcerated population lowers conventional employment about 2 points in 1980 and 9 points in 1999. While conventional statistics suggest that employment increased slightly for young white dropouts from 1980 to 1999, correcting for the size of the penal population shows that employment actually declined.

The discrepancy between conventional (unadjusted) employment rates and adjusted employment rates that count penal inmates is much larger for black men. Among working age black men, conventional figures overstate employment by about 5 percentage points in 1999. Among young black men, excluding prison and jail inmates from the population leads us to overestimate employment by 9 percentage points. The adjustment to employment rates is particularly dramatic for young black high school dropouts. The conventional employment rate overstates employment by 9 points in 1980. By 1999, this discrepancy had increased to 21 percentage points. Conventional statistics indicate that about half

of young black male dropouts had jobs, in contrast to the true employment rate of only 29.9 percent.

More detail about the employment rates for young unskilled men is provided in figure 23.2, which plots the unadjusted and adjusted employment series for black and white male high school dropouts. Although the gap between standard employment rates and those adjusted for incarceration widened for whites, both employment statistics show similar trends. Employment among young white male dropouts increased through the 1980s, and then again from 1995 to 1999. Adjusting employment rates for the penal population results in a much larger correction for young black dropouts. Conventional statistics suggest that employment among young black unskilled men declined in the decade after 1984, but increased through the second half of the 1990s. Counting prison and jail inmates in the population shows that the decline in employment through the 1980s and early 1990s was steeper than standard measures suggest. Furthermore, there was no recovery in employment through the 1990s for black male dropouts in their twenties.

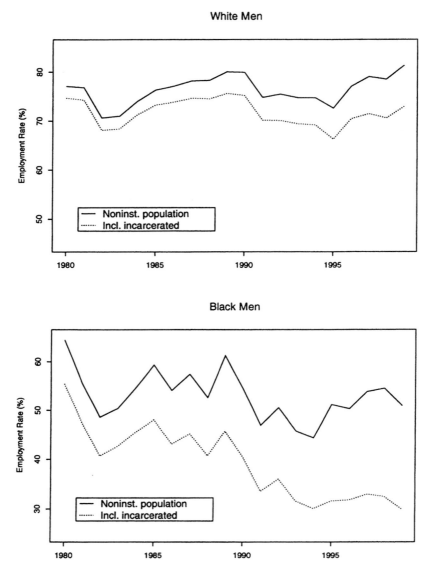

Figure 23.2   Adjusted and unadjusted employment–population ratios for black and white male high school dropouts, ages 22–30

The relatively large correction for incarceration in the employment rate of blacks also affects measures of black–white inequality in employment. The top panel of figure 23.3 shows that the white–black ratio in standard employment rates for young black male dropouts grew slightly in the 1980s, but remained constant through the 1990s. Throughout most of the last decade of the century, standard employment rates showed that young white dropouts were about 1.5 times more likely to have a job

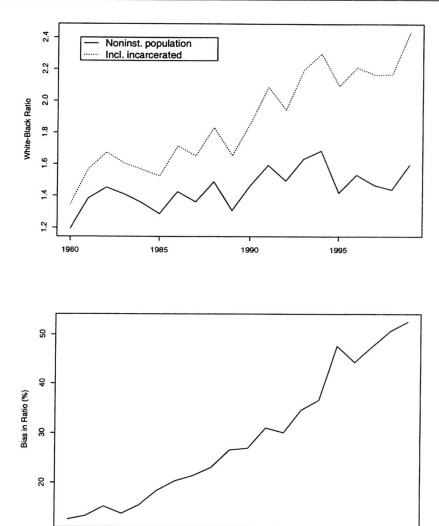

Figure 23.3 Black–White inequality in incarceration. Top panel: White–black employment ratios measured by adjusted and unadjusted employment–population ratios, for black and white male high school dropouts, ages 22–30. Bottom panel: the percent difference in black–white ratios measured by adjusted and unadjusted employment series

than young black dropouts. Correcting for incarceration, we see that the black–white ratio in employment for this group increased steadily in the two decades following 1980. The lower panel of figure 23.3 plots statistical bias in inequality calculated from standard employment statistics. The bias increases with the growth in the penal population. By 1999, standard employment rates understate racial inequality in employment among unskilled men by about 50 percent.

Inequality in wages is also affected by the invisible disadvantaged in prisons and jails. The penal system raises average wages by removing low-wage workers from the labor force. The rise in average wages doesn't represent a real improvement in living standards, however. Instead, it is an artifact of incarceration which is concentrated among low earners. We estimate that the wage gap between young black and white men would be 20 percent higher if all those not working, including those in prison and jail, were fully employed. Labor force surveys also show that the wage gap between black and white young men has narrowed over the last 15 years. However, about half the decline in inequality results from falling employment among black men due to imprisonment and more conventional joblessness.

Does Incarceration Increase Black–White Inequality?

While black–white inequality is obscured by high incarceration rates among African Americans, the penal system also increases inequality by reducing the employment and earnings of ex-inmates after release. Labor market researchers explain the low earnings and irregular employment of ex-convicts in three main ways. First, criminal conviction carries social stigma. Employers view job candidates with criminal records as untrustworthy. Surveys thus show that employers would rather hire welfare recipients or inexperienced applicants than ex-convicts. The stigma of conviction also has legal significance. Commonly, a felony record can temporarily disqualify employment in licensed or professional occupations. These prohibitions typically extend beyond the professions to include jobs in health care and skilled trades.[4]

Second, incarceration can also erode job skills. At a minimum, time in prison or jail limits the acquisition of work experience that is otherwise obtained on the open labor market. In addition, behaviors that are adaptive for survival in prison are likely to be inconsistent with work routines outside. Incarceration may also exacerbate pre-existing mental or physical illnesses. These effects may be especially large in the recent period as support declines for job training, drug treatment, and health care.

Third, incarceration may also undermine the social connections to good job opportunities. Criminologists find that juvenile delinquency embeds young offenders in social contexts with weak connections to stable employment. There is also evidence that in adult facilities, particularly those with significant gang activity, inmates build social connections to those promoting opportunities for further criminal activity after release. Social ties to legitimate employment are weakened as a result.[5]

Although social stigma, eroded skills and social networks indicate how incarceration undermines employment, it is difficult to calculate precisely the economic effect of imprisonment. The young unskilled minority men who are most likely to go to jail have poor job opportunities, even without incarceration. Statistical studies try to compare the wages and employment of men who are similar in all respects except for their criminal records. Many of these studies estimate that the ex-convicts earn between 10 and 30 percent less than similarly situated workers who have not been to prison or jail. Still, when very stringent comparisons are attempted, a few studies find there is no negative effect of incarceration on the labor market. This research implies that men at high risk of incarceration have such poor job prospects, prison time confers no additional economic penalty.[6]

Much of the statistical research is based on a very simple model in which incarceration generates a one-time decline in earnings or employment among ex-convicts. However, the economic effects of incarceration on poor and minority communities may be more complicated. One alternative approach places the effects of incarceration in the context of the life course of young men as they try to make the transition from school to stable employment. Another approach examines the impact of incarceration not just on individuals, but on the communities from which individuals are drawn.

The life course perspective argues that the experience of incarceration is a punctuating event that can interrupt a young man's transition into stable employment. While many young men leave school and ultimately find steady jobs that provide regular growth in earnings, men with criminal records experience virtually no growth in earnings at all. This suggests that ex-convicts have few job opportunities outside of day labor or other kinds of precarious employment.[7] Ethnographers paint a similar picture. Mercer Sullivan's vivid account of young ex-convicts in New York City describes a cycle of disadvantage resulting from entanglement with law enforcement and correctional authorities: "participation in income-producing crime and the resulting involvement in the criminal justice system in turn kept the [research subjects] out of school and forced them to abandon their occupational goals . . . By the end of their teens most of these youths had found and lost several jobs . . . Wages, though irregular, replaced theft as their major source of income . . . They were still frequently unemployed and generally made low wages when they did work."[8] From the life course perspective there is not a single earnings gap between non-convicts and ex-convicts. Instead, the earnings of ex-convicts diverges from the earnings of non-convicts as men get older. Non-convicts by their late twenties have settled into a stable path of earnings growth, while ex-convicts follow an unstable trajectory of irregular employment.

Although most research on the economic effects of incarceration focuses on the earnings or employment loss of individuals, the penal system may also have large aggregate-level effects. In a very simple sense, incarceration widens the earnings gap between black and white men because incarceration lowers earnings and blacks are more likely to be incarcerated than whites. A rough estimate of the impact of incarceration on the black–white earnings gap can be obtained from figures on the lifetime risk of incarceration and average earnings. A Bureau of Justice Statistics study suggests that about 24.6 percent of black men have prison records by age 30 in contrast to 3 percent of white men.[9] The earnings gap between black and white men under age 30 is around 18 percent. Following the statistical studies, we can assume that prison or jail time lowers earnings by around one-tenth. Some simple calculations show that the black–white gap in earnings would be reduced from 18 to 12 percent if blacks and whites were incarcerated at the same rate.

Beyond statistical aggregation, incarceration may have spillover effects for entire demographic groups or communities. Highly concentrated incarceration may create discrimination. For example, employers often report avoiding job candidates from high-crime neighborhoods. In these cases, an individual's employment opportunities are limited by coming from a particular neighborhood, rather than having a criminal history. Similar effects may follow the contours of demography. About a third of black men born since the late 1960s with only a high school education have been sentenced to time in prison. Under these conditions, incarceration may be collectively, rather than individually, stigmatizing. Employers may assume that all young low-skill black men are ex-convicts. This would help explain the finding in some studies that the employment penalty of incarceration is smaller for blacks than for whites. In addition, the high incarceration rates experienced by poor minority neighborhoods may reduce neighborhood employment rates. Studies of urban poverty show that neighborhood concentrations of crime, alcohol and drug use, and low educational attainment can promote such outcomes in individuals.[10] Similar neighborhoods effects could also influence employment. Poor urban communities with high incarceration rates are likely to have large numbers of idle young men recently released from prison or jail. These men may form peer groups or reference groups that offer the community few normative or social links to legitimate employment.

Implications and Conclusions

The bare facts surrounding the impact of the prison boom on the economic position of African Americans are striking. Incarceration rates are 7 to 8 times higher for blacks than whites. By 1999, young black male high school dropouts were more likely to be incarcerated than employed. Incarceration has become a routine stage in the life course for young black men with just a high school education. By removing poor men from labor force statistics, the penal system obscures inequality. Standard accounts of inequality in employment and wages under-estimate the gap between black and white men, particularly in recent birth cohorts at low levels of schooling. Official statistics suggest that young, low-skill, black men joined in the benefits of the economic expansion of the 1990s. When prison and jail inmates are accounted for, however, economic divisions between young black and white men appear to have widened.

After release from prison, ex-inmates have limited job opportunities. Their wages are low and employment unstable. In contrast to most men whose earnings increase through their twenties and thirties, ex-prisoners experience little or no wage growth. Wage stagnation among ex-prisoners also widens the earnings gap between black and white men. Again, the effects are especially large among those without a college education. The effects of highly-concentrated incarceration among low-skill minority men may spill over to affect entire neighborhoods and stigmatize broad demographic categories. Although the evidence here is less clear cut, we can speculate that high incarceration contributes to discrimination and undermines local labor markets.

The great irony of the prison boom is that it comes at a time when policymakers have set out to roll back the role of government in the lives of the disadvantaged. Despite anti-government rhetoric in policy debates, the government has not regulated the lives of unskilled minority men so intensively since depression or wartime. The policy offensive was wide-ranging, affecting policing, sentencing, prison construction, post-release supervision and a variety of other measures at the state and Federal levels of government. The sheer commitment of public resources is comparable in magnitude to social welfare efforts in the 1960s and 1970s. Unlike anti-poverty policy, however, the punitive trend in criminal justice policy conceals and deepens economic inequality between blacks and whites.

This represents a significant departure from the thrust of public policy through the 25 years following World War II. Beginning in the 1950s, school desegregation led to improved quality of schooling for black children, ultimately raising the relative wages of black workers. Bars on discrimination resulting from the Civil Rights Act, affirmative action and equal employment opportunity all narrowed the economic gap between blacks and whites. Black workers also found secure employment in public sector jobs which helped create the basis for a well-paid black middle class. For much of the postwar period, public policy played an important progressive role that helped offset the negative effects of declining manufacturing industries in urban labor markets. Weighed against these achievements, the prison boom can be seen as one of the most important developments in American race relations in the last 30 years.

While we often consider how welfare, employment, and education policy affect inequality, criminal justice policy is usually judged by other standards. This essay has focused on the social costs of incarceration that are typically uncounted in assessments of the recent growth in the US penal system. Much of the analysis of this chapter treats prison and jail inmates simply as disadvantaged and not as dangerous. Yet critics will warn that residents of the penal system should be thought of as criminal first, and poor second. From this perspective, nearly half the prison population are violent offenders. Many prisoners are also repeat (although not violent) offenders. For partisans in the war on crime, incarceration may affect economic inequality, but the criminal propensity of most young black and white men with little schooling demands an aggressive policy response. The inegalitarian effects of criminal justice policy must be balanced against the goal of public safety.

This counter-argument raises a complex question: Can public safety be achieved by policies that deepen social inequality? To answer this question, much depends on the link between inequality and crime. If inequality causes crime – and a large research literature indicates that it does – the recent reliance on punishment as the first option in criminal justice policy may be a self-defeating route to public safety. The connection between crime and inequality is well-trodden ground for students of criminology. The prison boom and its effects on racial inequality give this question renewed urgency. In earlier research and policy, the contours of social inequality were viewed as fixed and external to the patterns of crime that they generated. Our new challenge involves viewing inequality as, in part, a product of the expansion of the American system of punishment.

NOTES

Chapter prepared for *Collateral Damage: The Social Cost of Mass Incarceration* (New Press, 2002), edited by Meda Chesney-Lind and Marc Mauer. We gratefully acknowledge Marc Mauer's comments on an earlier draft. Research for this paper was supported by grant SES-0004336 from the National Science Foundation and a grant from the Russell Sage Foundation.

1   This discussion builds on an analysis by Bruce Western and Becky Pettit (2000), "Incarceration and Racial Inequality in Men's Employment," *Industrial and Labor Relations Review*, vol. 54, pp. 3–16.

2   These ratios were calculated using figures from the U.S. census and table 1, p. 22, in Alfred Blumstein and Allen J. Beck, "Population Growth in U.S. Prisons, 1980–1996," in *Prisons: Crime and Justice, a Review of Research*, vol. 26, pp. 17–62. They include both men and women and do not include jail inmates.

3   Becky Pettit and Bruce Western (2001), "Inequality in U.S. Prison Incarceration," paper prepared for the annual meetings of the American Sociological Association, Anaheim, California.

4   Results from an employer survey are reported by Harry Holzer (1996), *What Employers Want: Job Prospects for Less-Educated Workers*, New York, Russell Sage Foundation, p. 59. Employment restrictions resulting from a felony conviction are surveyed by the Office of the Pardon Attorney (1996), *Civil Disabilities of Convicted Felons: A State-by-State Survey*. Washington, DC, U.S. Department of Justice.

5   The idea that incarceration can generate social connections to illegal rather than legal employment is suggested by John Hagan (1993), "The Social Embeddedness of Crime and Unemployment," *Criminology*, vol. 31, pp. 465–91. On gang recruitment in prison see John M. Hagedorn (1988), *People and Folks: Gangs, Crime, and the Underclass in a Rustbelt City*. Chicago: Lake View Press. Also, Martin Sánchez Jankowski (1991), *Islands in the Street: Gangs and American Urban Society*. Berkeley: University of California Press.

6   The research is reviewed by Bruce Western, Jeffrey R. Kling, and David F. Weiman (2001), "The Labor Market Consequences of Incarceration," *Crime and Delinquency*, vol. 47, pp. 410–27.

7   Daniel Nagin and Joel Waldfogel (1998), "The Effect of Conviction on Income Through the Life Cycle," *International Review of Law and Economics*, vol. 18, pp. 25–40;

Shawn David Bushway (1996), *The Impact of a Criminal History Record on Access to Legitimate Employment*, Ph.D. dissertation, Carnegie Mellon University.

8   Mercer Sullivan (1989), *"Getting Paid": Youth Crime and Work in the Inner City*, Ithaca, NY: Cornell University Press.

9   Thomas P. Bonczar and Allen J. Beck (1997), *Lifetime Likelihood of Going to State or Federal Prison*, Bureau of Justice S.tatistics Bulletin, NCJ 160092.

10 The effect of incarceration on employment is lower for blacks than whites according to the estimates of Bruce Western and Katherine Beckett (1999), "How Unregulated is the U.S. Labor Market? The Penal System as a Labor Market Institution," *American Journal of Sociology*, vol. 104, pp. 1030–60. Research on the effects of spatial concentrations of economic and social disadvantage is summarized by Ronald B. Mincy (1996), "The Underclass: Concept, Controversy, and Evidence," in *Confronting Poverty*, edited by Sheldon Danziger, Gary Sandefur, and Daniel Weinberg, New York, Russell Sage Foundation, pp. 119–22.

Additional Reading

Part I   On the Origins and Causes of Wealth and Poverty: Systemic Explanations

Sheldon Danziger and Peter Gottschalk, "Why Inequality of Earnings Increased," pp. 124–50 in *America Unequal* (Cambridge, MA and New York: Harvard/Russell Sage Foundation, 1995).

Henry Hansmann, pp. 12–22 in *The Owner-ship of Enterprise* (Cambridge, MA: Belknap, Harvard University Press, 1996).

Bennett Harrison and Barry Bluestone, *The Great U-Turn: Corporate Restructuring and the Polarizing of America* (New York: Basic Books, 1988).

Gerhard Lenski, *Power and Privilege: A Theory of Social Stratification* (Chapel Hill, NC: University of North Carolina Press, 1984).

Georg Simmel, "The Poor," pp. 150–78 in *Georg Simmel: On Individuality and Social Forms* (edited by Donald Levine, Chicago, IL: University of Chicago Press, 1971).

Max Weber, "The Market: Its Impersonality and Ethic," pp. 635–40 in *Economy and Society* (Berkeley and Los Angeles: University of California Press, 1968).

Part II   Who's Rich, Who's Poor: How Resources Affect Life Chances

Peter Blau and Otis D. Duncan, *The American Occupational Structure* (New York: Wiley, 1967).

Greg Duncan and Jeanne Brooks-Gunn, "Income Effects Across the Life Span: Integration and Interpretation," pp. 596–610 in Greg Duncan and Jeanne Brooks-Gunn, eds., *Consequences of Growing up Poor* (New York: Russell Sage Foundation, 1997).

Claude Fischer et al., *Inequality by Design: Cracking the Bell Curve Myth* (Princeton, NJ: Princeton University Press, 1996).

Robert Havemann and Barbara Wolfe, pp. 22–50 in *Succeeding Generations: On the Effects of Investments in Children* (New York: Russell Sage Foundation, 1994).

Christopher Jencks et al., *Who Gets Ahead? The Determinants of Success in America* (New York: Basic Books, 1979).

Part III   Lifestyles of the Rich and Famous

Tom Bottomore, *Elites and Society* (London and New York: Routledge, 1993).

E. Digby Baltzell, *The Protestant Establishment: Aristocracy and Caste in America* (New York: Random House, 1964).

G. William Domhoff, *Who Rules America?* (New York: Prentice Hall, 1967).

Gaettano Mosca, *The Ruling Class* (Westport, CT: Greenwood Publishing Group, 1980).

Francine Owstrower, *Why the Wealthy Give* (Princeton, NJ: Princeton University Press, 1997).

Villefredo Pareto, *The Rise and Fall of Elites: An Application of Theoretical Sociology* (New Brunswick, NJ: Transaction Publishers, 1991).

Thorstein Veblen, *The Theory of the Leisure Class: An Economic Study of Institutions* (1899; New York: Viking Press, 1953).

Part IV   Lifestyles of the Poor and Anonymous

Dalton Conley, "Getting it Together: Social and Institutional Obstacles to Getting Off the Streets." *Sociological Forum* 11: 25–40, 1996.

Kathryn Edin and Laura Lein, *Making Ends Meet: How Single Mothers Survive Welfare and Low-Wage Work* (New York: Russell Sage Foundation Press, 1997).

Michael Katz, ed., *The Underclass Debate: Views from History* (Princeton, NJ: Princeton University Press, 1992).

Eliot Liebow, *Tally's Corner: A Study of Negro Streetcorner Men* (Boston, MA: Little Brown, 1968).

Katherine Newman, *No Shame in My Game: The Working Poor in the Inner City* (New York: Knopf, 1999).

David Snow and Leon Anderson, *Down on Their Luck: A Study of Homeless Street People* (Berkeley and Los Angeles, CA: University of California Press, 1994).

Charles Valentine, *Culture and Poverty: Critique and Counter-Proposals* (Chicago, IL: University of Chicago Press, 1968).

Part V   What is to be Done? Wealth, Poverty, and Public Policy

Gosta Esping-Anderson, *The Three Worlds of Welfare Capitalism* (Princeton, NJ: Princeton University Press, 1992).

Christopher Jencks, "Welfare," pp. 204–35 in *Rethinking Social Policy* (Cambridge, MA: Harvard University Press, 1992).

National Academy of Sciences, *Measuring Poverty: A New Approach* http://www.nap.edu/readingroom/books/poverty/summary.html

Mollie Orshansky, "Children of the Poor," *Social Security Bulletin* 26, 7: 3–13, July 1963.

John Rawls, pp. 3–22 of *A Theory of Justice* (Cambridge, MA: Belknap, Harvard, 1971).

Patricia Ruggles, "Setting the Poverty Threshold," pp. 31–62 in *Drawing the Line: Alternative Poverty Measures and their Implications for Public Policy* (Washington, DC: Urban Institute Press, 1990).

Michael Sherradan, "Individual Development Accounts," pp. 220–32 in *Assets and the Poor: A New American Welfare Policy* (Armonk, NY: M.E. Sharpe, 1992).

Edward Wolff, "Current Systems of Wealth Taxation," pp. 33–40 in *Top Heavy: The Increasing Inequality of Wealth and What Can be Done About It* (New York: The New Press, 1995).

Index

Note: Because this book focuses primarily upon the USA, no separate index entry for this subject has been made. Page numbers in bold type indicate a main reference.

CPSIA information can be obtained at www.ICGtesting.com
Printed in the USA
LVOW11s1437180913

353041LV00006B/201/P

3 4711 00218 2899

9 780631 231806